WHEN SCOUTS WORSHIP

Prepared by

**CHURCH COMMISSION ON
SCOUTING (NATIONAL)**

Worship Services, Guides, Resources
Hymns, Folk Songs, Fun Songs

Published by

THE BETHANY PRESS, ST. LOUIS, MISSOURI

Printed in the United States of America

WHEN SCOUTS WORSHIP

When Scouts Worship is a project of the Church Commission on Scouting (National). This Commission, representative of the Protestant churches, is concerned that Scout units have worship sources readily available when they are away from home. It is hoped that this book will fill this need.

The Commission feels that it is particularly fortunate in being able to incorporate its worship suggestions with the songs of Chapbook 2. By doing this, all printed resources necessary for worship, with the exception of the Bible, are contained in one pocket-sized volume.

Special thanks goes to the work group and the author who prepared this manuscript on behalf of the Commission. It is recommended that Scout units and Scout Camps make this book available to all so that it may help worship become a very real experience in the life of the Scout.

C. F. MESSINGER, *Chairman*

a brief word about worship . . .

Worship is an experience of people which is theirs at moments when they feel God's presence.

Worship is sometimes spontaneous; it is sometimes the result of structured praise of God; and it is always revealed in the life of service for God and His children.

We may never understand worship as something one may perform for another; nor is worship something which must employ a bystander to lead, and who, possibly, does not participate.

Again, worship is that personal, intimate experience of people which is most really theirs at moments when they most really feel God's presence.

FOREWORD

Ideas Relative to the Ways Leaders May Use *When Scouts Worship:*

In the report of the work group concerned with the proposed *When Scouts Worship* are these statements: "This should be a resource book, not a directory for worship"; include "several orders of worship, some informal and short with no meditation, some more formal and liturgical"; compose "one order containing prayers, responses, etc.—ready for use." With this in mind the writer sought to prepare materials which were illustrative of the great varieties and possibilities available.

Scouts are persons who live in a world of variety. Why should their worship not express also this real situation of contemporary life? Friends, schools, clothes, food vary. But in all these things some factors remain the same. Each boy must always pull his own load; but each boy also leans on others and other boys lean on him. Therefore we envision these worship services to be used in various situations of interpersonal relationships in which personal identity must be maintained and understood.

Likewise, worship experiences for Scouts should not be rigidly patterned into one form. This would be unreal. Changes are necessary. Worship is large, flexible, thrilling, exciting, corporate, individual. Valid worship experiences are those which may be described by these foregoing words. One of the services of worship found here provides for frank discussion of a scriptural passage. Who knows the outcome of such a service? Who would dare predict the glimpses of real social and humanitarian concern such a service can create in a boy? Another service of worship calls for the use of paper and pencil. Boys are asked to make notes as scriptural passages are being read. This is all done in an effort to illustrate for the boys ways they can become more familiar with certain aspects of the life and ministry of Jesus Christ.

This is simply saying that worship is much too varied, changing, thrilling to be always confined to definite, fixed forms.

These services hopefully show the Scouts the truth that newer translations of the Scriptures are often more easily understandable than the King James Version and the Revised Standard Version, although these translations may be helpful at times.

Sometimes leaders may feel that none of these services of worship answers the particular needs of his particular Scouts at a certain time. It is then that the leader is heartily encouraged to create his own services of worship. The leader is reminded that a rich and varied listing of resources is included in this book. Among these resources are the several denominational books of worship. The leader is especially directed to the section of this book which has prayers and readings provided for immediate use.

These services of worship are designed to cause the individual to evaluate his place within the Christian community and mission. It is hoped that the leader will allow ample time for individual expression during and after the services. Without this type of freedom in these types of services, all is lost. The leader is warned not to be afraid of silence. It must be a part of these services.

FRANK A. BROOKS, JR.

Richmond, Virginia
December, 1967.

CONTENTS

WORSHIP SERVICE I

(Morning)

An Order for Daily Prayer

Leader: Let us worship God.

Jesus said: I am the light of the world; he who follows me will not walk in darkness, but will have the light of life.

Unison: This is the day which the Lord has made, **Let us rejoice and be glad in it.**

HYMN OF PRAISE: (Suggestions for hymns: 67, 68, 69, 71, 72, 74, 75, 105, 107, 120, 122)

Leader: Let us pray.

O Lord, our heavenly Father, almighty and everlasting God, who has safely brought us to the beginning of this day: defend us in the same with your mighty power; and grant that this day we fall into no sin, neither run into any kind of danger; but that all our doings, being ordered by your wisdom, may be righteous in your sight; through Jesus Christ our Lord.

Unison: Amen.

A PSALM, AN OLD TESTAMENT READING, OR A RESPONSIVE READING: (Suggestions for responsive readings: 40 through 66)

Gloria Patri in unison:

Glory be to the Father, and to the Son, and to the Holy Ghost; as it was in the beginning, is now, and ever shall be, world without end. Amen.

Leader: Let us pray.

God of wisdom, grant us your Holy Spirit, that we may hear your word and obediently do your will; through Jesus Christ our Lord.

Unison: Amen.

A LESSON FROM SCRIPTURE, which *may* be followed by a brief interpretation.

Leader: The Lord be with you.

Unison: And with your spirit.

Leader: Let us pray.

God of mercy, God of grace: we bring you prayers for all mankind and beg your favor in every need. Let your Spirit direct your people that they may serve you in peace and proclaim your Word through all the world.

Look upon your servant _____(name)_____, the President of the United States, and upon all those in positions of public trust. Cause them to seek your perfect will.

Help us forgive those we don't like as we are forgiven by you.

Bless our friends and every earthly friendship.
Cause some relief to come to the troubled, and those who suffer in sickness.

Deliver the people who are worried and discouraged from these conditions.

Enrich the needy.

Enable us to do your will, that we may be faithful disciples to the honor of Jesus Christ our Lord, in whose name we pray.

Unison: Amen.

O God, our Father, creator of this pleasant world and giver of all good things: we thank you for our home on earth and for the joy of living. We praise you for your love in Jesus Christ, who came to set things right, who died rejected on the cross and rose triumphant from the dead: because he lives, we live to praise you, Father, Son, and Holy Spirit, our God forever. Amen.

Our Father who art in heaven,
Hallowed be thy name.
Thy kingdom come,
Thy will be done,
   On earth as it is in heaven.
Give us this day our daily bread;
And forgive us our debts,
   As we also have forgiven our debtors;
And lead us not into temptation,
   But deliver us from evil.
For thine is the kingdom and the power
   and the glory, forever. Amen.

HYMN: (Suggestions for hymns: 76, 77, 90, 93, 94, 96, 100, 101, 102, 108, 111, etc.)

Leader: Go in peace.

The grace of our Lord Jesus Christ and the love of God and the fellowship of the Holy Spirit be with you all.

Unison: Amen.[1]

---

[1]From *The Book of Common Worship,* PROVISIONAL SERVICES. The Westminster Press. Copyright © 1966, W. L. Jenkins. Used by permission.

WORSHIP SERVICE II

(Evening)

The Presence of Jesus Christ

WHAT IS NEEDED: *A song leader on shore if the service is to be a Galilean one*

Three leaders in the boat. See suggestions below.

A copy of the New Testament

Copies of WHEN SCOUTS WORSHIP *or mimeographed copies of songs and hymns to be used*

PROCEDURE: *This may be a Galilean service, if desired. Such a service would begin after the Scouts have gone quietly to some designated lakeside area. As they arrive and are seated, some folksongs may be sung. After everyone has arrived, those who are to participate and lead in the service should arrive by boat coming from some distance away. There should be at least three in the boat: a leader to read or tell the story "The Presence of Jesus"[1]; a Scout to read the Scripture passages and lead in singing the hymns; and a Scout who is capable of paddling and keeping the boat in a stationary position while the service lasts.*

It is suggested not to try this service as a Galilean one in some simulated surrounding such as a swimming pool. It will be best suited to a natural surrounding. However, in case of inclement weather, it may be adapted easily for the indoors.

AN OPENING PRAYER

HYMN: "Now, On Land and Sea Descending" No. 98

SCRIPTURE PASSAGES: Mark 3:7-9
Luke 5:1-3

MEDITATION: *The Presence of Jesus*

It is evening. The Sea of Galilee lies before your eyes.

In the west the splendid scarlets and golds have faded. It is the moment of daffodil and pale green sky. To your left, mountains run down steeply to the sea. Jesus is climbing up a spur of one of these mountains, seeking quietude in the bosom of the hills and in the hush of night; seeking to push back the tumultuous demands of all there is to do, to make a silence in which the soul can breathe, to pray. You can see his figure outlined for a moment against the fading light of that last glow of evening. But, in the east, clouds have gathered; clouds that mean storm. Rank upon rank . . . they sweep westward. The water of the lake turns from amber to steel. The wind . . . strikes chill and cold, menacing almost. Then the swish of the rain. Jesus hears it long before it reaches him. He sees in front of him a shepherd's hut on the hillside. He makes for it to avoid the discomfort of a soaking, lights the single lamp he finds within, and kneels to pray.

Now imagine that you are on the mountain, too. The storm is on you. You see a light shining from the window of the hut. Panting and disheveled, you rush up to it, seeking shelter. Glancing through the window, you see who is there, and you turn away. Shelter or no shelter, you feel you cannot intrude on his seclusion. But he has heard you. He rises, flings open the door. For very you there is his smile, his word of welcome. Then the door closes. Just you and Jesus, Jesus and you.

I will not try and imagine what he would say to you . . . I know, I think, some of the things he would have to say to me . . . and you know some of the things he would say to you. But if he said nothing, his presence would say everything. I think at first you would lift your eyes to his. Then somehow you would drop them. It is hard to look into eyes that search the uttermost secret you have guarded from the world so long. Yet, if it be hard to look at him, it is harder not to look at him. After a while you would look again into those dark, clear, steady, quiet eyes, and find them not only searching but shining; shining, not with any light regard for sin, but with a compassion that goes below the sin to the pure desire beneath. And in eyes that are the homes of all your dreams you would see the answer to all your prayers. You would *know* that he believed in you. A tremendous confidence would drive away all your fears and possess your whole being. Just because you could never belie a faith in you like his, a new faith in yourself would be born forthwith, and you would know yourself to be "able for anything."

Now the storm has passed. It is long after midnight, but you do not care. He sees you a little way on your path homeward. Then he turns back to pray. You have half a thought to go back with him. The thought of parting seems for a moment more than you can bear. Then you feel that you never *can* really be parted from him, though he goes his way and you yours unto the end of the earth. Something marvelous has happened. He is still with you. He hasn't gone back after all. He is dwelling within you. There has been a new birth. He will express himself through you. It is as though your heart has become the hut; as though you had gained him forever. . . . You are not just "you" any longer. You have become a self whose highest joy and truest life will forever be to express Jesus, and bring to others the wealth and beauty he has brought to you. . . .

The wind is hushed now. A crescent moon sails quietly through the last racks of stormcloud. Here and there a star. . . . You stride back to your job again on feet that scarcely touch the mountain turf; back to a life that can never, never be the same again. For in your heart there is an inward strength, an exultant radiance . . . an outgoing love, and an ineffable peace. They do not belong to this world and *nothing* in this world can destroy them.

"Ah," you say, "but this is imagination." The hut, the light, the mountain, yes. But not the Presence. Unless the New Testament is a lie, then this experience is for you . . . look and listen and you will see and hear. "Our fellowship is with the Father and with his Son Jesus Christ" . . . think quietly of him. He is nearer to you than any figure of speech can describe. He will receive you. He will understand you. He will know what to do with you. He will tell you where to begin *now*. And you will go back to a life that has become quite different because you have been with Jesus. You will find him everywhere, both within and without. And for you the whole earth will be full of his glory.[2]

HYMN: "Be Thou My Vision"　　　　　　No. 105

A CLOSING PRAYER

---

[1]It will add greatly to this service if the leader does not have to refer constantly to the script.

[2]From *The Presence of Jesus* by Leslie D. Weatherhead, published by Abingdon Press.

WORSHIP SERVICE III

Understanding Jesus of Nazareth

WHAT IS NEEDED: *Two leaders to read Scripture responsively*

Copies of the New Testament in modern language such as: THE NEW TESTAMENT IN MODERN ENGLISH, *by J. B. Phillips;* THE NEW ENGLISH BIBLE, GOOD NEWS FOR MODERN MAN, *ed. by R. G. Bratcher.*

Paper

Pencils

For small groups, one leader with Bible for each group

PROCEDURE: *Having determined previously which translations are to be used with which passages, the two leaders shall read the passages listed below responsively so that the entire group hears well. The boys are encouraged to make notes on each passage. They are not required to do so. They are reminded of the theme of this service and are urged to keep in mind portions of these passages which seem to help them understand Jesus of Nazareth.*

RESPONSIVE READINGS:

John 6:60-61   Mark 5:1-9a
Mark 14:32-42   John 8:3-11
Luke 22:54-62   Matthew 19:16-22

SMALL GROUPS: *Each boy will decide which Scripture passage best described Jesus of Nazareth in his own understanding. He will list on paper the reasons for this decision. After sufficient time has been given for this, a general sharing period will end the service. This sharing will be primarily conversation and discussion from the entire group, directed and led by the leader. Other ideas may be gotten by the leader as he considers suggestions for sharing in WORSHIP SERVICE V, "Let's Use Our Imaginations" service.*

WORSHIP SERVICE IV

Expressing Our Christian Beliefs in Singing

MOMENTS OF SILENCE

THE DOXOLOGY: "Praise God from Whom All Blessings Flow"

Unison: I believe in God the Father Almighty . . .

HYMN: "Holy, Holy, Holy"   No. 72

Unison: **Maker of heaven and earth . . .**

HYMN: "He's Got the Whole World in
                      His Hands"   No. 154

Unison: **and in Jesus Christ, his only Son our Lord,
who was conceived by the Holy Spirit, born of the
Virgin Mary . . .**

HYMN: "Go Tell It on the Mountain"   No. 90
        (or stanza one of No. 155)

Unison: **suffered under Pontius Pilate, was crucified,
dead, and buried . . .**

LITANY: "Preparation for Easter"   No. 48

Unison: **the third day he rose again from the dead;
he ascended into heaven, and sitteth on the right
hand of God the Father Almighty. From thence he
shall come to judge the quick and the dead.**

HYMN: "Thine Is the Glory"   No. 123
        (or stanzas 4 and 5 of No. 155)

Unison: **I believe in the Holy Spirit . . .**

HYMN: "Spirit of the Living God"   No. 124

Unison: **the holy Christian church . . .**

HYMN: "O God of Every Nation"   No. 112

Unison: **the communion of saints . . .**

HYMN: "Let Us Break Bread Together"   No. 150

Unison: **the forgiveness of sins, the resurrection of the
body, and the life everlasting. Amen**

HYMN: "A Mighty Fortress Is Our God"   No. 78

CLOSING PRAYER

WORSHIP SERVICE V

Let's Use Our Imaginations

WHAT IS NEEDED: *Groups of six to eight Scouts*
One leader for each group

> *The leader will be helped by a thorough considera-*
> *tion of the suggestions listed under "A Period of*
> *Sharing."*

Bibles

Paper and pencils

OUR SCRIPTURE PASSAGE: One day at three in the
afternoon, the hour of prayer, Peter and John [two
disciples of Jesus] were on their way up to the
temple. Now a man who had been a cripple from
birth used to be carried there and laid every day by
the gate of the temple called 'Beautiful Gate,' to beg
from people as they went in. When he saw Peter
and John on their way into the temple he asked for
charity. But Peter fixed his eyes on him, as John did
also, and said, 'Look at us.' Expecting a gift from
them, the man was all attention. And Peter said, 'I
have no silver or gold; but what I have I give you:
in the name of Jesus Christ of Nazareth, walk.' Then
he grasped him by the right hand and pulled him
up; and at once his feet and ankles grew strong; he
sprang up, stood on his feet, and started to walk. He
entered the temple with them, leaping and praising
God as he went. Everyone saw him walking and
praising God, and when they recognized him as the
man who used to sit begging at Beautiful Gate, they
were filled with wonder and amazement at what had
happened to him. (Acts 3:1-10, *New English Bible*)[1]

[1]From *The New English Bible, New Testament.* © The Delegates
of the Oxford University Press and the Syndics of the Cambridge
University Press 1961. Reprinted by permission.

With pencil on sheets of paper, each boy will jot down his feelings upon finishing each sentence of the passage as each boy imagines he is the cripple in the passage. For example, each boy asks himself at the conclusion of each sentence, "How would I feel if I had been cripple from birth and watched Peter and John enter the temple on good, strong legs and feet?"

Have each boy write down his feelings and emotions in first person in the style of a narrative. For example, "a cripple since the day I was born, I was sick and tired of having to be brought to the gate and watching those strong men walk past me day after day. I was resentful and bitter."

Encourage the use of IMAGINATION. Each boy needs to imagine seriously how he would feel BEFORE the experience, DURING the experience, and AFTER the experience of the cripple.

A PERIOD OF SHARING: *Make this a time of discussion which naturally and freely comes forth from the Scouts. The leader will always guide the discussion so that it remains relevant.*

Perhaps the leader will suggest that the passage of Scripture lends itself well to a simple venture into the area of drama. If so, the Scouts may have a profitable learning experience as they dramatize the passage.

A conversation which follows a time during which each Scout records his feelings about the passage could be very helpful. The leader will let each Scout verbalize his feelings. Questions from the group will help stimulate conversation. Sample questions might be: "What would I say to you if I were the cripple?" "What would you say to me if you were the cripple?" The leader may refer to such things as the Scout

Law, the God and Country manual, and selected merit badge pamphlets as he seeks to lead the Scouts in consideration of the passage of Scripture.

CLOSING PRAYER

Other Scripture passages which might be used include: 1 Samuel 28:3-14; The Book of Jonah; Luke 10:29-37; Acts 27:3-44.

WORSHIP SERVICE VI

Scattering in Order to Be the Love of God

WHAT IS NEEDED: *Leaders to read the passage from the Bible and to lead discussion.*

The meeting should be divided into . groups of six to eight Scouts with a leader for each.

MOMENTS OF SILENCE

Leader: Jesus said, "I assure you that whatever you did for the humblest of my brothers, you did for me." (Matthew 25:40)

HYMN: "Where Cross the Crowded Ways of Life"
No. 111

(stanzas 1, 2, 4 and 6)

PRAYER

Leader: O God, we seek to hear you above the cries of race, clan and selfishness.

Unison: Give us, we pray, the listening ear. Then give us the power to help restore courage and dignity where these have been lost by those who have refused to listen.

Leader: O God, we seek to serve you within the ugly attitudes of fear and greed.

Unison: Give us, we pray, the concern for unlikables. Then give us the willingness and grace to understand hurt and bewildered people whose actions seem to us rude and whose speech sarcastic.

Leader: O God, we seek to serve Christ by helping him bear the burdens of those now ready to faint from the needs of their troubles caused by location and people.

Unison: Give us, we pray, desires to strengthen those whose bodies are torn, needful, and sore. Provide, we pray, the ability to minister and serve in love toward your creatures.

Leader: O God, we seek not to forget that you call us to use the work of our hands in sharing the love of Christ.

Unison: Give us, we pray, the firm belief that your kingdom is already in our midst and that our deeds for the humblest of our brothers are those which hasten the coming of your reign among us.

Leader: Through Jesus Christ, our Lord,

Unison: Amen.

SCRIPTURE READING BY LEADER: "But when the Son of Man comes in his splendor with all his angels with him, then he will take his seat on his glorious throne. All the nations will be assembled before him and he will separate men from each other like a shepherd separating sheep from goats. He will place the sheep on his right hand and the goats on his left.

"Then the king will say to those on his right: 'Come, you who have won my Father's blessing! Take your inheritance—the kingdom reserved for you since the foundation of the world! For I was hungry and you gave me food. I was thirsty and you gave me drink. I was lonely and you made me welcome. I was naked and you clothed me. I was ill and you came and looked after me. I was in prison and you came to see me there.'

"Then the true men will answer him: 'Lord, when did we see you hungry and give you food? When did we see you thirsty and give you something to drink? When did we see you lonely and make you welcome, or see you naked and clothe you, or see you ill or in prison and go to see you?'

"And the king will reply, 'I assure you that whatever you did for the humblest of my brothers, you did for me.'" (Matthew 23:31-40)

A PERIOD OF MEDITATION: *Each worshiper shall silently consider the above passage.*

A PERIOD OF DISCUSSION: *The leader shall lead a group discussion of the following questions by asking one person to begin the discussion in answering each question.*

Leader: What does our passage of Scripture say about group life such as we are presently experiencing?

Discussion

Leader: What are some things our passage of Scripture suggests which possibly need changing in our minds; in our actions toward each other here; in our attitudes and actions at large?

Discussion

Leader: What has our passage of Scripture caused us to consider regarding our personal life from this very moment forward?

Discussion

Leader: What has the passage of Scripture taught us about our REAL place in God's plan for his world?

Discussion

PRAYER

Unison: O God, grant us freedom to move into the unknown. Grant us strength to explore the untried. Grant us vision to see the opportunities of the new day. Make us know that there is no place, no event, no meeting upon which we enter alone. You are with us. Then, lead us to the hungry, the thirsty, the lonely, the naked, the ill and the prisoner. Serve through us to them. For Christ's sake. Amen.

HYMN: "Lord, Whose Love Through Humble Service"
No. 103

SCATTERING

CALLS TO WORSHIP

The Church and Christian Fellowship

1 There is one body and one Spirit, just as you were called to the one hope that belongs to your call, one Lord, one faith, one baptism, one God and Father of us all, who is above all and through all and in all.
Ephesians 4:4-6

2 As in one body we have many members, and all the members do not have the same function, so we, though many, are one body in Christ, and individually members one of another. *Romans 12:4-5*

3 "The cup of blessing which we bless, is it not a participation in the blood of Christ? The bread which we break, is it not a participation in the body of Christ? Because there is one loaf, we who are many are one body, for we all partake of the same loaf."
1 Corinthians 10:16-17

World Outreach and Witness

4 Blessed be the name of the LORD
   from this time forth and for evermore!
From the rising of the sun to its setting
   the name of the LORD is to be praised!
The LORD is high above all nations,
   and his glory above the heavens! *Psalm 113:2-4*

5 "The harvest is plentiful, but the laborers are few; pray therefore the Lord of the harvest to send out laborers into his harvest." *Luke 10:2*

6 Let us not grow weary in well-doing, for in due season we shall reap, if we do not lose heart. So then, as we have opportunity, let us do good to all men, and especially to those who are of the household of faith. *Galatians 6:9-10*

Beloved, let us love one another; for love is of God, and he who loves is born of God and knows God. He who does not love does not know God; for God is love.

7

1 John 4:7-8

Stewardship

Let the favor of the Lord our God be upon us,
and establish thou the work of our hands upon us,
yea, the work of our hands establish thou it.

8

Psalm 90:17

Bless the LORD, O my soul;
   and all that is within me, bless his holy name!
Bless the LORD, O my soul,
   and forget not all his benefits.

9

Psalm 103:1-2

God's Seeking Love

"Blessed be the Lord God of Israel,
for he has visited and redeemed his people,
and has raised up a horn of salvation for us
in the house of his servant David,"
"to give light to those who sit in darkness
   and in the shadow of death,
to guide our feet into the way of peace."

10

Luke 1:68-69, 79

Jesus Christ

And the Word became flesh and dwelt among us, full of grace and truth; we have beheld his glory, glory as of the only Son from the Father. And from his fullness have we all received, grace upon grace.

11

John 1:14, 16

"I am the door; if any one enters by me, he will be saved, and will go in and out and find pasture. The thief comes only to steal and kill and destroy; I came that they may have life, and have it abundantly."

12

John 10:9-10

Prayer and Commitment

13 They who wait for the Lord
    shall renew their strength,
they shall mount up with wings like eagles,
    they shall run and not be weary,
they shall walk and not faint.
                        Isaiah 40:31

14 Draw near to God and he will draw near to you.
Humble yourselves before the Lord and he will exalt
you.
                        James 4:8a, 10

15 "God is spirit, and those who worship him must
worship in spirit and truth." I appeal to you therefore, brethren, by the mercies of God, to present your
bodies as a living sacrifice, holy and acceptable to
God, which is your spiritual worship.
                  John 4:24; Romans 12:1

Easter

16 How beautiful upon the mountains
    are the feet of him who brings good tidings,
who publishes peace, who brings good tidings of good,
    who publishes salvation,
who says to Zion, "Your God reigns."
                    Isaiah 52:7

17 For to this end we toil and strive, because we have
our hope set on the living God, who is the Savior
of all men, especially of those who believe.
                  1 Timothy 4:10

Forgiveness and Reconciliation

18 God shows his love for us in that while we were yet
sinners Christ died for us.
                  Romans 5:8

19 Blessed be the God and Father of our Lord Jesus
Christ, who has blessed us in Christ with every
spiritual blessing. He destined us in love to be his
sons through Jesus Christ, according to the purpose
of his will.
                  Ephesians 1:3, 5

Service and Vocation

"He has showed you, O man, what is good;
   and what does the LORD require of you
but to do justice, and to love kindness,
   and to walk humbly with your God?"   Micah 6:8

20

Let the word of Christ dwell in you richly, as you
teach and admonish one another in all wisdom, and
as you sing psalms and hymns and spiritual songs
with thankfulness in your hearts to God. And whatever you do, in word or deed, do everything in the
name of the Lord Jesus, giving thanks to God the
Father through him.   Colossians 3:16-17

21

God of the Universe

LORD, thou hast been our dwelling place
   in all generations.
Before the mountains were brought forth,
   or ever thou hadst formed the earth and the world,
   from everlasting to everlasting thou art God.
                                        Psalm 90:1-2

22

Make a joyful noise to the LORD,
   all the lands!
Serve the LORD with gladness!
Come into his presence with singing!
Know that the LORD is God!
   It is he that made us, and we are his;
   we are his people, and the sheep of his pasture.
                                        Psalm 100:1-3

23

Thanksgiving

O give thanks to the LORD,
   for he is good;
   for his steadfast love endures for ever!
Let the redeemed of the LORD say so.
Let them thank the LORD for his steadfast love,
   for his wonderful works to the sons of men!
                                        Psalm 107:1, 2a, 8

24

Peace

25 Thou dost keep him in perfect peace,
    whose mind is stayed on thee,
    because he trusts in thee.
Trust in the LORD for ever,
    for the LORD GOD
    is an everlasting rock.
                  Isaiah 26:3-4

Crisis

26 God is our refuge and strength,
    a very present help in trouble.
Therefore we will not fear though the earth should
    change,
    though the mountains shake in the heart of the sea;
though its waters roar and foam,
    though the mountains tremble
    with its tumult.
                  Psalm 46:1-3

27 "Be still, and know that I am God.
I am exalted among the nations,
I am exalted in the earth!"
The LORD of hosts is with us;
    the God of Jacob is our refuge.
                  Psalm 46:10-11

Christmas

28 The people who walked in darkness
    have seen a great light;
those who dwelt in a land of deep darkness,
    on them has light shined.
For to us a child is born,
to us a son is given;
and the government will be upon his shoulder,
    and his name will be called
"Wonderful Counselor, Mighty God,
    Everlasting Father, Prince of Peace."
                  Isaiah 9:2, 6

29 "Be not afraid; for behold, I bring you good news of
a great joy which will come to all the people; for
to you is born this day in the city of David a Savior,
who is Christ the Lord."
                  Luke 2:10-11

PRAYERS

Christian Fellowship

30

Dear God of all persons, who created us to depend on finding our delight in fellowship, we worship thee. We are grateful for the pleasure that comes in knowing others and being known by them. May our seeking of friendship glorify thee and build relationships with others on a foundation of Christian love. We rejoice in thy church which declares thy love and provides the nurturing warmth of fellowship to us all. Amen.

Witness and Outreach

31

Father, you who are the end of our ultimate quest, help us know that human life is made good through you. Help us order our lives in light of this knowledge.

God of the nations and of every one of us, help us be your people throughout the length and breadth of the earth.

Establish your rule in our lives, O Father, that we may be as lights in the midst of darkness and that our lives may bear praises of your goodness to all those among whom we dwell. Amen.

Appreciation for Resources

32

Dear Father, we thank you for the good gifts of life: for shelter at night, for the food we eat, for the clothing and comforts we enjoy in abundance. We thank you for the richness of the earth and this universe which nourishes us and sustains us, delights us and speaks to us of your love and concern. Help us be more worthy builders and users of these resources, more grateful participants with you in all that is creative and conserving in our world. In Jesus' name. Amen.

Understanding Vocation

33

O God, what are we called to be and do? Where would you have us go? Help us discern purpose in our lives and respond as far as our faith can lead us. Help us reach beyond immediate pleasures toward a more lasting goal. Help us see our lives in the perspective of your love and will for us. Earnestly we pray, in Jesus' name. Amen.

Christmas

34

Our Father, we thank you for so loving the world of men that you sent your Son. With grateful hearts and joyous spirits we celebrate an anniversary of his coming. We praise you and thank you for Jesus who began to be recognized as he grew to manhood as one in whom love had completely taken over, and whose life was devoted to loving and serving others.

We pray that in our own time and place we may understand and imitate that love so that we may serve others in the world and help bring the world under your eternal love. In the name of Jesus. Amen.

Easter

35

Humbly we offer our thanks, O Lord, for Jesus Christ, and for his unconditional, unsparing love, service and suffering for all of us. We praise you for the assurance of victory over death and the grave which you gave us by raising your Son from the dead. May the triumph celebrated on Easter Day renew our faith, redirect our purposes and energies, free us from all fears and deadening attitudes, and strengthen our loyalty to Jesus Christ, who was and is "the resurrection and the life." In his name. Amen.

Reconciliation

O God, Father of all mankind, in this broken world, so tragically pulled apart and fragmented, we seek to serve you and do your work in the world. Show us how we can be a strong force for good, and how we can heal the divisions that exist between person and person, and between persons and you. Forgive us, we pray, when we insist on our own way above your way. Unite us as we can be united in worship or service. This we ask in the name of Jesus who prayed that we might be one, as you and he are one. Amen.

Peace—Understanding

O God, in our anxiety to push ahead, we often lash out at others in foolish action or words, or ignore the great issues of our day, trying to pull what security we have close about us. O Lord of all of life, help us face the present and the future with courage and hope. May we triumph over our fears and gloom, trusting that you will lead us now as in the past. Help the leaders of this and every nation rise above hurtful pride and ambition. Give them the wisdom and the courage to do what your wisdom dictates. May all men learn to live peaceably together in freedom, providing justice for all. We ask this in the name and spirit of the Prince of Peace. Amen.

Forgiveness

From You, our Father,
We need not beg forgiveness,
Using thick yet fragile words.
Forgiveness is asked and granted
As we stand mute,
Aware of You and of our sin.
You are Love,
And love, in essence,
Cannot help forgiving.

You forgave David,
Forgiving adultery and murder.
You forgave Peter,
Forgiving denial of your Son.
Your son, loving,
Forgave Mary Magdalene,
Forgiving faithlessness and prostitution.
He forgave Zacchaeus,
Forgiving dishonesty and thievery.
Your Son, loving,
Forgave those who conspired against and killed him.
From You, Father,
We need but ask forgiveness, and
Our sins, small and large,
Your love forgives.
Help us, our Father,
To accept your forgiveness,
And then—forgive ourself.

39 Love

Dear God and Father of us all, help us to understand the nature of love, as you demonstrated it by sending your Son. Help us develop the kind of loving spirit that responds first to you, so that we may love ourselves in such a way that we may live honest and worthwhile lives. Finally help us love others in ways that free them to be their best selves.

Help us to be friendly and courteous to others, even in the face of rejection or misunderstanding. Grant that we may not use our affections in evil or perverse ways. May we feel privileged to bring to our families and friends, to our associates and acquaintances, to unknown persons in need as well as to that special young man or woman in our lives, the genuine love and warmth that builds good relationships.

May we put into the word "love" all the best, the finest meanings and attitudes that we know. We pray in the name of Jesus who was the gift of love. Amen.

RESPONSIVE READINGS

Our Church

Leader: For the church, which through the years has nourished, healed, guided, and renewed our spirits,

Everyone: We thank you humbly, O God.

Leader: For the sanctuary and pulpit, for the leadership of clergy and members, for the devotion of choir and church school teachers, and all who attend faithfully,

Everyone: We thank you humbly, O God.

Leader: For our ties to Christians of all ages; for the courage we gain from their faithfulness amid praise and persecution,

Everyone: We thank you humbly, O God.

Leader: For the times when two or three of us are gathered together in Jesus' name for quiet prayer or enthusiastic discussion, or serious planning—for the times when we become, ourselves, the church,

Everyone: We thank you humbly, O God.

Leader: Enlarge our understanding of the church, Father. May we see it not only as our congregation which assembles on this corner, but also the church in India, the church in Congo, and the church in Russia. May our dream of the ecumenical church—the church of the whole family of Christians—be one that we help bring to reality, according to your will;

Everyone: Use us in the building of your church, O God.

Leader: May our church become truly open to all races, all nationalities, all classes of men on earth as we build toward your kingdom on earth;

Everyone: Use us in the building of your church, O God.

Leader: Make us impatient with pretense and laziness within the church. Help us speak to one another with affection. Support us as we try to witness to others concerning your judgment and love.

Everyone: Use us in the building of your church, O God. Transform our personal lives so that they become "living" sacrifices, "holy and acceptable" to you.

Leader: "Like living stones" may we be "built into a spiritual house."

Everyone: Reorganize the rules and practices of our congregations and conventions and councils where we fail to do your will. Help us bring a clearer, brighter, more appealing image of the church to the world. For such an opportunity to *be* the church, we thank you humbly, O God.

41 This Fellowship

Leader: Sometimes in daily experiences we try desperately to join the crowd, but are left out;

Everyone: We try to be a friend, and are rejected. We try to serve some cause, and are overlooked. Yet we can turn to you, O God, and to Christians in this place and say, "Thank you for caring about us."

Leader: All around us there are people in classrooms, people on crowded streets, people jammed in

Romans 12:1
1 Peter 2:5

stores and buses and theaters—and all wear masks of politeness or bitterness or unconcern.

Everyone: **We have reached out for association with some of them and they have turned away, unwilling to be known. We are often frightened by what we see in ourselves, as well, and what we show to others. Yet we can turn to you, O God, and to Christians in this place and say, "Thank you for seeing the good within us."**

Leader: Sometimes we pretend to be what we are not for fear that our real selves are unacceptable. We commit ourselves to activities which we despise. We are afraid.

Everyone: **Yet we can turn to you, O God, and to Christians in this place and say, "Thank you for understanding; help us be courageous."**

Leader: We need this continuous contact with you, Father, and the continuing concern of these people.

Everyone: **Herein we have a place. Here we enlarge our knowledge and our faith. We find meaning and direction for our lives. We learn to know others, and to be truly known. Thank you, God, for this Christian fellowship.**

Leader: "So then you are no longer strangers and sojourners, but you are fellow citizens with the saints and members of the household of God, built upon the foundation of the apostles and prophets, Christ Jesus himself being the cornerstone, in whom the whole structure is joined together."

Everyone: **We thank you, Father, for such a household and such acceptance. Amen.**

———

Ephesians 2:19-21

Something to Share

(Witness and Outreach)

Leader: "Therefore, if any one is in Christ, he is a new creation; the old has passed away, behold, the new has come."

Everyone: Perhaps we do not want to be a new creation. We like our present way of pleasing others. We do not wish to miss out on the excitement of life. Being a new person is too hard.

Leader: "All this is from God, who through Christ reconciled us to himself and gave us the ministry of reconciliation."

Everyone: How can we reconcile others to God when we do not know what it means? We feel isolated from people and from God. Who would listen to us? Who would care?

Leader: "God was in Christ reconciling the world to himself, not counting their trespasses against them, and entrusting to us the message of reconciliation."

Everyone: But we are so busy—so young. Reconciliation is meant for those who are older—those who are wiser—those who want to preach and teach and heal and go into all the world.

Leader: "We are ambassadors for Christ, God making his appeal through us."

Everyone: There is no place to run. We must bear our witness if we believe in God. If we accept Jesus Christ, then we must offer our faith to all. "We are ambassadors for Christ, God making his appeal through us."

Leader: "Behold, now is the acceptable time; behold, now is the day of salvation."

2 Corinthians 5:17-20; 6:2

The Good Gifts   43
(Stewardship)

Leader: What do you bring to dedicate to God?

Everyone: We bring our lives, imperfect though they are. We bring our time and money—

FEMALE VOICES: That sounds so fine. But our abilities are spent on so many little things. Our calendars are crammed with many activities. We fritter away our money on frivolous things we see and admire.

Everyone: It is true, O God. We are often guilty of misusing time and money which we have. Guide us that we may find the greater values.

Leader: "Do your best to present yourself to God as one approved, a workman who has no need to be ashamed, rightly handling the word of truth."

Everyone: We bring our talent and ability, our vigor and curiosity. O Father, help us develop those abilities, that we may make a worthy contribution with our life.

MALE VOICES: Good-sounding phrases—but how stingy we often are with the time granted to us to live. How cautiously we enter into worship. How seldom do we work for others. How little thought we give to money earned and spent. How little time we spend in building up and using talent.

Everyone: **It is true, O God. Help us separate the important choices from the unimportant. Help us desire to spend ourselves in more meaningful pursuits. May we allot some time to all good things. Help us play and work, get to know others and serve, laugh, and pray, each in its time.**

Leader: "Where your treasure is, there will your heart be also."

FEMALE VOICES: Where is our treasure tied up? Too often we strain to get a car, records, clothes, recreation equipment, musical instruments, and other things that may not seem so valuable when we get them.

Everyone: **What can we answer, O God? Help us as Christians discern the relative value of things. Guide us in the use of our possessions, that we may not be tricked into believing that they are our greatest treasures.**

Leader: What do you bring to dedicate to God?

Everyone: **We bring our lives, yet frequently withhold a portion for ourselves.**

MALE VOICES: What do we withhold? Perhaps our freedom . . . our occupation . . . our future plans . . . our personal behavior with our friends.

Everyone: **Forgive us, Father, giver of each good and perfect gift. Help us want to give thee a worthy measure of our time and talent, money and possessions, worship and love.**

---

2 Timothy 2:15
Matthew 6:21

Leader: "Bless the LORD, O my soul!
O LORD my God, thou art very great!
Thou art clothed with honor and majesty,
who coverest thyself with light as with
a garment,
who hast stretched out the heavens like a
tent,
Thou didst set the earth on its foundations,
so that it should never be shaken."

MALE VOICES: We have brought into being the
Atomic Age, nuclear warheads, space exploration,
with all their possibilities for either good or evil.
We have the power to rattle the very foundations
of our world.

**Everyone: Forgive us, Lord God, for willingness to
waste and destroy. Teach us to use and
conserve.**

Leader: "Thou makest springs gush forth in the
valleys;
they flow between the hills,
they give drink to every beast of the field."
"From thy lofty abode thou waterest the
mountains;
the earth is satisfied with the fruit of
thy work."

FEMALE VOICES: In our own selfish way we have
often polluted the streams and wasted our water.
There is scarcely enough that is fit to drink.

**Everyone: Forgive us, Lord God, for willingness to
waste and destroy. Teach us to conserve.**

Leader: "Thou dost cause the grass to grow for
the cattle,
and plants for man to cultivate,
that he may bring forth food from the
earth."

MALE VOICES: Some eat too well, some not at all.

Everyone: Forgive us, Lord God, for willingness to waste and destroy. Show us how to share.

Leader: "The trees of the LORD are watered abundantly,
In them the birds build their nests;
Thou hast made the moon to mark the seasons;
the sun knows its time for setting."

FEMALE VOICES: Even the air is contaminated by our smoky cities and endless cars. We fill the air with fighter planes and missiles. We reach out for the moon—which may be good or bad.

Everyone: Forgive us, Lord God, for our willingness to waste and destroy. Help us create with thee for all men's good.

Leader: "O LORD, how manifold are thy works!
In wisdom hast thou made them all;
the earth is full of thy creatures."

MALE VOICES: So full, in fact, is the earth, that population has become a frightful problem. How can we feed the people? What can we do with them all?

Everyone: Forgive us, Lord God, for our willingness to waste and destroy—even people, created in thy image.

Leader: "When thou hidest thy face, they are dismayed;
when thou takest away their breath, they die
and return to their dust.

When thou sendest forth thy Spirit, they are created;

and thou renewest the face of the ground."

FEMALE VOICES: The people need their Creator to live. We must learn how to build with the God of our salvation. Otherwise we die.

Everyone: Forgive us, Lord God, for our willingness to waste and destroy. Teach us to live and work with thee.
"May the glory of the LORD endure for ever, may the LORD rejoice in his works."

Psalms 104:1-2, 5, 10-11, 13-14, 16-17, 19, 24, 29-31

God's Seeking Love

Leader: "O LORD, thou hast searched me and known me!
Thou knowest when I sit down and when I rise up;
thou discernest my thoughts from afar.
Even before a word is on my tongue,
lo, O LORD, thou knowest it altogether."

MALE VOICES: Is this true? Does God know when we deliberately lie to impress our friends? Does he hear our unspoken, angry thoughts?

Leader: "Thou dost beset me behind and before,
and layest thy hand upon me.
Such knowledge is too wonderful for me;
it is high, I cannot attain it."

FEMALE VOICES: What can be wonderful about being so well known by God? Who wants to be exposed to such knowledge?

Leader: "Whither shall I go from thy Spirit?
Or whither shall I flee from thy presence?"

Everyone: We must hide from God. We are afraid to be seen and known by him.

Leader: "If I take the wings of the morning and
dwell in the uttermost parts of the sea,
even there thy hand shall lead me, and thy
right hand shall hold me."

MALE VOICES: Can we not escape God? Why does
he seek us out—to judge us? To condemn us?

FEMALE VOICES: Can it be that God seeks us out to
love? To forgive us? To use us?

Leader: "If I say, 'Let only darkness cover me,
and the light about me be night,'
even the darkness is not dark to thee,
the night is bright as the day;
for darkness is as light with thee."

**Everyone: So it is with God's love. He seeks us
out with forgiveness and longing. He
turns our darkness to light. Such a gift
of love is scarcely deserved, but we can
receive it if we will.**

Leader: "Search me, O God, and know my heart!
Try me and know my thoughts!

**Everyone: "And see if there be any wicked way in
me,
and lead me in the way everlasting!"**

Psalms 139:1-2, 4-7, 9-12, 23-24

46   Jesus, the Man and the Son

Leader: Let us remember the man, Jesus. He walked
the ways men walk today, working at common
tasks, talking with neighbors, laughing with children, watching the flight of birds, thinking about
life and dreaming beyond his daily tasks.

Everyone: We remember Jesus, the man.

Leader: He thought of the races of mankind and
dreamed of a God whose love contained all the
nations of the world; but when he spoke of this
the people of his home town almost lynched him.

Everyone: We remember the man—Jesus.

Leader: He thought that people and their needs were more important than the sabbath rules. But when he helped a blind man or fed his disciples on the sabbath, the religious leaders were enraged.

Everyone: We remember Jesus, the man.

Leader: He dreamed of a temple that was holy, men who dedicated themselves to God; but when he drove out the corrupt money-changers, the priests plotted his death.

Everyone: We remember the man—Jesus.

Leader: Let us remember Jesus, the Son. He walked the ways men walk today, glorifying the common tasks, transforming strangers into neighbors, blessing the children, teaching and healing wherever he went.

Everyone: We remember Jesus, the Son.

Leader: The blind saw and the lame walked. The captive was set free and the lonely learned to love. The poor at last received good news, and the sinful were forgiven.

Everyone: We remember the Son—Jesus.

Leader: He defied the corrupt leaders of his day, and both state and temple replied by nailing him to a cross. He died a painful death while asking God's blessing on his executioners. And that cross became a redeeming symbol in the history of mankind.

Everyone: We remember Jesus, the man and the Son.

Leader: "The L ord came and stood forth, calling as at other times, 'Samuel! Samuel!'

M ale V oice : " 'Speak, for thy servant hears.'

Leader: "And Samuel grew, and the L ord was with him."

Everyone: So it was with Samuel. He heard the call of God. His life was changed.

Leader: "At Gibeon the L ord appeared to Solomon in a dream by night; and God said, 'Ask what I shall give you.'

M ale V oice : " 'Thou hast shown great and steadfast love to thy servant David my father, because he walked before thee in faithfulness, . . . And now, O L ord my God, thou hast made thy servant king. . . . Give thy servant therefore an understanding mind to govern thy people, that I may discern between good and evil . . .' "

Leader: "It pleased the Lord that Solomon had asked this."

Everyone: So it was with Solomon, and David— and the faithful kings of Israel. They heard the call of God. Their lives were changed.

Leader: "And I heard the voice of the Lord saying, 'Whom shall I send, and who will go for us?'

M ale V oice : " 'Here am I! Send me.'

Everyone: So it was with Isaiah and Amos and Jeremiah and all the worthy prophets. They heard the call of God. Their lives were changed.

Leader: "After three days [Joseph and Mary] found him in the temple, sitting among the teachers, listening to them and asking them questions. And when they saw him they were astonished.

MALE VOICE: "'How is it that you sought me? Did you not know that I must be in my Father's house?'"

Leader: "And Jesus increased in wisdom and in stature, and in favor with God and man."

Everyone: So it was with Jesus, who heard the call of his Father God. His life was changed.

Leader: "Paul, a servant of Jesus Christ, called to be an apostle, set apart for the gospel of God."

MALE VOICE: "I am not ashamed of the gospel: it is the power of God for salvation to every one who has faith."

Leader: "It is not the hearers of the law who are righteous before God, but the doers of the law who will be justified."

Everyone: So it was with Paul the Apostle and other followers of Jesus Christ. They heard the call of God.

MALE VOICE: Am I asked to live out my faith as a student, a scientist, a doctor, a mechanic, a preacher, a politician, a salesman? How do I answer the call of God in such a world as this?

Leader: We share a common call to be Christian in all we do, to the best of our understanding. The Lord calls to us as clearly as to all his servants in the past.

Everyone: So it is with us. We hear the call of God through Jesus Christ. We hear it through the needs of those around us. We pray that we might be strong enough to answer now, "Here am I. Send me."

_____
1 Sam. 3:10, 19; 1 Kings 3:5-7, 9-10; Isaiah 6:8-9, 8:11; Luke 2:46-49, 52; Romans 1:1, 16; 2:13

Leader: Almighty God, prepare us in these days to stand before the cross of Jesus Christ with deeper knowledge of its truth.

Everyone: Let us know the truth.

Leader: Almighty God, prepare us in these days to stand before the open tomb of Jesus with deeper understanding of the resurrection.

Everyone: Let us know the truth.

Leader: Almighty God, let the cross of Christ compel all men to face the tragic sin that scars the human race with war and famine, poverty and hate.

Everyone: Help us face the truth.

Leader: Almighty God, free us from our sin and heal us by the power of the risen Christ that we may live by his righteousness.

Everyone: The spirit of life in Jesus Christ has set us free from the law of sin and death.

Leader: Almighty God, let the cross of Jesus Christ stand as a lonely symbol of the loneliness of men, cut off by his own self-interest from God and man, groping for love, hoping for friendship, seeking relationship.

Everyone: Help us find one another.

Leader: Almighty God, restore us to our right relationship with thee and to others, that we may love again and live again by the power of the risen Christ.

Everyone: God was in Christ, reconciling the world.

Leader: "We are afflicted in every way,

Everyone: "but not crushed.

Leader: "We are perplexed,

Everyone: "but not driven to despair.

Leader: "We are persecuted,

Everyone: "but not forsaken.

Leader: "We are struck down,

Everyone: "but not destroyed."

Leader: "Our outer nature is wasting away,

Everyone: "Our inner nature is renewed."

Leader: "All flesh is grass,
    and all its beauty is like the flower
        of the field.
    The grass withers, the flower fades, . . .
        surely the people is grass."

**Everyone: " 'I am the resurrection and the life; he
who believes in me, though he die, yet
shall he live, and whoever lives and believes in me shall never die.' "**

2 Cor. 4:8-9, 16; Isa. 40:6-7; John 11:25-26

The Meaning of Easter   49

Leader: "Blessed be the God and Father of our
Lord Jesus Christ, who has blessed us in Christ
with every spiritual blessing."

**Everyone: "For he has made known to us in all
wisdom and insight the mystery of his
will."**

Leader: "We who first hoped in Christ have been
destined and appointed to live for the praise of
his glory."

Everyone: For he has given the greatness of his power to those who believe in Christ.

Leader: "He raised him from the dead and made him sit at his right hand . . . above all rule and authority and power and dominion, and above every name that is named, not only in this age but in that which is to come."

Everyone: "And he has put all things under his feet and has made him the head over all things for the church."

Leader: "God, who is rich in mercy, out of the great love . . . made us alive together with Christ."

Everyone: By such grace we have been saved.

Leader: "We are his workmanship, created in Christ Jesus for good works, which God prepared beforehand, that we should walk in them."

Everyone: By such grace we have been saved.

Leader: "You are no longer strangers and sojourners, but you are fellow citizens with the saints and members of the household of God."

Everyone: "For he is our peace, who has made us both one, and has broken down the dividing wall of hostility."

Leader: "I bow my knees before the Father, from whom every family in heaven and on earth is named, that . . . he may grant you to be strengthened . . . in the inner man."

Everyone: May Christ dwell in our hearts.

Leader: "May Christ dwell in your hearts through faith; that you, being rooted and grounded in love, may have power to comprehend . . . the breadth and length and height and depth, and to know the love of Christ which surpasses knowledge."

Everyone: May "we all attain to the unity of faith . . . and to the stature of the fullness of Christ."

Leader: Praise be to God who through Christ Jesus enables us to put aside our old ways and be directed anew.

Everyone "Grace be with all who love our Lord Jesus Christ with love undying."

Ephesians 1:3, 9, 12, 20-22; 2:4-5, 10, 19, 14; 3:14-19; 4:13; 6:24

Forgiveness   50

Leader: "Forgive us our debts,
As we also have forgiven our debtors."

Everyone: There is a string attached. God offers to forgive us—as we forgive. That is a hard bargain. What about the relative who wrongs us or whom we have wronged, so that we come to church with angry or guilty thoughts?

Leader: "If you are offering your gift at the altar, and there remember that your brother has something against you, leave your gift there before the altar and go; first be reconciled to your brother, and then come and offer your gift."

Everyone: What about the person at school who torments us and picks on us until we could scream or retaliate?

Leader: "Do not resist one who is evil. But if any one strikes you on the right check, turn to him the other also."

Everyone: Such an idea is alien to our world. We want to hit back when we are struck. We want to hurt others when we are hurt. It is hard to be kind when others are cruel, hard to love when others hate. Ask any believer in nonviolent protest. It is hard.

Leader: " 'Love your enemies and pray for those who persecute you, so that you may be sons of your Father who is in heaven; for he makes his sun rise on the evil and on the good, and sends rain on the just and on the unjust.' "

Everyone: There must be a limit to what we can endure. Perhaps we can forgive a person once—or twice—but if he still abuses us and misuses our trust, what then?

Leader: "Then Peter came up and said to him, 'Lord, how often shall my brother sin against me, and I forgive him? As many as seven times?' Jesus said to him, 'I do not say to you seven times, but seventy times seven.' "

Everyone: Lord God, it is a hard bargain. Forgiving others does not always seem realistic. Even forgiveness carries with it a temptation to be self-righteous. We may forgive someone and burden him forever with a debt of gratitude to us. We seek your forgiveness now for such pride and ego that we expect your full forgiveness for our sins, but deny full forgiveness to others. Help us learn what it is we say in prayer,
"Forgive us our debts,

As we also have forgiven our debtors."

Matt. 6:12; 5:23-24, 39, 44-45; 18:21-22

Reconciliation

Leader: What creates walls between men and between nations?

MALE VOICES: Fear! For many reasons we fear one another, and to fear people is to be separated from them.

FEMALE VOICES: Pride! When we are confronted by the truth about ourselves, our pride keeps us from facing our inadequacies. We are separated from others who might free us and allow us to know them.

MALE VOICES: Power! Wanting to control lives and governments we build walls of concrete or wood or ideas, and lock ourselves in as well as lock others out.

FEMALE VOICES: Hate! We are unable or unwilling to love each other. We hate people we do not know, and we wish them dead. Death of recognition is a hard cold wall.

Leader: Can these walls be broken down?

Everyone: Indeed! But we like the walls. They make us secure. As long as no one scales the walls there is a kind of peace, or should we say silence—the silence of the dead. We seem to prefer the peace of death to the struggles of life.

Leader: But can the walls be broken down?

MALE VOICES: Yes, with faith. If we dare to trust one another, if we dare to trust the Giver of all life, then fear can be banished and so, too, the wall made of it. But both sides of the wall must trust each other, and trust must have a foundation on which to build understanding.

FEMALE VOICES: Humility breaks walls of pride. Then we who dare to see ourselves as we are can begin to build relationships out of what is really there. But humility must first be cultivated in ourselves.

MALE VOICES: Love is the perfect breaker of walls that separate people. We all need the confirmation of love. Others need such love from us. We all need to know that God cares for us.

Leader: If what you say is true, the walls come down only at tremendous cost to us as we try to break them down.

Everyone: Sometimes the cost is death. Jesus died on a cross, but though he was killed, yet he loved the killers. The walls of hate and power and pride and fear could not prevail.

Leader: "For he is our peace, who has made us both one, and has broken down the dividing wall of hostility."

Everyone: Help us, Father, where we are, begin to tear down the walls of our own isolation from people—our little fears of change, our personal prejudices, our protective natures. Show us how wonderful a view we get of people when the walls come down.

Ephesians 2:14

52   Service to Others

Leader: O God, we appreciate Jesus Christ, who stirs us to good works. We recall that he healed the sick, taught the uninformed, preached to the uncommitted, worked in his father's carpenter shop, counseled individuals in trouble, and spoke out about the shortcomings of political and religious leaders of his day.

Everyone: **May we as followers be shaken out of our comfortable ruts in church.**

Leader: Help us evaluate our present jobs as students, laborers, professional people-to-be in terms of our commitment to Christ.

Everyone: **May we work hard, giving our devotion to our jobs, using our abilities fully, knowing we serve you in our efforts.**

Leader: Whenever we think of those who are sick, hungry, imprisoned, poorly clad, or strange in the community, may we hear again the voice of Jesus saying, " 'Truly, I say to you, as you did it to one of the least of these my brethren, you did it to me.' "

Everyone: **May we accept our responsibility to the refugee, the orphan, the unemployed, the alcoholic, the unmarried mother and her child, the victims of war, flood, tornado and fire, the sick, the lonely, the handicapped.**

Leader: Help us minister also to the deep yearning of people for meaning in life.

Everyone: **May we be worthy witnesses to the Christian gospel so that in our actions and words, people may sense a purpose greater than our own which gives life significance.**

Leader: O God, make us more like Jesus Christ who became a servant to all. Help us do your will without reservation, without complaint.

Everyone: **May we be given jobs to do, O Lord, so that in serving others we may know the pleasure of serving you as well.**

Matt. 25:40

Leader: Help us, Father God, in our friendships, to be loyal and trustworthy,

Everyone: **That we may learn what fidelity means to all human relationships, beginning in our own homes and among our closest companions.**

Leader: Instill in us a faithfulness of word and action,

Everyone: **That we may be the kind of friends we expect our friends to be to us.**

Leader: Teach us to communicate freely and without fear,

Everyone: **That we may know the fulfillment of sharing our deep feelings and longings with those who care.**

Leader: Help us, Lord, discover the uniqueness of each person that we meet, and help us learn respect for personality, even when people differ from us greatly,

Everyone: **That we may never use friends or dates for selfish purposes or wrong motives.**

Leader: Father, lead us in our choices of activities that we may neither embarrass nor bring harm to our companions,

Everyone: **And help us acquire the wisdom of having fun that is acceptable in your sight.**

Leader: May we learn to look beyond the obvious appearance of a person, into the inner person,

Everyone: **And may those we love look beyond our walls and shields and see the person we long to be.**

Leader: Help us sense the beauty which is in the attraction of one person to another;

Everyone: **Turn attraction into a creative sharing which will enrich, not destroy, our lives.**

Leader: Fill us with the wonder of discovering thee, O God, through our personal relationships with others. May each friend with whom we share leave a portion of himself with us to beautify our lives.

Everyone: **May we give to our relationships the qualities of love and concern which sustain life. Help us be better persons because of our friends. Grant that our friendship may bless the lives of others. Draw us close to our Master who told his followers, " 'You are my friends if you do what I command you. No longer do I call you servants . . . but I have called you friends.' "**

John 15:14-15

Love One Another

Leader: "If I speak in the tongues of men and of angels, but have not love,

Everyone: **"I am a noisy gong or a clanging cymbal."**

Female Voices: Winged is the heart that knows love,

Male Voices: And like bird songs at dawn Is our discovery of one another,

Everyone: **For love is the grand procession, The triumph of God over chaos.**

Leader: Love is our own search for stature, God's gift of power to grow; The music of our minds and bodies;

Everyone:	Speak to us, God, of the design of creation, Revealed in the dreams that enthrall us.
FEMALE VOICES:	Help us reveal ourselves to each other In ways that enable togetherness,
MALE VOICES:	Let us see in the eyes of each other The persons we long to be,
Everyone:	Out of our dreams of today Let us build a temple tomorrow, Becoming through friendship and courtship Persons worthy of the future.
Leader:	Cause our love for one another, And for all persons everywhere To cast out fears of differences, And free us to be understanding.
Everyone:	Help us bear hostility, And strengthen us when we are rejected. Translate our love into action.
FEMALE VOICES:	Winged is the heart that knows love,
MALE VOICES:	And like bird songs at dawn Is our discovery of one another,
Everyone:	For love is the grand procession, The triumph of God over chaos.

Leader: "For now we see in a mirror dimly, but then face to face.

Everyone: "Now I know in part; then I shall understand fully, even as I have been fully understood. So faith, hope, love abide, these three; but the greatest of these is love."

1 Cor. 13:1, 12-13

God at Work in the Universe

Leader: O LORD, our Lord,
how majestic is thy name in all the earth!

Everyone: **God is the Giver and Sustainer of all life. But with limited understanding, we have tried to bind him to the earth. We confess that we have secretly wondered if intelligent life exists on another planet, and if so, is there a plan of salvation for those? Is our God their God as well?**

Leader: God is Lord of the atoms and molecules, the mysterious world known through the microscope, as well as the Lord of the far flung universe beyond the telescope.

Everyone: **God is the Giver and Sustainer of all life. But we, with selfish interests, have tried to bind him to our nation. Feeling ourselves especially favored as a nation, we forget God's love and compassion for every man, woman, and child in every nation.**

Leader: God is not partial to cultures and races, nations, and creeds. He is the Lord of all.

Everyone: **God is the Giver and Sustainer of all life. But we have wanted to tie him to our definition of decency. We refuse to believe that God despises self-righteousness that calls itself "decency," and fails to act in a world of need. He loves the decency of genuine love, and he is with those who suffer ugliness and pain and neglect.**

Leader: "All the paths of the LORD are steadfast love and faithfulness,
for those who keep his covenant and his testimonies."

Everyone: God is the Giver and Sustainer of all life. But in our ignorance we try to secure him to the past when we feel self-sufficient. We seek to make him Lord of our own time when we fear change. Yet we know he is the Creator and Sustainer of the very change we fear.

Leader: The Lord is with us though we try to hide from him, though we try to contain him in an era or an hour.

Everyone: God is the Giver and Sustainer of all life. But we often act as if he is Lord only of the church. We confess to smothering his creative words too often in ritual, church busyness and piety, and have seemed to make him a stranger to his own world. Let us not forget, "In the beginning God created the heavens and the earth."

Everyone: We cannot bind God to anything. O God, forgive our attempts to find our security by trying to hold you where we want you. We give thanks for knowing finally we are secure only when we are able to trust in your continuing acts of love for all your creation. Help us be more courageous agents of that love in the heights and depths of your creation.

Psalms 8:1; 25:10
Genesis 1:1

56   God at Work in History

Leader: We praise thee, O God, for thy mighty deeds by which the worlds were formed and by which man came into the stream of time and experience we call history which glorifies thee because of man and in spite of men.

Everyone: We praise thy name, O God, for thy creation.

Leader: For great leaders whose keen minds, courageous spirits, wise statesmanship, warm compassion have been the instruments by which thy spirit has spoken to the human race.

Everyone: We praise thy name, O God, for thy redeeming Word.

Leader: For men of science, searching for new ways of healing diseases, increasing supplies of food, and extending the knowledge of men.

Everyone: We praise thy name, O God.

Leader: For those in every nation of the earth whose talents are dedicated to the creating of peace and security and the frustrating of warfare in all its forms.

Everyone: We praise thy name, O God.

Leader: For men in industry and commerce who by their honesty and integrity give stability to the economic life of the world and guarantee fair employment and good working conditions.

Everyone: We praise thy name, O God.

Leader: For education in schools of all kinds whose knowledge and compassion combine to aid the seeking student in finding his place in the world.

Everyone: We praise thy name, O God.

Leader: For entertainers and all those who know the secret of making people laugh; for artists and poets and all who call forth dreams from the human heart; for lovers and all who restore tenderness to the soul of man.

Everyone: We praise thy name and give thee thanks, O God.

Leader: "The LORD by wisdom founded the earth;
by understanding he established the
heavens:

"My son, keep sound wisdom and discretion;
let them not escape from your sight."

Everyone: Learning is not easy, and wisdom is a
far goal. May I appreciate the blessing
I have in education. May all my learning opportunities lead me toward understanding and wisdom.

Leader: "The beginning of wisdom is this;
Get wisdom;
and whatever you get, get insight."

Everyone: Wisdom is the climax of my learning
along the way. It is the completion of
the jigsaw puzzle of learning. May I put
together the pieces of information and
knowledge well, so that wisdom may result.

Leader: "Keep hold of instruction, do not let go."

Everyone: May I not be tempted to quit school,
even when things are rough. May I
realize, deep inside me, the value of
education in all forms.

Leader: "Let your eyes look directly forward, and
your gaze be straight before you.
Take heed to the path of your feet,
then all your ways will be sure."

Everyone: May my learning help me be a better
person, upright, able to fulfill my purposes and use my abilities. May I find joy

in education and strength in my tasks
of learning. I am thankful for all who
aid me in the learning process, in school,
in church, at home, and among friends.
May my delight in learning never end
as long as I live.

Prov. 3:19, 21; 4:7, 13, 25-26.

I, Myself

Leader: "What is man that thou are mindful of him,
and the son of man that thou dost care
for him?"

Everyone: We are restless. There's no place to
turn. What shall we do? What's it all
about? Why are we here? What is man?

Leader: Life is flying. Time is wasting. Settle down.
Grow up. Use your head. Make up your mind.

Everyone: But how can we do all these conflicting
things? What's it all about? Where are
we going? Why are we here?

Leader: Life is a blast. Live it up. Have fun while
you're young. Get to the top. That's what you hear.

Everyone: But we are confused by life's pace,
frightened by what we do not under-
stand, bored by the foolishness of people,
disgusted with what some persons do.
And we are lonely. What is the answer
to "What is man?"

Leader: Get with it. You can't just drift in this time
of automation. Be superior. No—conform. That's
what you hear when you raise the question.

Everyone: Such answers are not enough for us . . .
such competition . . . such conformity.
What is life all about?

Leader: "What is man that thou are mindful of him, and the son of man that thou dost care for him?

Yet thou hast made him little less than God, and dost crown him with glory and honor."

Everyone: But what does this mean to us now? We are young people among the world's billions of people. How can we know God cares for us, and how can we find our particular place?

Leader: Do not sell yourself short. God made only one you. No one else can have your style, or wear your smile, or think your thoughts, or feel exactly the way you do, or do your work for you.

Everyone: It is hard to find the answers to existence, and to know what to think, and do, and be.

Leader: You are a unique creation among other creatures. The church, your Bible, perhaps your family will help guide you toward the meaning of life. But finally, no one can tell you exactly who you are or where you fit. You must discover that yourself.

Everyone: Father, help us discover who we are in your divine plan. Help us discover that stranger who dwells somewhere deep inside of us, beneath the outer shell we sometimes wear in public. Lift us above the pressures and confusion, that we may see clearly where we fit into the scheme of things. Then, let us go down into the mainstream of life to take our place. Amen.

———

Psalms 8:4-5

Thanksgiving

Leader: "Great is our Lord, and abundant in power;
his understanding is beyond measure."

Everyone: **"For he is our God,**
and we are the people of his pasture."

Leader: "I give thee thanks, O LORD,
with my whole heart."

Everyone: **"Enter his gates with thanksgiving,**
and his courts with praise!
Give thanks to him, bless his name!
For the LORD is good;
his steadfast love endures forever."

Leader: "For God so loved the world that he gave
his only Son, that whoever believes in him should
not perish but have eternal life."

Everyone: **"Thanks be to God for his inexpressible**
gift!"

Leader: There is a splendor in our lives,
A glory not of our making.

Everyone: **At the heart of all our thanks is God,**
And his love comes forth to meet us;
The burden then is ours.

Leader: "Every one to whom much is given, of him
will much be required;

Everyone: **"and of him to whom men commit much**
they will demand the more."

Leader: Out of our having we must share;
Out of our living we must love.

Everyone: **Until we, in the fullness of Christ, are**
formed in a likeness to the Father.

Leader: We give thanks to God,

Everyone: **"For the LORD is good;**
his steadfast love endures forever,
and his faithfulness to all generations."

Psalms 147:5; 95:7; 138:1; 100:4-5   2 Cor. 9:15
John 3:16   Luke 12:48

Leader: "The LORD lift up his countenance
　　　　upon you, and give you peace."

MALE VOICES: So we hear. Peace is a quiet blessing
upon us. But there is no real peace around us.

FEMALE VOICES: No end to war. No end to quarrels.
No end to worry. No end to guilt.

**Everyone: O God, we pray for peace—but do not
know what it is—or how it comes. Hear
us in our distress.**

Leader: "Great peace have those who love thy law."

MALE VOICES: So we read and sing—but those who
"love thy law" are hurt by war and crime as well.
There is no peace.

FEMALE VOICES: What is peace? Is it the reward for
faithful practice of religion? Is that what Jesus
taught?

Leader: "Do not think that I have come to bring
peace on earth; I have not come to bring peace,
but a sword . . . he who does not take his cross
and follow me is not worthy of me."

**Everyone: O God, we pray for peace—but do not
know what it is—or how it comes. Hear
us in our distress.**

Leader: " 'Glory to God in the highest,
　　　　and on earth peace among men with whom
he is pleased!' "

MALE VOICES: There seems to be a condition on
peace. Peace is neither absence of war nor end
of conflicts.

FEMALE VOICES: What is peace? If not the absence of hostility, nor religious practice only—does Jesus give a clue to peace?

Leader: "Peace I leave with you; my peace I give to you; not as the world gives do I give to you. Let not your hearts be troubled, neither let them be afraid." "Therefore, since we are justified by faith, we have peace with God through our Lord Jesus Christ."

Everyone **Let us then pursue what makes for peace and for mutual upbuilding." O God, make us the instruments of thy peace—the peace that comes from knowing thee, the individual, inner peace of trusting our relationship with thee, even in times of stress. Amen.**

Numbers 6:26   Luke 2:14
Psalms 119:165   John 14:27
Matt. 10:34-38   Romans 5:1; 14:19

In Crisis   61

Leader: Dear Father, from the burdens of worry and overanxious fears that crowd our days,

Everyone: Deliver us, and help us learn to trust thee more.

Leader: From every minor and major crisis that pushes in upon us and causes us to panic or become irritable and rude; from misunderstandings with parents and friends, our thoughtless deeds,

Everyone: Deliver us, and help us learn to trust thee more.

Leader: From the temptation to give up in the face of defeat, or turn away from threatening conditions and inconsiderate people,

Everyone: Deliver us, and help us learn to trust thee more.

Leader: Dear Father, help us build up the necessary courage we need to face these times, to love people in spite of threats, to be concerned with important issues, to *care* when others cringe before the crises in their lives.

Everyone: Grant us the strength to live wisely and well, able to change and · grow as crises come.

Leader: We know that oftentimes the very situations we deplore are testing grounds and strengthening experiences. So let us learn from outside calamities and inner anxieties.

Everyone: Grant us the strength to live wisely and well, able to change and grow as crises come.

**"Be thou to me a rock of refuge,
a strong fortress, to save me,
for thou art my rock and my fortress."**

Psalms 71:3

---

62   The Coming of Christmas

Leader: "As it is written in the book of the words of Isaiah the prophet,

'The voice of one crying in the wilderness:
Prepare the way of the Lord,
make his paths straight.' "

Everyone: O God, in the confusion of our frequent wrongdoing, we turn to thee and await the continuing gift of thy love in Jesus Christ. Bring us to this Christmas season with simple faith.

Leader: "Every valley shall be filled,
and every mountain and hill shall be
brought low."

Everyone: Some of our life has been spent in
foolish fantasies and self-dislike. We
have struggled with our vain ambitions
and have often been disappointed with
ourselves. Sometimes our pride has
caused us to exalt ourselves. In worship
we have pretended to feel thy presence.
Help us clear our lives of folly and pretense. Bring us to this Christmas season
with simple faith.

Leader: "and the crooked shall be made straight,
and the rough ways shall be made smooth;"

Everyone: How often in our complicated life we
wish the choices were clearcut. How
grateful we are for this Advent season to
remind us of thy love. In Jesus Christ
there is a way for us to know thee.
Bring us to this Christmas season with
simple faith.

Leader: "and all flesh shall see the salvation of God."

Everyone: O God, prepare us so we may receive
anew the gift of thy love. Lift us up
from our despair, support us in our enthusiasm, bring us down from the lofty
places of our pride, guide us in the paths
of true righteousness, and send us running to others with the good news that
Christ is born again this day in the hearts
of all who believe.

Luke 3:4-6

One Body
(Unity)

Leader: We pray for the church of Jesus Christ scattered as it is through all the nations of the world, divided by its creeds and by its traditions, held apart by its organization and its attachment to existing powers. Unite thy church, O God, by the power of thy love that it may serve thee faithfully in these days.

Everyone: **We thank you, Father, for the hopeful signs of conversation and cooperation among the churches.**

Leader: Where we are separated from Christian brothers because of race or color, insisting on segregated worship, giving sanction to the tragic rift in social life by reflecting it in our religious life, forgive us and cleanse our churches of this iniquity.

Everyone: **We thank you, Father, for improvements that are made in all relationships from day to day.**

Leader: Where we are split by the cultural strata of society so that the rich are gathered in one church and the poor in another, the laboring man in one and his employer in another, grant us the courage and wisdom to bridge these chasms of caste and establish relationships of Christian love with all our neighbors.

Everyone: **We thank you, Father, when we discover common ties to one another and leave our class consciousness behind.**

Leader: Where the forces of history have left us sundered and bitter with the memories of strife, where loyalties to denomination have grown stronger than love of Christ, call us again to our true commitment so that the sheep of all the folds shall know the same shepherd and become one in him.

Everyone: We thank you, Father, for Jesus who prayed and worked for our unity in love.

Leader: Where sincere conviction and honest belief compel us to differ sharply with our fellow Christians, help us find a depth of fellowship in which dialogue may continue and we may know and cherish the faith of all.

Everyone: "There is one body and one Spirit, just as you were called to the one hope that belongs to your call, one Lord, one faith, one baptism, one God and Father of us all who is above all and through all and in all."

Eph. 4:4-6

Freedom with Responsibility   64

Leader: "For freedom Christ has set us free; stand fast therefore, and do not submit again to a yoke of slavery."

Everyone: But what is freedom? Everyone screams for it, "Freedom now!" We want to be free—but *from* what? For what?

Leader: "Do not use your freedom as an opportunity for the flesh, but through love be servants of one another."

Everyone: What kind of freedom is that—to serve one another?

Leader: "The whole law is fulfilled in one word, 'You shall love your neighbor as yourself.'"

Everyone: Are we bound to the love of Christ? Is this not a strange bondage and a strange freedom?

Leader: "If you are led by the Spirit you are not under the law. . . . But the fruit of the Spirit is love, joy, peace, patience, kindness, goodness, faithfulness, gentleness, self-control; against such there is no law."

Everyone: But how can we be led by such a Spirit? Surely God does not expect such noble use of freedom from us.

Leader: "Do not be deceived; God is not mocked, for whatever a man sows, that he will also reap."

Everyone Then we must earn our freedom as Christians. We are not free to violate each other's rights, or take advantage of the weak, or live as if we were alone upon the earth. Our freedom carries great responsibility. It is the freedom to choose WHO and WHAT we will serve.

Leader: "Live as free men, yet without using your freedom as a pretext for evil; but live as servants of God."

Gal. 5:1; 5:13-14, 18, 22-23; 6:7; 1 Peter 2:16

65   Morals and Ethics

Leader: "'You are a people holy to the LORD your God; the LORD your God has chosen you to be a people for his own possession. . . . Know therefore the LORD your God is God.'"

Everyone: We will listen, therefore, to his commandments and do them.

Leader: " 'You shall love the Lord your God with all your heart, and with all your soul, with all your strength, and with all your mind; and your neighbor as yourself.' "

Everyone: "Let us love one another; for love is of God, and he who loves is born of God and knows God.

Leader: "Let justice roll down like waters, and righteousness like an ever-flowing stream."

Everyone: " 'Blessed are those who hunger and thirst for righteousness, for they shall be satisfied.' "

Leader: "He shall judge between many peoples, and shall decide for strong nations afar off; nation shall not lift up sword against nation, neither shall they learn war any more."

Everyone: " 'Blessed are the peacemakers, for they shall be called the children of God.' "

Leader: "And he made from one every nation of men to live on all the face of the earth." "There is neither Jew nor Greek, there is neither slave nor free, there is neither male nor female; for you are all one in Christ Jesus."

Everyone: "And this commandment we have from him, that he who loves God should love his brother also."

Leader: "Do not be conformed to this world but be transformed by the renewal of your mind, that you may prove what is the will of God, what is good and acceptable and perfect."

Everyone: "Let love be genuine . . ."

Leader: "Do not be overcome by evil, but overcome evil with good."

Deut. 7:6, 9; Luke 10:27; 1 John 4:7; Amos 5:24; Matt. 5:6; Micah 4:3; Matt. 5:9; Acts 17:26; Gal. 3:28; 1 John 4:21; Romans 12:2, 9a; Romans 12:21

Leader: O thou who hast given to each one life and breath and hast called us into thy service to minister to the needs of all people and to share in thy marvelous works in the world:

Everyone: Make us worthy of the high calling with which we have been called.

Leader: O thou who hast created all the nations of men to dwell upon the face of the earth and hast called them to dwell in peace together so that righteousness may rule and freedom may abide,

Everyone: Make us loyal citizens of the land in which we live.

Leader: O thou who hast gathered the people together in cities and villages to live togahter in unity, supporting and encouraging one another, bearing one another's burdens, each doing his work and using his gifts for the well-being of all,

Everyone: Make us good neighbors in this community.

Leader: O thou who hast taught us by a thousand ways since the day of our birth and now hast set us within churches and schools where we continue to discover truth and to learn the skills of life and work,

Everyone: Make us keen-minded students, alert and creative in our search for truth.

Leader: O thou who hast surrounded us by family and friends that we may know the joy of giving and receiving love and be saved from despair and from loneliness by the depth of human belonging:

Everyone: Make us responsive to the love that is given us and true to the ties that bind us.

This Is My Father's World

67

Maltbie D. Babcock, 1858–1901

Franklin L. Sheppard, 1852–1930
Har. by Edward Shippen Barnes, 1887–

Joyfully

1. This is my Fa-ther's world, And to my lis-tening ears,
2. This is my Fa-ther's world, The birds their car-ols raise,
3. This is my Fa-ther's world, O let me ne'er for-get

All na-ture sings, and round me rings The mu-sic of the spheres.
The morn-ing light, the lil-y white, De-clare their Mak-er's praise.
That though the wrong seems oft so strong, God is the Rul-er yet.

This is my Fa-ther's world: I rest me in the thought Of
This is my Fa-ther's world: He shines in all that's fair; In the
This is my Fa-ther's world: The bat-tle is not done; Je-

rocks and trees, of skies and seas; His hand the won-ders wrought.
rus-tling grass I hear Him pass, He speaks to me ev-ery-where.
sus who died shall be sat-is-fied, And earth and heaven be one. A-men.

68 When Morning Gilds the Skies

German, c. 1800
Tr. by EDWARD CASWALL, 1814-1878

JOSEPH BARNBY, 1838-1896

Joyously and with dignity

1. When morn - ing gilds the skies, My heart a -
2. When - e'er the sweet church bell Peals o - ver
3. The night be - comes as day, When from the
4. Ye na - tions of man - kind, In this your

wak - ing cries, May Je - sus Christ be praised!
hill and dell, May Je - sus Christ be praised!
heart we say, May Je - sus Christ be praised!
con - cord find, May Je - sus Christ be praised!

A - like at work and prayer, To Je - sus I re -
O hark to what it sings, As joy - ous - ly it
The powers of dark - ness fear, When this sweet chant they
Let all the earth a - round Ring joy - ous with the

pair; May Je - sus Christ be praised!
rings, May Je - sus Christ be praised!
hear, May Je - sus Christ be praised!
sound, May Je - sus Christ be praised! A - MEN

Declare, O Heavens, the Lord of Space

ert Lansing Edwards, 1962

Har. & Arr. R. Vaughn Williams, 1872-1958

With dignity, in moderate time

1. De - clare, O heav'ns, the Lord of space, Re - ply broad lands in ev - ery
2. Launch forth, O man, and bold-ly rise, Be - yond our plan-et pierce the
3. Yet see this world with pro-blems filled, Earth cries for aid the Mas - ter
4. O Lord, whose pow'r all space ex - tols, Draw near our lives, en-large our

place, Tell his splen-dor! Al-le - lu - ia! New realms we find he
skies, Boundless ven - ture! Al-le - lu - ia! No soar-ing flight can
willed, Light its dark-ness! Al-le - lu - ia! Reach out all bro-ken
souls, Dwell with-in us! Al-le - lu - ia! Stir deeds of grace to

first hath made, All be-ing in his pow'r dis - played; Al-le - lu - ia!
e'er out-run Truth God has shown us in his Son; Al-le - lu - ia!
lives to mend, In Christ win peace no war will end; Al-le - lu - ia!
serve Thy plan, Wake joy the morn-ing stars be - gan; Al-le - lu - ia!

Al-le-lu - ia! Al-le-lu - ia! Al-le-lu - ia! Al-le - lu - - ia!

70   God, Our Father and Creator

Edward Krusen Ziegler
With exultation and joy

Welsh hymn melody
John Hughes, 1873-19

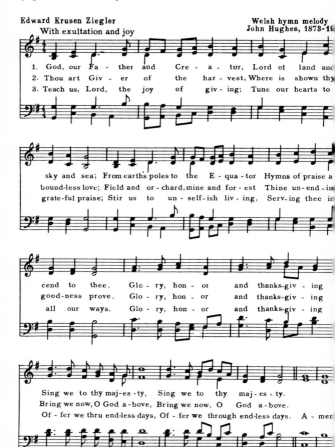

1. God, our Fa - ther and Cre - a - tor, Lord of land and
2. Thou art Giv - er of the har - vest, Where is shown thy
3. Teach us, Lord, the joy of giv - ing; Tune our hearts to

sky and sea; From earth's poles to the E - qua - tor Hymns of praise a
bound-less love; Field and or - chard, mine and for - est Thine un - end - in
grate-ful praise; Stir us to un - self - ish liv - ing, Serv-ing thee in

cend to thee. Glo - ry, hon - or and thanks-giv - ing
good-ness prove. Glo - ry, hon - or and thanks-giv - ing
all our ways. Glo - ry, hon - or and thanks-giv - ing

Sing we to thy maj - es - ty, Sing we to thy maj - es - ty.
Bring we now, O God a - bove, Bring we now, O God a - bove.
Of - fer we thru end-less days, Of - fer we through end-less days. A - mer

Music copyright by Dilys S. Webb. Used by permission.
Words from *Ten New Stewardship Hymns, 1961,* by the Hymn Society of America
used by permission.

Praise to the Lord, the Almighty

JOACHIM NEANDER, 1650–1680
Tr. by CATHERINE WINKWORTH, 1829–1878

STRALSUND GESANGBUCH, 1665
Arr. in PRAXIS PIETATIS MELICA, 1668

71

Majestically

1. Praise to the Lord, the Al-might-y, the King of cre-a-tion!
2. Praise to the Lord, who o'er all things so won-drous-ly reign-eth,
3. Praise to the Lord, who doth pros-per thy work and de-fend thee;

O my soul, praise Him, for He is thy health and sal-va-tion!
Shield-eth thee un-der His wings, yea, so gen-tly sus-tain-eth!
Sure-ly His good-ness and mer-cy here dai-ly at-tend thee.

All ye who hear, Now to His tem-ple draw near;
Hast thou not seen How thy de-sires e'er have been
Pon-der a-new What the Al-might-y can do,

Join me in glad ad-o-ra-tion!
Grant-ed in what He or-dain-eth?
If with His love He be-friend thee.   A-MEN.

72 Holy, Holy, Holy, Lord God Almighty

Reginald Heber, 1783-1826, Alt.

John B. Dykes, 1823-1876

With exaltation

1. Ho-ly, ho-ly, ho-ly, Lord God Al-might-y! Ear-ly in the
2. Ho-ly, ho-ly, ho-ly! all the saints a-dore Thee, Cast-ing down their
3. Ho-ly, ho-ly, ho-ly! tho' the dark-ness hide Thee, Tho' the eye of
4. Ho-ly, ho-ly, ho-ly, Lord God Al-might-y! All Thy works shall

morn - ing our song shall rise to Thee; Ho-ly, ho-ly, ho-ly,
gold-en crowns a-round the crys-tal sea; Cher-u-bim and ser-a-phim
sin-ful men Thy glo-ry may not see; On-ly Thou art ho-ly;
praise Thy name, in earth, and sky, and sea; Ho-ly, ho-ly, ho-ly,

mer - ci - ful and might-y! God in Three Per-sons, blessed Trin-i-ty!
fall-ing down be-fore Thee, Who wast, and art, and ev-er-more shalt be.
there is none be-side Thee, Per-fect in pow'r, in love, and pu-ri-ty.
mer - ci - ful and might-y! God in Three Per-sons, blessed Trin-i-ty! A-MEN.

73 God, Who Touchest Earth

Mary S. Edgar

C. Harold Lowden, 1883-1965

In moderate time

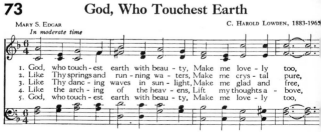

1. God, who touch-est earth with beau-ty, Make me love-ly too,
2. Like Thy springs and run-ning wa-ters, Make me crys-tal pure,
3. Like Thy danc-ing waves in sun-light, Make me glad and free,
4. Like the arch-ing of the heav-ens, Lift my thoughts a-bove,
5. God, who touch-est earth with beau-ty, Make me love-ly too,

With Thy Spir - it re - cre-ate me, Make my heart a - new.
Like Thy rocks of tower-ing gran-deur Make me strong and sure.
Like the straight-ness of the pine trees, Let me up-right be.
Turn my dreams to no - ble ac-tion, Min - is-tries of love.
Keep me ev - er, by Thy Spir - it, Pure and strong and true.   A - MEN.

Come, Thou Almighty King   74

Anonymous

Joyously, with dignity

FELICE DE GIARDINI, 1716-1796

1. Come, Thou al - might - y King, Help us Thy name to sing,
2. Come, Thou In - car - nate Word, Gird on Thy might - y sword,
3. Come, Ho - ly Com - fort - er, Thy sa - cred wit - ness bear,
4. To Thee, great One in Three, E - ter - nal prais - es be

Help us to praise! Fa - ther all - glo - ri - ous, O'er all vic -
Our pray'r at - tend; Come, and Thy peo - ple bless, And give Thy
In this glad hour: Thou who al - might - y art, Now rule in
Hence, ev - er - more: Thy sov-'reign maj - es - ty May we in

to - ri - ous, Come, and reign o - ver us, An - cient of Days!
word suc - cess; Spir - it of ho - li - ness, On us de - scend!
ev - ery heart, And ne'er from us de - part, Spir - it of power!
glo - ry see, And to e - ter - ni - ty Love and a - dore!   A - MEN.

75 For the Beauty of the Earth

FOLLIOTT S. PIERPOINT, 1835-1917

From a chorale by
CONRAD KOCHER, 1786-1872

Joyfully

1. For the beau-ty of the earth, For the glo-ry of the skies,
2. For the beau-ty of each hour Of the day and of the night,
3. For the joy of ear and eye; For the heart and mind's de-light;
4. For the joy of hu-man love, Broth-er, sis-ter, par-ent, child,

For the love which from our birth O-ver and a-round us lies:
Hill and vale, and tree and flower, Sun and moon, and stars of light:
For the mys-tic har-mo-ny Link-ing sense to sound and sight:
Friends on earth, and friends a-bove; For all gen-tle thoughts and mild:

Lord of all, to Thee we raise This our hymn of grate-ful praise. A-MEN.

76 God Moves in a Mysterious Way

WILLIAM COWPER, 1731-1800

Scottish Psalter, 161

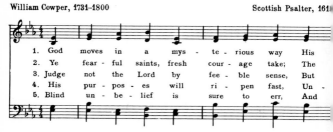

1. God moves in a mys-te-rious way His
2. Ye fear-ful saints, fresh cour-age take; The
3. Judge not the Lord by fee-ble sense, But
4. His pur-pos-es will ri-pen fast, Un-
5. Blind un-be-lief is sure to err, And

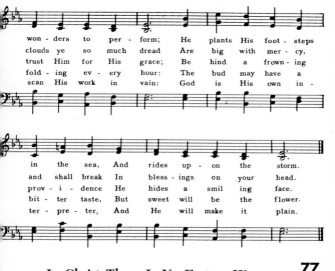

wonders to perform; He plants His foot-steps
clouds ye so much dread Are big with mer - cy,
trust Him for His grace; Be hind a frown-ing
fold-ing ev - ery hour: The bud may have a
scan His work in vain: God is His own in -

in the sea, And rides up - on the storm.
and shall break In bless-ings on your head.
prov - i - dence He hides a smil ing face.
bit - ter taste, But sweet will be the flower.
ter - pre - ter, And He will make it plain.

In Christ There Is No East or West 77

JOHN OXENHAM, d. 1941   ALEXANDER R. REINAGLE, 1799-1877

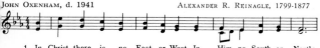

1. In Christ there is no East or West, In Him no South or North;
2. In Him shall true hearts ev - 'ry-where Their high com-mun - ion find;
3. Join hands, then, broth-ers of the faith, What - e'er your race may be.
4. In Christ now meet both East and West, In Him meet South and North;

But one great fel-low-ship of love Through-out the whole wide earth.
His serv - ice is the gold-en cord Close bind-ing all man-kind.
Who serves my Fa-ther as a son Is sure-ly kin to me.
All Christ-ly souls are one in Him Through-out the whole wide earth. A-men.

Words used by permission of American Tract Society, Oradell, New Jersey.

78   A Mighty Fortress Is Our God

MARTIN LUTHER, 1483-1546
Tr. by FREDERICK H. HEDGE, 1805-1890

In moderate time, with great dignity

MARTIN LUTHER, 1483-1546

1. A might-y for-tress is our God, A bul-wark nev-er fail-ing;
2. Did we in our own strength con-fide, Our striv-ing would be los-ing;
3. And though this world, with dev-ils filled, Should threat-en to un-do us,
4. That word a-bove all earth-ly powers, No thanks to them, a-bid-eth;

Our help-er He, a-mid the flood Of mor-tal ills pre-vail-ing:
Were not the right Man on our side, The Man of God's own choos-ing:
We will not fear, for God hath willed His truth to tri-umph through us:
The Spir-it and the gifts are ours Through Him who with us sid-eth:

For still our an-cient foe Doth seek to work us woe; His craft and power are great,
Dost ask who that may be? Christ Je-sus, it is He; Lord Sa-ba-oth, His name,
The Prince of Dark-ness grim—We trem-ble not for him; His rage we can en-dure,
Let goods and kin-dred go, This mor-tal life al-so; The bod-y they may kill:

And, armed with cru-el hate, On earth is not his e-qual.
From age to age the same, And He must win the bat-tle.
For lo, his doom is sure, One lit-tle word shall fell him.
God's truth a-bid-eth still, His king-dom is for-ev-er. A-MEN.

'9 Come, Ye Thankful People

HENRY ALFORD, 1810–1871

GEORGE J. ELVEY, 1816–1893

Joyfully

1. Come, ye thank-ful peo - ple, come, Raise the song of har - vest-home:
2. All the world is God's own field, Fruit un - to His praise to yield;
3. For the Lord our God shall come, And shall take His har - vest home;
4. E - ven so, Lord, quick-ly come, Bring Thy fi - nal har - vest home;

All is safe - ly gath-ered in, Ere the win - ter storms be - gin;
Wheat and tares to - geth - er sown, Un - to joy or sor - row grown;
From His field shall in that day All of - fens - es purge a - way;
Gath - er Thou Thy peo - ple in, Free from sor - row, free from sin;

God, our Ma - ker, doth pro - vide For our wants to be sup - plied:
First the blade, and then the ear, Then the full corn shall ap - pear:
Give His an - gels charge at last In the fire the tares to cast;
There, for - ev - er pu - ri - fied, In Thy pres - ence to a - bide:

Come to God's own tem - ple, come, Raise the song of har - vest-home.
Lord of har - vest, grant that we Whole-some grain and pure may be.
But the fruit - ful ears to store In His gar - ner ev - er - more.
Come, with all Thine an - gels, come, Raise the glo - rious har - vest - home. A-MEN.

80   Thanksgiving Hymn

Nancy Livingston Goff

1. Praise God for our bless-ings all, Al - le - lu - ia.
2. Praise God for the beau-ty known, Al - le - lu - ia.
3. Praise God for the joys we share, Al - le - lu - ia.
4. Praise God for the life we live, Al - le - lu - ia.

Poured out on both great and small, Al - le - lu - ia.
For the sea-sons as they flow, Al - le - lu - ia.
Friends we know who love and care, Al - le - lu - ia.
Know-ing that to live we give, Al - le - lu - ia.

Praise Him for his mer-cy kind, That with jus-tice is com-bined,
For the day and for the night, For the dark-ness and the light,
Fam - i - lies who give sup-port, Show-ing faith when we fall short
Praise Him for as - sur-ance givn, That our sin will be for-givn,

And with our lives in - ter - twined, Al - le - lu - ia.
For all things that give de - light, Al - le - lu - ia.
Of the goals that we hold forth, Al - le - lu - ia.
If we will re - turn to Him, Al - le - lu - ia.

O Come, O Come, Emmanuel

VENI EMMANUEL 8.8.8.8.8.8.
Adapted from Plainsong
Thomas Helmore, 1811-1890

81

c.9th century
John M. Neale, 1818-1866, Sts. 1,2, alt.
Henry S. Coffin, 1877-1954, Sts. 3,4

In unison

1 O come, O come, Emmanuel, And ransom captive
2 O come, thou Day-spring, come and cheer Our spirits by thine
3 O come, thou Wisdom from on high, And order all things,
4 O come, Desire of nations, bind All peoples in one

Israel, That mourns in lonely exile here, Un-
advent here; Disperse the gloomy clouds of night, And
far and nigh; To us the path of knowledge show, And
heart and mind; Bid envy, strife and quarrels cease; Fill

REFRAIN

til the Son of God appear.
death's dark shadows put to flight.   Rejoice! Rejoice! Em-
cause us in her ways to go.
the whole world with heaven's peace.

manuel Shall come to thee, O Israel! A-men.

82   Joy to the World!

Isaac Watts, 1674–1748

George F. Handel, 1685–175

With joy

1. Joy to the world! the Lord is come: Let earth re-
2. Joy to the world! the Sav - iour reigns: Let men their
3. No more let sins and sor - rows grow, Nor thorns in-
4. He rules the world with truth and grace, And makes the

ceive her King; Let ev - ery heart pre - pare Him room,
songs em - ploy; While fields and floods, rocks, hills and plains,
fest the ground; He comes to make His bless - ings flow
na - tions prove The glo - ries of His right - eous - ness,

And heaven and na - ture sing, And heaven and na - ture
Re - peat the sound - ing joy, Re - peat the sound - ing
Far as the curse is found, Far as the curse is
And won - ders of His love, And won - ders of His

And heaven and na - ture sing,
Re - peat the sound - ing joy,
Far as the curse is found,
And won - ders of His love,

And
Re
Far
And

sing, And heaven, and heaven and na - ture sing.
joy, Re - peat, re - peat the sound - ing joy.
found, Far as, far as the curse is found.
love, And won - ders, won - ders of His love. A - ME

heaven and na - ture sing,
peat the sound - ing joy,
as the curse is found,
won - ders of His love,

What Child Is This

WILLIAM C. DIX, 1837–1898

Old English melody

In unison

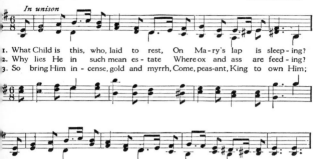

1. What Child is this, who, laid to rest, On Ma-ry's lap is sleep-ing?
2. Why lies He in such mean es-tate Where ox and ass are feed-ing?
3. So bring Him in-cense, gold and myrrh, Come, peas-ant, King to own Him;

Whom an-gels greet with an-thems sweet, While shep-herds watch are keep-ing?
Good Chris-tian, fear: for sin-ners here The si-lent Word is plead-ing.
The King of kings sal-va-tion brings, Let lov-ing hearts en-throne Him.

REFRAIN. *Unison or Harmony*

This, this is Christ the King, Whom shep-herds guard and an-gels sing:

Haste, haste to bring Him laud, The Babe, the Son of Ma-ry. A-MEN.

84 O Little Town of Bethlehem

Phillips Brooks, 1835–1893
With joy and serenity

Lewis H. Redner, 1831–190

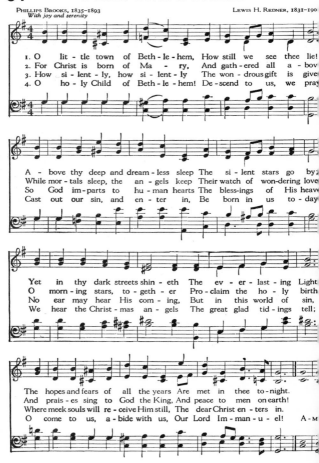

1. O lit-tle town of Beth-le-hem, How still we see thee lie!
2. For Christ is born of Ma — ry, And gath-ered all a-bove
3. How si-lent-ly, how si-lent-ly The won-drous gift is given
4. O ho-ly Child of Beth-le-hem! De-scend to us, we pray

A - bove thy deep and dream-less sleep The si-lent stars go by;
While mor-tals sleep, the an-gels keep Their watch of won-der-ing love
So God im-parts to hu-man hearts The bless-ings of His heaven
Cast out our sin, and en-ter in, Be born in us to-day

Yet in thy dark streets shin-eth The ev-er-last-ing Light
O morn-ing stars, to-geth-er Pro-claim the ho-ly birth
No ear may hear His com-ing, But in this world of sin,
We hear the Christ-mas an-gels The great glad tid-ings tell;

The hopes and fears of all the years Are met in thee to-night.
And prais-es sing to God the King, And peace to men on earth!
Where meek souls will re-ceive Him still, The dear Christ en-ters in.
O come to us, a-bide with us, Our Lord Im-man-u - el! A-M

O Come, All Ye Faithful

Anonymous, Latin, 18th century
Tr. by FREDERICK OAKELEY, 1802–1880

From J. F. WADE'S
CANTUS DIVERSI, 1751

Joyously

1. O come, all ye faith-ful, joy-ful and tri-um-phant,
2. Sing, choirs of an-gels, sing in ex-ul-ta-tion,
3. Yea, Lord, we greet Thee, born this hap-py morn-ing,

O come ye, O come ye to Beth-le-hem! Come and be-hold Him,
O sing, all ye cit-i-zens of heav'n a-bove! Glo-ry to God, all
Je-sus, to Thee be all' glo-ry giv'n; Word of the Fa-ther,

REFRAIN

born the King of an-gels!
glo-ry in the high-est! O come, let us a-dore Him, O come let us a-
now in flesh ap-pear-ing!

dore Him, O come, let us a-dore Him, Christ, the Lord! A-MEN.

86 Angels We Have Heard on High

Traditional
Old French-English Carol

1. An - gels we have heard on high, Sweet - ly sing - ing o'er the plains
2. Shep-herds, why this ju - bi - lee? Why your joy - ous strains pro - long?
3. Come to Beth - le - hem, and see Him whose birth the an - gels sing;
4. See Him in a man - ger laid, Whom the choirs of an - gels praise

And the moun-tains in re - ply, Ech - o - ing their joy - ous strain.
What the glad-some ti - dings be Which in - spire your heav'n - ly song?
Come, a - dore on bend - ed knee, Christ the Lord, the new - born King.
Ma - ry, Jo - seph, lend your aid, While our hearts in love we raise.

Soprano only, or unison ad lib.

Glo - - - - - - ri - a

in ex - cel - sis De - o Glo - - -

- - - - ri - a in ex - cel - sis De - o.

Silent Night, Holy Night 87

JOSEPH MOHR, 1792–1848
Tr. compiled from various sources
In moderate flowing rhythm

FRANZ GRUBER, 1787–1863

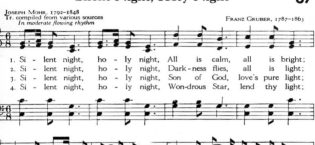

1. Si - lent night, ho - ly night, All is calm, all is bright;
2. Si - lent night, ho - ly night, Dark - ness flies, all is light;
3. Si - lent night, ho - ly night, Son of God, love's pure light;
4. Si - lent night, ho - ly night, Won - drous Star, lend thy light;

Round yon Vir - gin Moth - er and Child! Ho - ly In - fant, so ten - der and mild,
Shep - herds hear the an - gels sing, "Al - le - lu - ia! hail the King!
Ra - diant beams from Thy ho - ly face, With the dawn of re - deem - ing grace,
With the an - gels let us sing, Al - le - lu - ia to our King;

Sleep in heav - en - ly peace, Sleep in heav - en - ly peace.
Christ the Sav - iour is born, Christ the Sav - iour is born."
Je - sus, Lord, at Thy birth, Je - sus, Lord, at Thy birth.
Christ the Sav - iour is born, Christ the Sav - iour is born. A - MEN.

88   We Three Kings

JOHN H. HOPKINS, 1820-1891

JOHN H. HOPKINS, 1820-1891

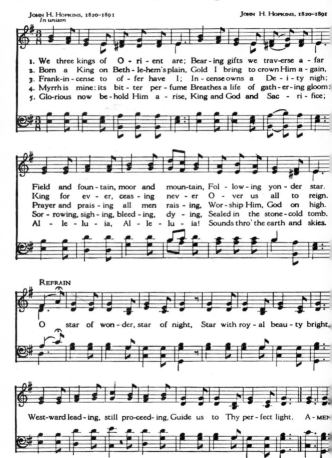

In unison

1. We three kings of O - ri - ent are; Bear-ing gifts we trav-erse a - far
2. Born a King on Beth - le-hem's plain, Gold I bring to crown Him a - gain,
3. Frank-in - cense to of - fer have I; In - cense owns a De - i - ty nigh;
4. Myrrh is mine: its bit - ter per - fume Breathes a life of gath - er-ing gloom;
5. Glo-rious now be-hold Him a - rise, King and God and Sac - ri - fice;

Field and foun - tain, moor and moun-tain, Fol - low-ing yon - der star.
King for ev - er, ceas - ing nev - er O - ver us all to reign.
Prayer and prais-ing all men rais - ing, Wor-ship Him, God on high.
Sor - rowing, sigh-ing, bleed-ing, dy - ing, Sealed in the stone-cold tomb.
Al - le - lu - ia, Al - le - lu - ia! Sounds thro' the earth and skies.

REFRAIN

O star of won - der, star of night, Star with roy - al beau - ty bright,

West-ward lead - ing, still pro-ceed-ing, Guide us to Thy per - fect light. A - MEN

While Shepherds Watched Their Flocks

NAHUM TATE, 1652-1715
With joyous rhythm

GEORGE FREDERICK HANDEL, 1685-1759

1. While shep-herds watched their flocks by night, All
2. "Fear not!" said he— for might-y dread Had
3. "To you, in Da-vid's town this day, Is
4. "The heaven-ly Babe you there shall find To

seat-ed on the ground, The an-gel of the Lord came down,
seized their trou-bled mind— "Glad tid-ings of great joy I bring,
born of Da-vid's line, A Sav-ior, who is Christ the Lord;
hu-man view dis-played, All mean-ly wrapped in swath-ing bands,

And glo-ry shone a-round, And glo-ry shone a-round.
To you and all man-kind, To you and all man-kind.
And this shall be the sign, And this shall be the sign:
And in a man-ger laid, And in a man-ger laid." A-MEN.

Thus spake the seraph; and forthwith
   Appeared a shining throng
Of angels praising God, who thus
   Addressed their joyful song:

6 "All glory be to God on high,
   And to the earth be peace:
Good will henceforth from heaven to men,
   Begin and never cease!"

90   Go Tell It on the Mountain

Christmas Spiritual

Go tell it on the moun - - - tain,
Tell on the mou - - - tain,

Tell it, tell it on the moun - tain,
Tell on the mou - - - tain,

O - ver the hills and ev - 'ry - where, Go tell it on the

Tell it,
Tell on the

Fine

moun - - - tain that Je - sus Christ is a born.

Tell it on the moun - tain
moun - - - tain

1. When I was a sin - er, I prayed both night and day; I
2. When I was a seek - er, I sought both night and day; I
3. He made me a watch - man up - on the cit - y wall; And

D.

asked the Lord to help me, and He showed me the way.
asked my Lord to help me, and He taught me to pray.
if I am a Chris - tian, I am the least of all.

Of the Father's Love Begotten

Latin: Prudentius, 348 c. 410
Tr. John M. Neale, 1818-1866, St. 1, alt.
Henry W. Baker, 1821-1877, Sts. 2, 3

Divinum Mysterium 8.7.8.7.8.7.7.
13th century Plainsong, Mode V

Of the Fa-ther's love be - got - ten, Ere the worlds be - gan to be,
O ye heights of heaven a - dore him; An-gel hosts, his prais-es sing;
Christ, to thee with God the Fa - ther, And, O Ho - ly Ghost, to thee,

He is Al - pha and O - me - ga, He the source, the end - ing he;
Powers, do-min - ions, bow be - fore him, And ex - tol our God and King;
Hymn and chant and high thanks-giv - ing, And un - wea-ried prais-es be:

Of the things that are, that have been, And that
Let no tongue on earth be si - lent, Ev - ery
Hon - or, glo - ry, and do - min - ion, And e -

fu-ture years shall see, Ev - er-more and ev - er-more!
voice in con - cert ring, Ev - er-more and ev - er-more!
ter-nal vic - to - ry, Ev - er-more and ev - er-more! A - men.

92   Within the Shelter of Our Walls

Elinor Lennen

Frederick C. Maker, 1844–19

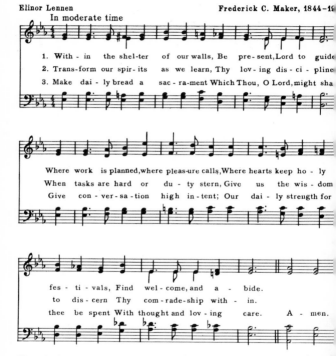

In moderate time

1. With - in the shel-ter of our walls, Be pre-sent, Lord to guide
2. Trans-form our spir - its as we learn, Thy lov-ing dis-ci-pline
3. Make dai - ly bread a sac - ra-ment Which Thou, O Lord, might sha

Where work is planned, where pleas-ure calls, Where hearts keep ho - ly
When tasks are hard or du - ty stern, Give us the wis - dom
Give con - ver - sa - tion high in-tent; Our dai - ly strength for

fes - ti - vals, Find wel-come, and a - bide.
to dis - cern Thy com - rade-ship with - in.
thee be spent With thought and lov - ing care. A - men.

Come Forth, O Christian Youth

ry Ellen Jackson, 1955

George J. Elvey, 1868

1. Come forth, O Chris-tian youth, A task be-fore us lies;
2. Stand firm, O Chris-tian youth, With trust in God a - lone,
3. Grow strong, O Chris-tian youth, Be loy - al, brave and true,
4. Give all, O Chris-tian youth, And nought from Christ with - hold;

The world a-waits the strength and zeal Which youth-ful heart sup-plies.
That we may live our Chris - tian faith And make Christ tru - ly known.
And strive with cour-age for the right In what we say and do.
His King-dom claims us for its own; His Spir - it keep us bold!

We seek to win man - kind To choose Christ's no - bler way,
Be ours to show all men The path His feet have trod,
Thus may our words and deeds Be wor - thy in God's sight,
As pil-grims in the world Yet fol-lowers of the Way,

And u - sher in true broth-er-hood For ev - 'ry man to day.
To make all life a sa-cra-ment And ho - ly un-to God.
And man - i - fest to all man-kind His way of truth and light.
God make us faith-ful cit - i - zens Till His e - ter-nal day. A - men.

om *Two Hymns for Youth by Youth*, copyright 1956 by the Hymn Society of America; ed by permission.

94   The Son of God, Our Christ

Edward M. Blumenfeld, 1956   Calvin W. Laufer, 19

1. The Son of God, our Christ, the Word, the Way,
2. In ev - 'ry test, in tri - als man - i - fold,
3. To - day, as then, Christ sum - mons men to dare
4. In ci - ty street, in town or on the soil,
5. Wher - e'er we find our wit - ness should be made,

Shared hu - man life and toiled through-out the day;
These ser - vants wit - nessed, by their faith made bold;
His path to fol - low and his work to share,
May each serve Christ in faith-ful dai - ly toil,
What - e'er our task, be thou, O Christ, our aid,

From com - mon folk he called twelve men to be
And with the gifts and tal - ents which they brought,
To help and heal the sick, the lame, the blind,
And in each thought and kind - ly word and deed
That we may glad - ly give for thee our best

Co - work - ers in his sa - cred min - is - try.
The Church was found-ed and God's mes - sage taught.
To make his Gos - pel known to all man - kind.
O - bey Christ's call, and go where he shall lead.
And find each task di - vine - ly sent and blest. A - men.

Christ the Lord Is Risen Today

CHARLES WESLEY, 1707–1788, and others

From LYRA DAVIDICA, 1708

Joyously

1. Christ the Lord is risen to-day, Al — — le - lu - ia!
2. Lives a - gain our glo - rious King, Al - — - le - lu - ia!
3. Love's re - deem - ing work is done, Al — — le - lu - ia!
4. Soar we now where Christ has led, Al — — le - lu - ia!

Sons of men and an - gels say, Al — — le - lu - ia!
Where, O death, is now thy sting? Al — — le - lu - ia!
Fought the fight, the bat - tle won, Al — — le - lu - ia!
Fol - lowing our ex - alt - ed Head, Al — — le - lu - ia!

Raise your joys and tri - umphs high, Al — — le - lu - ia!
Once He died, our souls to save, Al — — le - lu - ia!
Death in vain for - bids Him rise, Al — — le - lu - ia!
Made like Him, like Him we rise, Al — — le - lu - ia!

Sing, ye heavens, and earth re - ply, Al — le - lu - ia!
Where's thy vic-tory, boast-ing grave? Al — le - lu - ia!
Christ hath o - pened Par - a - dise, Al — le - lu - ia!
Ours the cross, the grave, the skies, Al — le - lu - ia! A-MEN.

96   I Bind My Heart This Tide

LAUCHLAN MACLEAN WATT

GRACE WILBUR CONANT

In moderate time

1. I bind my heart this tide To the Gal - i - le - an's side,
2. I bind my heart in thrall To the God, the Lord of All,

To the wounds of Cal - va - ry,— To the Christ who died for me.
To the God, the poor man's Friend, And the Christ whom he did send.

I bind my soul this day To the broth - er far a - way,
I bind my - self to peace, To make strife and en - vy cease,

And the broth-er near at hand, In this town, and in this land.
God! knit thou sure the cord Of my thral-dom to my Lord. A - MEN.

Praise the Lord, His Glories Show

From Psalm cl
HENRY F. LYTE, 1793–1847

ROBERT WILLIAMS, c. 1781–1821

Joyously

1. Praise the Lord, His glo - ries show, Al - - le - lu - ia!
2. Earth to heaven, and heaven to earth, Al - - le - lu - ia!
3. Praise the Lord, His mer - cies trace, Al - - le - lu - ia!

Saints with - in His courts be - low, Al - - le - lu - ia!
Tell His won - ders, sing His worth, Al - - le - lu - ia!
Praise His prov - i - dence and grace, Al - - le - lu - ia!

An - gels round His throne a - bove, Al - - le - lu - ia!
Age to age and shore to shore, Al - - le - lu - ia!
All that He for man hath done, Al - - le - lu - ia!

All that see and share His love, Al - - le - lu - ia!
Praise Him, praise Him ev - er - more! Al - - le - lu - ia!
All He sends us through His Son. Al - - le - lu - ia! A - MEN.

98 Now, on Land and Sea Descending

Samuel Longfellow, 1819–1892, alt.

Dimitri S. Bortniansky, 1752–18

In moderate time

1. Now, on land and sea de-scend-ing, Brings the night its peace pro-fou
2. Soon as dies the sun-set glo-ry, Stars of heaven shine out a-bo
3. Now, our wants and bur-dens leav-ing To His care who cares for a
4. As the dark-ness deep-ens o'er us, Lo! e-ter-nal stars a-ri

Let our ves-per hymn be blend-ing With the ho-ly calm a-rou
Tell-ing still the an-cient sto-ry—Their Cre-a-tor's change-less lo
Cease we fear-ing, cease we griev-ing: At His touch our bur-dens fa
Hope and faith and love rise glo-rious, Shin-ing in the spir-it's sk

Ju-bi-la-te! Ju-bi-la-te! Ju-bi-la-te! A-me

Let our ves-per hymn be blend-ing With the ho-ly calm a-round.
Tell-ing still the an-cient sto-ry—Their Cre-a-tor's changeless love.
Cease we fear-ing, cease we griev-ing: At His touch our bur-dens fall.
Hope and faith and love rise glo-rious, Shin-ing in the spir-it's skies. A-M

O God, Thy Hand the Heavens Made **99**

Leroy Cross

William Croft, 1678–1727

1. O God, thy hand the heav-ens made And all that they con-tain; The world ap-peared at thy com-mand, And in it thou shalt reign.

2. The rest-less sea, the land, the sky, Thy hand-i-work de-clare; The touch of thy cre-a-tive pow'r Is pre-sent ev-'ry-where.

3. To men are giv-en gifts di-vine, All tal-ents thou dost send; In-spire us now to use them well, Thy King-dom to ex-tend.

4. We hold each gift a trust from thee, Nor claim it as our own; We grate-ful-ly ac-knowl-edge, Lord, All things are thine a-lone.

5. De-liv-er us from self-ish aims, True stew-ards we would be; En-dow us with a deep de-sire To share with men and thee.

6. A full ac-count-ing we must give, The Mas-ter we shall face; Let us ap-proach his throne with joy Sup-port-ed by thy grace. A-men.

100 Take My Life, and Let It Be

FRANCES R. HAVERGAL, 1836-1879   H. A. CESAR MALAN, 1787-18

In moderate time

1. Take my life, and let it be Con-se-crat-ed
2. Take my hands, and let them move At the im-
3. Take my voice, and let me sing, Al-ways, on-ly
4. Take my will, and make it Thine; It shall be n
5. Take my love; my Lord, I pour At Thy feet its

Lord, to Thee, Take my mo-ments and my days; Let them flow
of Thy love. Take my feet, and let them be Swift and beau-
for my King. Take my in-tel-lect, and use Ev-ery power
lon-ger mine. Take my heart, it is Thine own; It shall be
treas-ure-store. Take my self, and I will be Ev-er, on-

cease-less praise, Let them flow in cease-less praise.
ful for Thee, Swift and beau-ti-ful for Thee.
Thou shalt choose, Ev-ery power as Thou shalt choose.
roy-al throne, It shall be Thy roy-al throne.
all for Thee, Ev-er, on-ly, all for Thee. A-

101 O Master, Let Me Walk with Thee

WASHINGTON GLADDEN, 1836-1918   (*Second Tune*)   H. PERCY SMITH, 1825-18

In moderate time

1. O Mas-ter, let me walk with Thee In low-ly paths of serv-ice true;
2. Help me the slow of heart to move By some clear, win-ning word of lo
3. Teach me Thy pa-tience; still with Thee In clos-er, dear-er com-pa-r
4. In hope that sends a shin-ing ray Far down the fu-ture's broad-ening

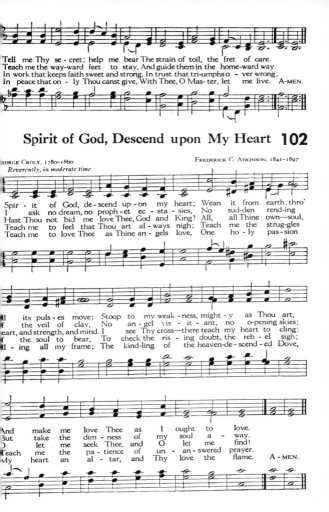

Tell me Thy se - cret; help me bear The strain of toil, the fret of care.
Teach me the way-ward feet to stay, And guide them in the home-ward way.
In work that keeps faith sweet and strong, In trust that tri-umphs o - ver wrong;
In peace that on - ly Thou canst give, With Thee, O Mas - ter, let me live. A-MEN.

Spirit of God, Descend upon My Heart 102

GEORGE CROLY, 1780–1860

FREDERICK C. ATKINSON, 1841–1897

Reverently, in moderate time

Spir - it of God, de - scend up - on my heart; Wean it from earth; thro'
I ask no dream, no proph - et ec - sta - sies, No sud - den rend - ing
Hast Thou not bid me love Thee, God and King? All, all Thine own—soul,
Teach me to feel that Thou art al - ways nigh; Teach me the strug-gles
Teach me to love Thee as Thine an - gels love, One ho - ly pas - sion

all its puls - es move; Stoop to my weak - ness, might - y as Thou art,
of the veil of clay, No an - gel vis - it - ant, no o-pening skies;
heart, and strength, and mind. I see Thy cross—there teach my heart to cling:
of the soul to bear, To check the ris - ing doubt, the reb - el sigh;
fill - ing all my frame; The kind - ling of the heaven-de-scend - ed Dove,

And make me love Thee as I ought to love.
But take the dim - ness of my soul a - way.
O let me seek Thee, and O let me find!
Teach me the pa - tience of un - an - swered prayer.
My heart an al - tar, and Thy love the flame. A - MEN.

103 Lord, Whose Love Through Humble Service

Albert F. Bayly, 1961

Rowland Hugh Prichard, (1811–

1. Lord, whose love through hum-ble ser-vice Bore t
2. Still thy chil-dren wan-der home-less; Still
3. As we wor-ship, grant us vi-sion, Till t
4. Called from wor-ship un-to ser-vice, Forth i

weight of hu-man need, Who did'st on t
hun-gry cry for bread; Still the cap-t
love's re-veal-ing light, In its height a
thy dear name we go, To the child, t

Cross, for-sak-en, Work thy mer-cy's per-fect deed
long for free-dom; Still in grief men mourn their dead
depth and great-ness Dawns up-on our quick-ened sigh
youth, the a-ged, Love in liv-ing deeds to show

We, thy ser-vants, bring the wor-ship Not
As, O Lord, thy deep com-pas-sion Healed
Mak-ing known the needs and bur-dens Thy
Hope and health, good-will and com-fort, Coun-

Alternative tune: *St. Asaph.*
Copyright 1961 by Albert F. Bayly. Used by permission of the
Society of America from *Seven New Social Welfare Hymns.*

voice a - lone, but heart; Con - se - crat - ing to thy
sick and freed the soul, Use the love thy Spir - it
pas - sion bids us bear, Stir - ring us to tire - less
aid and peace we give, That thy chil - dren, Lord, in

pur - pose Ev - 'ry gift thou dost im - part.
kin - dles Still to save and make men whole.
striv - ing Thine a - bun - dant life to share.
free - dom May thy mer - cy know, and live. A - men.

Help Us, O Lord, to Learn 104

m W. Reid, Jr. From Cantica Laudis, 1850

In moderate time

1. Help us, O Lord, to learn The truths thy word im - parts;
2. Help us, O Lord, to live The faith which we pro - claim,
3. Help us, O Lord, to teach The beau - ty of thy ways,

To stud - y that thy laws may be In - scribed up - on our hearts.
That all our thoughts and words and deeds May glo - ri - fy thy name.
That yearn - ing souls may find the Christ And sing a - loud his praise. A - men.

105 Be Thou My Vision

Ancient Irish; tr. by Mary Byrne
Versified by Eleanor Hull

Ancient Irish traditional m
Harmonized by David Evans,

Unison. Moderately slow, with great dignity

1. Be Thou my Vi - sion, O Lord of my heart;
2. Be Thou my Wis - dom, and Thou my true Word;
3. Rich - es I heed not, nor man's emp - ty praise,
4. High King of heav - en, my vic - to - ry won,

Naught be all else to me, save that Thou art—
I ev - er with Thee and Thou with me, Lord;
Thou mine in - her - it - ance, now and al - ways:
May I reach heav - en's joys, O bright heaven's Sun!

Thou my best thought, by day or by night,
Thou my great Fa - ther, I Thy true son;
Thou and Thou on - ly, first in my heart,
Heart of my own heart, what - ev - er be - fall,

Wak - ing or sleep - ing, Thy pres - ence my light.
Thou in me dwell - ing, and I with Thee one.
High King of heav - en, my treas - ure Thou art.
Still be my Vi - sion, O Rul - er of all. A - M

Hymn for the Motor Age

Thomas Tiplady, 1957

moderate time

O God, by whom the clouds are spread And by whose hand each
Up - on the road be thou re-vealed To trav - el - ers as
Cre - a - tor of the Milk - y Way Where count-less stars make

ar is led; No spar - row falls by thee un - seen
ide and shield; The a - ged and the young pro - tect
eav - ens gay, The hearts and minds of men in - spire

In bus - y town or wood-land green; O hear us, Lord, for
rom heed-less driv - ing or neg-lect; O hear us, Lord for
To free our roads from per - ils dire; And may each driv - er

all who ride Through cit - y street or coun - try - side.
ll who ride Through cit - y street or coun - try - side.
l - ways feel Thy guid-ing hand up - on the wheel. A - men.

107   Love Divine, All Love Excelling

Charles Wesley, 1707-1788

John Zundell, 1815

In moderate time

1. Love di-vine, all love ex-cell-ing, Joy of heav'n, to earth come
2. Breathe, O breathe Thy lov-ing Spir-it In-to ev-ery trou-bled
3. Come, Al-might-y to de-liv-er, Let us all Thy grace re-
4. Fin-ish, then, Thy new cre-a-tion; Pure and spot-less let us

Fix in us Thy hum-ble dwell-ing, All Thy faith-ful mer-cies cr
Let us all in Thee in-her-it, Let us find the prom-ised r
Sud-den-ly re-turn, and nev-er, Nev-er more Thy tem-ples le
Let us see Thy great sal-va-tion Per-fect-ly re-stored in T

Je-sus, Thou art all com-pas-sion, Pure, un-bound-ed love Thou a
Take a-way our love of sin-ning; Al-pha and O-me-ga b
Thee we would be al-ways bless-ing, Serve Thee as Thy hosts a-b
Changed from glo-ry in-to glo-ry, Till in heaven we take our pl

Vis-it us with Thy sal-va-tion, En-ter ev-'ry trem-bling heart.
End of faith, as its be-gin-ning, Set our hearts at lib-er-ty.
Pray, and praise Thee with-out ceas-ing, Glo-ry in Thy per-fect love.
Till we cast our crowns be-fore Thee, Lost in won-der, love and praise. A-

God of Grace and God of Glory

Harry Emerson Fosdick, 1878–

Henry Smart, 1813–1879

In moderate time, with earnestness

1. God of grace and God of glo - ry, On Thy peo - ple
2. Lo! the hosts of e - vil round us Scorn Thy Christ, as -
3. Cure Thy chil - dren's war - ring mad - ness, Bend our pride to
4. Set our feet on loft - y pla - ces; Gird our lives that
5. Save us from weak res - ig - na - tion To the e - vils

pour Thy power; Crown Thine an - cient church's sto - ry;
sail His ways! From the fears that long have bound us
Thy con - trol; Shame our wan - ton, self - ish glad - ness,
they may be Ar - mored with all Christ - like grac - es
we de - plore; Let the search for Thy sal - va - tion

Bring her bud to glo - rious flower. Grant us wis - dom,
Free our hearts to faith and praise: Grant us wis - dom,
Rich in things and poor in soul. Grant us wis - dom,
In the fight to set men free. Grant us wis - dom,
Be our glo - ry ev - er - more. Grant us wis - dom,

Grant us cour - age, For the fac - ing of this hour.
Grant us cour - age, For the liv - ing of these days.
Grant us cour - age, Lest we miss Thy king - dom's goal.
Grant us cour - age, That we fail not man nor Thee!
Grant us cour - age, Serv - ing Thee whom we a - dore. A - MEN.

109 Here at Thy Table, Lord

May P. Hoyt

William F. Sherwin, 1826–1888

In moderate time

1. Here at Thy ta - ble, Lord, This sa - cred hour, O let us
   feel Thee near, In lov - ing pow'r; Call - ing our thoughts a - way
   From self and sin, As to Thy ban-quet hall We en - ter in.

2. Sit at the feast, dear Lord, Break Thou the bread; Fill Thou the
   cup that brings Life to the dead; That we may find in Thee
   Par - don and peace; And from all bond-age win A full re - lease.

3. So shall our life of faith Be full, be sweet; And we shall
   find our strength For each day meet; Fed by Thy liv - ing bread
   All hun - ger past, We shall be sat - is - fied, And saved at last.

4. Come then, O ho - ly Christ, Feed us, we pray; Touch with Thy
   pierc - ed hand Each com - mon day; Mak - ing this earth - ly life
   Full of Thy grace, Till in the home of heav'n We find our place. A - ME

110 That Cause Can Neither Be Lost nor Stayed

Christian Ostergaard
Tr. by J. A. Aaberg

Danish folk tune

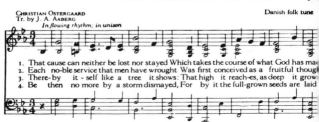

In flowing rhythm; in unison

1. That cause can neither be lost nor stayed Which takes the course of what God has ma
2. Each no-ble service that men have wrought Was first conceived as a fruitful thoug
3. There-by it - self like a tree it shows: That high it reach-es, as deep it grow
4. Be then no more by a storm dismayed, For by it the full-grown seeds are laid

And is not trusting in walls and towers, But slow-ly growing from seeds to flowers.
Each worthy cause with a future glorious By qui-et growing becomes vic-to-rious.
And when the storms are its branches shaking, It deep-er root in the soil is tak-ing.
And though the tree by its might it shatters, What then, if thousands of seeds it scatters! A-MEN.

Where Cross the Crowded Ways of Life 111

FRANK MASON NORTH 1850–1935

Adapted from SACRED MELODIES
WILLIAM GARDINER, 1770–1853

In moderate time

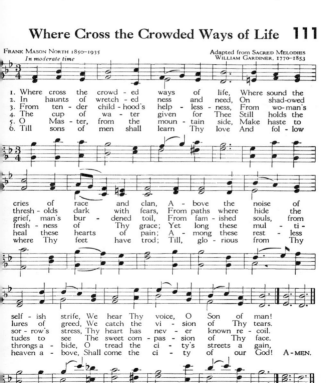

1. Where cross the crowd - ed ways of life, Where sound the
2. In haunts of wretch - ed ness and need, On shad-owed
3. From ten - der child-hood's help - less - ness, From wo-man's
4. The cup of wa - ter given for Thee Still holds the
5. O Mas - ter, from the moun-tain side, Make haste to
6. Till sons of men shall learn Thy love And fol - low

cries of race and clan, A - bove the noise of
thresh - olds dark with fears, From paths where hide the
fresh - ness of Thy grace; Yet long these mul - ti -
grief, man's bur - dened toil, From fam - ished souls, from
heal these hearts of pain; A - mong these rest - less
where Thy feet have trod; Till, glo - rious from Thy

self - ish strife, We hear Thy voice, O Son of man!
lures of greed, We catch the vi - sion of Thy tears.
sor - row's stress, Thy heart has nev - er known re - coil.
tudes to see The sweet com - pas - sion of Thy face.
throngs a - bide, O tread the ci - ty's streets a - gain,
heaven a - bove, Shall come the ci - ty of our God! A-MEN.

112   O God of Every Nation

William W. Reid, Jr., 1958   Melchior Teschner, c. 1615

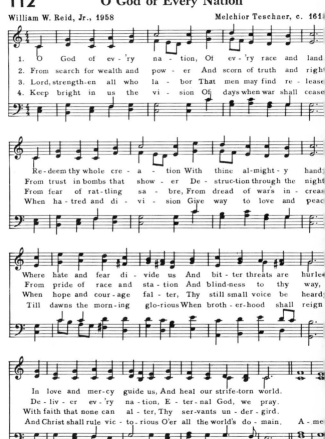

1. O God of ev-'ry na-tion, Of ev-'ry race and land
2. From search for wealth and pow-er And scorn of truth and right,
3. Lord, strength-en all who la-bor That men may find re-lease
4. Keep bright in us the vi-sion Of days when war shall cease,

Re-deem thy whole cre-a-tion With thine al-might-y hand;
From trust in bombs that show-er De-struc-tion through the night,
From fear of rat-tling sa-bre, From dread of wars in-creas
When ha-tred and di-vi-sion Give way to love and peace,

Where hate and fear di-vide us And bit-ter threats are hurled,
From pride of race and sta-tion And blind-ness to thy way,
When hope and cour-age fal-ter, Thy still small voice be heard;
Till dawns the morn-ing glo-rious When broth-er-hood shall reign,

In love and mer-cy guide us, And heal our strife-torn world.
De-liv-er ev-'ry na-tion, E-ter-nal God, we pray.
With faith that none can al-ter, Thy serv-ants un-der-gird.
And Christ shall rule vic-to-rious O'er all the world's do-main. A-men

Alternative tune: *Aurelia or Llangloffan*. From *Twelve World Order Hymns*, copyright 1958 by the Hymn Society of America, used by permission.

Lord, We Believe

113

Thomas Paul Slavens, 1957

Charles Henry Purday, 1860

1. Lord, we be-lieve; help thou our un-be-lief; Show us the way.
2. Lord, we be-lieve; O speak to us to-day In ac-cents clear
3. Lord, we be-lieve; help us our faith to live And sted-fast be.

Till thee we seek, we can-not find re - lief Or fears al - lay.
Throw thy bright beams of love a-cross our way; Cast out our fear.
Thou hast so loved, help us our love to give With joy to thee.

Where now we grope for faith to meet our needs,
Grant us the faith in God which Christ re - vealed
Let doubt give way and faith our spir - its fill

Help us to find the way the true path leads.
That un - be - lief to sure be-lief may yield.
With power to know and do thy ho - ly will. A - men.

114 We Would Be Building

FINLANDIA. 10. 10. 10. 10. 10. 10.

Purd E. Deitz

Jean Sibelius, 1865–1

In moderate time and flowing rhythm

1. We would be build-ing; tem-ples still un-done O'er crum-bling walls the
2. Teach us to build; up-on the sol-id rock We set the dream th
3. O keep us build-ing, Mas-ter; may our hands Ne'er fal-ter when th

cross-es scarce-ly lift; Wait-ing till love can raise the bro-ken stone,
hard-ens in-to deed, Ribbed with the steel that time and change doth mock,
dream is in our hearts, When to our ears there come di-vine com-mands

And hearts cre-a-tive bridge the hu-man rift; We would be build-in
Th' un-fail-ing pur-pose of our no-blest creed; Teach us to build; C
And all the pride of sin-ful will de-parts; We build with Thee, C

Mas-ter, let Thy plan Re-veal the life that God would give to man.
Mas-ter, lend us sight To see the tow-ers gleam-ing in the light.
grant en-dur-ing worth Un-til the heav'n-ly King-dom comes on earth. A-mi

God Almighty, God Eternal

115

ary Jackson Cathey

Ludwig van Beethoven, 1770–1827

1. God al-might-y, God e-ter-nal, To thy throne we bring our prayer.
2. God un-chang-ing, God for-ev-er, In these times of sky and space,
3. God the Sov'reign, our Cre-a-tor, Thou to whom all things be-long,

Ask-ing help and seek-ing guid-ance For thy peo-ple ev-'ry-where.
When has come a new di-men-sion To our wide-spread hu-man race,
Thou who speak-est through the a-ges To the u-ni-ver-sal throng,

In this age of chang-ing boun-dries, Wid-'ning spac-es, spread-ing spheres,
Lend to us thine un-der-stand-ing, Lov-ing spir-it, fer-vent zeal,
Speak a-gain to all thy chil-dren, Voice thy truth to us we pray,

Give to us the strength to fol-low When thy will for us ap-pears.
That our dai-ly, liv-ing wit-ness May be filled with Christ's ap-peal.
As the world of na-ture wid-ens, Teach us how to live Christ's way. A-men.

116 Once to Every Man and Nation

James Russell Lowell, 1819-1891, alt.

EBENEZER
Welsh hymn melody

In moderate time, with dignity

1. Once to ev-ery man and na-tion Comes the mo-ment to de-cide,
2. Then to side with truth is no-ble, When we share her wretched crust,
3. By the light of burn-ing mar-tyrs, Christ, Thy bleed-ing feet we trace,
4. Though the cause of e-vil pros-per, Yet 'tis truth a-lone is strong;

In the strife of truth with false-hood, For the good or e-vil side;
Ere her cause bring fame and prof-it, And 'tis pros-perous to be just;
Toil-ing up new Cal-varies ev-er With the cross that turns not back;
Though her por-tion be the scaf-fold, And up-on the throne be wrong:

Some great cause, God's new Mes-si-ah, Of-fering each the bloom or blight,
Then it is the brave man choos-es While the cow-ard stands a-side,
New oc-ca-sions teach new du-ties, Time makes an-cient good un-couth;
Yet that scaf-fold sways the fu-ture, And, be-hind the dim un-known,

And the choice goes by for ev-er 'Twixt that darkness and that light.
Till the mul-ti-tude make vir-tue Of the faith they had de-nied.
They must up-ward still and on-ward, Who would keep a-breast of truth.
Standeth God with-in the shad-ow Keep-ing watch a-bove His own. A-MEN

God of Our Fathers

117

DANIEL C. ROBERTS, 1841–1907

GEORGE W. WARREN, 1828–1902

With martial rhythm

Trumpets, before each stanza

1. God of our fa - thers, whose al-might - y hand
2. Thy love di - vine hath led us in the past;
3. From war's a-larms, from dead-ly pes - ti-lence,
4. Re - fresh Thy peo - ple on their toil-some way;

Leads forth in beau - ty all the star - ry band
In this free land by Thee our lot is cast;
Be Thy strong arm our ev - er sure de - fense;
Lead us from night to nev - er - end - ing day;

Of shin - ing worlds in splen - dor through the skies,
Be Thou our Rul - er, Guard - ian, Guide, and Stay,
Thy true re - li - gion in our hearts in - crease,
Fill all our lives with love and grace di - vine,

Our grate - ful songs be - fore Thy throne a - rise.
Thy Word our law, Thy paths our cho - sen way.
Thy boun - teous good - ness nour - ish us in peace.
And glo - ry, laud, and praise be ev - er Thine. A - MEN.

118

Renew Thy Church

Kenneth L. Cober

Old English Melody

1. Renew thy church, her min-is-tries re-store: Both to serve
2. Teach us thy word, re-veal its truth di-vine, On our path
3. Teach us to pray, for thou art ev-er near, Thy still voice
4. Teach us to love, with strength of heart and mind, Ev-er-one,

and a-dore. Make her a-gain as salt through-out the land,
let it shine; Tell of thy works, thy might-y acts of grace.
let us hear. Our souls are rest-less 'til they rest in thee,
all man-kind. Break down old walls of pre-ju-dice and hate,

And as light from a stand. 'Mid som-ber shad-ows of the night, Wh
From each page show thy face. As thou hast loved us, sent thy Son, An
This our glad des-ti-ny. Be-fore thy pres-ence keep us still, Tha
Leave us not to our fate. As thou hast loved and given thy life, To

greed and ha-tred spread their blight, O send us forth with
our sal-va-tion now is won, O let our hearts with
we may find for us thy will And seek thy guid-ance
end hos-til-i-ty and strife, O share thy grace from

power en-dued, Help us, Lord, be re-newed.
love be stirred, Help us, Lord, know thy word.
ev-ery day, Teach us, Lord, how to pray.
heav'n a-bove, Teach us, Lord, how to love. A-men.

Praise to the Lord

Nancy Livingston Goff

1. Praise to the Lord, e - ter - nal, with - out end;
Sing to his name; His wor - ship now at - tend,
This hour we come, and so pre - pare our hearts To
know and re - ceive, the joy that he im - parts.

2. Praise to the Lord, the source and strength of life,
   Giving support in both our joy and strife;
   We give ourselves into his loving care
   And sing forth our thanks for this great gift we share.

3. Praise to the Lord, who comforts us and heals,
   Binding our souls and spirits as a seal
   Of his great love, renewing us to live
   Revived and refreshed, a witness now to give.

4. Praise to the Lord, O sing unto his name!
   With joyful voice our gratitude proclaim.
   We bring ourselves to give as offering
   In grateful response and homage to our King.

120 O Worship the King

ROBERT GRANT, 1785-1838

FRANZ JOSEPH HAYDN, 1732-1809

With dignity but joyously

1. O wor-ship the King, all glo-rious a-bove, And grate-ful-ly
sing His won-der-ful love; Our Shield and De-fend-er, the
An-cient of days, Pa-vil-ioned in splendor, and gird-ed with praise.

2. Thy boun-ti-ful care, what tongue can re-cite? It breathes in the
air, it shines in the light; It streams from the hills, it de-
scends to the plain, And sweet-ly dis-tils in the dew and the rain.

3. Frail chil-dren of dust, and fee-ble as frail, In Thee do we
trust, nor find Thee to fail; Thy mer-cies, how ten-der! how
firm to the end! Our Mak-er, De-fend-er, Re-deemer, and Friend.

4. Our Fa-ther and God, how faith-ful Thy love! While an-gels de-
light to hymn Thee a-bove; The hum-bler cre-a-tion, though
fee-ble their lays, With true ad-o-ra-tion shall lisp to Thy praise. A-MEN.

121 Dear Lord and Father of Mankind

JOHN G. WHITTIER, 1807-1892

FREDERICK C. MAKER, 1844-1927

In moderate time

1. Dear Lord and Fa-ther of man-kind, For-give our fool-ish ways;
2. In sim-ple trust like theirs who heard, Be-side the Syr-ian sea,
3. O Sab-bath rest by Gal-i-lee! O calm of hills a-bove,
4. Drop Thy still dews of qui-et-ness, Till all our striv-ings cease;
5. Breathe through the heats of our de-sire Thy cool-ness and Thy balm;

Re - clothe us in our right - ful mind; In pur - er lives Thy
The gra - cious call - ing of the Lord, Let us, like them, with-
Where Je - sus knelt to share with Thee The si - lence of e-
Take from our souls the strain and stress, And let our or - dered
Let sense be dumb, let flesh re - tire; Speak through the earth-quake,

ser - vice find, In deep - er rev - er - ence, praise.
out a word, Rise up and fol - low Thee.
ter - ni - ty, In - ter - pret - ed by love.
lives con - fess The beau - ty of Thy peace.
wind, and fire, O still small voice of calm! A - MEN.

Music copyright by the Psalms and Hymns Trust.   Used by permission.

Fairest Lord Jesus   **122**

German, 17th century

From SCHLESISCHE VOLKSLIEDER, 1842
Arr. by RICHARD S. WILLIS, 1819–1900

In moderate time, and graceful rhythm

1. Fair-est Lord Je - sus, Rul-er of all na - ture, O Thou of God and man the Son,
2. Fair are the mead-ows, Fair-er still the woodlands, Robed in the bloom-ing garb of spring:
3. Fair is the sun-shine, Fair-er still the moon-light, And all the twink-ling star-ry host:

Thee will I cher-ish, Thee will I hon-or, Thou, my soul's Glo-ry, Joy, and Crown.
Je - sus is fair-er, Je - sus is pur-er, Who makes the woe-ful heart to sing.
Je-sus shines bright-er, Je-sus shines pur-er Than all the an-gels heaven can boast. A-MEN.

123 Thine Is the Glory

Anonymous
Tr. by R. Birch Hoyle, 1923

George F. Handel, 1685-1759

With majestic rhythm

1. Thine is the glo-ry,— Ris-en, con-qu'ring Son,
2. Lo! Je-sus meets thee,— Ris-en from the tomb;
3. No more we doubt Thee,— Glo-rious Prince of Life!

End-less is the vic-t'ry— Thou o'er death hast won.
Lov-ing-ly He greets thee,— Scat-ters fear and gloom;
Life is nought with-out Thee;— Aid us in our strife;

An-gels in bright rai-ment—Rolled the stone a-way.
Let His Church with glad-ness—Hymns of tri-umph sing,
Make us more than con-qu'rors,—Through Thy death-less love.

Kept the fold-ed grave-clothes—Where Thy bod-y lay.
For her Lord now liv-eth;—Death hath lost its sting.
Bring us safe through Jor-dan— To Thy home a-bove.

Thine is the glo-ry, Ris-en, con-qu'ring Son,

End-less is the vic-t'ry Thou o'er death hast won. A-MEN.

Spirit of the Living God   **124**

Daniel Iverson   Daniel Iverson

Spir-it of the liv-ing God, fall fresh on me; Spir-it of the

liv-ing God, fall fresh on me. Break me! Melt me! Mold me!

Fill me! Spir-it of the liv-ing God, fall fresh on me.

125   Grant Us True Courage

Henry Wilder Foote

A. Fritsch, 1679
Harmonized by J.S.

Grant us true cour-age, Lord, To front each new en-deav-or; Con-fid-ing in Thy word Thou wilt leave us nev-er; A-like in gloom or joy Each du-ty to ful-fill, Our faith-ful hearts em-ploy To do Thy per-fect will. A-men

The World One Neighborhood 126

Jeanette E. Perkins

German, c 1784

1. We thank thee, God for eyes to see The beau-ty of the
2. Help us re-mem-ber that to some The eye and ear and
3. O may our eyes be o-pen, Lord, To see our neigh-bors'

earth; For ears to hear the words of love And
mind Bring sights and sounds of ug-li-ness And
need; And may our ears be kept a-lert Their

hap-py sounds of mirth; For minds that find new
on-ly sad-ness find; Help us re-mem-ber
cries for help to heed; Make keen our minds to

thoughts to think, New won-ders to ex-plore; For
that to them The world has seemed un-fair; That
plan the best For one an-oth-er's good, That

health and free-dom to en-joy The good thou hast in store.
we should strive to bring to them The beau-ty all may share.
all the world may be at last One friend-ly neigh-bor-hood.

From *As Children Worship* by Jeanette E. Perkins.
Copyright 1936, 1964, by The Pilgrim Press. Used by permission.

127 Jesu, Joy of Man's Desiring

Robert Bridges

J. S. Bach

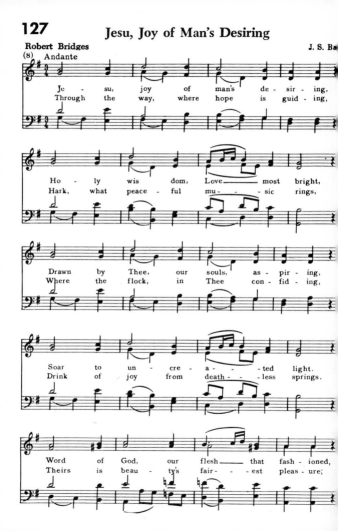

With the fire of life_____ im - pas - sioned,
Theirs is wis - dom's ho - -liest trea - sure;

Striv - ing still to Truth un - known,
Thou dost ev - er lead Thine own

Soar - ing, dy - ing round Thy throne.
In the love of joys un - -known.

umerals refer to measures of rest if Bach's accompaniment is played.

ords reprinted by permission of the Church Music Society and the ford University Press.

The Lord Is in His Holy Temple 128

Calvin W. Laufer, 1874 - 1938

The Lord is in His ho - ly tem - ple; let all the

earth keep si - lence be - fore Him, keep si - lence be - fore Him.

usic copyright, 1927, by C. W. Laufer, abr., alt., 1933; renewed, 1955, by B. Laufer, from *The Hymnal*, 1933; used by permission.

129   Joyful, Joyful We Adore Thee

HENRY VAN DYKE, 1852-1933

LUDWIG VAN BEETHOVEN, 1770-182

With exultation

1. Joy-ful, joy-ful, we a-dore Thee, God of glo-ry, Lord of love
2. All Thy works with joy sur-round Thee, Earth and heaven re-flect Thy rays
3. Thou art giv-ing and for-giv-ing, Ev-er bless-ing, ev-er blest
4. Mor-tals, join the hap-py cho-rus Which the morn-ing stars be-gan

Hearts un-fold like flowers be-fore Thee, Open-ing to the sun a-bov
Stars and an-gels sing a-round Thee, Cen-ter of un-bro-ken prai
Well-spring of the joy of liv-ing, O-cean depth of hap-py rest
Fa-ther love is reign-ing o'er us, Broth-er love binds man to man

Melt the clouds of sin and sad-ness, Drive the dark of doubt a-way
Field and for-est, vale and mountain, Flow-ery meadow, flash-ing sea
Thou our Fa-ther, Christ our Broth-er, All who live in love are Thine
Ev-er sing-ing, march we on-ward, Vic-tors in the midst of strife

Giv-er of im-mor-tal glad-ness, Fill us with the light of day.
Chant-ing bird and flow-ing foun-tain, Call us to re-joice in Thee.
Teach us how to love each oth-er, Lift us to the Joy di-vine.
Joy-ful mu-sic leads us Sun-ward In the tri-umph song of life. A-ME

Wondrous Love

What won-drous love is this, O my soul, O my soul! What won-drous love is this, O my soul! What won - drous love is this, That caused the Lord of bliss To send this per - fect peace to my soul, to my soul. To send this per - fect peace to my soul.

2

When I was sinking down, sinking down, sinking down,
When I was sinking down, sinking, sinking down;
When I was sinking down, Beneath God's righteous frown,
Christ laid aside His crown for my soul, for my soul. (Repeat)

3

To God and to the Lamb, I will sing, I will sing,
To God and to the Lamb, I will sing, will sing;
To God and to the Lamb, Who is the great I Am,
While millions join the theme, I will sing, I will sing. (Repeat)

4

And when from death I'm free, I'll sing on, I'll sing on,
And when from death I'm free, I'll sing on, sing on;
And when from death I'm free, I'll sing and joyful be,
And through eternity I'll sing on, I'll sing on. (Repeat)

131 Evening Skies

Evelyn Thompson To...

Eve-ning skies! Sun - rise! Lakes and rush-ing wa-ter;
Star-ry skies! Moon - rise! Far, e-ter-nal heav-ens;

Make all things un - love-ly From my soul de - part;
Take a-way my small-ness, Make me long to grow;

With grandeur

Pur-ple moun-tains ris-ing high! Trees a-gainst the sky;
Vast-ness of the u-ni-verse! Time-less-ness of space;

Thoughtfully

Life is beau-ti-ful be-cause God speaks with-in my heart!
Life is won-der-ful be-cause God speaks with-in my soul!

132 Hear Our Prayer

EDNA BRUNE...

Hear our pray'r, O Fa - ther, We be - seech Thee. A - ME...

Tallis' Canon

133

With dignity * Succeeding voices enter

Glo - ry to Thee, my God, this night, For all the bless-ings of the light;

Keep me, oh keep me, King of Kings, Be-neath Thine own Al might-y wings.

Round of Thanks

134

For health and strength and dai-ly food we praise Thy name, O Lord!

135

Gratitude Grace

OLIVE HASKINS

Old Hundredth

Lord, grat - i - tude we of - fer all Who la - bor

that we may be fed; O dig - ni - fy our toil for them,

Bring kin - ship thru our dai - ly bread. A - men.

Wesley Grace

136

Be present at our table, Lord,
Be here and everywhere adored,
These mercies bless, and grant that we
May feast in fellowship with Thee. Amen.

DRESDEN AMEN **137**

pp

A - men, A - men.

THREEFOLD AMEN **138**

mf

Danish

A-men, A-men, A - men.

139 Praise for Bread

Morn - ing
Noon - time has come, the board is spread. Thanks be to
Eve - ning

Him who giv - eth bread Praise God for bread!

140 Praise and Thanksgiving

Paraphrase of the German

Lobet und Preiset
Alsatian Round

Praise and thanks - giv - ing let ev - ery - one bring

Un - to our Fa - ther for ev - ery good thing.

All to - geth - er joy - ful - ly sing!

From *The Whole World Singing* by Edith Lowell Thomas,
Copyright 1950 by Friendship Press, used by permission.

141 Abide with Us, O Lord

Luke 24: 29

German

Herr, blei - be bei uns, Denn es wird A - bend
A - bide with us, O Lord, For it is now the

wer - den, Der Tag hat sich ge - nei - get.
eve - ning, The day is past and o - ver.

From *Chansons de Notre Chalet*, Copyright 1957

Dona Nobis Pacem 142

3-part Canon

Source Unknown

PART I

Do - na no - bis pa - cem pa - cem

PART II

Do - na no - bis pa - cem

PART III

Do - na no - bis pa - cem

Do - na no - bis pa - - - cem.

Do - na no - bis pa - - cem.

Do - na no - bis pa - - cem.

Hiney Mah Tov 143

Ps. 133: 1

Israeli Round

Hi - ney mah tov u - mah na - yim She - vet a - chim gam
How good and pleas-ant it is for broth-ers to dwell to -

ya - chad. Hi - ney mah tov She - vet a - chim gam ya - chad.
geth - er. Good and pleas - ant for broth-ers to dwell to - geth - er.

As sung by Tova Ben-Tsvi, Jerusalem.

Almighty Father 144

Arr. from FELIX MENDELSSOHN, 1809-1847

Al-might-y Fa-ther, hear our prayer, and bless all souls that wait be-fore Thee. A - MEN.

145 Silvery Star

Italian
Arr. by A. D. Z

Slowly

1. I looked up in the star-light One night when I was
2. Its soft and sil-ver rad-iance Shone si-lent-ly a-
3. When night strews all its dia-monds A-cross the sky a-

lone-ly; One star of all the stars there Was our star on-ly.
bove me, And si-lent-ly I asked it How well you love me
bove you, I pray our star may tell you How well I love you.

English by Max Exner. Copyright 1962 Cooperative Recreation Service, Inc.

146 Vine and Fig Tree

Shalom Altman

And ev-'ry man 'neath his vine and fig tree, Shall live in

peace and un a-fraid. fraid. And in-to plough-shares

turn their swords, na-tions shall learn war no more. war no more.

Isaiah 2:4; Micah 4:3.
* Second Group singing B music may enter at * on second repeat of A.

147 All Night, All Day

All night, all day, an-gels watch-in' o-ver me, my Lord.

All night, all day, an-gels watch-in' o-ver me.

1. Day is dyin' in the West, Angels
2. Now I lay me down to sleep, Angels
3. Thy love stay with me thru the night, Angels

watch-in' o-ver me, my Lord
Sleep, my child, and
Pray the Lord my
And wake me with the

take your rest,
soul to keep, An-gels watch-in' o-ver me.
morn-ing light,

D. C.

Swing Low, Sweet Chariot

148

Negro Spiritual

Swing low, sweet char-i-ot,— Com-in' for to car-ry me home!

Swing low, sweet char-i-ot,— Com-in' for to car-ry me home.

Fine

I looked ov-er Jor-don, an' what did I see,—

Com-in' for to car-ry me home! A band of an-gels

Com-in' af-ter me,— Com-in' for to car-ry me home.

D. C.

2. If you get there before I do,
   Jes' tell my fren's that I'm a-comin' too, . . .

3. I'm sometimes up an' sometimes down,
   But still my soul feels heavenly boun'. . . .

These two songs may be sung together. Divide the group.

149 Let Us Break Bread Together

Negro Spiritual

Let us break bread to-geth-er On our knees, on our
Let us drink wine to-geth-er On our knees, on our
Let us praise God to-geth-er On our knees, on our

knees; Let us break bread to-geth-er on our knees, on our
knees; Let us drink wine to-geth-er on our knees, on our
knees; Let us praise God to-geth-er on our knees, on our

knees. When I fall on my knees, with my face to the ris-ing

sun, O Lord, have mer-cy on me. on me.

150 Kum Ba Yah

African (Angola)

Slowly

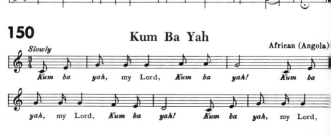

Kum ba yah, my Lord, *Kum ba yah! Kum ba*

yah, my Lord, *Kum ba yah! Kum ba yah,* my Lord,

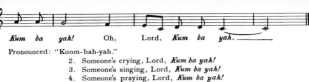

Kum ba yah! Oh, Lord, Kum ba yah.

Pronounced: "Koom-bah-yah."

2. Someone's crying, Lord, Kum ba yah!
3. Someone's singing, Lord, Kum ba yah!
4. Someone's praying, Lord, Kum ba yah!

Oh, Freedom! 151

mf SOLO   UNISON

1. Oh, free-dom! oh, free-dom! oh,
2. No mo' moan-in' 'no mo' moan-in' no mo'
3. There'll be sing-in', there'll be sing-in', there'll be

free-dom
moan-in' o-ver me! An' be-fo' I'd be a slave, I'll be
sing-in'

o-ver me!

bur-ied in my grave, An' go home to my Lord an' be free.

4. There'll be shoutin'. . .   5. There'll be prayin'. . .

From *Religious Folk Songs*, 1927. By permission of the Hampton Institute Press.

152

Balm in Gilead

Arr. by Francis Ames

REFRAIN

There is a balm in Gil-e-ad To make the wound-ed whole._ There is a balm in Gil-e-ad To heal the sin-sick soul._ There is a soul.__

1 | Don't
You
Some-

2 | Fine: soul.

hm ____ hm ____

times I feel dis-cour-aged an' think my work in vain, But
ev-er feel dis-cour-aged, our Fa-ther is our friend, And
may not preach like Pe-ter, you may not pray like Paul, But

hm ____ hm ____

Fine: soul.

hm ____ hm ____

then the Ho-ly Spir-it re-vives my soul a-gain.
if you lack for know-ledge He'll not re-fuse to lend. There is a
you can tell the sto-ry of one who died for all.

D.S. %

hm ____ hm ____

He's Got the Whole World in His Hands

Negro Spiritual

1. He's got the whole _____ world ___ in His hands,
wind and the rain ___ in His hands,

He's got the big round ___ world ___ in His hands,
He's got the sun and the moon ___ in His hands,

He's got the whole _____ world ___ in His hands,
He's got the wind and the rain ___ in His hands,

He's got the whole world in His hands. He's got the

Fine 2 *D. S.*

m the Marion Kerby collection of Negro Exaltations.

3. He's got the little bitsy baby in His hands,
He's got the tiny little baby in His hands.
He's got the little bitsy baby in His hands.
He's got the whole world in His hands.

4. He's got you and me, brother, in His hands,
He's got you and me, sister, in His hands,
He's got you and me, brother, in His hands,
He's got the whole world in His hands.

5. He's got everybody in His hands,
He's got everybody in His hands,
He's got everybody in His hands,
He's got the whole world in His hands.

6. He's got the whole world in His hands,
He's got the big, round world in His hands,
He's got the whole world in His hands,
He's got the whole world in His hands.

154   Amen

CHORUS

A - - men, A - - men, A - men, A

SOLO OBBLIGATO

See   the ba - by,
See Him in   the tem - ple,
See Him at   the sea - side,
See Him in   the gar - den,
Yes, He is   my Sav - ior.

|1 CHORUS |2

men, A - men.   men, A - men.

A

Ly - ing in a   man - ger   One Christ - mas   morn - ing.
Talk - ing to the El - ders, How they marvelled at His wis - dom.
Preach - ing and heal - ing, To the blind and the fee - ble.
Pray - ing to His Fa - ther, In   deep - est   sor - row.
Je - sus died to save us, And He rose on Eas - ter.

men,   A - - men,   A -

6. Hal - le - lu -   jah   In the king -

men, A - men, A - men.   A - - men,

dom   with my Sav - ior   A - men, A - men.

A - - men,   A - - men, A - men, A - men.

Amen– pronounce A as in bay.

NOTES: (1) Sing chorus thru twice before beginning obbligato lead and softening back
ground singing with beginning of lead. (2) Swell the 2nd and 3rd "Amen" when going u
scale. (3) In last verse be sure to observe break, and all hold last "A-men".

Garden Hymn

155

Traditional
Southern Folk-hymn

Andante

1. The — Lord in - to His gar - den comes; — The
2. Oh, that this dry and bar - ren ground — In
3. Come, — breth - ren, ye that love the Lord, — And

spic - es yield a rich per - fume; The — lil - ies grow and
springs of wa - ter may a - bound, A — fruit - ful soil be -
taste the sweet - ness of His word, In — Je - sus' ways go

thrive, — the lil - ies grow and thrive. — Re -
come, — a fruit - ful soil be - come, — The
on, — in Je - sus' ways go on, — Our

fresh - ing showers of grace di - vine From —
des - ert blos - soms as the rose When —
trou - bles and our tri - als here Will —

Je - sus flow to ev - 'ry vine And — make the dead re -
Je - sus con - quers all His foes And — makes His peo - ple
on - ly make us rich - er there When — we ar - rive at

vive, — And make the dead re - vive. —
one, — And makes His peo - ple one. —
home, — When we ar - rive at home. —

ginia version. Found in many shape-note hymnals.

156   The Lord's Prayer

Tune set down by
Olive Pattison

West Indian Folk Tu

Our Fa-ther, which art in heav-en, Hal-low-ed-a-be thy Name.

Thy king-dom come, Thy will be done, Hal-low-ed-a-be thy Name.

On the earth as it is in heav-en, Give us this day our

dai-ly bread, And for-give us all our tres-pas-ses,

As we for-give those who tres-pass a-gainst us,

And lead us not to the dev-il to be temp-ted.

But de-liv-er us from all that is e-vil.

For thine is the king-dom, The pow-er and the glo-ry,

For ev-er, for ev-er, for ev-er and ev-er,

men, A - men. Hal - low - ed - a - be thy Name.

peat A....* or B....* as indicated after alternate lines.
om the EDRIC CONNOR COLLECTION OF WEST INDIAN SPIRITUALS.
pyright 1945 by Boosey and Co., Ltd. Reprinted by permission.

Every Time I Feel de Spirit   **157**

CHORUS

Ev - 'ry time I feel de Spir - it Mov - in'

in my heart, _ I will pray; _ Ev - 'ry time I _ feel de

Spir - it _ Mov - in' in my heart, _ I will pray. _

Fine

Hum   *Hum*

1. Up - on the moun - tain, when my Lord spoke, _ Out of His
2. Oh, I have sor - rows and I have woe, _ And I have

Hum   *Hum*

mouth came _ fire and smoke; Looked all a - round _ me, it looked so
heart - ache _ here be - low; _ But while God leads _ me, I'll nev - er

Hum   *Hum*   *D. C.*

fine, _ Till I asked my Lord if all were mine. _
fear, _ For I am shel - tered _ by His care. _

NOTE: Male voices sing the verse melody. Women's voices hum the obbligato. Keep synco-
pated rhythm.

158

King of Kings

Arr. by Olive J. Willia[m]

He is King of Kings. He is Lord of Lords.

Je - sus Christ the first and last,— No man works like Him.

1. I know that my Re - deem - er lives—
2. He builds a plat - form in the air— No man works like Him,
3. O sin - ner if you will be - lieve—

And by His love sweet bless - ing gives.
And calls the saints from ev - 'ry - where No man works like Him.
Grace of the Lord you will re - ceive

NOTE: Repeat refrain at beginning and end, last time *pp*.
Sing refrain once after each stanza.

159

Steal Away

Negro Spiritu[al]

Steal a - way, steal a - way, steal a - way to Je - sus! Steal a - way, steal a - way

1. My Lord ___ calls me, He calls me by the
home, I ain't got long to stay here. 2. Green trees are bending, Poor sin-ners stand a-
3. My Lord ___ calls me, He calls me by the

thun-der;
trembling; The trumpet sounds with-in-a my soul; I ain't got long to stay here.
lightning;

Michael Row the Boat Ashore 160

160

Descant

1. Mich-ael   row   the   boat   a - shore,
2. Jor-don's ri - ver is deep   and   wide, Hal-le-lu - jah.
3. Jor-don's ri - ver is chil-ly and   cold,

Mich-ael   row   the   boat   a - shore,
Milk and hon-ey on the oth-er side, Hal-le-lu - jah.
Chills the bo-dy but   not   the   soul,

permission of Anthony Saletan, who discovered it in an 1886 Collection of Slave
ngs; Arr. by W. H.
pyright 1963 by Cooperative Recreation Service, Inc.

161
I Want to Live in a Friendly World

Lyric by
Hy Zaret

Music by
Lou Sing

skin, Or the church I wor-ship in, Or the town from which I came, Or my great grand - fa - ther's name. name. I want to live in a friend - ly world, a friend - ly world, a friend - ly world__ I want to live in the kind of world that's kind to folks like me.

162 Kommt Herbei

Ps. 106: 1

Traditio

Kommt her - bei dan - ket dem Herrn; denn barm - her - zig ist dei
Come and sing to __ the __ Lord, love and mer - cy in His

Gott, sei - ne Güt und Wahr - heit wäh - ren __ e - wig - lich.
word show us truth and good - ness ev - er, __ ev - er more

English by Ursula Stechow

163 We Shall Overcome

Slowly

American Freedom S

1. We shall o - ver - come, We shall o - ver

come, __ We shall o - ver - come some

day; __ Oh! __ Deep in my heart

I do be - lieve, We shall o - ver - come some day. __

2. We'll walk hand in hand some day. . .
3. We are not afraid to-day. . .
4. The truth shall make us free. . .
5. We shall live in peace . . .

Alouette

164

CHORUS

French-Canadian

A - lou - et - te, gen - tile A - lou - et - te, A - lou - et - te,

Fine LEADER

je te plu - me - rai. 1. Je te plu - me - rai la tête,

ALL LEADER ALL D.C.

Je te plu - me - rai le - tête, Et la - tête, Et la - tête, Oh,____

2. Le bec   4. Le dos   6. Le cou
3. Le nez   5. Les pattes

Brothers Not

165

ds: Beth Dunlop

Music: Jackie Spitz
Arranged: Larry Trettin

G   Em   Am   D7

1. Down   this   road,   a   lone - ly   road,
2. Here's   the   spot   where they   stood   fish - ing
3. Walk -   ing   home,   one   fish   be -   tween them;
4. Years   have   passed, the   road's for -   got - ten,

G   Em   Am   D7   G   Em

Walked two young-sters hand in hand.   Broth-ers they,   by
On   the coarse and rock - y sand.   Spoke they not,   yet
Down that road still hand in hand.   Vowed that they'd be
And   the coarse and rock - y sand   Sep - a - rate lives, no

C   D7   G   Em   Am D7   G Em Am D7

word   of God;   Broth - ers   not   by   word   of   man.
both   were wish - ing,   Broth - ers   to   be   in   word   of   man.
friends for - ev - er   'Spite   the   fool - ish   word   of   man.
vow   re - main - ing   Broth - ers   not   by   word   of   man!

166   Linstead Market

Adapted from
Jamaica folk so[ng]

Carry mi' ack - ee go-a Lin-stid Mar - ket,
Ev - er - y bod - y come-a feel - a feel - a,
Come all you pick - ney; come-a ling - a ling - a,

Not a quat-tee would sell; Car-ry mi' ack - ee go-a
Not a quat-tee would sell; Ev - er - y bod - y come-a
What yo' ma-ma no bring; Come all you pick-ney; come-a

Lin - stid Mar - ket, Not a quat-tee would sell.
feel - a feel - a, Not a quat-tee would sell.
ling - a ling - a, What yo' ma-ma no bring.

REFRAIN

Why not a light, not a bite, what a Sat-ur-day night.

Why not a light, not a bite, what a Sat-ur-day night.

ackee — vegetable   pickney — children
quattee — quarter-penny's worth   linga — listen
feel-a — "feel for me" (sympathize)

167   Hey, Ho! Nobody Home

3-Part R[ound]

Hey, ho! No-bod - y home, Meat nor drink nor

mon - ey have I none, Yet will I be me - e - e - e - rr[y]

Are You Sleeping?

168

Round

Are you sleep-ing? Broth-er John, Morn-ing bells are ring-ing, Ding, ding, dong!

The Ash Grove

169

Welsh folk song

mp

The ash-grove, how grace-ful, how plain-ly 'tis speak-ing, The
My laugh-ter is o-ver, my step los-es light-ness, Old

harp thro' it play-ing has lan-guage for me; When-ev-er the
coun-try-side meas-ures steal soft on my ear; I on-ly re-

light thro' its branch-es is break-ing, A host of kind
mem-ber the past and its bright-ness, The dear ones I

fac-es is gaz-ing on me; The friends of my child-hood a-
mourn for a-gain gath-er here. From out of the shad-ows their

gain are be-fore me, Each step wakes a mem-'ry as free-ly I
lov-ing looks greet me, And wist-ful-ly search-ing the leaf-y green

roam; With soft whis-pers la-den, its leaves rus-tle o'er me, The
dome, I find oth-er fac-es fond bend-ing to greet me, The

ash-grove, the ash-grove a-lone is my home.

Descant by Janet E. Tobitt

170   Green Grow the Rushes

I'll sing you one - ho! Green grow the rush-es ho; What is your one-ho?

One is one and all a - lone and ev - er-more shall be so.

I'll sing you two-ho! Green grow the rush-es-ho; What are your two-ho?
(three etc.)

Two, two, the lil - y-white boys, cloth - ed all in green - ho,

D. S. Fine

One is one and all a - lone and ev - er-more shall be so.

Three, three the ri - vals, (to 2) Four for the gos-pel mak - ers. (to 3

(4, 6, 10)

5. Five for the symbols at your door and four for the gospel makers, (to 3)
6. Six for the six proud walkers, (to 5)
7. Sev'n for the sev'n stars in the sky and six for the six proud walkers, (to 5)
8. Eight for the April rainers, (to 7)
9. Nine for the nine bright shiners, (to 8)
10. Ten for the ten commandments, (to 9)
11. Elev'n for the 'lev'n went up to heav'n and ten for the ten commandments, (to 9)
12. Twelve for the twelve Apostles, (to 11)

Possible meaning: I refers to Deity; II, Hebrew version Tables of the Law. III, Trinity or Patriarchs; IV, Gospel writers, or wives of Patriarchs; VII, Ursa Major, or days of the week. X, All versions agree here; XI Apostles minus Judas, or 11 stars seen by Joseph: XII, Apostles, or tribes of Israel.

Let Us Sing Together

Adapted from Czech Folk Tune

Let us sing to geth - er, Let us sing to - geth - er, One and
all a joy - ous song. Let us sing to - geth - er,
One and all a joy - ous song. Let us sing a - gain and
a - gain, Let us sing a - gain and a - gain, Let us sing a -
gain and a - gain, One and all a joy - ous song.

Shalom, Chaverim

Israeli Round

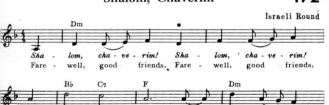

Sha - lom, cha - ve - rim! Sha - lom, cha - ve - rim!
Fare - well, good friends, Fare - well, good friends,

Sha - lom, sha - lom! Le - hit - ra - ot,
Fare - well, fare - well! Till we meet a - gain,

le - hit - ra - ot, Sha - lom, sha - lom.
till we meet a - gain, Fare - well, fare - well.

Pronounced "Shah-lohm chah-vay-reem"; ch like German "noch".
* Succeeding voices enter. English by A. D. Z.

From *Chansons de Notre Chalet*, copyright 1957 by Cooperative Recreation Service, Inc. Used by permission.

173 Evening Star

Chr. Richardt, 1861
Trans. by S. D. Rodholm

Carl Mortensen

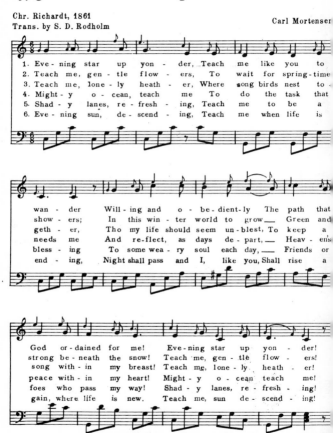

1. Eve-ning star up yon-der, Teach me like you to wan-der Will-ing and o-be-dient-ly The path that God or-dained for me! Eve-ning star up yon-der!
2. Teach me, gen-tle flow-ers, To wait for spring-time show-ers; In this win-ter world to grow__ Green and strong be-neath the snow! Teach me, gen-tle flow-ers!
3. Teach me, lone-ly heath-er, Where song birds nest to-geth-er, Tho my life should seem un-blest, To keep a song with-in my breast! Teach me, lone-ly heath-er!
4. Might-y o-cean, teach me To do the task that needs me And re-flect, as days de-part,__ Heav-en's peace with-in my heart! Might-y o-cean teach me!
5. Shad-y lanes, re-fresh-ing, Teach me to be a bless-ing To some wea-ry soul each day,__ Friends or foes who pass my way! Shad-y lanes, re-fresh-ing!
6. Eve-ning sun, de-scend-ing, Teach me when life is end-ing, Night shall pass and I, like you, Shall rise a-gain, where life is new. Teach me, sun de-scend-ing!

Upward Trail

174

We're on the up-ward trail! We're on the up-ward trail!

Sing-ing, sing-ing, ev-'ry-bod-y sing-ing, As we go!

We're on the up-ward trail! We're on the up-ward trail!

Sing-ing, sing-ing, ev-'ry-bod-y sing-ing, Home-ward bound!

Zum Gali Gali

175

Palestine

1. He-cha-lutz le 'man a-vo-dah;
2. A-vo-dah le 'man he-cha-lutz;
3. He-cha-lutz le 'man ha-b'tu lah;
4. Ha-sha-lom le 'man ha-'a-mim;

Zum ga-li ga-li ga-li Zum ga-li ga-li,

A-vo-dah le 'man he-cha-lutz.
He-cha-lutz le 'man a-vo-dah.
Ha-b'tu lah le 'man he-cha-lutz.
Ha 'a-mim le 'man ha-sha-lom.

Zum ga-li ga-li ga-li, Zum ga-li ga-li.

An approximate translation of the various Hebrew phrases:
1 and 2. The pioneer's purpose is labor: labor is for the pioneer.
3. The pioneer is for his girl: his girl is for the pioneer.
4. Peace for all the nations: all the nations are for peace.

Pronounce: a as in father; he like hay; le with very short e; i as in machine; o as in come; u as in rule; ch as in German ach.

Sarasponda

Spinning Son

GIRLS: Sa - ra - spon - da, Sa - ra -
BOYS: Boom - da, Boom - da, Boom - da, Boom - da, Boom - da, Boom - da,

spon - da, Sa - ra - spon - da, Ret - set - set! Sa - ra -
Boom - da, Boom - da, Boom - da, Boom - da, Boom - da, Boom - da.

spon - da, Sa - ra - spon - da, Sa - ra - spon - da, Ret - set - set!
Boom - da, Boom - da, Boom - da, Boom - da, Boom - da, Boom - da, Boom - da.

ALL
Ah - do - ray - oh! Ah - do - ray - boom - day - oh! Ah

do - ray - boom - day - ret - set - set! Aw - say - paw - say - oh!

The "Boom-da," which is sung very softly by the boys, represents the "burr" of the
spinning wheel.

Day Is Done

Day is done, Gone the sun From the lake, From the hills,
Thanks and praise. For our days 'Neath the sun, 'Neath the stars,

From the sky, All is well, Safe - ly rest, God is nigh.
'Neath the sky, As we go, This we know, God is nigh.

Black Is the Color

178

Early American

Black is the color of my
I love my love and well she

true love's hair, Her lips are some thing won-drous fair; The
knows. I love the grass on where she goes, If

pur - est eyes and the dain - t'est hands I
she on earth no more I'd see, My

love the grass on where she stands. **Repeat first phrase**
life would quick-ly fade a - way.

179   Song of Youth

Amar Utari
English by Max Exner

Amar U
In

1. For-ward, O youth! For - ev - er ad - vanc - ing,
2. Wak - en! This hour is no time for sleep-ing,
3. Go we with sing - ing o - ver the land, Whe

Look to ho - ri - zons far. Eyes do not grope in
Wel-come the ris - ing sun. Na-tions are stir - ring,
ev - er the road - ways lie. Free-dom shall be the

depths of the night That look on a shin-ing star.
out of their slum-bers; Great is the work un - done.
theme of your song, The watch-word of peace your cry:

Na-tions, fear-ful in a - part-ness, Need your sight to
Wak-en, sis-ters! Wak-en, broth-ers! Rise up, now, and
E - qual right for ev - 'ry broth-er, Lands at peace with

light their dark - ness. Look up, O youth for
wak - en oth - ers! Wel - come the morn: a
one an - oth - er. Loy - al to truth, the

ev - er ad-vanc - ing; Look to ho - ri - zons far.
new day is born When peo-ples shall live as one.
sing-ing of youth Shall ech - o from hill to sky.

The Instruments

Willy Geisler, 1927
Arr. by J. G. H.

180

The vi - o - lin's ring - ing like love - - -
The clar - i - net, the clar - i - net makes dood - le, dood - le,

The trump - et is bray - ing ta - ta - ta ta - ta - te - ta, ta -

The horn, the horn, a - wakes me
The drums play - ing two tones and al - ways

ly sing - ing. The vi - o - lin's
dood - le, dood - le det. The clar - i - net, the

ta - ta ta - ta - te - ta The trump - et is

at morn. The horn, the
the same tones: five one, one

ring - ing like love - - ly song.
clar - i - net makes dood - le, dood - le, dood - le det.

bray - ing ta - ta - ta - ta - ta - te - ta, ta - ta ta.

horn a - wakes me at morn.
five, five, five, five, five, one.

181 Marianina

David Stevens   Italian Popular Tune

Brightly

1. Where the Tus-can sun is warm and bright, Dwells a
2. I have loved her ev-er since we met, She is

maid whose laugh is pure de-light; Tho' her charm is yet un-
mine, but does-n't know it yet; I shall tell her so to-

known to fame, Still I love her just the same.
mor-row day, She will nev-er an-swer nay.

CHORUS

Ma-ri-a-ni-na, tra, la, la, Ma-ri-a-ni-na, tra, la, la.

O Ma-ri-a-ni-na! O Ma-ri-a-ni-na! The
O Ma-ri-a-ni-na! O Ma-ri-a-ni-na! My

wild red rose Was nev-er half so fair.
Tus-can belle With pop-pies in her hair.

Waltzing Matilda

B. Paterson

Once a jol-ly swag-man camped by a bill-a-bong,
Down came a jum-buck to drink at the bill-a-bong,
Down came the squat-ter mount-ed on his thor-o-bred,
Up jumped the swag man, sprang in-to the bill-a-bong,

Un-der the shade of a cool-i-bah tree, And he
Up jumped the swag-man, grabbed him with glee, And he
Up came the troop-ers, one, two, three,
"You'll nev-er catch me a-live!" said he. And his

sang as he sat and wait-ed while his bill-y boiled,
sang as he shoved that jum-buck in his tuck-er-bag:
"Whose that jol-ly jum-buck you've got in your tuck-er-bag?"
ghost may be heard as you pass by that bill-a-bong:

Fine

"You'll come a-waltz-ing Ma-til-da with me." "Waltz-ing Ma-til-da,

D. S.

waltz-ing Ma-til-da, You'll come a-waltz-ing Ma-til-da with me."

183 Doktor Eisenbart

Pennsylvania Dutch

1. I am Herr Dok-tor Ei-sen-bart, Twil-li wil-li witt, boom
2. My pa-tients call me "I-ron Beard,"

boom! I'll cure your ills with heal-ing art, Twil-li wil-li witt, boom
For all my cures I am re-vered,

boom! Now I can make the dumb to walk, Twil-li wil-li witt, boom

boom boom boom! The lame to see, the blind to talk,

Twil-li wil-li witt, boom boom! Sing to-ri-ay sing to-ri-ay!

Twil-li wil-li witt, boom boom boom boom! Sing to-ri-ay, Sing

to-ri-ay! Twil-li wil-li witt, boom boom!

184 Fellowship

May this our fel-low-ship fore-tell, That men may learn in peace to dwell,

This Old Man

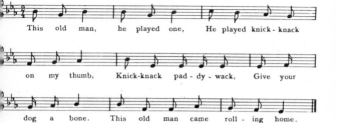

This old man, he played one, He played knick-knack on my thumb, Knick-knack pad-dy-wack, Give your dog a bone. This old man came roll-ing home.

On my shoe

On my knee

On my door

5. On my hive

6. On my stick

7. Up in heaven

8. On my pate

9. On my spine

10. Once again

Alleluia

Mozart, Adapted by H. R. W.

Allegro

Al-le-lu-ia, al-le-lu-ia,— al-le-lu-ia, al-le-lu-ia, Al-le-lu-ia, al-le-lu-ia.— al-le-lu-ia, al-le-lu-ia, Al-le-lu-ia, al-le-lu-ia.

om *Rounds and Canons*.
d by permission of the publishers, Schmitt, Hall & McCreary Co.,
neapolis, Minn.

Music Notes

69—Words for "Declare, O Heavens, the Lord of Space," were written by Robert Lansing Edwards in 1962.

70—Words for "God, Our Father and Creator," were written by Edward Krusen Ziegler in 1961; he is a pastor for the Church of the Brethren, and served as a missionary to India and as a director of evangelism for his denomination.

80—Words and music for the "Thanksgiving Hymn," were written by Mrs. Nancy Livingston Goff in 1965 for her youth choir at First Christian Church, Centralia, Illinois. Mrs. Goff is a minister of Christian education. She also wrote words and music for No. 119.

92—Words for "Within the Shelter of Our Walls," was written by Miss Elinor Lennen, a Christian educator for Christian Churches (Disciples of Christ) and writer of poetry. It was written in 1961.

93—Words for "Come Forth, O Christian Youth," were written in 1955 by Miss Mary Ellen Jackson, a director of Christian education for the Presbyterian Church, U.S.

94—Words for "The Son of God, Our Christ," were written in 1956 by Edward M. Blumenfeld, a Congregational pastor who served in both the Navy and the Army, and has served churches in Vermont.

99—Words for "O God, Thy Hand the Heavens Made," published in 1961, were written by Frank Leroy Cross, literary editor for Lorenz Publishing Company of Dayton, Ohio, and a pastor of the Evangelical United Brethren church.

104—Words for "Help Us, O Lord, to Learn," were written by William W. Reid, Jr. in 1959. The author is a Methodist minister, and author of several hymns, including "O God of Every Nation," No. 112.

106—Words for "Hymn for the Motor Age" were written in 1957 by Thomas Tiplady, a native of England and a Methodist clergyman.

113—Words for "Lord, We Believe," were written in 1957 by Thomas Paul Slavens, a Christian Churches (Disciples of Christ) minister.

114—"God Almighty, God Eternal," written in 1958 by Mary Jackson Cathey, was one of the winning World Order Hymns published by the Hymn Society of America.

118—"Renew Thy Church," was written by Kenneth L. Cober, executive director of the Division of Christian Education for American Baptists, and was published in 1960, is set to an Old English melody.

127—"Jesu, Joy of Man's Desiring," is Bach's tune with words written by Martin John. It can be sung to the accompaniment of the original Bach melody.

160—"Michael, Row the Boat Ashore" is an arrangement of a popular folk song.

165—"Brothers Not" is an original folk song written by Beth Dunlop and Jacqueline Spitz, both of Shaker Heights, Ohio, and members of the First Baptist Church in Cleveland; the song was written when the girls were in high school, and was arranged by Larry Trettin for this publication.

Alphabetical Index of Songs

ACKNOWLEDGMENT

lev	Write at a level appropriate to your subject and audience. *59*	
mm	Misplaced modifier: place it elsewhere so that it clearly modifies the intended word. *25*	
mo	Use the mood required by your sentence. *57*	
ms	Follow conventional manuscript form. *77, 78*	
p	Correct the punctuation	

| |	brackets *40*	( )	parentheses *39*
:	colon *37*	.	period *33*
,	comma *29–32*	?	question mark *34*
–	dash *38*	" "	quotation marks *40*
...	ellipsis *40*	;	semicolon *36*
!	exclamation point *35*		

pred	Make the subject and predicate of this sentence relate to each other logically. *26*
ps	Know the parts of speech and their uses. *83*
ref	Make this pronoun refer clearly to its antecedent. *52*
rep	Eliminate the obvious repetition. *70*
shift	Correct the shift in verb or pronoun use. *58*
sp	Proofread for proper spelling, and work on your spelling weaknesses. *47*
sub	Use subordination to relate secondary details to main ideas. *20*
t	Use the correct verb tense. *55*
trite	Replace this trite expression with fresher language. *67*
ts	Use a topic sentence to focus each paragraph on one point. *16*
u	Unify this paragraph by making all sentences relate to the topic sentence. *17*
vague	Use specific and concrete words. *62*
vb	Use the correct form of this verb. *56*
wdy	Tighten this wordy expression. *70*
ww	Wrong word: choose a more exact word. *63, 64*

The Practical Handbook for Writers

Seventh Edition with MLA Updates

Gerald J. Schiffhorst
University of Central Florida

Donald Pharr
St. Leo University

Academic Media Solutions

Affordable - Quality Textbooks, Study Aids, & Custom Publishing

The Practical Handbook for Writers, 7th Edition with MLA Updates

Print version - black/white:	ISBN-13: 978-1-942041-53-5
	ISBN-10: 1-942041-53-5
Print version - color:	ISBN-13: 978-1-942041-52-8
	ISBN-10: 1-942041-52-7
Online version:	ISBN-13: 978-1-942041-54-2
	ISBN-10: 1-942041-54-3

Printed in the United States of America by Academic Media Solutions.

Contents

Preface

This handbook has been helpful to writing students and others since 1979, when the first edition appeared. Over the years, *The Short Handbook for Writers* served as an authoritative guide to the conventions of grammar, punctuation, mechanics, usage, and style. This updated, seventh edition, now titled *The Practical Handbook for Writers*, continues in the same tradition.

Like the earlier editions, this revision of what has become a standard textbook is intended to provide users with a handy source of reference as well as with essential information on the composing process. You can use this handbook either as a textbook in any course that requires writing or as an independent tool that answers your questions about grammar, punctuation, usage, documentation, and other essentials.

The three divisions of this text indicate its distinct purposes: Part I guides you through the writing process, including rhetorical emphasis on the sentence and paragraph; Part II serves as a source of reference on matters of grammar, punctuation, and diction; and Part III presents most of the major practical writing applications that composition students encounter.

Part I will interest you if you are looking for guidance on planning and writing an essay. You will find tips on topic selection, development, revision, and writing effective paragraphs and sentences. Included in the chapter on sentences are exercises intended to help you review the material covered in each section of the chapter.

Refer to Part II when you wish to edit your work and need help with language, punctuation, grammar, or usage. The exercises in these sections will test your knowledge. Please note that a complete set of extra exercises is also available.

Part III concentrates on applied writing. If, for example, you are looking for information on how to write a documented essay or research paper, Chapter 10 offers a thorough guide, including sample papers using the current MLA and APA documentation styles. We have thoroughly revised this chapter so that it covers both traditional print research and the ever-expanding world of online research. The MLA section concentrates on the eighth edition of the *MLA Handbook* and shows, point by point, how the formats prescribed by this edition differ from the older, seventh-edition formats.

At the end of the text you will find a Glossary of Terms, as well as a Glossary of Usage that draws distinctions between accepted usage and usage not appropriate in today's college-level writing.

Our book provides clear, brief answers to the basic questions that arise whenever people write. By avoiding unnecessary technical terms, *The Practical Handbook for Writers* provides an accessible yet authoritative guide to the essentials of English.

We are indebted to the innumerable students who have used earlier editions of this book and to the many college instructors who have made suggestions about these editions. We are grateful to Dan Luciano, to Academic Media Solutions, and to the editors at Textbook Media. We extend special thanks to Victoria Putman for her amazing ability to create books.

We hope that you enjoy *The Practical Handbook for Writers,* and we invite you to contact us with any comments, questions, or suggestions: info@academicmediasolutions.com.

Gerald J. Schiffhorst
Donald Pharr

The
Writing
Process

PART

I

The Writing Process

Finding Something to Say

Overview

Instead of reading this book straight through, you will probably refer to various chapters and parts of chapters as you need them. Even so, to put things in perspective and to help you get the most from your time, we will begin with an overview of the whole subject of writing.

We are not going to present a simple, foolproof formula guaranteed to make you a competent writer. Unfortunately, there is no such formula. Writing is like playing golf or the piano: you learn and improve by doing—by practicing, by listening to criticism, and by practicing some more. Good writing does more than just avoid blunders. It holds the reader's interest. When you write well, you begin by thinking through what you want to say. Then you say it, in clear, logical sentences and carefully chosen words, expressing your thoughts and feelings so that your audience will understand them just as you want them to be understood.

Most writing—certainly all the writing we will be concerned with here—has a purpose and a method suited to it. Writers tell stories: they say what happens (narration). Or they argue: they speak for or against something (argument). Or they describe: they tell how something looks, sounds, or moves (description). Or they explain: they tell how something works (process analysis) or why something happens (causal analysis). Writers have other methods available as well: classification, definition, comparison/contrast.

As you plan what you want to say in a paper, you will also be deciding which approach that you will use. This does not mean that you will choose one approach and ignore the rest. You may be called on to classify, argue, describe, analyze, or narrate, or define and argue, or describe and narrate, or do all of these in one paper. Nevertheless, the assignment, your own purpose, or a combination of your assignment and your purpose will usually make one approach predominant. For example, you may start out by describing ways in which consumers are deceived by television commercials and then end up arguing that there should be stricter regulation of such advertising. Because the emphasis in this case should fall on the argument, your purpose in describing commercials is to prepare your reader to believe as you do about regulation.

If you chose to write an essay on Alateen, an organization that provides support to young people affected by problem drinking by other family members, your main purpose might be to explain what this group does and how it functions. You might compare it with Alcoholics Anonymous, or you might classify various programs for substance abusers and their families in relation to in-patient or out-patient treatment centers. You might also analyze different theories of alcoholism and drug abuse, using quotations from magazine and newspaper articles dealing with the causes of these problems. Perhaps you could attend an Alateen meeting and then describe the range of people you met or provide a narrative account of your visit. Finally, you might conclude an essay with your opinion of the issues involved: Is Alateen helping to solve the problems of adolescents faced with substance abuse in their family? Still, your essay would remain mostly exploratory: to explain the role of Alateen, based on your experience and reading.

To a certain degree, all writing must be persuasive. It must persuade readers that it is worth their time and attention. What you have to say will get a fair hearing only if you make sure it deserves one. Writing that deserves to be read is the kind we will be concerned with throughout this book.

Writing is a process of generating ideas, and the first four chapters divide this ongoing process, for convenience, into prewriting, considering the reader, drafting, and revising. At each stage, focus on a few things at a time. Allow yourself time to plan and develop ideas by learning to think on paper, and do not worry about editing or correcting what you write until the composing process has run its course. Because writing is a complex activity, the stages often overlap or double back: you will simultaneously generate and react while considering your purpose and reader. But you must first find something to say.

1 Explore what you want to say.

Most writers have experienced the frustration of being unable to think of a fresh idea—or of discovering one too late. Thinking through some of the many possible subjects for writing and exploring what you already know about those subjects can keep you from becoming "stuck." Anything can be turned into material for writing; how to do so through invention, the first stage in the writing process, is the topic of this chapter.

If you are new to college or university life, for instance, you might jot down whatever comes to mind as you think about your experience. Here are one student's notes:

big campus	online courses
dorm living	a lot of reading
freedom—on my own	major—in what?
working—how many hours?	

You could then underline some of the more promising points on such a list, ones that could easily be developed with examples. If living away from home sounds like a good topic, you could write about the need to budget your time so that daily chores do not consume too much of it. Or you could consider the pros and cons of Greek life or the problems of working while pursuing a degree. Listing ideas in the order they occur to you is an easy way to get started. Such invention strategies are helpful both in locating subjects and in exploring them before you write your essay.

Sometimes, however, a subject is readily available or is assigned. For example, you are upset by a news story about the state legislature's plans to raise tuition rates and decide to send an e-mail to the newspaper's "Letters" column. Or your employer asks for a report on building security. Or your instructor suggests five topics for an essay. Yet even when the subject is provided or limited for you, you will have to determine your own approach and decide what to say about it. In any case, careful planning is essential; successful writers seldom produce effective work without it.

In exploring what to say about a subject, try out some of the following invention strategies to determine which works best for you:

1. *Brainstorming* is one of the simplest ways to begin the writing process. You can generate ideas by talking about possible topics with a friend or group of friends. The result will be uneven, but ideas will emerge. If you don't have a friend willing to brainstorm with you, try using a digital voice recorder, talking freely about your subject for fifteen minutes. Then play the file back, noting any important ideas. To explore a point you have discovered, try another fifteen minutes on the recorder.

2. *Freewriting* is like voice recording on paper. Jot down your thoughts about your topic, writing continuously for fifteen minutes without stopping. Try to record your thoughts as fast as they occur. Ignore correctness or neatness. If you get stuck, write "I'm stuck"—or something similar—and keep going. After fifteen minutes, select anything from your notes that looks worthwhile. When you discover something promising, you can use the freewriting exercise again on this new idea. Here is an example of a student's freewriting exercise:

> Raise the minimum driving age to 18? There'd be chaos! You spend half your life waiting to get a driver's license, and then they tell you to wait two more years? Kids would start hitchhiking too— they've got jobs, and school, and their parents don't have time to take them everywhere. But there would be less accidents, I have to admit. And insurance would surely go down (?). All in all it's an interesting idea—I'm just glad that I'm already 18.

Even in this short excerpt, several possible points emerge for further exploration: fair treatment under the law, the high rate of traffic accidents involving young drivers, the dangers of hitchhiking, how insurance companies determine premiums.

Freewriting is most successful if you try to capture your mind in action without planning, structuring, or editing.

3. *Clustering* can also help you generate ideas and see the relations between them. Instead of sentences, clustering uses single terms, which are easier to jot down quickly. And instead of moving down the page, you begin clustering by writing down a possible subject in the middle of the page inside a circle (or balloon). From there you can take off in any direction with another term. Each new balloon may give rise to additional ideas, which get attached to the balloon that sparks them.

Clustering

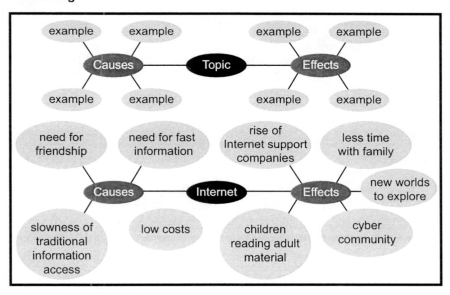

Again, work freely and quickly for fifteen minutes; then look at the clusters to see which ones look most promising. Using this technique, you could explore the causes and effects of the growth in popularity of the Internet.

4. *Asking questions* can help you recall specific experiences or attitudes. If, for example, the subject of tattoos arises, you could ask yourself these questions:

* Do I like tattoos? Why?

* Do I like only certain types of tattoos? Which ones?

* Is it a good idea to alter your skin permanently when you may change as a person as you grow older?

Such exploratory questions involve classifying, analyzing, and persuading as you determine your own feelings about the subject. Various possible ideas can emerge:

- Tattoos can be visually appealing.

- Some tattoos seem tasteful enough, but others are disgusting.

- Permanently altering your skin might seem a good idea when you are young, but twenty years from now you may well curse the day you thought of it.

Asking questions about the meaning of a word, the design of an object, or your reactions to a book or a movie can produce numerous topics for writing.

5. The *pentad* is an especially valuable form of asking questions. According to this technique, developed by Kenneth Burke, every human action is influenced by five elements: act (what), scene (where, when), agent (who), agency (how), and purpose (why). *Act* refers to anything that happens (or could happen) or anything that is the result of an activity. *Scene* is the setting or background of the action. The *agent* is the person (or force) responsible for (or influenced by) the action. *Agency* is the method that makes a thing happen, and *purpose* is the reason or motive for an action. These five elements parallel the journalist's familiar questions *who, what, where, when, how,* and *why,* but they also go further.

   You can use these five terms to analyze current, historical, or fictional events; to explore characters in novels or films; to learn more about the people involved in a narrative; or to analyze your audience in an argument. However, the pentad is not applicable to objects (computers, for example).

   Imagine, for a moment, that your college or university has announced a new policy to test incoming students for drugs. Those who test positive must undergo counseling while their admission is delayed. As a student senator, you are asked to write a column in the campus newspaper evaluating this ruling. You think through the topic in terms of the pentad:

What was done? (act)	new ruling?
	unconstitutional act?
	bold initiative?
When/where was it done? (scene)	after long consultation?
	in private?
	on campus?

Who did it? (agent)	governor?
	legislature?
	president of college?
	outsiders?
How was it done? (agency)	by open vote?
	secret agreement?
	outside pressure?
Why was it done? (purpose)	to protect young people?
	to keep out undesirables?
	to earn votes?
	to appear strong?
	to appear innovative?
	to take a stance against drug dealing?

When we compare and relate the five terms, here is what happens when we think about the act (mandatory testing) in terms of the scene (university):

- How does the campus setting influence this act?

- Is the university being "used"?

- Are students being singled out because they are unsympathetic victims?

- Do officials hope the students will protest, hence turning public opinion against the students?

This example shows some of the many questions that can be generated when each of the five terms is considered in relation to the other four.

6. *Cubing* means examining a subject from six perspectives (a cube has six sides):

   1. Describe the subject. (What is its content?)

   2. Compare it. (What is it similar to or different from?)

   3. Associate it. (What does it remind you of?)

   4. Analyze it. (Explain how it was made.)

   5. Apply it. (Explain how it can be used.)

   6. Argue for or against it. (Take a stand.)

1

Write briefly (for three to five minutes) about the subject from *each* of the six points of view, beginning with what you know. Unlike the pentad, this exercise can be used for objects (a car, building, sculpture) as well as for persons, events, and ideas.

7. Writing informally in a *journal* can provide valuable ideas for assigned essays. Or you can create your own blog. Unlike a diary or class notebook, a journal is a record of interesting impressions and experiences that you can share with others. It provides an opportunity for private writing and thinking. Some suggestions for writing in a journal:

   a. Find a quiet spot where you can write for about fifteen minutes a day, freely recalling what you have observed and read. Do not worry about correct form. You can include the people you met, the ideas you discussed, the movies or lectures you attended, the food you ate—but note your reactions, explaining why you liked or disliked what you experienced.

   b. Write about your progress in your writing and in other classes. What are you learning? What are your feelings about your work?

   c. Keep a record of a major local or national event (such as a political scandal) as it unfolds over several weeks.

Because writing is a way of learning, journal entries will help you observe and reflect on your experiences. And they will often be of use in other, more formal writing.

Considering Your Context, Reader, and Role

2

In collecting information for an essay, you initially focus on your observations, memories, and thought processes. However, your aim as a writer is not just to get facts and ideas on paper but to communicate them to a reader for a purpose. This chapter discusses the ways in which your writing is shaped by the need to communicate to others. People are involved in all aspects of the writing act: the human occasion for the writing, the real or presumed audience, and the human agent, the writer. Each of these—the occasion of the writing, the audience, and the writer—influences both the content and the form of a specific piece of writing.

2   Consider the writing context.

Every writing act responds to a specific occasion or context. A technician takes notes while reading an article to understand and retain important information. A police detective writes up the facts of an unsolved case to find a key to its solution. Writing is not spontaneous, like breathing; it is a deliberate act in response to a given situation.

What You Write

Your reason for writing greatly influences what you write, too. For instance, feeling guilty after a fight with the person you are dating, you sit down and send an apology. This situation calls for a personal expression of your feelings. But if a shirt you bought online has a flaw, the e-mail or letter you write should be factual, providing the information necessary to correct the error. And if you send a letter of application to a potential employer, your writing will be persuasive, attempting to make the reader consider you for an interview.

Why You Write

We often begin to write without first identifying what it is we want to accomplish. For example, a simple e-mail home may seem to be purely informational. But on further reflection, we may discover that this e-mail is really an attempt to explain a failing grade. Or a sarcastic letter to your college newspaper, after more careful thought, may prove to be defeating your intention of getting the editor to change her point of view.

As a writer, always be sure of your purpose. Is your aim to persuade? To inform? To scold? To disclose your feelings? To investigate? Different purposes call for different strategies, so know your aim before you begin.

How You Write

Context also helps to determine how you write; many situations have conventions that are often taken for granted. For instance, you would not mail an apology to your boyfriend or girlfriend on business stationery, using formal style, but a letter to your insurance company should be formal.

College Writing

College writing is also determined by context. The written report of a biology experiment must conform to the conventions of lab reports, and a review of a book for a history course must meet the standards of book reviews. Before beginning any kind of writing assignment in any of your classes, be sure you know the context and follow the expected conventions.

3 Consider your readers.

The greatest influence on the content and form of a piece of writing is probably your reader. For instance, children's fiction tells stories that are appropriate for young minds, using a simple, direct style. On the other hand, novels written for an adult audience often treat mature subjects, using irony, ambiguity, and symbolism. The sophistication of the audience determines the difference.

Because we usually write to communicate some idea or feeling to another person, that person becomes central to the writing act. Nearly every piece of writing is aimed at a specific audience. Whenever you write, you should be actively imagining your readers, not writing at them but creating a dialogue with them that meets their expectations and needs.

You should think of these readers as intelligent people who want to be informed and pleased. You are addressing people who want to solve a problem, make a decision, or learn something new. They do not want you to repeat what they already know. They expect original approaches to ideas, clearly organized essays that are easy to follow, and writing that is free of errors in grammar and mechanics. They are sure to think less of you if they find any lack of care in the form and content of your writing.

Nonacademic Writing

When you are writing outside the classroom, the issue of audience is important but relatively easy to address because you have a clear idea of your readers. If you are writing an e-mail message to someone you know at work, you can be friendly; you can assume that the two of you share interests and information. If the same information is included in a report for a customer outside your office, your tone becomes less relaxed, and you assume less knowledge and interest on the reader's part. If exactly the same information is written for a professional journal, there is again a change. Now you use a more formal style and include more background information, references to other articles, and significant attempts at keeping your audience's interest.

Academic Writing

When you respond to an assignment from your instructor, you might have to imagine a reader. In such cases you create a fictional, sympathetic person and write to him or her. Your instructor, of course, will have a significant interest in the information you provide.

Having a sense that your work is directed to specific readers—your instructor, your classmates, your fellow employees, imagined citizens, or club members, for example—will help you establish your purpose.

Identify Your Audience

The one constant audience for academic writing is the person who assigns it. This is an easy audience to identify. Whether you are writing a physics exam, a marketing report, or even a teacher evaluation, the product of your efforts will be aimed at your instructor.

When you are assigned writing that addresses readers in addition to your instructor, take time to identify the multiple audiences. To do this, think of yourself as the starting point of the activity and follow your writing as it leaves you and passes through other hands.

For instance, your instructor assigns you the task of writing an editorial for your school newspaper. Before you begin to write, imaginatively trace the journey of your writing after it leaves your desk. First, your boyfriend or girl-friend may volunteer to type the essay for you: Audience Number One. Then, of course, your essay will find its way into the hands of the newspaper editorial board, which will consider it for publication: Audience Number Two. If your editorial is published, the obvious audience comes into play, your fellow students: Audience Number Three. However, faculty, staff, alumni, and parents also have access to the school newspaper: Audience Numbers Four, Five, Six, and Seven. And should you be unlucky enough to libel someone, your writing may go to court: Audience Number Eight.

Identify as many of the types of readers as you can who may read the following pieces of writing:

- a letter to the regional unemployment office complaining about a local manager

- a complaint to the college dean about your sociology instructor

- a short autobiography to accompany your application to law school

- a letter to the local newspaper complaining about unsafe intersections

Define Your Audience

Have you ever written a nasty letter to a company that cheated you or an e-mail to a public personality who angered you? That sort of writing is intended to make you feel good and make your reader feel bad. But most writing tries to create a common ground between the reader and writer. Writers—in order to persuade, entertain, or teach readers—try to convince the audience that they have mutual backgrounds, interests, beliefs, aspirations, and needs. Successful writing reflects a feeling of concern for the reader and tries to gain the reader's trust; it wants to generate a dialogue. To do this, writers must not just identify their readers; they must also learn what their readers are like. In short, a good writer defines the personalities of his or her readers. For example, are your readers

young or old?
male or female?
Southern, Northern, Eastern, or Western?
well educated or not?

In addition to these traits over which your readers have no control, consider those characteristics that they have chosen. Are they

single or married?
urban or rural?
liberal or conservative?
people who work with their hands or with their minds?
religious or nonreligious?
physically fit or couch potatoes?

Most important, think about how your readers relate to your subject matter. What is their level of knowledge about your subject? Must you provide extensive background information? Must you define terms, identify aspects, and explain concepts, or will you insult your readers by explaining things that they already know?

Think about the level of knowledge that each of these audiences has about the following subjects, considering what would and would not be appropriate in an essay:

Audience	Subject
college students	Medicare
senior citizens	skateboards
hunters	National Rifle Association
college students	National Rifle Association
senior citizens	Medicare

3

In addition to what your readers know, their interest in your subject is also important. For example, if your subject is important to them, you will immediately have their attention. If not, then you will have to work harder to get them involved.

Finally, would your readers be likely to look favorably on your subject, or would they be likely to disagree with you? If they favor what you say, you can approach your topic more aggressively than you would if you knew you had a hostile audience.

Asking yourself these questions can help you create a vivid picture of your audience and can aid you in writing to "real" people in convincing prose. Try to think of readers as partners in the writing process, people who ask questions, require information, and need to be satisfied.

If you imagine your readers as people seriously interested in what you have to say and if you imagine that they see you as a competent, self-assured friend, your tone will be friendly, relaxed, and conversational. This is the case in most informal essays. If you see yourself as the expert and your readers as learners, as in a research report, your tone will be more formal (see **59**).

Your Instructor

Although you may be writing for a variety of audiences, your instructor will ultimately evaluate your assigned writing. Because your instructor must read what you write (you have a captive audience), you might unconsciously assume that you have no need to excite, interest, or persuade your instructor. But every reader wants to enjoy fresh insights and original or amusing approaches to familiar subjects. This is especially true of busy, critical readers—and of teachers who have evaluated thousands of student essays.

To avoid putting both you and your instructor to sleep, try to see your instructor simply as another human being. As you get to know this person, what idea of his or hers would you like to change? What important issue would you like to disclose to this person? What fascinating point would you like to explain? What would you like to think through, consider, or test with this person? Analyze your audience—your instructor—to discover those subjects that you might argue or investigate with her or him.

At the same time, this human being is still your instructor, an audience to whom you must demonstrate your competence in the handling of your material, the structuring of your thought, and the quality of your style.

4 Consider your role as writer.

Each of us assumes various roles in life—as someone's child, grandchild, or parent and as a member of some civic, social, or religious group. Similarly, as a writer you may assume one of many different roles. You may be an adult writing to children, or you may be a child (no matter how old) writing to your parents. You may be an expert writing to amateurs or an angry person trying to communicate that anger. The role that you assume in a piece of writing has a major influence upon what you write.

Be Aware of Your Role

Are you addressing your readers as a college student, bank employee, hip hop musician, or family member? Selecting one of the roles you play in everyday life means drawing on specific experiences and interests, and these roles affect the way you "talk" to your readers. Here, for example, is one student's list of roles:

college student	keyboard player
consumer	amateur auto mechanic
taxpayer	fraternity member
U.S. citizen	film fanatic
Catholic	computer programmer
son	swimmer
brother	soccer player

Each of these roles could suggest possible topics and readers:

Topic: Safety Tips for Beginning Divers
Readers: People interested in learning to dive

Topic: Majoring in Computer Science
Readers: Many college students

Topic: The Problem of Date Rape
Readers: Parents, all college students, general readers

Be consistent throughout a composition in the role you choose to assume. If you write as a clarinet player, stick with that role rather than—in the same essay—also trying to be a streetwise teenager. If you write as a student researcher on cognitive psychology, keep in mind that you are not an expert on your topic and that you are reporting the results of your reading. When writing an exam, remember that you are a student trying to reveal your mastery of the subject matter. Be consistent in displaying your knowledge and understanding.

Whether you write as a credit-card holder seeking an increase in your limit, as an outraged citizen, or as a well-prepared student, be aware of the identity you take on. If you are an authority, act like one. If you are committed to your subject, don't be afraid to show it. If you lack information, locate the necessary facts or data before you proceed. If you are not enthusiastic

4

about your subject, don't pretend you are; you will probably sound insincere. If you are not an expert, don't pose as one; the chances of being found out are almost certain.

Know How Your Audience Perceives You

It is important that you anticipate how your audience will respond to you and your subject. The way an audience perceives you as a writer influences how you approach your topic, what level of detail you need, and what tone you should use.

If your readers respect you as an authority, you will not have to establish your expertise as much as you would if they thought of you as a beginner. Of the following student topics, determine which ones reflect a student's experience. Ask yourself this question: How does the reader's perception of my expertise affect what I will write about each topic?

The Benefits of Joining the Business Fraternity

The Personal Gains of Ethical Behavior

Increasing Sales by Using the "Fear" Appeal

Malcolm X, Martin Luther King, Jr., and the U.S. Civil Rights Movement

Also work toward creating a sense of trust between you and your readers. Is your writing objective? Do you show some personal bias toward your subject? Is your tone reasonable and mature?

Finally, does your audience like you? If your readers don't like you, they won't feel any commitment to what you write, no matter how expert or how credible you may be as an author. Because readers are usually busy people, they respond favorably to a writer who can

- present information clearly

- structure ideas so readers can easily follow them

- avoid obnoxious or insulting language

- provide all the details an audience needs

- be generous, understanding, and modest

- hold the reader's interest by freshness of thought

Being aware of who you are in each writing act and anticipating how your audience sees and reacts to you is an important step in the writing process.

3

Drafting Your Essay

5

This chapter will help you compose the first draft of an essay. Having collected information and considered your purpose and readers, you now come to the point when you must direct and arrange this information. You might begin by looking over your prewriting material to see what interesting insights or connections you can explore. Look for points to be developed, subdivided, or deleted. Next, you can make the subject your own by turning it into a manageable topic, one that you know and have an opinion on. Before you write, you will probably ask yourself these basic questions, which are covered in the following pages:

- How can I limit my subject?

- What is my main idea?

- How will I plan the essay?

- How will I begin?

5 Limit your topic.

Before you write the first draft, examine your subject for a topic that will interest your reader and that will be possible for you to handle. Consider whether you have enough information about your topic to develop it effectively. Do you have sources available? Do you have enough time for research? Return to your prewriting strategy to narrow your subject. For example, if you had begun with a broad subject such as physical fitness, your prewriting might have helped you limit your focus to jogging. Now, with further thought, you find that this topic is also too broad. Continue to narrow your focus:

Jogging
↓
Benefits of Jogging
↓
Benefits of Jogging for Cardiovascular Improvement

Many beginning writers choose the broadest possible topic because they fear that they have too little to say. However, a more limited topic will actually be easier to develop and will provide more opportunities for specific details. For instance, if you were to write about the meaning of love or the value of moral behavior, the result would likely be a series of general statements that would be both boring and unconvincing. Choose instead your experience with caring for a terminally ill relative or the benefits of a difficult moral choice that you once made. For an essay on the latter subject, you realize that you cannot discuss everything that led up to your moral dilemma, so you select one revealing or unusual episode:

Not: Life Isn't Always Easy or
Some Choices Can Tear You Apart

But: Why I Can't Be Friends with a Shoplifter or
Vandalism Isn't Funny When the Police Arrive

There are several ways to narrow a subject. You might ask yourself these questions: What aspect of the subject do I know the most about? What aspect most interests me? What aspect would most interest a reader? Your prewriting might also help you narrow the subject. For instance, in addressing the issue of football safety, you might have subdivided this subject into specific areas, such as head injuries, improved helmets, artificial turf, and the role of coaches. Any one of these points can become a limited topic for a short essay:

Broad subject: Football Safety

Still too broad: Reasons for Football Injuries

Limited topic: The Role of Artificial Turf in Football Injuries

Broad subject: Cable Television

Still too broad: How Cable Television Differs from Broadcast Television

Limited topic: Creative Freedom and "Adult" Topics on Cable Television

Broad subject: Modern Technology and the Environment

Still too broad: Industrial Chemicals and Global Warming

Limited topic: Long-Term Possible Effects of Global Warming

To convince others that what you write is worth reading, make sure that you find the topic interesting. Picking a topic that you care about will make planning and developing the paper easier and more pleasant. It will also give the finished paper an authenticity, authority, and enthusiasm that will capture and hold your reader's interest. (If a topic is assigned to you, make sure that you are comfortable with it before you start to write.) You must understand just what is being asked of you, and you must know—or find out—enough about the subject so that you can handle it with sufficient confidence.

If you are given a general topic, begin by studying the broad assignment ("For your classmates, write an explanation of a process or a technique that you have found useful") and the specific suggestions ("Possibilities range from planting tomatoes to imaging a laptop to housebreaking a puppy").

Here are examples of topics that students chose for papers addressed to an audience of classmates:

Inappropriate: A Simple Method of Determining Chi-Square with a Pocket Calculator

Appropriate: A Foolproof Method of Balancing a Checkbook with a Pocket Calculator

Inappropriate: U.S. Policy in the Middle East

Appropriate: Reasons for U.S. Involvement in Pakistan

The first inappropriate example assumes a stronger background in statistics than most readers have. It would be appropriate for a group of students who use chi-square in interpreting research data, but not for students in the average writing class. The second inappropriate topic deals with a broad subject that most students could treat successfully only through extensive research. A thorough paper on that topic would require more time and space than the typical college essay permits.

The first appropriate topic has a broad appeal. Many of us know nothing about chi-square, but almost all of us know about unbalanced checkbooks. The second appropriate topic is more sensible in scope than the overly ambitious topic on the Middle East as a whole, and it gives the writer more opportunity to present personal judgments.

6 Clarify your purpose with a thesis statement.

Stating your main idea—your thesis—will help you define your purpose in writing: to inform, analyze, describe, or argue, among others. What, you ask yourself, will I say about my topic? What main point do I hope to make in my essay? Although your prewriting exercises will probably have focused on such questions, it is important to solidify your central idea as you begin to write.

Sometimes it is helpful to complete this open-ended sentence: "In this paper I hope to _____." (Note that such a statement would not be included in your paper.) This technique allows you to clarify your goal as well as some plan for achieving this goal. Rather than stating, "My purpose is to write an essay on animal research," define more explicitly your goal, plan, and audience: "My purpose is to persuade my classmates of the need for stronger government regulations on the use of animals in scientific research." This more clearly focused statement includes a basic writing strategy: to argue.

In organizing your material, determine your basic aim in presenting the topic: to explain how a thing works, to analyze its parts, to define what it means, to describe what it looks like, to tell what happened to it, or to argue for or against it. In an essay you will often use several of these rhetorical strategies. When you decide on your principal rhetorical aim, you can often identify a method of organization, such as listing events in chronological order or presenting the causes of a problem in the order of their importance. Often the topic itself will suggest a method of organization: an essay on how to pre-pare for a job interview would follow a step-by-step order; an essay analyzing the differences between a novel and a film would employ comparison and contrast.

Having decided what you want to do, construct a sentence that expresses the main idea you intend to present to your audience. This thesis statement should reflect a clear, definite expression of your stand on the topic. Your statement of purpose will help you formulate a tentative thesis statement: "Better government regulations are needed to reduce the suffering of animals used in laboratory research." Such a statement, subject to change, will guide you as you compose, helping you to ensure that the essay will make one main point. Also, including the thesis in the introduction of your paper will clearly identify your most important point for your audience.

A thesis statement does not announce the subject you are going to write about. (Never include a thesis statement like this one: "This paper will discuss tax increases.") Rather, it specifies the point that you will make about the topic. For example, you may want to use one of the following sentences:

Tax increases tend to favor the rich at the expense of the poor.

Or: Tax increases are not justified unless there is a clearly defined, lim-ited need for more revenues.

Or: Tax increases should not be used to fund "corporate socialism."

Each of these thesis statements serves three functions:

1. It identifies the limited subject and thus provides a test for what material should go into your essay.

2. It makes clear your attitude toward the subject.

3. It focuses the reader's attention on the specific features of the subject that you will discuss.

6

The inadequate thesis statements that follow perform only one or two of those three functions:

Inadequate:	The health professions are very promising today.
Improved:	Many new, well-paying, challenging positions are opening up in medical technology.
Inadequate:	Police officers today are different from the way they used to be.
Improved:	As increasing numbers of college-educated men and women join police forces, the stereotypical cop is a thing of the past.

The inadequate thesis statements do not provide a limited focus or indicate the writer's feelings or stance: Why are health professions promising? How are police officers different—and what does the writer think of this change? The revised statements answer such questions by revealing a more specific approach to the topics. The improved thesis statements point to the kind of material that should be presented in the paper and indicate the writer's attitude. Such thesis statements make it much easier to locate information. For instance, if you were developing the essay on jobs in medical technology, you would know that you need data on recent developments in the field, on salaries, and on jobs that call for more than routine performance; you would also know that you should ignore information with no bearing on these matters.

Despite the importance of a thesis statement, you need not feel bound to the first one you write. If you come upon contradictory information or if your attitude changes as you think about the topic, you can always revise your thesis. For example, you might decide to change your thesis statement on the new breed of police officers to something like this one:

> The change in big-city police forces today results not so much from college graduates entering police work as from policemen and policewomen taking advantage of in-service opportunities for advanced education and specialized training.

A good thesis statement, one that is complete and specific, will guide you in developing and supporting it. It will help you know what to emphasize and what to exclude. An effective thesis clarifies your aim: you know why you are writing on the topic and what it means to you. Because nearly all our writing tries to persuade the reader to accept our opinion, try to think of your topic in arguable terms, as one side in a debate. Sharpening your topic so that it has an argumentative edge will help you clarify your stance and purpose.

7 Plan your draft with a rough outline.

As you begin to write, you need to consider a plan to help you group the various points that you have developed. Your first (rough) draft allows you to think through the topic fully, concentrating on the larger issues of content and organization, not style. Sometimes you may begin writing at once, referring to your prewriting notes, and sketch out the body of the essay before returning to the introduction. More often you will start with a rough outline to give you a clear sense of direction and to make sure that your essay has a logical sequence that the reader can follow.

Most writers make rough outlines before they compose and then continue to organize as they write. They use outlines to guide the development of their ideas and do not feel restricted by them. Outlines are meant to be changed, not followed as though they represented a contract. Rough outlines, consisting of phrases arranged to show some relationship, can emerge from your prewriting material, as in this example:

Thesis: Modern cars are much more sophisticated than older ones.

1. Computerized fuel injection
2. Enhanced safety features: air bags, antilock brakes, GPS systems
3. Expert mechanical attention a must

Conclusion: A 2014 automobile is a huge improvement over a 1994 version, but the day of the shade-tree mechanic seems to be over.

Such an outline suggests the overall plan of the typical essay with its beginning, middle, and end:

Introductory paragraph

Body paragraphs
1. First point
2. Second point
3. Third point, etc.

Concluding paragraph

With your thesis in mind, write out three or four major points in the order that seems most logical. As you write, you can place the supporting information (facts, examples, details) under the headings in your list. Again, these

7

headings are flexible: if you discover considerable new material, you might need to adjust your outline or simply compose freely, with the rough outline as your initial guide.

Here is a sample thesis statement with two rough outlines—one unsuccessful, one more effective.

Thesis: AIDS is a disease that is both deadly and cunning.

Ineffective outline:
1. AIDS must be taken seriously
2. AIDS is a ghastly disease
3. How do you get AIDS
4. Many people ashamed to go to a doctor
5. Having blood drawn can be painful

Effective outline:
1. AIDS is very dangerous and can be fatal
2. Many people confused about how it is contracted
3. Many people would rather be in the dark than undergo testing
4. Blood tests not always accurate
5. Possible ten-year gap between infection and symptoms

The second rough outline is superior because each point develops from, and clearly relates to, the thesis statement, whereas the first outline contains generalities and less relevant points (2, 4, 5).

A more formal topic outline can provide a complete point-by-point layout of your entire essay. To develop a good topic outline, start by using the points on your rough outline as the major divisions (labeling them with Roman numerals I, II, III, etc.). Then develop subdivisions (labeling them A, B, C, etc.) for each major point. Although two levels may be enough for a short paper, a third level (labeled 1, 2, 3, etc.) will help you organize details in longer projects. Sometimes even a fourth level is useful (labeled a, b, c, etc.).

Topic outline

Thesis: Businesses should not use credit reports to screen job applicants.

I. Why businesses use credit reports
   A. To determine the stability of job applicants
   B. To determine the honesty of job applicants
II. What kind of businesses use credit reports

III. What the credit report assesses
   A. How much credit one has or has had in the past
   B. One's record of repaying debt
   C. One's "credit score"
IV. Why businesses should not use credit reports
   A. Potentially good employees turned away
   B. Applicants not able to contest results
   C. Lack of consistency—different credit-reporting companies produce different results
   D. Unethical uses of confidential information
   E. Questionable invasion of privacy

A sentence outline can do even more, if you wish to devote the time to creating one. It can provide topic sentences to organize your explanations for all of your points. Detailed topic or sentence outlines are excellent guides to organization and can be especially helpful in preparing a long paper. See Chapter 10 for an example.

8 Your introductory paragraph should focus the reader's interest on your thesis.

A good introduction serves two important functions: it attracts the reader's interest and focuses that interest on the thesis. Therefore, to write a good introduction, you need to know what your thesis is and why your reader might care about what you have to say. If you can be sure that your reader is already interested in your topic and if your essay is short, then you might not need an introduction. You could start with the thesis statement and move to the first point:

> Anyone who has ever received an e-mail promising an electronic transfer of wealth should be aware of three issues. The first and most obvious of these. . . .

To treat the same subject in a longer paper, involving more than just a few paragraphs, you might need to mention all three issues in the introduction so that the reader would know what to expect. Then the next paragraph could begin discussing the first issue.

If your reader needs background information in order to understand why your topic is significant, provide that information in your introductory paragraph. For example, if you were going to report on new techniques for catching shoplifters at the store where you work, you could first discuss what shoplifting costs the average consumer and then lead your reader to the specific case of your store and finally to your thesis statement.

8

The pattern just discussed for the introductory paragraph on shoplifting is the most reliable way of introducing college papers:

General statement(s) related to topic and to reader's interests

↓

Any necessary background material

↓

Thesis statement

Sometimes you will start with your thesis and include an outline of your main points in the introductory paragraph:

> *Chinatown* is Roman Polanski's greatest movie. Released in 1974, this classic has multiple areas of appeal. One is the theme, a study of Noah Cross's addiction to power and the horrifying acts that he is drawn to. His foil is J. J. Gittes, an honest private investigator who is as much driven by his need to understand Noah Cross as he is to see justice done. The movie is very much in the *film noir* style, except at its most basic requirement: Polanski uses "natural" color to play off the darkness of Cross's deeds. Finally, the three principal actors, John Huston (as Cross), Jack Nicholson (as Gittes), and Faye Dunaway (as Cross's estranged daughter), give top-level performances.

The body paragraphs would analyze these issues in detail.

One effective way to capture the reader's interest is to open with an interesting example, experience, or anecdote. Sometimes a quotation or proverb is effective:

> "It is better to be silent and thought a fool than to open your mouth and remove all doubt." I remember this old saying whenever I choose to listen in class rather than speak. . . .

Instead of stating his thesis—that football is unnecessarily brutal—this student begins with his own experience:

> I spent the Christmas of my senior year in the hospital with my neck in a brace, wondering if the cut nerves in my right arm would leave me permanently crippled. In the next room, a classmate was recovering from spinal surgery to correct a massive herniation that made him, a strong young man of 21, immobile. He took a year to recover; I spent three months in traction. We still undergo therapy and face further hospitalization. Although we both survived, we paid a terrible price for playing football.

Sometimes you will find that the revision stage of the writing process provides the best opportunity to produce a good introduction. After you have completed a first draft and have clarified your ideas, you can then return to the opening and rework it. Consider these introductory paragraphs:

First draft: Elvis Presley, who died in 1977, lives in the minds of many of his fans and in the pages of tabloids, which proclaim his reincarnation. Books, too, recount psychic experiences involving the dead singer and stories of his reincarnation. Visitors pour into his home and buy memorabilia, making his estate much more valuable than it was when he was alive. To thousands of loyal worshippers, the King is not dead. He and the Elvis phenomenon have become larger than life.

Revised draft: Each year on August 16, the anniversary of Elvis Presley's death, the faithful converge on Memphis to hold a candlelight vigil at the "shrine" of the King. Many of them look forward to his return or recount psychic experiences in which Elvis appears to them. Books and tabloids proclaim "The King lives," thus adding fuel to the reports of his reincarnation. Millions of dollars are spent on statues, records, pictures, and other memorabilia because of a belief that if Elvis is not alive, he is a saint. Elvis worshippers have formed a religious cult unlike anything associated with other dead celebrities.

In revising, the writer has developed an introduction with specific examples that clarify the suggestion of a religious cult.

9 Your concluding paragraph should reemphasize your main points.

The conclusion should restate your thesis in different words and reemphasize its importance. Merely repeating your ideas is unnecessary and tedious, but a concluding paragraph can effectively summarize the main points of a long essay. Here is the conclusion of an essay on the importance of lifelong exercise:

Although older people often have reduced physical abilities and must be wary of broken bones, exercise programs can be tailored to meet the needs of every age group. Just as very young children can be taught to swim or jog for exercise and pleasure, the elderly can continue a tradition of fitness and good health by exercising in a safe and appropriate manner. Physical fitness is never "age-specific."

9

Sometimes you can recommend a course of action or solution to problems presented in the paper, as in this ending of an essay on low voter turnouts in U.S. elections:

> After all that our ancestors went through to secure political freedom and establish a democratic republic, it is shameful that so few Americans bother to vote. By adopting the Australian model and requiring adults to vote in national elections, we will inevitably have a better-informed populace, one more like the vision of our nation's founders. There will be problems at first, as I have illustrated, but the eventual result will be a vast improvement on our current state of voter apathy.

Whether you cover all of your main points or just your thesis, follow these guidelines in writing concluding paragraphs:

1. Do not introduce new topics; everything you present should emphasize points that you have already made.

2. Do not repeat the same words and examples you used earlier.

3. Make your writing forceful; do not overestimate the importance of what you have said, but do not hesitate or apologize, either.

Although it should be concise, a conclusion cannot be so vague and general that the reader feels let down, as in this ending of a literary analysis that compares two short stories:

> **First draft:** These two stories, despite their many differences, have much in common. They show how two writers, using different subjects and styles, can say similar things.

To satisfy the reader with an appropriate conclusion, the writer should restate the reason for comparing the stories and then sum up what the analysis has revealed:

> **Revised draft:** These two stories, though different in subject and tone, force us to think about what a successful life is. By presenting their readers with failures, both authors imply that success does not come from possessing material goods but from living according to the enduring values of love, self-sacrifice, and honesty.

Revising

10

Revision means to "look again," to rethink and clarify what you have written. You step back from your work to examine it from a new perspective. Revision does not mean simply recopying or correcting errors but recognizing that your draft is unfinished, that words and ideas can be added, deleted, or rearranged. A good writer is never satisfied with a first draft and never forgets that writing involves rewriting. Rarely would you want to hand in an essay without making changes in its content as well as in its structure and style. If you assume that nearly every piece of writing can be improved, you will not hesitate to drop entire paragraphs, to condense, shift, and rearrange. As you revise, you are examining your initial ideas, purpose, and audience to get a more objective perspective on your work; after you revise, you then edit, making changes and corrections to the altered text.

Revision occurs throughout the writing process. After you complete a sentence, for example, you read and react to it, considering whether to expand it or delete from it. But most rewriting occurs after you have written a first draft. You read that draft with your own intentions in mind, and you also read with your reader in mind. To satisfy the reader's needs, you consider what you have produced and what might be missing. Reading your own work objectively and considering the comments of other readers will help you discover if your meaning is clear and if your structure and style express your meaning effectively.

When you read your first draft, you may need to change your thesis, purpose, and writing strategy as you compare what you have written with your original intention. When you proceed from large overall concerns to specific sentence and word changes, your focus will shift from yourself to the reader. First, read what the draft says, then read from the reader's viewpoint, and finally read with an eye for problems to be solved. Here are some basic tips for revising:

1. If you write your draft by hand, leave plenty of space for changes. If you compose on the computer, remember that inserting, deleting, pasting, cutting, and so on make revising fast and easy.

2. When you revise, try to work from a typed or printed, not handwritten, draft so that you can approach your work more objectively.

3. Revise in stages, setting the draft aside for a "cooling off" period. When you return to it, you can then view it more critically.

4. Read each draft aloud. If a sentence sounds awkward, reword it until it sounds right. Listen also for omissions and repetitions.

5. Let someone else read your drafts, and ask this person to react honestly to your ideas and style. Collaborative work is especially useful as you revise. The comments of your fellow students and instructor can help you develop a more objective view of your work.

6. Be willing to discard anything that does not relate to your purpose and thesis. But revising does not involve changing everything; your prewriting will have produced some valuable material.

In making your work clearer for your reader, you make it clearer for yourself. This point has been made by Donald M. Murray, who suggests a three-stage "clarification" process. With each reading, he says, the writer should focus on a different aspect of the writing:

1. meaning

2. structure

3. style

10 Revise for overall meaning.

Consider the major areas of your essay before worrying about the minor ones. First, read your draft quickly for content and ideas. Try to be objective, ignoring word choice and other details as you ask yourself these questions about the content:

1. What is my main point?

2. Does everything in the draft relate to this point?

3. Do I have enough solid evidence to develop my point?

4. What else does the reader need to know?

5. Is the draft too short or too long?

6. Are there parts I could cut?

7. Does the draft follow through on what the title and introduction promise?

To make sure that your essay has unity, compare your thesis and introduction with the body of the paper. If they do not match, rewrite the introduction or revise paragraphs that stray from the main point. Use arrows to indicate any paragraphs that need to be altered.

11 Revise for structure.

Read the draft quickly a second time, this time with your method of organization in mind. Again, avoid questions of style and try to be as objective as you can. Focus on whether each part of the essay is developed well and is in the right order by asking yourself these questions:

1. Is my title effective?

2. Will my introduction capture the reader's interest? (see **8**)

3. Do I have a clear thesis statement? (see **6**)

4. Is every paragraph related to my thesis?

5. Does each paragraph make one point? Is each paragraph fully developed? (see **16, 19**)

6. Am I using facts and examples, not just general statements, to support my thesis? (see **19**)

7. Have I defined my major terms?

8. Am I bringing myself into the paper too much, distracting the reader from the subject?

9. Does the conclusion sum up the main points and return to the thesis? (see **9**)

At this stage in the revision, look for any irrelevant information that can be cut. Then examine your paragraphs. If they are skimpy, consider what examples or facts you can add from your prewriting. Remember that making changes is easier than starting from scratch.

To make sure that your essay is effectively organized, make a rough outline of your draft or, if you prefer, briefly summarize each paragraph. This will allow you to stand back from your work and see if your points flow naturally and proceed logically and if each point is properly developed.

Read the first draft of the paragraph that follows, then the revised version. Notice how the writer has eliminated one irrelevant sentence and kept himself out of the piece while reducing wordiness and clarifying vague, impersonal subjects.

First Draft   Although you can find many differences between rugby and football, I believe that the major difference is that rugby is unlike professional football because you get involved with it for the love of the sport. Participating in the game means that outside jobs are necessary to support the players and their hobby. And expenses on the road must be paid by the players. This is not so much the case in England, where the

12

game was first played and where it is much more popular than American football. In this country, the problem with attracting large crowds to support rugby is no doubt due to the fact that it is an amateur sport that is less well promoted and so less popular than football.

Revised Draft   The major difference between rugby and football is that rugby players play the sport not for pay but for love. To participate in the sport, players must have outside jobs to support themselves, and they must pay their expenses on the road. Rugby in this country does not attract large crowds because it is an amateur sport that is not as well promoted as football or as popular.

12 Revise for style.

After a short break, read the draft a third time for style. Now that the content is well established and the structure is firm, slowly read your essay out loud, line by line. Examine your sentence patterns and word choice. Ask yourself these questions:

1. Are my sentences all starting the same way? If so, could I use subordination and variety (combining)? (see **20**)

2. If any of my sentences contain series or lists, are the items grammatically parallel? (see **28a**)

3. Are there any unnecessary repetitions, wordy phrases, clichés, or jargon? (see **24, 67, 69**)

4. Are there any words whose meanings I am unsure of? Is my word choice appropriate for my audience and purpose? (see **59, 63**)

5. Have I avoided unnecessary passive verbs? (see **23e**)

6. Are my tenses consistent? (see **58a**)

7. Have I deleted all unnecessary words and phrases? (see **70**)

8. Do I lead the reader smoothly from one point to another and from start to finish?

12a Check the point of view.

As you polish your essay, make sure that you have selected the proper person and that you have not shifted person: first person (*I, we*), second person (*you*), third person (*he, she, it, one,* or *they*). Most academic and professional writing uses third person because it emphasizes the subject, not the writer.

12

Weak:	I found as I read the novel that the plot was implausible.
Revised:	The novel's plot was implausible.

In this example, the use of *I* distracts the reader from the subject. However, some beginning writers mistakenly think that *I* is never suitable in college writing and go out of their way to avoid it:

Weak:	It is this writer's contention that watching most movies on DVD is nothing like seeing them at a theater.
Improved:	Watching most DVDs is nothing like seeing the movies at a theater.

Or, if your audience is such that you can use a more informal tone,

For me, watching a DVD is a pale imitation of going to the theater to see a "real" movie.

The *I* point of view is appropriate if you are writing from your own experience. In this example the writer is the subject:

Most writers I have known are like me: they agonize over their stories. Writing and worrying, it seems, are inseparable. Even after twenty years of writing and publishing fiction, I find that old fears about who will read my work, and what these imagined readers will say, get in the way of what should be a smooth, flowing process. Some days, it is easier for me to talk or do almost anything else than write.

The *you* point of view, which emphasizes the reader, is used in instructional materials—such as this book, which talks directly to the student. The indefinite *you* (referring to anyone in general) is inappropriate:

Inappropriate:	Being sent to prison makes you stop and take account of your life. (see **52b**)

12b Rely on topic sentences.

When revising for style, examine the topic sentence of each of your paragraphs to see if that sentence clearly defines the doer (subject) and the action (verb). By asking *who, what, where, when, how,* and *why,* you can give each paragraph a more specific focus and place the emphasis where it is needed.

Weak:	There are numerous differences between the administration of President George W. Bush and that of his successor, Barack Obama.
Revised:	The administration of President George W. Bush and that of his successor, Barack Obama, have differed significantly in their use of diplomacy in foreign affairs.

The first topic sentence in the preceding example is weak because it fails to address how the two administrations differed. The following paragraph is poorly developed because the writer did not ask any of the basic questions about the doer, the action, and the purpose:

> Beginning life on a college campus is exciting yet difficult and frustrating in many ways. For the first time there are new ideas, responsibilities, and attitudes that are challenged. Yet with these challenges come many problems for the new freshman.

The first sentence has no doer: Who is beginning life? The writer uses *there are* (in the second sentence) rather than a human subject, such as "the freshman for the first time encounters new. . . ." The use of *many ways* and *many problems* gives the reader no mental picture. To revise this vague paragraph, the writer examines each sentence to see how it can become more specific and then draws on her experience to generate examples. Here is a later version of that paragraph with final revisions included:

A freshman's ~~One's~~ introduction to college life is less often exciting ~~as well as~~ than difficult and ~~very~~ frustrating. I spent most of my first day at the Ʉniversity standing in lines, ~~I waited~~ first at registration, ~~and~~ then at the bookstore. When I returned exhausted to the dorm after getting none of the classes I had wanted, ~~and~~ I went to the cafeteria, hoping to ~~see~~ find my roommate, but ended up eating alone. That night I was ~~really~~ ready to ~~call it quits and~~ go home. But now, after two weeks here, I have learned to cope with dorm problems and to enjoy the independence. Having made new friends, ~~in my classes and at several parties,~~ I find college challenging and fun. My experience shows that if ~~one~~ freshmen can handle the hassles of the first week, they can manage to enjoy [life in] college.

13

Revising should also help you develop your own style. Your aim is to express your convictions clearly and honestly, not to try to impress readers with a formal, stilted style of borrowed phrases and unfamiliar words. Pay close attention to sentence structure (see Chapter 6) and word choice (see **63**), simplify wordy phrases (see **70**), reduce the passive voice (see **23e**), and reword for emphasis (see **23**). Note the following troublesome sentences and their revisions:

Not: There is no reason single mothers should not be allowed to stay in high school. *(confusing double negative)*

But: Single mothers should be allowed to finish their high school education.

Not: The house was purchased for $115,900, but Carlos sold it for $250,900. *(shifts from passive to active)*

But: Carlos purchased the house for $115,900 but sold it for $250,900.

Rather than worry about having an inadequate number of words, imagine that you will be rewarded for the words you can delete. Consider the advice of Strunk and White in *The Elements of Style:* "A sentence should contain no unnecessary words, a paragraph no unnecessary sentences, for the same reason that a drawing should have no unnecessary lines and a machine no unnecessary parts."

Notice how each of these sentences can be more concise:

Weak: The reason why I was late was due to the fact that I overslept.

Improved: I was late because I overslept.

Weak: What that machine does is enable the blind to read without Braille.

Improved: The machine enables the blind to read without Braille.

13 Use collaboration in revising.

Writing need not be an entirely solitary activity. By having others respond to your work, you can receive valuable help, and you can see that your instructor is not your only reader. Moreover, by reading another student's paper, you can also become a better reader of your own writing.

Friends and family members can react to your work as outsiders. Fellow students or tutors in a campus writing center, who know the assignment and the standards for evaluating it, can approach your work more objectively; they are insiders who know the problems involved with incomplete drafts. As partners, for example, they can help you reexamine your ideas.

Here are some suggestions for collaborative revising:

14

1. Make helpful, positive suggestions and comments. Your aim is not to "play teacher." Recognize also that the criticism you receive is directed at your work, not at you. Respect others' responses, but know that you must decide what to accept and what to reject.

2. Be prepared with a legible draft and with specific questions about your work.

3. Do not focus on errors, style, or word changes.

4. If your instructor divides the class into groups, you can focus on three or four specific aspects of your partners' work. For example, you can determine if there is a clear purpose and thesis, adequate development, and an introduction that captures the reader's attention and indicates how the paper will be structured.

5. Outside of class, you could exchange a draft with another student and agree to examine each other's work before it is due. Don't try to focus on everything; examine the introductory paragraph, the first sentence of each subsequent paragraph, and the conclusion to determine if the structure is clear and logical. Or work with your partner to develop some of your own criteria for evaluating each other's writing. Try writing a short summary of the student's thesis and purpose; then write a short comment, indicating your assessment of the paper's strengths and weaknesses.

14 Revising on a computer.

Most writers are more objective and critical when reacting to computer-printed drafts than to handwritten ones. Writing undergoes an important transformation when you move from reading your own penmanship to seeing your words in type, and you become aware of problems not apparent before. Also, revising from a printed copy can help you spot smaller stylistic problems as well as larger problems of organization and development.

If you compose your first drafts on a computer, you are ahead of the game. Computers allow you to make multiple changes: with the text on the computer screen, it is easy to add, delete, or rearrange elements. However, many writers prefer to edit on hard copy (paper), which they mark up before entering the changes into the computer file. Similarly, proofreading can be done more effectively on hard copy before you print the final text. Remember that you should not rely exclusively on a spelling-check function, which cannot help you distinguish between easily confused words (*their* and *there*, for example). Writers must be responsible for editing their own errors and

15

correcting their own spelling. Grammar-checking software is also available, but remember that *you* will receive the grade on your essay—the software is merely a tool. Whether you revise by working onscreen or by marking up your printout, be sure to save and print copies of each stage of your essay. You may want to return to earlier drafts as you progress through the assignment.

15 Edit for errors.

The final stage in revising is editing the final draft for correctness. If your work is to make a good impression, you will need to give your completed essay a thorough word-by-word examination for errors and omissions. No matter how interesting the topic, and no matter how imaginative your development, if the essay contains errors, the reader is sure to think less of your work.

The proofreading stage is the time not for major changes but for checking keyboarding errors or slips of the pen. Put the draft aside for a while; then read it carefully, looking at individual words, not at whole statements. To locate misspellings, read backwards, starting with the last word. Check for repeated words as well as for spelling, punctuation, and grammatical errors. Check a dictionary for the meanings of any words you are unsure of. To change a wrong or misspelled word, draw a line through it and write the correction directly above. If you have omitted a word, place a caret (^) below the line at the place where the omission occurs. Then write the word directly above the caret. The following passage includes most of the frequently used proofreading marks:

Most of us have difficulty	
proof reading our own work properly	close up
because of the way we read it: for	
content. Our eyes normally move	transpose
across a line of print in a series	transpose
of "jumps" that Allow us to focus	lowercase
^ one point of information, then	insert
another. in proofreading, we must	caps
interrupt this normal reading-for-	insert space
information method and read words	insert
as words, concentrating on form	
(spelling, grammar, etc.), on not	transpose
meaning.	

15

After you have proofread your essay, carefully make your final corrections in your text file. A good way to ensure that you haven't missed anything is to make a small check mark beside each correction on the hard copy. When you have finished, run your spell-checker function one last time, or output your finished work so that you can compare it to your marked-up draft.

As you read these drafts of a student's paragraph, notice where changes were made and the overall effect of the revision:

First Draft   There are many reasons why Star Trek was a huge success world wide, the main reason being that it offered a hopeful view of the future. Life in what we call present reality is filled with violence and conflicts of all types, but Star Trek and The Next Generation give an optimistic view of life in the future. It is a time when negotiation and compromise are seen as possible in solving social issues. It was the creator, Gene Roddenberry's vision that the future will not be overwhelming or complex but human. His belief was in a logical, rational approach to life, and this is the other major reason for the success of these shows, which have moved millions of people, who might otherwise not identify with science fiction plots or futuristic stories. The idea that the human mind has the power to solve life's eternal questions is a major reason why this adventure series has become a popular classic and will remain so.

Second Draft   Of the many reasons Star Trek has been a huge, worldwide success, perhaps the main reason is that it offered a hopeful view of the future. In contrast to the very violent, conflict-ridden world of present reality, Star Trek and Star Trek: The Next Generation picture life in the future optimistically. This is due to creator Gene Roddenberry's vision that future centuries will not be overwhelmingly complex but human. His belief in a rational approach to life is what has moved millions of viewers. The idea that the mind has the power to solve life's eternal questions is a major reason why this adventure series has become, and will remain, a popular classic.

Final Draft   Star Trek has been a huge, worldwide success mainly because it offers a hopeful vision of the future. In contrast to the present, with its cynicism, violence, and racial conflicts, Star Trek and Star Trek: The Next Generation picture the future optimistically. This hopeful view is due to creator Gene Roddenberry's belief that life in the twenty-third century need not be overwhelmingly technical and complex. Rather, his future is one in which

15

negotiation and compromise can solve national rivalries and racial bigotry. Millions of viewers have been moved by the emphasis in this adventure series on the mind's power to solve life's eternal questions. Because of this positive philosophy, Star Trek has become, and will remain, a popular classic.

Paragraphs and Sentences

5

Writing Paragraphs

16

Writers use paragraphs to build sentences into blocks of thought that can then join other paragraphs to develop the main idea of an essay or other piece of writing. A paragraph can introduce a thesis (the main idea of an essay), develop one of the points supporting the thesis, conclude the discussion, or supply a transition between parts of a fairly long paper. The paragraphs that support the thesis often correspond to the points in a rough outline—for example, you might begin an essay on ways of controlling pollution with a paragraph outlining three main solutions to the problem. Then, in three longer paragraphs, you would discuss each of these solutions in turn.

Paragraphs come in various sizes. The length of a paragraph depends on the difficulty of the subject, the size of related paragraphs, and the background of the intended audience. An essay consisting of very brief paragraphs (fewer than three sentences each) will suggest inadequate thought. If your paragraphs are frequently less than one hundred words in length, you are probably not giving them the development they deserve. More important than paragraph length, however, is making sure that each paragraph develops essentially one point.

A good paragraph presents enough facts and examples to satisfy the reader that its topic has been properly developed, and it does so in sentences that fit together, or cohere, to form a single unit. The following sections examine the main qualities of effective paragraphs.

ts 16 Use a topic sentence to focus each paragraph on one point.

The topic sentence of a paragraph states the central idea that the rest of the paragraph clarifies, exemplifies, or otherwise supports. It promises what is to come. Therefore, a good topic sentence is useful both to you, the writer, and to your reader. You can use it to guide the development of the rest of the paragraph; your reader uses it as a clue to what lies ahead. Although a topic sentence is often the first sentence in a paragraph, it sometimes follows a transitional opening sentence. It may even appear at the end of a paragraph, leading the reader to a climactic conclusion. Experienced writers often do not give every paragraph a topic sentence, but beginning writers are usually well advised to use topic sentences consistently and to make them easily recognizable.

A good topic sentence identifies the subject of the paragraph and the specific issue to be developed. When the focus is blurred, the topic sentence offers no direction to the reader, who may suspect that the writer was not sure where the paragraph was heading. In the following examples, note how the sharpened topic sentences point to the supporting sentences:

Not focused: A business plan does more than just indicate the initial direction of a new company.

Sharpened: *A business plan not only specifies goals and procedures of the new company but also outlines how the lender will be repaid.*

16

A more specific topic sentence will help you find examples and details to develop the paragraph.

Not focused: The 1957 Thunderbird is a classic automobile.

Sharpened: *The appearance of the 1957 Thunderbird is both striking and simple.* The body is devoid of heavy amounts of chrome that tend to be ostentatious. The style, with its low-slung design and smooth curves, is very sleek and aerodynamic. The tail fins, which begin at the door handle and continue straight back to just over the taillights, are tasteful and not as outlandish as the fins of the 1960 Cadillac, for example. Even though many people refer to the Thunderbird as a sports car, its rear wheel skirts still retain the aura of a luxury automobile. The side porthole hardtop and the low-profile hood scoop are stylish additions to a classic car.

—*Scott Wilson (student)*

Not focused: Video games are useful for young people.

Sharpened: *Video games give many young people their first experience with computer technology.* In fact, despite the ongoing controversy over questionable content and the amount of time some children expend, these games play a large part in educating youths about our information-driven society. Students lacking formal instruction in computers usually find that a video game is the first computer they learn to control. And the skills involved in playing the game can help prepare them for more-complex computer systems. Most middle-class children have computers or game systems at home, but less fortunate youngsters may have to learn about this technology in video game arcades, which have been criticized by parents as a waste of time and money. However, adults who object to video games should realize the educational value that they can provide.

Not focused: Early-morning classes are not always wise.

Sharpened: *Most young people don't function well enough in the early morning to benefit from 8 A.M. classes.* As my psychology professor told us, recent studies of sleep disorders show that teenagers naturally function poorly in the early morning. A hormone that regulates the body's cycles of sleep and waking has more impact on morning sleepiness than staying up late. As a result, many students are deprived of the amount of sleep they need and can't be expected to get up early and perform well before 10 o'clock. So it seems better to blame biology, not late-night hours, for students' morning yawns.

—Alison Smith (student)

In a first draft, begin every paragraph with a topic sentence. Doing so will help you make sure that the paragraph accomplishes its purpose. When you revise your early draft, you may want to move the topic sentence to another position or get rid of it entirely. Occasionally, you may choose to place the topic sentence at the end of the paragraph to give it special emphasis.

ᵘ 17 Make all other sentences in the paragraph relate to the topic sentence.

If a paragraph is to succeed, it must be unified (see also **18**). In a unified paragraph, each sentence contributes to the central idea. Every detail supports the topic sentence to produce a single, unfolding idea.

Examine your paragraphs to make certain that each sentence follows from and develops the topic sentence. Details not directly relevant to the central point do not belong in the paragraph. For instance, if your topic sentence is "I support our university's policy of recruiting student athletes because it benefits the students academically and the school economically," your supporting sentences should deal with the advantages to student athletes and to the university recruitment budget. Sentences about the problems raised by the policy of building winning teams would violate the unity of the paragraph. To write about such problems, you would need a new paragraph.

The first step in achieving paragraph unity is to construct a clear, specific topic sentence. The next step is to develop, throughout the rest of the paragraph, the idea that the topic sentence expresses. When you revise your rough draft, eliminate all irrelevant points, no matter how interesting or well stated they may be. The two underlined sentences in the following paragraph violate unity:

Psychoanalysis, as developed by Sigmund Freud at the end of the nineteenth century, was originally a therapy, but it eventually evolved into a theoretical system. <u>As a therapy, psychoanalysis experienced its greatest popularity in this country during the 1950s and 1960s.</u> According to Freudian theorists, along with or underneath the conscious mind, we have an unconscious mind, a type of mental energy we are unaware of. Therefore, nothing that happens, consciously or unconsciously, is without some cause. Another basic part of psychoanalytic theory is that, in everyday life, we often use defense mechanisms to hide from unpleasant truths about ourselves. <u>In his celebrated break with Freud, C. G. Jung rejected the idea that major problems can be traced to sexual disturbances.</u>

Note that the last sentence in the preceding paragraph could well be the topic sentence of a new paragraph.

coh 18 Provide coherence within and between paragraphs.

For an essay to be effective, it must be coherent: its parts must fit together. The content of your paragraphs should lead the reader from the beginning of your essay to the end in a logical order. When you move from one paragraph to a new one, include signals that show the relationship between the two. These signals are transitional devices to indicate, for example, that you are moving from an introductory paragraph that states a problem to supporting paragraphs that explain causes and effects, offer solutions, or provide examples.

In a paragraph, coherence is the natural flow from one sentence to the next. The sentences interlock so that the first idea leads to the second, the second to the third, and so on. You can't write a succession of isolated sentences and expect your reader to supply the words and phrases that tie them together. You must make the reader feel that by the end of the paragraph you have made your point clearly and smoothly.

18a Achieve coherence by following a clear order.

The first step in achieving coherence is to follow a clear, logical order. That is, point *A* might precede point *B* because *A* happened before *B*, because *A* led to *B* or caused *B*, or because *B* illustrates *A*. Or your purpose might determine the order: you might put *A* first to give it special prominence; you might lead up all the way to point *G*, leaving it until last for emphasis. Always try to find a pattern that will seem sensible to your reader.

The main patterns involve the order of time, space, and climax as well as the general-to-specific and specific-to-general order. In all cases, the structure determines the coherence.

18

Time order Paragraphs that relate either a series of incidents or steps in a process often follow chronological order. The first example is a narrative; the second is a factual explanation of a process:

First: The most terrifying day in my life came in July of 1946. I was washing lunchtime dishes in our farmhouse in middle Georgia when my husband unexpectedly appeared at the door. "Appeared" is the best word that I can think to use,

Second: because he was not walking but crawling, dragging his left leg. I got out of him as quickly as possible that he had been bitten by a copperhead of some three feet, a snake large enough for its venom to be fatal. We lived thirty miles from the nearest hospital, I did not have a driver's license (and, in

Third: fact, had never driven a car), but my husband was dying before my eyes. I pushed/pulled him into the back seat of our Chevrolet and pointed the car toward Atlanta.

Every angler knows that fishing can be a bewildering sport. Days that look perfect frequently turn into casting exercises, and awful, dreary days sometimes produce huge yields. So what is the "ideal" time to catch fish? Roughly, two elements should be involved. **First**, a reasonable amount of food supply should be present—normally insects or minnows—so that fish are in the "habit" of eating. Weather is the **second** question mark. Fish are moved to eat not only by hunger but also by the effects of lowering barometric pressure in the atmosphere (a process that affects the sensory organ called the "lateral line," which runs along the body of most fish). Thus, when a storm is approaching, fish are sometimes moved to violent feeding activity, a phenomenon that produces the strange—and sometimes dangerous—sight of an angler hauling in fish after fish while a storm rages overhead.

Spatial order An arrangement in space (from top to bottom, left to right, and so on) is often possible in descriptive paragraphs, such as in the following excerpt:

Melanie's first impression of the apartment was not favorable. How, she wondered, could she coexist for a year with the riot of colors that she had inherited? The door she had entered was painted bright red on one side, black on the other. Her eye was at once attracted to the open window, straight ahead of her as she came into the cramped space— an inviting sight except that it was painted shocking pink and outlined with old red-and-green Christmas lights. Next to the window was a bright-green desk with a tall yellow-and-blue lamp, the only other source of light. The desk chair had been upholstered in faded leopard skin, and there was a small, tiger-striped rug on the dark wooden floor. A green bookshelf, mostly empty except for a few old paperbacks, stood to the right of the desk. On the bare wall above the bookshelf was a welcome splash of color: a poster of Van Gogh's sunflowers. Looking eagerly for her bed, Melanie spied on her left a narrow cot covered in purple and decorated with red pillows. On one of the pillows she was glad to see her new roommate's plump, long-haired white cat.

Climactic order Some topics will suggest an order of increasing importance. In this example, the sentences lead up to the highest point of interest:

> In the center of the grove an oak stood, tall and stately but bulging in the middle. On this venerable bulge a pair of ravens had taken up residence for so many years that the tree was known as the "raven tree." Children often tried without success to get at the nest, the difficulty of the task whetting their appetites. But when they climbed up to the swelling, it jutted out so far beyond their grasp that they found the undertaking too hazardous. And so the birds lived on, building nest after nest in perfect security until a February day when the grove was to be cleared. Men came with their saws, the woods echoed the clamor, but the mother raven remained on her nest, even when the tree began to tilt. At last, when it gave way, the bird was flung from her nest, whipped to the ground by twigs. She deserved a better fate.
>
> —*adapted from Gilbert White*

General-specific Paragraphs often begin with a general statement or topic sentence (see **16**), followed by supporting details and examples. However, many writers start with specifics and end with a general comment that summarizes the point of the paragraph, as in this example:

> Jared is just beginning the tenth grade, but already "the big test" is something for him to worry about. He watches his older sister, Margot, preparing feverishly for the SAT exam. She reviews math and vocabulary questions twice a week in the hope of landing a college scholarship or even admission to a selective university. These high school students are among millions each year who spend considerable time, energy, and money preparing for a rite of passage called the Scholastic Aptitude Test, developed by a New Jersey company, the Educational Testing Service. This company established a system that, for the past eighty years, has been able to determine the success or failure of many young people in America.

18

In contrast, the following paragraph offers a good example of the general-to-specific pattern:

> A new style of movies called *film noir* because of their dark settings and grim characters came out of Hollywood, capturing a prevailing feeling of the times. In these black-and-white films from the middle of the last century, the use of light and shadow enhances the menacing nighttime mood of urban despair. The stories of love, betrayal, and murder involve men caught in a net of treachery from which they cannot escape. The mood of film noir is one of confusion, anxiety, and danger. The male protagonists encounter sexually overpowering women, who often betray them. *Kiss Me Deadly, Detour,* and *Double Indemnity* are among the famous noir films. Other well-known examples of the style can be found in *Touch of Evil, The Third Man,* and *Sunset Boulevard.*

18b Use transitional devices to improve coherence.

On reading over your rough draft, you may find that, logical as your pattern is, the sentences do not flow from one to the next. Sentence A ends with a thump. Then sentence B starts up. And so on. Transitional devices can bridge the gaps. These devices connect the sentences and bind the paragraph into a single, coherent unit. The most common transitional devices are presented here.

Pronouns Because each pronoun must refer to an antecedent, a pronoun and its antecedent form a link. You can often make a paragraph cohere merely by using pronouns properly. On the other hand, incorrectly used pronouns can weaken coherence (see **51–53**). In the following examples, notice how pronouns in the second sentence of each pair provide coherence by referring to the important subjects in the first:

> *Self-help* books continue to proliferate. *They* appeal to the anxieties of many people in our society.

> *Patients* must fast for twelve hours before the test. *They* should also avoid eating red meat for seventy-two hours before coming in.

Repetition Substituting a pronoun for a noun is actually a kind of repetition. Direct repetition of a word or expression will give a similar effect:

> Exposure to too much sun can *damage* the skin. This *damage* is irreversible and can result in skin cancer.

18

Use direct repetition with care. Overdoing it will give an awkward, immature ring to your writing ("Daily receipts are transmitted to the central office. *Daily receipts* are then analyzed . . ."). You can get much the same transitional effect by using synonyms or slightly altered forms of the repeated expressions:

> *Bill Clinton* has been busy since leaving the White House. *The former President* has raised money for AIDS relief and other world-health issues.

Transitional terms Transitional terms make a paragraph coherent by relating ideas. Like pronouns, many of these terms come to mind automatically, but you should carefully choose among them. Here is a partial list of common transitional terms:

1. *Time:* next, then, after, before, during, while, following, shortly, thereafter, later on, the next day, secondly, finally
2. *Place:* over, above, inside, to the left, just behind, beyond
3. *Contrast:* however, but, nevertheless, on the other hand, nonetheless, notwithstanding, on the contrary, conversely, yet
4. *Cause-effect:* so, therefore, thus, accordingly, consequently, as a result, hence, because of this
5. *Addition:* and, furthermore, moreover, likewise, similarly, in a like manner, too, also
6. *Emphasis:* indeed, in fact, especially, most important
7. *Summary:* in other words, in short, to sum up, in conclusion
8. *Example:* for instance, for example, that is, in particular

The following examples illustrate the use of transitional terms:

Pronoun

Contrast

Emphasis

In the 1980s, media experts were prophesying the death of the book. The printed word, *they* said, was being replaced by the electronic age. *But* these prophets were wrong because books remain alive and well in the twenty-first century. Along with e-books, Internet blogs, and instant messaging, the printed word seems destined to retain its place in the world of reading. *In fact,* Microsoft founder Bill Gates said that reading anything more than a few pages on the screen is vastly inferior to

18

Pronoun

Repetition

Example

Repetition

reading on paper. *He* prefers to print anything more than

four pages long to carry around with him and annotate.

This feature—usability—has been one of the book's virtues

since its earliest days. *For example,* the book has always been

easy to carry, easy to store, convenient to thumb through, and

comfortable to curl up with. *This handiness,* which has made it

the basic tool of learning for thousands of years, continues to

make the printed book indispensable.

> Sometimes it seems that Thomas Jefferson the man hardly exists for us. *That is, he* seems to be mainly a symbol of what we as Americans are or think we are. *He* appears almost to have been invented so as to reveal something about ourselves. *In fact,* no one else in our history embodies so much of our democratic heritage and so many of our democratic hopes. *Yet* the man himself has proved to be a fascinating, complex character, the worthy subject of several recent biographies.

Transitional sentences and paragraphs Pronouns, repetition, and transitional terms can provide coherence within paragraphs and can even link two consecutive paragraphs, but to link two paragraphs that differ significantly in content, you occasionally will need a transitional sentence or even a short paragraph. If, for instance, you have devoted three or four paragraphs to the theories of one authority and are ready to shift to those of another, you will probably need a sentence to help the reader make the transition. For example: "However, a critic who approaches Shakespeare's plays differently is Maynard Mack, who. . . ."

If you have written three paragraphs on the ways in which your school district can provide better education for high school students and are now ready to shift to differing views on the subject, you might use a short transitional paragraph:

> However, several experts disagree with these conclusions and believe that the problem has been misinterpreted. As we will see, their views have one thing in common: parental responsibility.

19

Here are two versions of a student's paragraph. In the first, transitional devices are omitted. In the second, they have been inserted and italicized.

Less effective: There is no Nobel Prize for mathematics, and mathematicians rarely make the headlines. It is not a glamorous profession. There are no exotic, expensive pieces of equipment—no cyclotrons, body scanners, or electron microscopes—for the public to identify with. Research tools are plain. Pencil, paper, chalk, and a computer are about all one needs. In a time when some scientists' names—Einstein, Oppenheimer, Freud, and others—have become household words, few people could name even one great modern mathematician. Mathematics is so basic to most scientific subjects that it has been called the language of all experimental dialogue.

More effective: There is no Nobel Prize for mathematics, and mathematicians rarely make the headlines. It is not a glamorous profession. *For example,* there are no exotic, expensive pieces of equipment—no cyclotrons, body scanners, or electron microscopes—for the public to identify with. *In fact,* research tools are plain. Pencil, paper, chalk, and a computer are about all one needs. *And* in a time when some scientists' names— Einstein, Oppenheimer, Freud, and others—have become household words, few people could name even one great modern mathematician. *Yet* mathematics is so basic to most scientific subjects that it has been called the language of all experimental dialogue.

Note how the four transitional devices make explicit the connections between the ideas. The last transition—*yet*—clarifies the contrast between the final, climactic sentence and the preceding points.

dev

19 Develop paragraphs fully.

If your paragraph is to be interesting and convincing, you must clarify and support its main point. Effective development is quite different from "padding": think of development as growth and increasing depth, not as mere expansion. This section shows some of the various ways that writers, depending on their subject and purpose, develop effective paragraphs.

19a Examples

19

Including examples and details is one of the best ways to achieve good paragraph development. Examples provide readers with the specific information that they need to understand the controlling idea. Merely asserting a point is never sufficient; each idea must be developed with facts and examples. Although too much detail is sometimes a problem, bad writing usually suffers from too little detail rather than too much. Short paragraphs often indicate lack of effort or thought.

In the following passage, notice how using the example of Japanese culture helps make the author's initial point concrete and convincing:

> Poetry provides an important outlet for expressing emotion. This is certainly true in Japan, where I lived as an exchange student for a year. In Japanese society, people are often reluctant to express their feelings directly, so poetry has become unusually popular. Millions of people write poetry regularly, buy best-selling books of poetry, and attend poetry meetings. Television programs have made some poets into national celebrities, and newspapers carry daily poetry columns on the front page. Nearly everyone, from the Emperor on down, enjoys the freedom and challenge of writing haiku and other forms of verse. Other arts that we think of as elite also flourish in Japan, but none as widely as poetry.
>
> —*Jason Clarke (student)*

In the following example, the weak paragraph is general, whereas the improved version is developed with specific illustrations:

Weak development:	In many earlier cultures, salt was viewed not only as a preservative but also as a powerful religious and symbolic substance. Valued because it was essential to life, salt had such a symbolic significance that it came to represent health, virtue, and friendship. From biblical to medieval times, there are references to salt in many cultures. At the same time, this valuable substance contributed to a number of fascinating legends and superstitions.
Improved development:	In many earlier cultures, salt was viewed not only as a preservative but also as a powerful religious and symbolic substance. Valued because it was essential to life, salt had such a symbolic significance that it came to represent health, virtue, and friendship. For example, Moses commanded the Israelites to sprinkle offerings of wheat with salt. And because covenants were usually made over a sacrificial meal, the expression "covenant of salt" was established. Arabs who shared bread and salt with guests were committed to protecting them, and the Persian expression "untrue to salt" means disloyal

and ungrateful. This valuable substance also contributed
to a number of superstitions. Some medieval Frenchmen
said that the devil was often seen without a tail because
courageous folk had once sprinkled it with salt. The devil
was so agonized by the virtuous substance that he
chewed his tail off.

19b Comparison and Contrast

Comparison notes the similarities of two subjects; contrast notes the differences. Writers most often discuss both similarities and differences, following
one of these two methods:

1. *Subject by subject* presents all the details of one side of the
   comparison or contrast first and then the details of the other side.

> Thomas Jefferson had an insatiable curiosity that made him a sort
> of Renaissance man. The third American president, author of the
> Declaration of Independence, and founder of the University of Virginia
> was also an architect, inventor, musician, and scholar of philology,
> meteorology, archeology, astronomy, chemistry, and anatomy, among
> other fields. The idea that such a man could master all knowledge and
> put it into practice was an invention of the Italian Renaissance, as
> seen in the career of Leon Battista Alberti, whose interests parallel
> Jefferson's. Alberti, also a self-confident innovator, studied languages,
> law, and mathematics and wrote treatises on painting, sculpture, and
> moving weights. In 1444, he wrote the first book on architecture since
> antiquity; a classical scholar, he was concerned with the practical
> application of his studies. His relaxations were the same as
> Jefferson's: music and horsemanship. Although Jefferson, unlike
> Alberti, was a politician and statesman, the similarities between the
> two men show that Jefferson's achievement owes much to the Italian
> Renaissance and its dream of the universal man.
>
> —*adapted from Kenneth Clark*

2. *Point by point* moves back and forth between the subjects, item by item:

> Generally, Americans who can be classed as liberals believe that
> government should be responsible for protecting the defenseless and
> for righting wrongs caused by inequities in wealth and privilege.
> However, conservatives believe that the government is an inefficient
> "protector" and causes more harm than good. Furthermore, they see
> large differences in wealth and privilege as part of the natural order.
> Liberals believe that taxation of the wealthy is the logical method for
> government to finance its social programs, but conservatives, who
> disagree with liberals on both the cause of social problems and the
> possibility of fixing them, react angrily to having their incomes reduced
> by what they claim to be an ever-greedy federal government.

19

19c Definition

A definition explains the meaning of a word or concept by placing it into a general class and then supplying details that distinguish it from other items of the same class. Writers often expand upon historical definitions, using examples or comparison and contrast to distinguish one thing from another and thus provide a thorough explanation of an idea or term, as in this paragraph:

> Happiness is something everyone wants but few people can define. Its meaning seems to differ according to each individual. We Americans think we have a right to the "pursuit of happiness," and probably to achieving it, but what is it that makes us happy? In earlier times, Darrin McMahon states in his book *Happiness: A History*, the word *happiness* was usually linked to the word for luck or chance. The ancient Greeks had a saying: "Call no one happy until he [or she] is dead." Only then, when the person has passed beyond the world of chance, could his or her life be called happy. For the Greek thinkers and many later philosophers, happiness had to do with well-being, with living a rational and virtuous life. Many today would associate happiness with love; many others would agree with the ancients that if more good things than bad things happen to you, you are a happy person—whether you feel that way or not. But it does seem clear that true happiness is more than just a sense of pleasure.

19d Analogy

Writers use analogies to make comparisons of items that seem to have little in common. Analogies help make something that is unfamiliar or complex easier to understand, as in this example:

> Having a too-busy, stressful life is like always having a buzzing fly in the room. The irritation never goes away because nothing ever seems to get done. The sense of completion that comes from finishing work and chores is absent: you are always being interrupted and finding it hard to concentrate on the issue at hand. And at night, when you are trying to sleep, the fly is still there, buzzing around the periphery of the restless mind.

19e Classification

Classification organizes material into categories to reveal the nature of each category. A writer might want to show the differences and relationships among the categories, as in explaining three types of instrumental music, or an author might outline several psychological theories before indicating which one that she will discuss. In the following example, a student lists three reasons that student evaluations of faculty are biased:

Student evaluations of faculty are biased for several reasons. First, students' grade expectations influence their rating of an instructor. Those who are likely to receive a high grade will be more favorably disposed toward the instructor than those expecting low grades. A second area of bias is more subtle. It involves age, sex, and appearance. A study in the *Journal of Educational Psychology* found that unattractive, middle-aged female instructors and unattractive, elderly male instructors frequently received lower ratings than their younger, more attractive counterparts. Related to this is a third factor: men are generally rated higher than women because of gender stereotyping that associates masculinity with success and authority. For these reasons alone, it is apparent that any effort to conduct student evaluations of faculty will be far from objective.

—*Cynthia Wilson (student)*

19f Cause and Effect

Cause-and-effect paragraphs explain why something happened. They may proceed from cause to effects or may simply list the causes of an obvious effect. For example, a writer might explore the reasons for the real estate crash of 2007 without showing that the crash was disastrous. The following paragraph deals with some of the causes of jealousy and envy in a famous play:

Most people think of jealousy and envy as interchangeable, but, although closely related, they are different emotions. Simply stated, jealousy usually means a fear of losing someone (or something) you love, whereas envy means a hatred of someone who has something you want. Like jealousy, envy begins with fear of being denied what you think you deserve. How these powerful feelings develop, and the effects they have, can be seen in Shakespeare's tragedy *Othello*. The title character, the Moor of Venice, fears losing his wife, Desdemona, to another man; this jealousy is stirred by his ensign, Iago. Iago hates Othello for several reasons, which include the promotion of another man over Iago and the fact that Othello is black. As a result, the villain Iago is envious of and destroys Othello, who is jealous. Both emotions stem from fear, which leads to anger and then to hatred: Iago has always hated the Moor, and Othello, believing Iago's hateful lies, thinks he has lost control of his wife and, fearing his loss of control, comes to hate the wife he really loves and so kills her and himself.

6

Writing Effective Sentences

Because the sentence is your main means of expressing ideas, look carefully at each sentence you write to make sure that it is clear, emphatic, and mature. Chapter 8 focuses on correct grammatical patterns; this chapter focuses on effectiveness, describing ways to express your thoughts with skill and style.

20

The principal types of sentences (see also **84**) are as follows:

1. Simple sentence (one subject and one predicate)

> I have never played tennis.

2. Compound sentence (two or more independent, or main, clauses)

> I have never played tennis, but I hope to start taking lessons next year. (independent clauses joined by coordinating conjunction)

3. Complex sentence (one independent clause and at least one dependent, or subordinate, clause)

> Although I have never played tennis, I hope to start taking lessons next year. (dependent clause + independent clause)

4. Compound-complex sentence (at least two independent clauses and one dependent clause)

> Although I have never played tennis, I hope to start taking lessons next year; I really need the aerobic exercise that tennis provides. (dependent clause + two independent clauses)

> Although I have never played tennis, I really need the exercise, so I hope to start taking lessons next year. (dependent clause + two independent clauses)

sub

20

Use subordination to relate secondary details to main ideas and to improve choppy sentences.

Two or more ideas can be connected in a sentence by two means: *coordination* and *subordination*. Coordination gives the ideas equal grammatical emphasis; subordination presents one as the main idea and puts the other(s) in a dependent or deemphasized relation to the main idea. Therefore, your sentence structure should depend upon the relationship you want to show between your ideas. Notice how the meaning subtly changes in the following sentences:

20

Two sentences:	Comedians can make outrageous statements. They must make sure that no one takes these statements seriously.
Coordination:	Comedians can make outrageous statements, but they must make sure that no one takes these statements seriously.
Subordination:	Although comedians can make outrageous statements, they must make sure that no one takes these statements seriously.
Subordination:	Comedians can make outrageous statements if they make sure that no one takes the statements seriously.

Subordination allows you to include a number of details in one sentence; some of these details you need but do not want to emphasize. In this sentence, the emphasis is in the main clause, with the subordinate *(italicized)* elements adding additional information:

> I started my car, *a white 2001 Buick with over 180,000 miles,* and drove to the lawyer's office, *which was not my favorite destination that summer.*

20a Use subordinate clauses to relate secondary details to your main idea.

Relative pronouns *(who, whom, which, that)* and subordinating conjunctions (such as *because, although,* and *since*—see others in the list below and the list on page 295) introduce subordinate clauses and signal specific relationships between them and the main clause. Notice in the following examples how each subordinate clause has a different relationship to the main clause:

Effective:	Antonio, *who* had slept for ten hours, still felt tired.
Effective:	*Although* Antonio had slept for ten hours, he still felt tired.
Effective:	*After* he had slept for ten hours, Antonio still felt tired.
Effective:	*Because* Antonio had slept for only ten hours after working a double shift, he still felt tired.

The following list of subordinating conjunctions shows the variety of relationships that subordination can indicate:

Cause:	since, because, if, so that, in order that
Contrast or concession:	although, though, whereas, while
Time:	when, whenever, as, before, since, after, as long as, once, until, while

Place:	where, wherever
Condition:	if, unless, whether, provided that, as long as
Manner:	as, as though, as if, how
Similarity:	as . . . as

Some subordinate clauses can be used in the same way as nouns (as subjects or objects):

Ms. Wallace argued *that command of a foreign language should be required for an advanced degree.* (clause as direct object of the verb *argued:* What did Wallace argue?)

Some subordinate clauses can also function as modifiers—that is, as adjectives or adverbs. An adjective clause modifies (or qualifies) a noun or pronoun and most often begins with a relative pronoun:

Golf is a sport *that can reduce one to tears.* (The clause modifies *sport* and thus functions as an adjective.)

An adverb clause modifies a verb, adjective, adverb, verbal (such as a gerund or participle), or the rest of the sentence:

When Dr. Santiago speaks, people listen. (The clause modifies the verb *listen.*)

Be sure to place your main idea, the one you want to stress, in the independent clause. When possible, put the main clause last:

When you arrive at a fork in the road, take it. (Yogi Berra)

Do not misplace the emphasis in a sentence by putting the main idea in a subordinate clause:

Misplaced emphasis:	The American Medical Association issued a report which warned that many doctors tend to ignore nutrition.
Improved:	According to an American Medical Association report, many doctors tend to ignore nutrition.

20

20b Use subordination to improve long, rambling sentences.

Inexperienced writers often use long, stringy sentences composed of a series of main clauses hooked together with *and* or some other coordinating conjunction. If you subordinate one or more clauses, you will usually make your meaning clearer and the sentence more readable:

Ineffective:	Some business leaders are unhappy with the skills of the average entry-level applicant, and they argue that schools should better prepare students for the workplace and that college standards need to be raised in general.
Effective:	Business leaders who are unhappy with the skills of the average entry-level applicant argue that schools should better prepare students for the workplace and that schools should raise their overall standards.
Ineffective:	Ms. Li is a hard worker, and she is a good teacher, and she pushes her students to excel.
Effective:	Ms. Li, who is a hard worker and a good teacher, pushes her students to excel.
Effective:	Ms. Li, who pushes her students to excel, is a hard worker and a good teacher.
Ineffective:	I watched the start of the movie and had the strange sense that I had seen it before, and I wondered if, in my haste, I had bought a ticket for the wrong film.
Effective:	When I watched the start of the movie, I had the strange sense that I had seen it before, as if I had hastily bought a ticket for the wrong film.

20c Use subordination to improve a series of short, choppy sentences.

Numerous short, choppy sentences are another common sign of an inexperienced writer. Such sentences are awkward to read and fail to show the relationships between their ideas. Notice in these examples how using subordination improves the short, choppy sentences:

Ineffective:	Carl wanted a new truck very much. He took a second job. Then he went to his bank for a loan.
Effective:	Carl wanted a new truck so much that he took a second job before he went to his bank for a loan.
Ineffective:	Nick expected to enjoy reading *The Life of Pi*. He failed to understand it fully at first. Then he saw the movie.
Effective:	Although he expected to enjoy reading *The Life of Pi*, Nick failed to understand it fully until he saw the movie.

20d Avoid excessive subordination.

Although using subordination is a valuable strategy, too many subordinate structures in a sentence can make it awkward, monotonous, or even confusing:

Ineffective:	Ms. Rivera works in Tropical Business Center, the new office park near Portside Mall on the south side of the interstate.
Improved:	Ms. Rivera works in Tropical Business Center, the new office park near Portside Mall; TBC is on the south side of the interstate.

Ineffective:	I caught a grayling, which is a kind of small salmonid, which is found in Alaska and Canada.
Improved:	I caught a grayling, the small salmonid found in Alaska and Canada.

In this last example, notice how you can eliminate nonessential information (and wordiness) by deleting *which is, which are,* and so on at the beginning of a clause.

Exercise

A. Read the following sentences. Mark *E* for those that are effective and *X* for those needing less or more subordination.

1. Feline leukemia is a deadly disease. It affects domestic cats. It is easily transmitted.

2. Exchange-traded funds (ETFs) have become a popular investment vehicle, and they are starting to replace individual stock purchases for investors and have a vast influence on the health of the stock market.

3. The realtor has bought a GIS system, which gives her an efficient way to pinpoint sites for new housing developments.

4. I did not finish my term paper, so I got an extension from my humanities instructor, so I'm off to the library.

5. The afternoon grew cold. Dusk was coming. Gloria sighed.

6. My friend Bobby is sick, and he could not accompany me to the races; I went with my friend Mario instead.

7. A national lottery has been debated for years, and its supporters believe that it would raise revenues and morale but that it would not cause problems for compulsive gamblers or open the door for organized crime.

21

8. At lunch I had a bacon cheeseburger, which is not real food but junk food, which is something that I'm trying to avoid.

9. Yuko specialized in the butterfly stroke, a style of swimming hard to master.

10. I find opera depressing. This is not because I have trouble following the story. It is because I have no appreciation for that style of singing.

B. Rewrite the sentences that you marked *X*.

co-ord
21 Use coordination when you want to give equal emphasis to two or more points.

You can use coordination to join two or more independent clauses and create one compound sentence that gives equal grammatical emphasis to each clause (see **83h**). A compound sentence is less choppy than two separate simple sentences that contain the same information. And compound sentences signal to the reader the similarity or equivalence of the material in the independent clauses.

> **Effective:** I never forget a face, but in your case I'll make an exception. (Groucho Marx)
>
> **Effective:** Jerry went to buy a camouflage outfit, but he couldn't find one.

Coordination implies an equal relationship between the clauses. If the content of one clause is more important than that of the other, subordinate the less important clause.

> **Ineffective:** It was snowing, so we had to allow extra travel time.
>
> **Effective:** Because it was snowing, we had to allow extra travel time.

comb
22 Use coordination to combine sentences.

Parallel coordinate phrases can help you develop mature, expressive sentences. Instead of constructing separate sentences, skillful writers often combine and relate sentence elements so that a single sentence carries more weight.

You can add colorful or clarifying details to a sentence by adding modifiers to the subject, to the predicate, or to the sentence as a whole. You can add modifiers in front of the main clause to form a periodic sentence (see **23c**), or you can pile up modifiers after the main clause to avoid using a string of short, choppy sentences.

Ineffective:	Computerized inventory systems have many uses. They allow businesses to monitor supplies. Businesses can also make efficient purchases from wholesalers. Shoplifting will be reduced. Employees will be less likely to steal.
Effective:	Computerized inventory systems have many uses, allowing businesses to monitor supplies, to make efficient purchases from wholesalers, and to combat shoplifting and employee theft.
Effective:	By allowing businesses to monitor supplies, to make efficient purchases from wholesalers, and to combat shoplifting and employee theft, computerized inventory systems have many uses.

The repetition in sentences that all begin alike can be eliminated by creatively combining them into one richer, more complex sentence. However, too many modifiers can overload a sentence and make it hard to read; also, not every sentence need be developed in this way. But combining can be especially valuable in generating effective descriptive and narrative sentences.

Ineffective:	Steven stands on the bridge. He drops pieces of wood upstream. He times how long it takes them to come out the other side and calculates the rate of flow.
Effective:	Steven stands on the bridge, dropping pieces of wood upstream, timing how long it takes them to come out the other side, calculating the rate of flow.

—*Margaret Atwood*

1. *Noun phrases* can develop a sentence by vividly restating a noun in the main clause:

Nancy bought a 1963 Corvette Stingray, a beautiful car that is a true collector's item.

2. *Verbal phrases* can provide details of the action, object, or scene mentioned in the main clause. In a narrative sentence, verbal phrases enable a writer to picture simultaneously all the separate actions that make up the action. The following sentence is broken to distinguish the verbal phrases from the main clause that follows them:

Working more than eighty hours per week,
    trying desperately to support her three small children,
      Terri somehow managed to stay ahead of the bill collectors.

22

3. *Absolute phrases,* like the indented phrases in the sentence below, can also add details to a single sentence, often by developing one aspect of the subject:

> The waterfall loomed ahead,
>> its rocks forbidding,
>> its force tremendous,
>> and its sound deafening.

Note that the use of coordinate modifiers requires parallelism (see **28**).

Exercise

A. Develop each of the following into one sentence, using coordinate noun, verb, or absolute phrases.

1. The old man came to the door. His smile was kind. His voice was friendly.

2. The strip mall was abandoned. Its stores were boarded up. Its parking lot was covered with trash.

3. I once wanted to be a pirate. I saw myself standing in the wind on the bow of my ship. I dreamed of boarding the ships of the evil king's fleet and taking the plunder back to my island fortress.

4. Harry was seventeen when he got his first car. It was a fifteen-year-old sedan. Its doors would not lock. Its radio was broken.

5. My mother glared at the mess I had made. Her frown was severe. Her silence indicated that I was in real trouble this time.

B. Combine the following groups of sentences, using whatever method works best, to form effective sentences.

Ineffective: Jerry's room was a mess. The floor was littered with empty beer cans. The bed was piled high with dirty clothes. The desk was stacked with books.

Effective: Jerry's room was a mess, its floor littered with empty beer cans, its bed piled high with dirty clothes, and its desk stacked with books.

1. Some of the stranded travelers were quiet. They read or dozed in their seats. Others seemed angry. They talked about suing the airline.

2. The rain fell in sheets. It lashed the barn and the utility shed. The two buildings looked like the last survivors of some terrible weather war.

3. The movie took me to a place I had never been before. It was a place where technology was king. The people in the movie were the slaves of their machines.

4. Ann's cat is about five pounds above the average. It is a tortoiseshell. It is mostly black. Its eyes are very green.

5. My grandfather's feed store was very small. It was in a cinderblock building. The floor was made of hard pine. The walls were covered with manufacturers' advertisements.

emp
23 Vary word order and sentence length for emphasis.

Effective writing not only expresses ideas clearly and relates them to one another appropriately but also emphasizes the most important ideas. Skillful writers also vary the structure of their sentences to avoid relying on the same patterns.

23a Emphasize an important word by placing it at the beginning or end of the sentence.

The most emphatic position in most essays, paragraphs, or sentences is at the end. The next most emphatic position is the beginning; therefore, you can emphasize key words by starting and ending sentences with them. Because semicolons operate much like periods, words immediately before and after semicolons also receive emphasis. Notice how altering the key words in the following examples improves the emphasis:

Ineffective:	All the villagers were killed, as Bob reported. (leaves the reader thinking about Bob, not about the tragedy)
Ineffective:	It was Bob who reported that all the villagers were killed. (empty words at the beginning of sentence)
Effective:	Bob reported that all the villagers were killed.
Ineffective:	For us, time was brief and money was a problem.
Effective:	We had little time; we had little money.

23

23b Use an occasional short sentence.

A very short sentence contrasting with longer sentences stops the flow and catches the reader's attention. You can also use a short sentence to emphasize an especially important point. Notice how effective the short sentences are in the following passages:

> **Effective:**   In the middle of a block of tasteful, quiet homes stood a two-story house with green paint and lavender trim, diamond-shaped windows, and gargoyles perched to strike. It was ghastly.

> **Effective:**   If we read of one man robbed, or murdered, or killed by accident, or one house burned, or one vessel wrecked, or one steamboat blown up, or one cow run over on the Western Railroad, or one mad dog killed, or one lot of grasshoppers in the winter, we never need read of another. One is enough.
>
> —*Henry David Thoreau*

If you have written three or four long sentences, use a short one for variety. If you find that every sentence begins the same way, following the subject-verb-object pattern, for example, vary the word order and use subordination to express the relation among ideas.

> **Weak:**   People suffering from depression sometimes find it difficult to confront their problem. It is easier to let life slide by. But this medical condition will worsen if not treated. Depression requires prompt medical attention.

> **Improved:**   Although people suffering from depression sometimes find it difficult to confront their problem, preferring to let life slide by, this medical condition will worsen if not treated. Depression requires prompt medical attention.

23c Use an occasional balanced or periodic sentence.

Most English sentences are *loose* or *cumulative* sentences—that is, the main clause comes first, followed by details supporting the main idea. The order is reversed in a periodic sentence, in which the main idea follows the subordinate details. Because it saves the most important idea for last and because it is less commonly used, the periodic sentence is more emphatic. However, do not overuse the periodic sentence; save it for those ideas you especially want to emphasize.

> **Loose:**   *The family farm is becoming an endangered species,* criticized by agricultural economists as inefficient, scorned by banks as a poor credit risk, and threatened by huge multinational food producers.

Periodic:	Criticized by agricultural economists as inefficient, scorned by banks as a poor credit risk, and threatened by huge multinational food producers, *the family farm is becoming an endangered species.*

23

In a *balanced* sentence, coordinate structures are enough alike that the reader notices the similarity. You can use a balanced sentence to emphasize a comparison or contrast. Notice how a repeated word points up the contrast between the two balanced parts of the sentence:

Balanced:	Many of us resent shoddiness in cars, food, and services; few of us resent shoddiness in language.
Balanced:	We used to admire a man's valor, his worth and bravery; today we admire a man's value, his material assets.

23d Use a climactic word order.

By arranging a series of ideas in order of importance, you can gradually build emphasis:

Climactic:	Like all great leaders, Lincoln was hated by many; like all strong presidents, he was embattled by Congress; and, like many heroes, he was popular only after his death.

23e Write primarily in the active voice.

In most active-voice sentences, the subject does something:

Vanessa → started → the car.

In passive-voice sentences, the subject receives the action of the verb:

The car ← was started ← by Vanessa.

The active voice is usually more direct, natural, and economical:

Passive:	Never put off until tomorrow what can be avoided altogether.
Active:	Never put off until tomorrow what you can avoid altogether.

Passive:	On May 7, a bill to establish permanent curfews for minors was introduced to the legislature by its sponsor, Representative Cooke. The issue at hand was discussed by legislators, and criticisms were offered by members from small towns and rural districts. It was suggested by Representative Blythe that the bill be sent back to committee. A vote on this motion was held, but a decision was not made because of an objection by Representative Cooke.

23

> **Active:** On May 7, Representative Cooke, the sponsor of a bill to establish permanent curfews for minors, introduced the bill to the legislature. Legislators discussed the issue, and members from small towns and rural areas offered criticisms. Representative Blythe suggested that the bill be sent back to committee. The legislature voted on this motion but did not make a decision because of Representative Cooke's objection.

There are appropriate uses for the passive voice, as in these examples:

> **Passive:** Franklin D. Roosevelt was elected to an unprecedented fourth term.
>
> **Passive:** Jane Martin's article will be published next summer.

In each case, to rewrite the sentence in the active voice, the writer has to reconstruct the subject (and alter the original intention):

> **Active:** American voters elected Franklin D. Roosevelt to an unprecedented fourth term.
>
> **Active:** *Current Anthropology* will publish Jane Martin's article next summer.

If the writer is discussing Roosevelt or the article (or its author), not voters or *Current Anthropology,* the passive voice is more logical. But in general, writing in the active voice is better. Passive-voice sentences tend to be artificial, wordy, and dull. They are less emphatic, especially when they obscure the doer of the action:

> A tax increase was announced yesterday.

Passive-voice sentences can also lead to dangling modifiers (see **25f**):

> To be a CPA, a college education and a state exam are needed.
>
> By doing a few simple blood tests, the cause of the patient's illness can be isolated.

Finally, the passive voice is not an effective way to vary your style. Unnecessary shifts in voice can be distracting for the reader (see **58a**).

Exercise

A. Study the following sentences. Mark *X* for those that need rephrasing for emphasis, *E* for those that are effective.

1. It was suggested by Professor Cho that the biology curriculum needs to be revised.

2. Although not everyone agrees about the afterlife, many people claim not to fear death.

3. One of the most important battles of the American Revolution was fought at Saratoga, an upstate New York village now known for its horseracing season.

4. For the experiment to be successful, detailed procedures must be followed.

5. Women students today constitute roughly half of college populations, a large increase since 1930, when men predominated.

6. One possible effect of global warming is the loss of beaches, and the extinction of certain animal species is another.

7. In the first half of the twentieth century, African Americans were prohibited from playing Major League Baseball, but this ban was lifted in 1949.

8. Gas mileage is usually not improved by fuel additives, which are available at all auto-parts stores.

9. Sam Snead was a great golfer, Jimmy Demaret was a good one, but Ben Hogan was outstanding.

10. Breathing large amounts of gasoline vapor may cause cancer, according to various studies.

B. Rephrase the sentences that you marked *X*.

awk   Avoid awkward repetitions and omitted words.

24

Awkward sentences are difficult to read. They may or may not be clear, but they always require extra effort and usually interrupt the flow of thought. In this section we discuss two common causes of awkwardness. But many awkward sentences do not fit into neat categories; they often result from the ineffective choice or arrangement of words, as described in this chapter and in Chapter 9. If awkwardness is a problem for you, try reading your sentences aloud: an awkward sentence usually does not sound right.

24a Repeat words only for emphasis or transition.

Repeating a prominent word or expression can provide an effective transition between sentences or paragraphs (see **18b**). Occasional repetition of a key word can also emphasize an idea. But use repetition sparingly, for too much can create awkward sentences:

Awkward repetition:	A writer who writes about gender must be careful to be balanced.
Improved:	A writer who concentrates on gender must be careful to be balanced.
Effective repetition:	An external audit is valuable because it allows a company's managers to verify the firm's accounting procedures, to verify the firm's financial stability, and to verify the firm's perception by stockholders.
Effective repetition:	Cormac McCarthy's *The Road* is a great novel as well as a great read.

One especially confusing type of repetition is the use of two different senses of the same word in the same or adjoining sentences. Find a synonym for one instance of the word.

Awkward repetition:	No one knew the major reason for the major's sudden retirement.
Improved:	No one knew the principal reason for the major's sudden retirement.

24b Include all necessary words.

Many sentences are awkward because they use unnecessary words, but many others are awkward or confusing because they omit words. Following are some of the more common types of omissions:

Awkward omission:	I could see almost all the puppies were active and healthy. (*That* has been omitted after *see*. Omitting *that* in this case produces a confusing and awkward sentence.)
Improved:	I could see that almost all the puppies were active and healthy.
Awkward omission:	The children were happy and talking freely. (*Were* has been omitted before *talking*. *Happy* and *talking* are not parallel.)
Improved:	The children were happy and were talking freely.
Awkward omission:	In her will, Mrs. Johnson left money to Myra Rhodes, a neighbor; Charles Johnson, her nephew; and Paula J. Stephens, her granddaughter. (*To* is omitted before *Charles Johnson* and *Paula J. Stephens*. Repeating the preposition shows the parallel elements more clearly.)
Improved:	In her will, Mrs. Johnson left money to Myra Rhodes, a neighbor; to Charles Johnson, her nephew; and to Paula J. Stephens, her granddaughter.

24

When you use two verbs that require different prepositions, be sure to include both prepositions:

Awkward omission:	Richard could neither comply nor agree to the proposal. (*With* has been omitted after *comply*.)
Improved:	Richard could neither comply with nor agree to the proposal.

Exercise

Mark *X* for sentences that are awkward and *E* for those that are effective. Rewrite the awkward sentences.

1. I felt my leg injury would keep me from training for the marathon.

2. Modern travelers frequently search and try to visit unspoiled destinations.

3. After the race, Lance was cold but talking a mile a minute.

4. Roxanne is less concerned about the future of the city than the past.

5. Dr. Hernandez is esteemed for her interest in her patients and her sense of them as individuals.

25

6. I found money is not essential for happiness.

7. The review board is willing to hear your demands and to comply with them, if at all possible.

8. The human rights team published a study that treated the plight of the refugees; the study focused on the refugees' treatment by the military at the border.

9. I advised my nephew to study, save his money, and to explore all available scholarship offers.

10. The governor could neither agree nor approve of the legislature's astounding proclamation.

mm dg 25 Place all modifiers so that they clearly modify the intended word.

The meaning of English sentences depends largely on word order. If you move words and expressions around, you will often change what a sentence means:

> Nancy Ruiz recently published the poem she wrote.

> Nancy Ruiz published the poem she wrote recently.

The rule of thumb is to place modifiers as near as possible to the words that they modify.

25a Place an adjective phrase or clause as near as possible to the noun or pronoun it modifies.

Single adjectives usually come immediately before the noun or pronoun they modify, adjective phrases and clauses immediately after. When other words come between an adjective and the word it modifies, the sentence may sound awkward, and its meaning may be obscured:

> **Misplaced:**   Vincent soaked an ankle he injured in an ice bucket.
> **Improved:**   Vincent used an ice bucket to soak an ankle he injured.

Often you have to do more than move the modifier; you have to revise the whole sentence:

> **Misplaced:**   Unless completely anesthetized, surgeons cannot operate on cardiac patients.
> **Revised:**   Surgeons cannot operate on cardiac patients who have not been completely anesthetized.

25

Misplaced: The ball grazed Jim's leg, which rolled into left field.

Revised: The ball, which rolled into left field, grazed Jim's leg.

25b Place a limiting adverb, such as *only* or *just,* immediately before the word it modifies.

In speech, most of us are casual about where we place adverbs such as *only, almost, hardly, just,* and *scarcely.* But writing should be more precise:

Misplaced: Tram almost completed all of her lab experiment.

Revised: Tram completed almost all of her lab experiment.

Notice how moving the modifier can change the meaning of a sentence:

I had five dollars only yesterday.

I only had five dollars yesterday. *(Think about what this sentence actually means and how the next one more accurately expresses the writer's intent.)*

I had only five dollars yesterday.

25c Make certain that each adverb phrase or clause modifies the word or words you intend it to modify.

An adverb phrase or clause can appear at the beginning of a sentence, inside the sentence, or at its end:

After the awards ceremony, Irina Clarke found two new friends.

Irina Clarke, after the awards ceremony, found two new friends.

Irina Clarke found two new friends after the awards ceremony.

However, be careful that the adverb modifies only what you intend it to modify:

Misplaced: A woman found dead behind a local bar was thought to be murdered by the city police.

Revised: According to the city police, a woman found dead behind a local bar was thought to be murdered.

Misplaced: On Tuesday, Michael swore that he was going to quit his job three times.

Improved: On Tuesday, Michael swore three times that he was going to quit his job.

25

25d Move ambiguous (squinting) modifiers.

If you find that you have placed a modifier so that it refers to more than one word, move it to avoid the ambiguity:

Ambiguous:	The woman who was asked the question sincerely considered her response.
Clear:	The woman who was asked the question considered her response sincerely.
Or:	The woman who was asked the sincere question considered her response.

Ambiguous:	The student whom Professor Walker answered abruptly left the room.
Revised:	The student whom Professor Walker abruptly answered left the room.
Or:	The student whom Professor Walker answered left the room abruptly.

25e Avoid awkwardly split infinitives.

Conventional usage avoids inserting an adverb between *to*—called the sign of the infinitive—and its verb form (for example, *to quickly run*). In some instances, splitting the infinitive is natural; many writers would prefer the following sentence to an alternative: "To suddenly stop accepting discount coupons might upset our customers." But the following example is awkward:

Awkward:	The veterinarian proposed to, if Ms. Jones agreed, postpone the dog's surgery until August.
Revised:	The veterinarian proposed to postpone the dog's surgery until August, if Ms. Jones agreed.

25f Make certain that introductory verbal phrases relate clearly to the subject of the sentence.

Modifiers are said to *dangle* when they do not logically modify a word or expression in the sentence. Most often, a *dangling modifier* does not correctly refer to the subject of the sentence:

Dangling:	Driving to the old house, my left ear started to hurt.

In this sentence, the reader will mistakenly assume that the subject of the sentence *(ear)* is also the understood subject of the verbal *(driving)*. The result is absurd: Did the ear drive? The writer should have written the following:

25

Improved: While *I* was driving to the old house, my left ear started to hurt.

The improved sentence illustrates one way of correcting a dangling modifier: supply the necessary words to make the phrase into a complete dependent clause. It is relatively easy to supply missing words when the dangling modifier is an *elliptical phrase* (a predicate with the subject and part of the verb implied but not expressed):

Dangling: While watching the movie, their car was stolen.

Corrected: While *they* were watching the movie, their car was stolen.

At other times, the best way to correct a dangling modifier may be to revise the independent clause, as in the following examples:

Dangling: *Driving recklessly,* Allen's Miata crashed into a city bus. (dangling participial phrase)

Corrected: Driving recklessly, Allen crashed his Miata into a city bus.

Dangling: *To succeed in show business,* a great deal of hard work and luck are needed. (dangling infinitive)

Corrected: To succeed in show business, one needs a great deal of hard work and luck.

These examples illustrate two common causes of dangling modifiers. In the first sentence, the word that the phrase is intended to modify is not the subject of the sentence but a possessive modifying the subject *(Allen's).* In the second sentence, the independent clause is in the passive voice (see **23e**). Note that the revisions are both logical and more direct.

Some verbal phrases (called *absolute constructions*) refer not to a single word but to the whole idea of a sentence; hence, they do not dangle.

Acceptable: *Generally speaking,* most families have problems.

Acceptable: *Considering the cost of gasoline,* the bus fare looks quite reasonable.

25g Be certain that concluding clauses and phrases modify the word intended.

Illogical: Tom Hanks won an Oscar for *Forrest Gump,* his greatest role. (Was the movie his role?)

Corrected: Tom Hanks won an Oscar for his greatest role, Forrest Gump, in the movie of the same name.

Exercise

26

Rewrite the following sentences, correcting any dangling or misplaced modifiers.

1. Without money or prospects, Jonathan's future was dim.
2. While swimming in the mist of happy memories, my finger started to twitch.
3. She is only happy when she establishes a clear schedule for a project.
4. Jeremy nearly finished the race in 23 seconds, a school record.
5. Be it stupid or sublime, a reader should be able to experience a story's conclusion without having to wait for the next issue of the magazine.
6. I considered what Mr. Perkins had told me carefully.
7. To succeed at golf, a good grip is required.
8. Peering into the future, trouble was expected.
9. Yesterday, Roberta only worked three hours.
10. Considering all the time and expense that went into decorating the Christmas tree, the results are disappointing.

pred
26 Make subject and predicate relate logically to each other.

As a main verb, *be* links a subject with a complement: "The *piano is* an old *Steinway.* The *news is good.*" A common error called *faulty predication* occurs when the subject and complement cannot be logically joined:

Faulty:	His job was a reporter for the *Sun Times.*
Correct:	He worked as a reporter for the *Sun Times.* (he = reporter)
Faulty:	The art competition is a chance to prove what a painter can do.
Correct:	The art competition provides a chance to prove what a painter can do.
Or:	The art competition is an event that proves what a painter can do. (art competition = event)

In general, avoid following a form of *be* with adverb clauses beginning with *where, when,* and *because:*

26

Faulty:	Someone said that diplomacy is when one lies gracefully for his country.
Correct:	Someone said that diplomacy is lying gracefully for one's country.

Faulty:	The reason I got a new smartphone was because my old one was stolen.
Correct:	The reason I got a new smartphone was that my old one was stolen.
Or:	I got a new smartphone because my old one was stolen.

Faulty predication can occur with verbs other than *be* whenever the subject and predicate do not fit together logically:

Faulty:	Neglected children must be dealt with severely.
Correct:	Child neglect must be dealt with severely.

Exercise

A. Mark *E* for those sentences in which the subject and complement are compatible, *X* for those with faulty predication.

1. A malfunctioning computer is a ghastly experience for a writer working on deadline.

2. London, England, is where the 2012 Summer Olympics were held.

3. The city was a mob of athletes, media figures, and spectators.

4. September was when the city got back to normal.

5. Justin's new executive position is much better compensated than was his old one.

6. Exceeding the posted speed limit is the most common criminal violation in the United States.

7. The reason is because motorists believe these restrictions to be absurd.

8. Actual battle conditions are when the military can evaluate a soldier's ability.

9. However, virtual reality offers one way to test a soldier prior to military conflict.

10. A good detective novel is an evening well spent.

B. Reword the sentences that you marked *X*.

comp Compare only things that are logically comparable.

27

A common fault involves comparing a characteristic of one thing with another thing instead of with its corresponding characteristic:

Faulty:	Disney's theme parks are visited by more people than any other company. (comparing *parks* to *company*)
Correct:	Disney's theme parks are visited by more people than *those of* any other company.

Faulty:	A technician's income is generally lower than a scientist. (*income* compared to *scientist*)
Correct:	A technician's income is generally lower than a scientist's.
Or:	A technician's income is generally lower than *that of* a scientist.

Many comparisons are faulty because the word *other* has been omitted:

Faulty:	Miranda is smarter than any child in her class.
Correct:	Miranda is smarter than any *other* child in her class.

Many faulty comparisons are ambiguous:

Faulty:	Tim likes Amy much more than George. (Who likes whom?)
Correct:	Tim likes Amy much more than George does.
Or:	Tim likes Amy much more than he likes George.

Faulty:	Pensacola is farther from Chicago than Miami.
Correct:	Pensacola is farther from Chicago than it is from Miami.

Many comparisons are incomplete because words such as *that* and *as* are omitted.

Faulty:	Reggae is as good if not better than other types of popular music.
Correct:	Reggae is as good as, if not better than, other types of popular music.
Or:	Reggae is as good as other types of popular music, if not better.

Faulty:	The poetic style of Vaughan is much like Traherne.

| **Correct:** | The poetic style of Vaughan is much like that of Traherne. |
| **Or:** | . . . is much like Traherne's. |

28

Exercise

A. Mark *E* for those sentences with effective comparisons and *X* for those with ineffective comparisons.

1. On one dismal Saturday, my golf score was higher than any golfer's in the tournament.

2. Bobby loves pork chops more than his wife.

3. Plagiarism is as serious if not more so than any other problem involving academic integrity.

4. Technically, failure to yield the right-of-way causes more accidents than speeding does.

5. Cats have an easier life than any animal on the planet.

6. The baseball cap is more common in the United States than any other type of hat.

7. The swimmer's graceful stroke was like a swan.

8. Ed could never tell Karen's voice from Anne.

9. The traffic flow is better this summer than it has been for years.

10. I am much colder than yesterday.

B. Reword the sentences that you marked *X*.

comp

28 Use parallel structures effectively.

When you express two or more ideas that are equal in emphasis, use parallel grammatical structures: nouns with nouns, infinitives with infinitives, adverb clauses with adverb clauses. Parallel structures clearly and emphatically indicate parallel ideas.

| **Effective:** | The old man was haunted by his past, tortured by his failures, confused by his successes, and terrified by his future. (verb phrases) |

Effective: It is better, Hippocrates said, for a doctor to do nothing than to do harm to the patient. (infinitive phrases)

Effective: Because of its acute hearing, because of its playful imagination, and most of all because of its amazing intelligence, the porpoise is a rare creature of the sea. (introductory phrases)

28a In parallel structures, use equal grammatical constructions.

A common error among inexperienced writers is faulty parallelism—treating unlike grammatical structures as if they were parallel. This practice upsets the balance that the reader expects in a coordinate structure. Below are some of the more common types of faulty parallelism:

Faulty: Albert has two great ambitions: running a business and to become a millionaire.

Correct: Albert has two great ambitions: running a business and becoming a millionaire.

Or: . . . to run a business and to become a millionaire.

Faulty: Andrea is intelligent, charming, and knows how to dress.

Correct: Andrea is intelligent, charming, and well dressed.

28b Repeat necessary words to make parallels clear to the reader.

Awkward, confusing sentences often result if you do not repeat needed prepositions, signs of infinitives (*to*), auxiliary verbs, or other words needed to make a parallel clear:

Faulty: North Carolina is well-known for its beautiful mountains, found in the western region of the state, and its beaches, rivers, and farms.

Correct: North Carolina is well-known for its beautiful mountains, found in the western region of the state, and *for* its beaches, rivers, and farms.

Faulty: I told my daughter that she should be more realistic and driving two more miles to work would not be a huge problem.

Correct: I told my daughter that she should be more realistic and *that* driving two more miles to work would not be a huge problem.

28c Always use parallel structures with correlative conjunctions such as *both . . . and* or *neither . . . nor.*

Correlative conjunctions can join two closely related ideas, but both ideas should be in the same grammatical form. The most common correlatives are *both . . . and, either . . . or, not only . . . but also, neither . . . nor, whether . . . or.*

> **Faulty:** Jack Nicklaus is well respected both for his outstanding career in golf and as a shrewd businessperson.
>
> **Correct:** Jack Nicklaus is well respected both for his outstanding career in golf and for his shrewd business sense.
>
> **Faulty:** He is admired not only by those who recognize his amazing athletic skills, but also financial analysts applaud his business career.
>
> **Correct:** He is admired not only by those who recognize his athletic skills but also by financial analysts, who applaud his business career.

Exercise

A. Mark with *E* those sentences that are effective and with *X* those containing faulty parallelism.

1. I have three desires: to succeed in business, to marry, and have children.

2. To follow the letter of the law is not the same as following the spirit of the law.

3. "Son, you need to decide whether to fish or to cut bait," said my father.

4. Driving into the sun can lead to fatigue, headaches, and is irritating.

5. The summer camp for children is safe, convenient, and to the benefit of working mothers.

6. Most people enjoy having a meal cooked for them, their food served, and someone to clean up the aftermath.

7. In my first year with the company, I received many financial bonuses and several new clients for the firm.

28

8. The students on this campus should be opposed to and protest this blatant disregard for their freedoms.

9. Ellen wants to be a teacher and develop her skills as a consultant.

10. The new car that I want is beautiful, fast, but costs an arm and a leg.

B. Reword the sentences that you marked *X*.

Punctuation and Mechanics

PART

II

A Guide to Style

Editing for Punctuation and Mechanics

29

Punctuation marks represent much of the information we transmit in speaking when we pause and raise or lower our voices—information such as where a sentence ends and whether the sentence is a question or a statement. Punctuation marks also signal things that we cannot communicate easily in speech, such as quoting someone directly. Although we can often "hear" when we need a punctuation mark, such as when we hear where we need commas in this sentence, we cannot always tell which mark to use. The only sure way to punctuate correctly is to know the conventions.

' 29 Use commas to separate certain elements of a sentence.

The comma is the most widely used—and misused—mark of punctuation. One of its most common uses is to separate clauses and phrases, as in these patterns: (1) commas used with coordinating conjunctions to form compound sentences, (2) commas used after introductory elements, (3) commas used to separate items in a series, and (4) commas used to separate coordinate adjectives.

29a Place a comma before a coordinating conjunction joining two independent clauses.

Use a comma before a coordinating conjunction *(and, but, or, nor, for, yet,* or *so)* when it joins two independent clauses to form a compound sentence. A comma without a coordinating conjunction between independent clauses is not enough and will cause a major error (see comma splice, **49**).:

Incorrect:	Everyone wants to live forever but no one wants to get old.
Correct:	Everyone wants to live forever, but no one wants to get old.
Incorrect:	Jack read innumerable warnings about smoking so he gave up reading.
Correct:	Jack read innumerable warnings about smoking, so he gave up reading.

Be careful with *so* as a connector:

Incorrect:	I took another job, so my wife could finish her degree.
Correct:	I took another job so [that] my wife could finish her degree.

As mentioned in Chapter 6, the subordinator *that* is frequently left out of sentences. The incorrect sentence above is a good example of a problem that can result from this habit. The sentence *looks* like a compound, but in reality it is made up of an independent clause followed by a dependent clause.

If the clauses are very short and closely related, you may omit the comma, but it is generally safer to include it. (Why take chances?)

Acceptable: It is dark and I am alone.

Better: It is dark, and I am alone.

Note the difference between a compound sentence (one with two independent clauses) and a sentence containing a compound predicate (double verb):

Correct: Ms. Hernandez *graded* the tests and *entered* the scores in her database.

Correct: Ministers *write* and *preach* many sermons each year.

In each of these sentences, no comma is used before *and* because it does not join two independent clauses.

29b Place a comma after an introductory dependent clause or a long introductory phrase.

A dependent clause resembles an independent clause in that it has a subject and a verb. However, an introductory dependent clause always begins with a subordinating conjunction (*although, because, since, while, after,* for example—see the list on page 295). Written alone, a dependent clause is a sentence fragment (see **48**), but it is properly used in conjunction with an independent clause. A phrase, on the other hand, is missing a subject, a verb, or both.

Incorrect: Although murder is seen as a crime this prohibition is largely voided during military combat.

Correct: Although murder is seen as a crime, this prohibition is largely voided during military combat. (introductory dependent clause—requires comma)

Incorrect: If the rain would stop we could play golf.

Correct: If the rain would stop, we could play golf. (introductory dependent clause—requires comma)

Incorrect: Fighting hard against the crashing waves and shifting currents the small boat barely managed to avoid capsizing.

Correct: Fighting hard against the crashing waves and shifting currents, the small boat barely managed to avoid capsizing. (long introductory phrase—requires comma)

Incorrect: Although it was hard to believe the story was true. (dependent clause incorrectly used as sentence fragment)

Correct: Although it was hard to believe, the story was true.

29

Commas are optional after brief introductory phrases. However, including the comma is a more conservative approach, and if there is any possibility of confusing the reader, use the comma. Also, always include a comma after an introductory element that comes before an imperative.

Acceptable:	After this month all my bills will be paid.
Better:	After this month, all my bills will be paid.

Acceptable:	In 1989 the Berlin Wall became an anachronism.
Better:	In 1989, the Berlin Wall became an anachronism.

Comma needed:	In 2011, 438 new employees joined our corporation.
Comma needed:	After today, start parking your car in its assigned place.

There is usually no need for a comma when an adverb clause follows the independent clause:

No comma:	He walked as if he owned the whole town.

However, a comma is needed before clauses that follow the independent clause and add a contrasting idea or are loosely connected to the independent clause:

Comma needed:	Mr. Walker decided to apply for the programming position, although he had not touched a computer in two years.
Comma needed:	An animal's habitat is the area in which that animal lives, whereas an ecosystem is made up of many habitats.

29c Place commas between items in a series.

Place a comma after each item except the last one in a series of words, phrases, or clauses unless all the items are joined by conjunctions. In a series with the last two items joined by a conjunction (a, b, *and* c), make sure that you place a comma before the conjunction to prevent a possible misreading. Some writers omit this comma, but the safer practice is to use it.

Incorrect:	My father's pickles are made from a combination of cucumbers vinegar and dill.
Correct:	My father's pickles are made from a combination of cucumbers, vinegar, and dill.

Incorrect:	In mountainous areas, hikers should dress carefully plan an exact route and let friends know how long the excursion will take.

29

Correct:	In mountainous areas, hikers should dress carefully, plan an exact route, and let friends know how long the excursion will take.

Incorrect:	Consider the feeding habits of the following mammals: bears wolves wildcats rabbits foxes and cats and dogs.
Correct:	Consider the feeding habits of the following mammals: bears, wolves, wildcats, rabbits, foxes, and cats and dogs. (Because the *and* before *cats* makes *cats and dogs* a single item, no comma is placed after *cats*.)

29d Use commas to separate coordinate adjectives.

Coordinate adjectives modify a noun equally:

 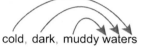

You can check for coordinate adjectives by placing *and* between them or by reversing their order:

long and windy speech   muddy, dark, cold waters

Do not place commas between cumulative adjectives, those in which one adjective modifies the rest of the expression:

In the above example, *severe* modifies not just *difficulties* but *economic difficulties. And* could not be inserted between *severe* and *economic,* nor could the adjectives be reversed. Therefore, no comma is used.

Incorrect:	One of the dusty, battered, antique violins sold for $23,000.
Correct:	One of the dusty, battered antique violins sold for $23,000.

Incorrect:	We replaced our old, food processor.
Correct:	We replaced our old food processor.

30

Exercise

Delete unnecessary commas and add commas where necessary in the following sentences. If the sentence is correct, mark it *C*.

1. Maria Rodriguez was born in Puerto Rico but she moved to Atlanta with her family.

2. Maria liked Atlanta very much but her family moved to Florida when she was nine.

3. Although Maria spoke only Spanish before the move, she learned English very quickly.

4. There were many Hispanic children in Maria's new school so she felt comfortable there.

5. Even though Eastwood Elementary was small it was well funded and carefully managed.

6. In fourth grade, Maria was taught by Ms. Karnes Mr. Rivera and Mrs. Ogletree.

7. Because Maria made very high grades in her first year at Eastwood Elementary the principal asked her parents about allowing Maria to go directly to sixth grade.

8. Despite the fact that Mr. Rodriguez thought that the idea was a good one his wife convinced him that Maria was better off staying in class with her friends.

9. Maria's mother was concerned that Maria would have been anxious about skipping a year that she still needed to adjust to the area and that she would have been a year younger than most of her classmates.

10. Maria was happy, and proceeded to do even better in fifth grade.

30 Use commas to set interrupting elements apart from the rest of the sentence.

Commas are also used to set apart groups of words that interrupt the normal flow of a sentence. Four such interrupters are especially common: (1) nonrestrictive modifiers, (2) nonrestrictive appositives, (3) parenthetical expressions, and (4) transitional adverbs or phrases.

30a Use commas to separate a nonrestrictive modifier from the rest of the sentence.

A **restrictive modifier** defines or restricts the noun or pronoun that it modifies. For example, the noun *candidate* can refer to any of those people seeking office, but *candidate who supports higher taxes* refers to someone from a much more limited group. In the sentence "A candidate who supports higher taxes cannot get elected in this state," the modifier *(who supports higher taxes)* is needed to limit the noun *(candidate)* so that it refers to someone in the smaller group. If the modifier is removed, the sentence is no longer accurate: "A candidate cannot get elected in this state."

A **nonrestrictive modifier,** on the other hand, is not needed to limit the noun or pronoun it modifies: "Phil Spender, *who supports higher taxes,* cannot get elected in this state." Here the subject already refers to just one person, so the modifier simply adds information. Thus, the modifier is non-restrictive.

Enclose a nonrestrictive modifier in commas:

Incorrect: My father who was born in Alabama retired in California.

Correct: My father, who was born in Alabama, retired in California.

Note: Be careful to place a comma at both ends of a nonrestrictive element (unless, of course, the element ends the sentence).

Do not set off a restrictive modifier with commas:

Incorrect: Children, who are hyperactive, should be examined regularly by a pediatrician.

Correct: Children who are hyperactive should be examined regularly by a pediatrician.

Incorrect: Stores, which have electronic checkpoints at exits, have noticed a decrease in shoplifting.

Correct: Stores that have electronic checkpoints at exits have noticed a decrease in shoplifting. (restrictive)

Correct: O'Brien Stores, which have electronic checkpoints at exits, have noticed a decrease in shoplifting. (nonrestrictive)

The pronoun *that* is normally used to begin restrictive modifiers, and *which* is used to introduce nonrestrictive modifiers. (If the subject is a person or people, *who* is used, whether the modifier is restrictive or nonrestrictive.) The usage of *that* and *which* can cause problems; in Standard English, *which* can replace *that* in a restrictive context:

Correct: The car *that* is at the end of the parking lot is mine.

Correct: The car *which* is at the end of the parking lot is mine.

30

However, *that* cannot replace *which* in a nonrestrictive context:

Incorrect: My apartment, *that* is located at the corner of Vine and Illinois, is being renovated.

Correct: My apartment, *which* is located at the corner of Vine and Illinois, is being renovated.

As much as possible, avoid using *which* to introduce a restrictive modifier. Your decisions about punctuation will be made easier.

It is often difficult to determine whether a modifier is restrictive or non-restrictive. Study the sentence both with and without the modifier. If the meanings are substantially different, the expression is restrictive and no commas are needed.

Correct: For many people who have severe vision problems, the exam for a driver's license is a traumatic experience.

30b Use commas to separate a nonrestrictive appositive from the rest of the sentence.

An appositive is a noun or a noun phrase that restates, explains, or supplements a preceding noun:

Jon Stewart, *the political satirist,* grew up in New Jersey.

Most appositives are nonrestrictive (see **30a**) and can be deleted from the sentence without changing its meaning. Enclose them in commas:

Incorrect: Flannery O'Connor the great American writer who lived in Georgia died at age thirty-nine in 1964.

Correct: Flannery O'Connor, the great American writer who lived in Georgia, died at age thirty-nine in 1964.

Incorrect: When I need to relax, I turn on Macy Gray my favorite singer.

Correct: When I need to relax, I turn on Macy Gray, my favorite singer.

A restrictive appositive, like a restrictive modifier, is essential to the meaning of the sentence and so should not be set off with commas:

Correct: My sister *Karen* always avoids using the word *dumb.*

In this sentence, the writer is a person with more than one sister. If, however, the writer had only one sister, the appositive would be nonrestrictive and would require commas:

30

> **Correct:**   My sister, *Karen*, always avoids using the word *dumb*.

30c Use commas to separate a parenthetical element from the rest of the sentence.

Parenthetical elements are words, phrases, or clauses inserted into a sentence to clarify or emphasize a point or to give extra information. They interrupt the basic sentence structure, so they should be set off with commas:

> **Correct:**   My husband, as I had predicted, hated the shirt I bought him for Christmas.
>
> **Correct:**   Reckless driving, of course, is something to be feared.
>
> **Correct:**   A vast number of exhibits, large and small, will be featured in the Exposition Building.

Use commas to set off nouns that name the reader or listener in direct address.

> **Correct:**   We've already gone over that, Bob.
>
> **Correct:**   Charles, Anne, and Sara, please see me after class.

Use commas for mild interjections:

> **Correct:**   Well, I guess I have no choice in the matter.

Commas also prevent misreadings:

> **Incorrect:**   From forty five were selected.
>
> **Correct:**   From forty, five were selected.

30d Use commas to set off conjunctive adverbs and transitional expressions.

Words such as *however, moreover,* and *nevertheless* and phrases such as *for instance* and *on the other hand* are often used as parenthetical expressions to provide transition between independent clauses, sentences, or paragraphs. (See the list on page 294.) Set them off with commas:

> **Correct:**   Hemingway's Americans sound more like Hemingway than Americans; *on the other hand,* they could not be anything other than Hemingway Americans.
>
> **Correct:**   *Therefore,* many readers find Hemingway's style American in a special way.

31 If the transitional word or phrase appears within the independent clause, use a pair of commas:

Correct: Many viewers, *for example*, object to the lack of character development in action films.

Exercise

Delete any unneeded commas in the following sentences, and add commas where needed. If a sentence is correct, mark it *C*.

1. One class Maria found difficult however was physical education.
2. Children like Maria who was small for her age are likely to find physical competition difficult.
3. Maria, who would undergo a growth spurt two years later, tried to be patient.
4. On the other hand the hour-long gym class seemed to take forever.
5. Everything Mrs. Rodriguez said will work out for the best.
6. Most children, at that age, hate mathematics.
7. Maria, however, found math intriguing.
8. Maria's best friend April stated that if math were to disappear, the world would be a better place.
9. Math, biology, and English April believed were ridiculously difficult.
10. Young students, who develop an aversion to one or more subjects, are likely to carry that aversion throughout their academic career.

31 Use commas in numbers, addresses, titles, and quotations.

Separate the day of the month from the year with commas:

October 24, 1987   December 23, 2006

When only a month and year are given, the comma is not used:

February 1941

The inverted form (for example, *1 December 2007*) also requires no commas.

Commas separate numbers into thousands, millions, and so on:

31

3,916   4,816,317,212

Within sentences (not on envelopes), items in addresses are separated by commas. Notice that no comma appears between the state name and the Zip code:

Toledo, Ohio

400 7th Street, New Kensington, PA 15068

121 87th Street, Brooklyn, NY 11209

In sentences, the final item of an address or a date is also followed by a comma:

Working in Phoenix, Arizona, has many compensations.

March 12, 1992, was a day he never forgot.

Use commas to separate titles and degrees from proper names:

Jane B. Nelson, Ed.D.

Joseph Hernandez, M.D.

Stephanie Pew, Ph.D., C.D.P., C.D.E.

Albert M. Johnston, Jr., took over as chief clerk.

Exception: Michael Raleigh III is our family attorney.

Use commas to introduce direct quotations and to separate quoted material from the rest of the sentence:

Dr. Guber asked, "When is her test scheduled?"

"I'm not sure," I answered, "that I really know."

Use commas to set off expressions such as *he said* and *she replied:*

"The future," she wrote, "is just the past getting younger."

He said, "I pull habits out of rats."

"No, you don't," she replied.

32

If the original quotation ends with a period, change the period to a comma when the quotation is followed by nonquoted material. In all cases, place the comma inside quotation marks. Omit the comma if the quotation ends with an exclamation point or question mark:

"Do you want to register?" *[no comma]* Ms. LaPorte asked.

Exercise

Supply needed commas in the following sentences. If a sentence is correct, mark it *C*.

1. The principal of Maria's new middle school located in Clickville was Lionel Jones M.Ed.

2. Maria started seventh grade on August 23 2010.

3. When Maria first saw the school, she said, "What a dump," even though she eventually came to like it.

4. Mrs. Rodriguez, not happy to hear Maria's comment, said "I hope you're not developing an attitude."

5. Andrea Walsh, Maria's biology teacher was born in Minneapolis, Minnesota on July 7 1965 and moved to Clickville Florida on August 3 1992.

6. After the first biology class, Maria said "Ms. Walsh is the coolest old person I've ever met."

7. On February 5, 2011, Ms. Walsh took her biology class on a field trip to the Reynolds Wildlife Preserve in Gidneyville, a nearby town.

8. February 2011 was a month Maria would remember.

9. Her father was promoted on 17 February.

10. Mr. Rodriguez's new contract started on March 1 2011, and continued through February 28 2012.

no ,

32 Omit all unnecessary commas.

Unnecessary commas will make your reader pause needlessly or look for connections that are not there. Use a comma only when any of the guidelines above calls for one or when you are certain that a comma is necessary to prevent misreading.

Do not use a comma to separate a subject from its verb:

Incorrect: The cholesterol problem caused by eating too many eggs, involves the yolk more than the white.

Correct: The cholesterol problem caused by eating too many eggs involves the yolk more than the white.

Do not use a comma to separate a verb from its object:

Incorrect: Ed always believed, that the weather was a farmer's enemy.

Correct: Ed always believed that the weather was a farmer's enemy.

Do not use a comma before a coordinating conjunction except when the conjunction precedes the last item in a series or joins two independent clauses:

Incorrect: Walking through the park, and lying in the shade of the water oaks are some of my favorite leisure activities.

Correct: Walking through the park and lying in the shade of the water oaks are some of my favorite leisure activities.

Do not separate a restrictive modifier from the rest of the sentence (see **30a**):

Incorrect: The two bills, that had the greatest popular support, failed in the Senate.

Correct: The two bills that had the greatest popular support failed in the Senate.

Do not use a comma before the first item or after the last item of a series:

Incorrect: History, language, and art, are prized elements of all cultures.

Correct: History, language, and art are prized elements of all cultures.

Exercise

Delete any unnecessary commas in the following sentences. If a sentence is correct, mark it *C*.

1. Initially, Maria said, that she didn't like middle school.

2. Her mother pointed out that you can't always judge a book, by its cover.

3. This is especially true, Mrs. Rodriguez pointed out, in terms of schools.

33

4. Mr. Rodriguez had just finished reading an article titled, "School Funding Problems in Florida."

5. Then he read a book, about the same subject, titled *Public Schools and Their Trauma.*

6. Mrs. Rodriguez, likes to say, that schools are a hundred times more important than sports stadiums.

7. Mr. Rodriguez both knows, and respects her beliefs.

8. Schools, that were built before 1990, have aged badly.

9. The problem of funding new schools, was debated at a public meeting in Click County.

10. Dr. Edwina Wallace, superintendent of schools, said, new state funds, and matching federal funds, were essential to the funding issue.

33 Use periods after statements or commands and in abbreviations and decimals.

The period ranks second to the comma as the most common mark of punctuation. It is one of the easiest to use properly, serving three basic functions: to end sentences, to end abbreviations, and to separate decimals.

33a Use a period after a sentence that is not a direct question or an exclamation.

The examples below show three types of sentences ended by periods:

Direct statement:	Spiritualism is alive and flourishing.
Indirect question:	I wonder why Miguel looks so happy.
Instruction or command:	Cut the nonsense, please.

33b Use periods according to conventions in abbreviations and decimals.

Periods are required after most abbreviations, as shown below. See **45** for help in using abbreviations.

Ms.   Mrs.   Mr.   Jr.   Dec.   a.m.   p.m.   e.g.   i.e.   A.D.   B.C.

Do not use periods in acronyms (abbreviations pronounced as words) and abbreviations of company names and governmental agencies:

NATO   CORE   ITT   FBI   CIA   NOW

Most writers omit periods from capitalized abbreviations:

JFK   USA   NJ

Use a period as the decimal point in a decimal fraction, between a whole number and decimals, and between dollars and cents:

.007   .95   98.6°   3.1416 $.19 $36,500.48

Include the period *inside* quotation marks (see **40c**):

Incorrect: "The only way to get rid of a temptation," Oscar Wilde said, "is to yield to it".

Correct: "The only way to get rid of temptation," Oscar Wilde said, "is to yield to it."

? 34 Use a question mark to indicate a direct question.

Question marks are end stops for direct questions; they can also be used within sentences, as shown here:

Correct: Why has Frank Herbert's *Dune* remained so popular through the years?

Correct: I want to go, but how can I?

Correct: "When will we get there?" she asked.

Correct: Sergeant Walsh called in three backup units (who knows why?) after the situation had been resolved.

Correct: You actually like Sean? (Notice that the question mark here shows the reader how to read the sentence; a period would produce an entirely different meaning.)

Use a period after an indirect question:

Correct: Brad asked if he could turn in his essay a day late.

35 ! 35 Use an exclamation point to show extreme emphasis.

An exclamation point shows extreme emotion or disbelief and can end a sentence, an interjection, or a clause or phrase. Do not overuse the exclamation point; instead, try to achieve emphasis through your choice of appropriate words. Do not use a comma or period following an exclamation point.

Correct:	What a night we've had!
Correct:	Get out of my way! Now!
Correct:	You can't be serious!

Exercise

Correct any punctuation errors in the following sentences. If a sentence is correct, mark it *C*.

1. Maria told April that she really liked history class!

2. April wondered how someone as old as Mr. Salinger could be such an interesting teacher?

3. "Why is age such a big deal," Maria inquired?

4. "I guess I don't know many older people—do you?"

5. "Just my parents, and they're almost forty!"

6. Maria learned that her grandfather—or was it her great-grandfather— lived to be ninety-seven.

7. "That's impossible," she shouted when her father told her the story.

8. "No one lives to be that old!"

9. "Did he really live that long?"

10. Maria asked her father to tell her more.

36 ; 36 Use semicolons to separate independent clauses and punctuated items in a series.

The semicolon is an intermediate mark, stronger than a comma but weaker than a period. It is used only between grammatically equal units—two or more independent clauses or two or more items in a series.

36a Use a semicolon to connect two independent clauses not joined by a coordinating conjunction.

36

In a compound sentence (two or more independent clauses), join the clauses with a semicolon unless you use a coordinating conjunction (*and, or, nor, for, but, yet,* and *so*) and a comma (see **49**):

Incorrect:	What is called "adult entertainment" is rarely adult, it is at best adolescent. (comma splice)
Correct:	What is called "adult entertainment" is rarely adult; it is at best adolescent.

Incorrect:	The student parking lot is half empty at 3:15 p.m. this must be a commuter campus. (fused sentence)
Correct:	The student parking lot is half empty at 3:15 p.m.; this must be a commuter campus.

Incorrect:	Personal safety is threatened not only in the home, it is also threatened on the highways and at the workplace. (comma splice)
Correct:	Personal safety is threatened not only in the home; it is also threatened on the highways and at the workplace.

Use a semicolon before a conjunctive adverb (*however, hence, therefore,* etc.) or transitional phrase (*on the contrary,* etc.—see the lists on page 294) that introduces an independent clause:

Incorrect:	The casual sports fan will always be interested in big-name athletes, however, their greed is threatening to destroy professional sports.
Correct:	The casual sports fan will always be interested in big-name athletes; however, their greed is threatening to destroy professional sports.

Incorrect:	My opponent's so-called tax overhaul is not a carefully designed and equitable system, on the contrary, it is clearly meant to appease the special interests that my opponent has always served.
Correct:	My opponent's so-called tax overhaul is not a carefully designed and equitable system; on the contrary, it is clearly meant to appease the special interests that my opponent has always served.

36

Before a coordinating conjunction joining two long independent clauses that already contain internal punctuation, it is acceptable to use a semicolon rather than a comma:

> My father never mentioned Louis Armstrong, except to forbid us to play his records; but there was a picture of him on our wall for a long time.
> —*James Baldwin,* Notes of a Native Son

Do *not* use a semicolon after a dependent clause when it precedes an independent clause:

Incorrect:	Although the skies looked threatening; the race began on time.
Correct:	Although the skies looked threatening, the race began on time. (dependent clause with independent clause)
Correct:	The skies looked threatening; nevertheless, the race began on time. (both independent clauses)

36b Use semicolons to separate items in a series when the items themselves contain commas.

When punctuating a series of items that contains commas, such as dates or cities and states, use semicolons between the items to avoid confusion with the internal commas:

Incorrect:	Bonnie has already attended colleges in Fort Collins, Colorado, Tempe, Arizona, and Galesburg, Illinois.
Correct:	Bonnie has already attended colleges in Fort Collins, Colorado; Tempe, Arizona; and Galesburg, Illinois.
Incorrect:	Vicky met several uninvited guests at the door: Bruno, her older brother, Tina, her former roommate, and Robert, her secretary.
Correct:	Vicky met several uninvited guests at the door: Bruno, her older brother; Tina, her former roommate; and Robert, her secretary.

Exercise

In the following sentences, replace incorrectly used commas with semicolons, and replace incorrectly used semicolons with commas. If a sentence is correct, mark it *C*.

1. For her research paper in Mr. Salinger's class, Maria decided to write about the history of Click County; choosing the subject after hearing Mr. Salinger speak on the radio.

2. Maria started work on her essay, April, however, was undecided.

3. Although the paper was not due for five weeks; Maria wanted to give herself plenty of time.

4. Click County was named after Major Ezekiel Click, who was born in Chattanooga, Tennessee; and joined the military during the Civil War.

5. Major Click traveled with his regiment to a small town in Florida; called Gidneyville.

6. The major was separated from his troops, he had been caught in a powerful storm while hunting in a swamp.

7. Myron Parker, a sergeant, Obidiah Welles, a corporal, and Johnson Baker, a private, searched for Click for three days.

8. Click eventually became frustrated, he abandoned his military career and bought a farm.

9. Everyone thought that nothing could be grown in the area of Click's farm, on the contrary, the soil was perfect for rutabagas.

10. In terms of the military, Click was a failure; as a farmer, however, he was a success.

11. Not only did Click become a wealthy man, he also became an author.

12. Despite the fact that Click was a horrible speller; he devoted his later years to his writing career.

13. Overall, Click published seven books; such as *The Virtues of Becoming Lost* and *Rutabagas and Moral Health.*

14. His books, however, did not find a wide audience.

15. Click continued writing until his death in 1918, he finished his last title, *Rutabagas and the War Effort,* three days before he died from indigestion at the age of seventy-five.

37   Use a colon to call attention to what comes next or to follow mechanical conventions.

The colon is a formal mark that calls attention to words that follow it. It also has special uses in titles, scriptural references, time references, and formal letters. Do not confuse it with the semicolon, which separates grammatically equal elements.

37

37a Use a colon to introduce a list, an explanation or intensification, an example, or (in certain cases) a quotation.

Place a colon at the end of an otherwise grammatically complete sentence to introduce a list of items, an explanation of the first part of the sentence, or an example. Do not use a colon after a verb or after *such as*. (When in doubt, ask yourself if the sentence is complete without a colon. If so, don't use the colon.)

Correct: Johnson's formula for success was simple: hard work, strict discipline, and a willingness to lie when necessary.

Correct: In my old neighborhood we lived lives of plenty: plenty of relatives, boarders, landlords, cats, fights, and cockroaches.

Incorrect: I enjoy a variety of sports, such as: baseball, swimming, tennis, and soccer.

Correct: I enjoy a variety of sports, such as baseball, swimming, tennis, and soccer.

Incorrect: The students who applied for the job were: Thomas, Sims, and Watkins.

Correct: The students who applied for the job were Thomas, Sims, and Watkins.

Incorrect: Peter is interested only in: his guitar, his motorcycle, and his girlfriend. (The words before the colon do not form a grammatically complete sentence.)

Correct: Peter is interested only in his guitar, his motorcycle, and his girlfriend.

Colons may separate two independent clauses when the clauses are very closely related and the second explains or intensifies the first:

Correct: Reynaldo couldn't decide what to do or where to turn: he was stymied.

Correct: Yesterday I realized my age: my son asked if I remembered an old-time singer named Jim Morrison. (The second part of the sentence explains the first part; the colon = *that is.*)

Use a colon to introduce a long quotation (more than one sentence) or a shorter quotation not introduced by a word such as *said, remarked,* or *replied:*

Correct: I remember my reaction to a typically luminous observation of Kierkegaard's: "Such a relation which relates itself to its own self (that is to say, a self) must either have constituted itself or have been constituted by another."

—*Woody Allen,* "My Philosophy"

38

| Correct: | Consider the words of John Donne: "No man is an island entire of itself. . . ." |

37b Use a colon between title and subtitle, between Bible chapter and verse, between hours and minutes, and after the salutation of a formal letter.

Scripture:	Genesis 1:7	John 3:1
Time references:	3:00	1:17 p.m.
Salutations:	Dear Ms. Jones:	Dear Sir or Madam:
Subtitles:	*Greek Tragedy: A Literary Study*	
	The Fields of Light: An Experiment in Critical Reading	

Exercise

In the following sentences, mark any incorrectly used punctuation and insert colons where necessary. If a sentence is correct, mark it *C*.

1. Maria found that Click County had one characteristic in common with the surrounding counties, its economy was based on agriculture.

2. Ezekiel Click had given the county its motto "The family farm is where the food is grown."

3. He believed the most important crop was, of course: rutabagas.

4. Maria planned to give copies of her report to: her mother, her father, and her Aunt Delores.

5. Her essay was titled "Ezekiel Click's Obsession with an Obscure Vegetable."

── 38 Use dashes to signal sharp changes or to set apart emphatic parenthetical elements.

The dash is a strong, dramatic mark that has several important uses. Unfortunately, it is often misused and overused. In college- and job-related writing, it should be used sparingly, not overused as a substitute for other punctuation.

39

38a Use a dash to signal a sharp change in thought or tone.

Correct: "There is a simple solution to every complex problem—the wrong one."

—H. L. Mencken

Correct: Wang's treatment of urban health problems is poorly researched, inaccurately documented, badly written—but why go on?

38b Use dashes to separate and emphasize a parenthetical element or to set off a parenthetical element that contains commas.

The dash is a stronger mark than the comma, indicating a longer pause in reading. It is used to give extra emphasis to parenthetical elements. It is also useful when parenthetical elements themselves contain commas:

Correct: Oviparous mammals—those that lay eggs—are strange descendants of the past.

Correct: The real Lawrence of Arabia—vain, secretive, obsessive, manipulative—remains both fascinating and infuriating.

In printed text, the dash is shown as a continuous line. However, you can also use two hyphens together with no space before or after. For hyphens, see **43**.

( ) Use parentheses to set off parenthetical material that is long or strictly supplementary.

Unlike dashes, which *emphasize* parenthetical material, and unlike commas, which relate parenthetical material to the rest of the sentence, parentheses set such material apart from the rest of the sentence and *deemphasize* it. Use parentheses for material that is not essential to the meaning of the sentence. Notice in the first example below that the period is inside the parentheses: the parenthetical material is a complete sentence and is not included in another sentence. Otherwise, put end punctuation after the final parenthesis.

Correct: Milton lived well into the Restoration period. (He died in 1674.)

Correct: Only one of the thirteen studies (see Appendix A) showed even minor irregularities.

Correct:	*Cajun* (from the word *Acadian*) refers to Louisiana culture and cuisine.

40

Exercise

In the following sentences, replace any incorrectly used parentheses or dashes with the proper punctuation. If a sentence is correct, mark it *C*.

1. Maria wrote her essay on her new PC (personal computer).

2. Her young cousin Roberto the one with the hyperactivity disorder was staying with the Rodriguez family that week.

3. Roberto's mother Mr. Rodriguez's youngest sister believed that Roberto's condition would improve over time.

4. Roberto's sisters (Xiomara, Tatiana, and Consuelo) all had to be treated for the same condition.

5. Maria believed that revising her essay should take around three hours (if she could have some privacy).

" "
40 Use quotation marks to indicate direct quotations.

Quotation marks enclose words quoted directly from another source. Use them only when you quote the exact words of your source. Indirect quotations, which report the gist of a message but not the exact words, do not need quotation marks.

40a Enclose direct quotations in double quotation marks.

Put double quotation marks around the exact words spoken or written by your source; do not enclose introductory or interrupting information, such as *she said.*

Correct:	According to Samuel Kaplan, "The social and economic segregation of suburbs also is resulting in the political segregation of suburbs."
Also correct:	Samuel Kaplan said that "the social and economic segregation of suburbs also is resulting in the political segregation of suburbs."
Correct:	"I'll beat you to the barn," Uncle Gene said, jumping onto his horse.

Do not enclose an indirect quotation in quotation marks:

Direct: According to *Robert's Rules of Order,* "The subsidiary motion to Amend . . . requires only a majority vote, even in cases where the question to be amended takes a two-thirds vote for adoption."

Indirect: *Robert's Rules of Order* says that an amendment needs only a simple majority, even when the main motion needs a two-thirds vote.

Combined: *Robert's Rules of Order* says that an amendment needs only a simple majority, "even in cases where the question to be amended takes a two-thirds vote for adoption."

For quotations of four or more typed lines, double-space, indent one inch from the left margin (use your word processing program's "format paragraph" option), and do not add quotation marks:

Correct: Roger Taylor comments on women writers:

> The Equal Rights Amendment has stimulated community interest in the issues of women's rights. Both men and women are taking a second look at the roles and expectations of women in society. The subject of women and "women writers," therefore, moves to the forefront of what should be offered to the community. (21)

In quoting poetry of more than three lines, indent each line one inch from the left margin (use your word processing program's "format paragraph" option), double-space, and do not add quotation marks (shorter quotations of poetry can be included within the text):

March storms are vast: sky split, the fall and rise,

Earth's strange sudden suckling of spring her caul.

But when stream banks are full, the beasts surprised,

Fish trapped in their sad pools, the moment falls.

Ah, me, to have the guts to face the skies:

"That week it did not need to rain at all."

40b Use single quotation marks to enclose a quotation within a quotation.

Correct: As John Ehrlichman wrote, "Nixon is the 'Man of a Thousand Facets' to me."

40c Place other punctuation marks inside or outside closing quotation marks, according to standard conventions.

40

Place periods and commas *inside* closing quotation marks.

Correct:	"No," she replied, "I wouldn't consider joining your company for that salary."
Correct:	His favorite short story is Faulkner's "That Evening Sun."
Exception:	The hero asserted, "Patience conquers all" (Joyce 21). (The period follows the source of the direct quotation; see **77a** and **78a**.)

Place question marks, exclamation points, and dashes inside the closing quotation marks when they apply directly to the quoted material:

Correct:	My mother asked her favorite question, "Where do you think you're going, young lady?"
Correct:	My response was, "Oh, no!"

When a question mark, exclamation point, or dash is not part of a direct quotation, place it outside the closing quotation marks. (If both an entire sentence and the quoted material are questions or exclamations, place the question mark or exclamation point inside the quotation marks.)

Correct:	Was it Pete Seeger or Woody Guthrie who wrote "This Land Is Your Land"?
Correct:	It was Guthrie, but wasn't Seeger the one who wrote "Where Have All the Flowers Gone?"
Correct:	Why did Jim Hubbard submit a theme with the title "An Immodest Proposal"?

Place all colons and semicolons *outside* closing quotation marks.

Correct:	In his first conference, he stated emphatically, "We will finish by July 30"; in his second conference, he hedged a bit.
Correct:	His first pronouncement was "I am not yet ready to quit": he resigned the next day.

40d Use an ellipsis (. . .) to indicate material omitted from a quotation.

An ellipsis consists of three spaced periods and is used to show that a word or words have been deleted from a quoted passage. It is usually unnecessary to use an ellipsis at the beginning of a quotation; the ellipsis is normally used

40

in the middle or at the end of a quoted sentence. When you omit material at the end of a sentence, use four dots (period plus ellipsis), with no space before the first one:

> **Correct:**   According to Dr. Peter LeWitt, "the brain may record short-term and long-term memory differently. . . . Long-term memory might be recorded more permanently."

> **Correct:**   "As soon as sensible birth control devices became widely available, women . . . began to use the new methods—when the front office allowed them to."
>
> —*Richard Cornuelle,* De-Managing America

40e Use brackets ([ ]) to mark an insertion into a quotation.

Brackets have only one commonly accepted function in text: to enclose editorial comments or other information inserted into a direct quotation. *Do not confuse parentheses with brackets.* Parentheses appear within quotations only when they are part of the quotation itself.

> **Correct:**   His response was a mild "Well, I do the best I can [debatable], but sometimes that isn't good enough."

> **Correct:**   "They [the staff] are all conscientious, honest people."

Always quote your original exactly, including errors. Insert *sic*—meaning "thus"—in brackets [*sic*] after an error to indicate that the error appears in the original:

> **Correct:**   "The civil rights movement picked up steam after President Kennedy's assassination in 1953 [*sic*]."

Exercise

Correct any errors in punctuation in the following sentences. Mark *C* if the sentence is correct.

1. In her essay, Maria quoted this passage: "One who becomes lost finds himself in a world of pure possibility. . . . Whilst others believe themselves to be in a secure environment, the one who is lost waits for Fortune's blessing."

2. Click defined the rutabaga as "a tuber [root] from heaven".

3. Maria wrote that "the rutabaga was much more important to Click than to anyone else".

4. When Maria finished her essay, her father said, "Congratulations!."

5. Mr. Rodriguez said that it was "the best thing she had ever written," Mrs. Rodriguez had some minor criticisms.

6. She asked Maria, "Don't you know how to spell *receive*"?

7. Maria found this error in one of Click's books: "The Civil War lasted seven *(sic)* years."

8. The error was in the chapter titled "Who Knows the Future?"

9. Later in this chapter, Click wrote that "harm [is] in the eye of the beholder".

10. "The future is the pudding" Click wrote, "that makes us appreciate the salad of life."

ital 41 Use underlining (italics) or quotation marks to designate titles and special types of words.

Enclose titles of articles, chapters, poems, short stories, and songs in quotation marks:

Correct:	Sergei thinks that John Updike's best short story is "A&P."
Correct:	I just read a helpful article titled "Theftproof Your Cell Phone."
Correct:	The best essay in the magazine is "Faulkner's Women."

Use italics to designate the title of a book, newspaper, periodical, play, motion picture, television program, painting or sculpture, and full-length musical composition (such as a symphony). In handwritten or typed materials, use underlining to indicate italic print.

Correct:	Dave Barry once wrote a humor column for the *Miami Herald*.
Correct:	Cheryl always keeps *The American Heritage Dictionary* and the *Information Please Almanac* close at hand.
Correct:	After becoming popular in the television series *Bosom Buddies,* Tom Hanks starred in such movies as *Philadelphia, Saving Private Ryan,* and *The Da Vinci Code.*

Avoid using both italics and quotation marks to indicate a title:

Incorrect:	One of my favorite paintings is *"The Naked Maja."*
Correct:	One of my favorite paintings is *The Naked Maja.*

41 Do not use italics or quotation marks to refer to the Bible or parts of the Bible:

> **Correct:**   Genesis is the first book of the Bible, Revelation the last.

Use italics to indicate a foreign word that is not yet a standard part of English; a scientific name of a plant, animal, disease, etc.; a word mentioned as a word; or letters or numbers used as examples:

> **Correct:**   The word *liberal* comes from Latin *liber,* meaning "free."
>
> **Correct:**   *Gauge* is now spelled *gage* in some professional journals.
>
> **Correct:**   *Dracaena marginata* is an easy plant to propagate by mound layering.
>
> **Correct:**   Social Security numbers beginning with *3* come generally from the Midwest.

Some writers use italics or quotation marks to give a word or phrase special emphasis, but you should do so very sparingly. Avoid enclosing slang in quotation marks as a form of apology. Using emphatic wording is a much more effective approach.

Exercise

Correct any sentences in which italics or quotation marks are improperly used. If a sentence is correct, mark it *C.*

1. Click always carried a copy of the "Old Testament."

2. Maria saw a copy of one of Click's letters and realized that his capital F's and T's were almost impossible to distinguish.

3. Click's writing style was modeled on that of T. R. Williams, editor of the "Florida Harvester."

4. *My Beginnings* is the first chapter of "The Virtues of Becoming Lost."

5. At a used bookstore, Maria found a biography of Click titled "Clickville's Pioneer."

6. Maria called this book a wonder.

7. She learned that Click's lucky number was 8.

8. "Lost in the Swamp," the fourth chapter of the biography, tells of Click's belief that moss always grows on the north side of trees.

9. This faux pas meant that Click had to spend six more days in the swamp.

10. Maria was bothered by the biographer's constant use of "per se" and "ipso facto."

Use apostrophes to form contractions, certain plurals, and the possessive form of nouns and indefinite pronouns.

42a Use an apostrophe to indicate the possessive of nouns and indefinite pronouns.

Add an apostrophe and *s* to form the possessive of indefinite pronouns (*everyone, someone, somebody,* etc.) and of most singular nouns:

Sally's coat	Ms. Cullom's office
anybody's game	one's chances
a dollar's worth	a cat's life

The same rule applies if a one-syllable singular noun ends with an -*s* sound:

boss's relatives   class's performance

But in words of more than one syllable, the -*s* following the apostrophe is optional when it might not be pronounced:

Sophocles' *or* Sophocles's   Perkins' *or* Perkins's

Add only the apostrophe to plurals ending in -*s*. Add an apostrophe and *s* to plurals not ending in -*s:*

girls' watches	cats' lives
ladies' shoes	two months' work
children's clothes	mice's cages

Add an apostrophe and *s* to the last word of a word group or compound:

the editor-in-chief's office   the chief of staff's car

Add an apostrophe and *s* to each name to indicate individual ownership; add the apostrophe and *s* to the last name to show joint ownership:

Jo's and Arnie's cars   David and Linda's apartment

42

42b Use an apostrophe to indicate the omitted letters in a contraction. Use it also to indicate omitted parts of dates or other numerals.

they'll (they will)   it's (it is)   can't (cannot)   class of '65

Note that the apostrophe is used only where letters are left out and not between the words joined in a contraction:

wouldn't   can't

42c Use an apostrophe to form the plural of lowercase letters and of abbreviations followed by periods. Use it also to prevent confusion in forming plurals of other abbreviations, of capital letters, of symbols, and of words used or singled out as words:

M.S.'s   *j*'s   *miss*'s
J's   DVDs *or* DVD's   @'s

Note that the *s* is not italicized.
    Never use an apostrophe to form a simple plural:

Incorrect: Three dog's barked.
Incorrect: Three Mazda Miata's were parked in a row.

Exercise

Correct the use of apostrophes in the following sentences. If a sentence is correct, mark it *C*.

1. When Maria started Mippallaupa High School, she found that it's environment was different.

2. Mippallaupa contains three *a*'s, three *p*'s, two *l*'s, and one *m*.

3. The school's locker's were more than a foot wide.

4. Each lockers' door was painted a different color than the one adjacent to it.

5. The assistant principals job was one of the most crucial in the school.

6. Her situation was made worse by her father-in-law's illness.

7. The Johnson's spent all their evenings at the hospital.

8. Ms. Johnson had planned to spend the time reviewing a proposed course in womens' studies.

9. Its true that the course could wait for a semester.

10. The lives of the Johnsons were put on hold.

Use a hyphen to join two words into a single adjective, to join a root word to a prefix or suffix, and to write out a fraction or compound number.

43

Compound words are sometimes written separately, sometimes hyphenated, and sometimes together as one word. When in doubt, consult a print or online college-level dictionary.

43a Use a hyphen to join two or more words serving as a single adjective before a noun.

up-to-date information	energy-related problems
seventeen-year-old son	late-night meeting
well-intentioned actions	claw-like arms

But do not hyphenate such adjectives following the noun:

The information was clearly not up to date.
His son was seventeen years old.
The agency's actions were well intentioned.

Do not use a hyphen between an adverb ending in *-ly* and an adjective:

unusually fine wine
carefully developed plot

43

43b Use hyphens to write out fractions and compound numbers greater than twenty.

twenty-two   three hundred sixty-one
a two-thirds majority   one-fourth complete

However, do not hyphenate a fraction used as a noun:

one fourth of a cup   two thirds of the members

43c Use hyphens to join root words to certain prefixes and suffixes.

The suffix *-elect* and the prefixes *pro-, anti-, ex-, self-,* and *great-* are normally joined with hyphens to root words. Check your dictionary when you are uncertain whether to use a hyphen with a prefix or suffix.

ex-convict   self-confessed   great-grandmother
anti-abortionist pro-abolitionist   congressman-elect

43d Use a hyphen to avoid a confusing combination of letters or syllables.

re-creation (*not* recreation)
steel-like (*but* froglike, etc.—the idea is to avoid using double *l*)

Exercise

Correct any misuses or omissions of hyphens in the following sentences. If a sentence is correct, mark it C.

1. As a healthy, intelligent fourteen year old girl, Maria found high school interesting.

2. The school was painted a light rosy-beige.

3. The exterior color was an attempted recreation of the appearance of the old Clickville Academy.

4. In Maria's sophomore year, Ms. Johnson, assistant-principal and self-described workaholic, was named as the new principal-to-be.

5. Thirty-seven teachers, more than three-quarters of the faculty, signed a petition supporting her promotion.

Always capitalize the first word of a sentence and the word *I;* capitalize proper nouns and important words in titles according to conventional practice.

cap

44

44

Appropriate capitalization is a matter of convention. This section will show you basic conventions, but conventions vary, and expert writers often disagree on what should be capitalized. Consult your college dictionary for specific problems; words commonly capitalized will be shown that way in the dictionary entry.

44a Capitalize the first word of a sentence and *I.*

Correct:	He advised our club on energy-saving devices.
Incorrect:	I would go if i could.
Correct:	I do not know whether I would go if I could.

44b Capitalize the names of persons, races, and nationalities.

Also capitalize derivatives of such words:

English	Maxwell R. Folger	Ms. Tucker
Chicano	Americanize	Cuban
Caucasian	Russian	Kentuckian

Neither *black* (African American) nor *white* (Caucasian) is capitalized; however, *Hispanic* is capitalized.

44c Capitalize place names.

Puerto Rico	Amazon River	Orange County
Zaire	Nile Valley	North Carolina

44d Capitalize the names of organizations, historical events, holidays, days of the week, and months.

World War II	BP	Thursday
Chrysler Corporation	Yom Kippur	Thanksgiving
Easter	NAACP	July

44

44e Capitalize titles preceding a name.

Professor Elizabeth Kirk
Chairman Dick Fisher

Titles following a name are capitalized in addresses and typed signatures of letters, but not in sentences:

Elizabeth Kirk, Professor of Chemistry
Dick Fisher, Chairman of the Board

The chairman of the board called the meeting to order.
Elizabeth Kirk is a professor of chemistry.

44f Capitalize common nouns such as *street, company, river,* or *aunt* only when they are part of a proper noun. Capitalize *north, south, east,* and *west* only when they refer to specific regions.

Huskey Company	my brother's company
Kirkman Road	on the road
Roosevelt University	at a university
Atlantic Ocean	in the ocean
American Airlines	a major airline
Uncle George	my favorite uncle
Oak Ridge High School	my old high school
The Midwest	go west
East Texas	toward the east

44g Capitalize the first word and all important words of the title of a book, periodical, article, report, or other document. Also capitalize the titles of chapters and other major divisions.

The Scarlet Letter	*Macbeth*
"Chapter Six: Projected Revenue"	*Writers on Writing*
Time	"Methods Used"

A, an, the, conjunctions, and prepositions of fewer than five letters should not be capitalized unless they are the first or last word in a title or subtitle.

Exercise

Correct any errors in capitalization in the following sentences. If a sentence is correct, mark it *C*.

1. After the High School year was over, Maria wondered what she would do that Summer.

2. Her family planned a picnic for the July 4 Holiday.

3. Some of their Puerto Rican relatives planned to come up to join them.

4. The picnic was to be held on the banks of the Gidney river.

5. In August, Maria planned to visit Clickville's rutabaga festival.

6. The rutabaga Queen would be crowned after an extensive Pageant.

7. This year's Queen was born in Mary Sherman hospital in Sullivan, Indiana, a small town South of Terre Haute.

8. For cultural reasons, many people considered it inappropriate to have a midwesterner win a north Florida Pageant.

9. Maria's mother said that it just proved that Clickville was moving out of the middle ages and into the early renaissance.

10. The pageant was hosted by a member of the Gidney Family, prominent republicans who owned a great deal of farmland in Click county.

ab 45 Capitalize and punctuate abbreviations according to conventional practice.

Abbreviations and figures are widely used in technical reports, tables, footnotes, and bibliographies. However, only a few abbreviations and figures are commonly used in the text of college writing.

45a Use only conventionally accepted abbreviations in college and general writing.

The following abbreviations are recommended:

Mr.	M.D.	Rev. (Rev. Jane Smith or the Rev. Mr. Jones)
Mrs.	M.S.	
Ms.	S.P.A.	Col. and other military titles
Dr.	A.D. or B.C.	C.E. or B.C.E.

45

St. (Saint)	a.m. or p.m.	Ph.D. and other degrees
Jr.	no.	CIA, IBM, NAACP, and other groups commonly known by initials
Sr.	D.C.	

45b Spell out the following in college writing:

Units of measure:	pounds, feet
Place names:	Arkansas, New York
Parts of addresses:	Street, Avenue, Road
Corporate identities:	Company, Incorporated (except in official titles)
Parts of written works:	page 3, Chapter Seven, Volume 14
Personal names:	Charles (not Chas.)
Names of courses:	English 101 (not Eng. 101)

Check your college dictionary for the proper spelling, punctuation, and capitalization of abbreviations.

Exercise

In the following sentences, correct any improper abbreviations or supply abbreviations as needed. If a sentence is correct, mark it *C*.

1. Maria found the capt. of her swim team to be an interesting case.

2. Edna Smith was born in Texarkana, Ark., on a Tues. morn.

3. She weighed three pounds, four oz.

4. Her family then moved to Washington, District of Columbia.

5. When Edna was five, her parents took her to a Dr., Kenneth Perkins, for a check-up.

6. Ken.'s clinic was named Healthy Children, Inc.

7. Doctor Perkins wanted to be an M.D. ever since he could remember.

8. His clinic is described on p. 367 of Vol. 4 of *America's Great Physicians.*

9. After Perkins started treating E. S. in D.C., she grew seven in. and gained fifty pounds in the year before the Smith family moved to Fla.

10. Edna's father, Robt., bought a big house on State St. in Clickville.

46 Spell out one- and two-word numbers in most situations.

Use figures for page numbers, numbers with units of measure, time followed by *a.m.* or *p.m.,* percentages, decimals, identification numbers, and numbers that cannot be written in one or two words. Otherwise, write out numbers.

Use figures		Write out	
428	5,687,414	eleven twenty-two	
		seventeen thousand	
3¾		three-quarters	
		one third of the population	
East 181st Street		East Eighty-first Street	
Channel 3			
page 17		seventeen-page report	
85° F	12 meters	eighty-five cadets	
6:30 p.m.		six-thirty that afternoon	
38%	10 percent		
3.1416	.005		
U.S. 66	I-84		
4 B.C.E.	2007		

Avoid beginning a sentence with a number, but if it is unavoidable, write out the number:

Four hundred twenty-eight people attended the opening ceremonies.

In a series, if one number must be written in figures, write all the numbers in figures:

Incorrect: Of the students who responded to the questionnaire, thirty had never used the university tennis courts, twelve had used them once, and 123 had used them more than once.

Correct: Of the students who responded to the questionnaire, 30 had never used the university tennis courts, 12 had used them once, and 123 had used them more than once.

Exercise

47

Correct any errors in number usage in the following sentences. If a sentence is correct, mark it *C*.

1. In the summer of Nineteen Seventy Nine, Clickville found itself in the national news for the 1st time.

2. A controversy occurred on County Road 546 near Interstate ninety-five.

3. 9 farmworkers went on strike against Gidney Farms.

4. Over twenty percent of the county deputies arrived and arrested the strikers.

5. The group became known as the Clickville 9.

6. A petition in support of the strikers was signed by 37 people and was printed on page two of section 2 of the *Clickville Clarion.*

7. Surveys revealed that only a third of area citizens believed the strikers to be guilty of a crime, but another 1/4 feared the powerful Gidney family.

8. Channel Thirteen covered the story extensively, but Channel 5 had other concerns.

9. Temperatures that summer were broiling, averaging just under ninety-four degrees.

10. The 16-page investigative report was completed by the District Attorney's office in thirteen days.

^{sp} **47** Proofread for proper spelling, and work on your spelling weaknesses.

Unfortunately, there is no easy shortcut to effective spelling. Some writers who are otherwise very skillful struggle all their careers with poor spelling. If you are a poor speller and cannot seem to improve much, allow extra time to look up spellings. If you frequently misspell the same words, make a list of them. The following suggestions should help you with some of the more common spelling problems; however, for many words, only memorization or reference lists will help.

47

ie or ei: Place *i* before *e*, except after *c* and in words pronounced with other than the long *e* sound:

Correct:	field	ceiling	sleigh	height
	grief	conceit	vein	stein
	niece	deceive	weigh	foreign
	relief	conceive	neighbor	heir

Exceptions: fiery, seize, species, weird, neither

Final e: Drop a silent final *e* before suffixes beginning with a vowel; keep it before suffixes beginning with a consonant:

Correct:	writ*ing*	hope*ful*	guid*ance*
	love*ly*	nine*teen*	sincere*ly*

Exceptions: dye*ing* (clothes), nin*th*, tru*ly*, courage*ous*

Changing y to i: When adding a suffix, change a final *y* to *i* except before a suffix beginning with *i:*

Correct:	fly, flying, flier
	rely, reliance
	forty, fortieth

Plurals: Most plurals add *-s* to the singular; plurals of nouns ending in *s, ch, sh,* or *x* add *-es:*

Correct:	girls	tables	typists	spoonfuls
	dishes	taxes	churches	bosses

Singular nouns ending in *y* preceded by a consonant change the *y* to *i* and add *-es:*

Correct:	cities, tragedies, replies, supplies

Singular nouns ending in *o* preceded by a consonant usually add *-es,* but note the exceptions:

Correct:	potatoes, tomatoes, heroes, zeroes, hypos, pros, jumbos, ghettos *or* ghettoes, mosquitos *or* mosquitoes

47 The Glossary of Usage at the back of this handbook (page G-5) lists some words easily confused because of similar spelling. Here are a few others:

advice, advise	inequity, iniquity
ascent, assent	paradox, parody
censor, censure	passed, past
decent, descent, dissent	prophecy, prophesy
definite, definitive	stationary, stationery
device, devise	to, too
idea, ideal	weather, whether

Here is a list of one hundred commonly misspelled words:

absence	continuous	imitation
accommodate	criticize	incredibly
acquaintance	definitely	independent
adequately	description	intelligence
aggravate	desirable	irrelevant
alleviate	desperate	irresistible
all right	develop	knowledge
a lot	disappoint	leisure
altogether	disastrous	license
amateur	dissatisfied	loneliness
analysis	embarrass	maintenance
apparent	environment	maneuver
argument	existence	mischievous
athletic	exaggerate	necessary
becoming	familiar	noticeable
bureaucracy	feasible	occasionally
calendar	February	occurred
category	forth	omitted
cemetery	gauge	parallel
committee	government	permissible
competition	grammar	personnel
condemn	guard	possess
conscience	harass	preceding
conscientious	hindrance	predominant
conscious	hurriedly	prejudice
consistent	hypocrisy	prevalent

privilege	repetition	susceptible
procedure	rhythm	temperament
proceed	ridiculous	thorough
prominent	schedule	unanimous
psychology	separate	undoubtedly
questionnaire	sergeant	villain
receive	succeed	
recommend	supersede	

47

Exercise

Underline the correctly spelled words. Write out the proper spelling of the words that are incorrect.

1. independent
2. resistence
3. indispensable
4. heighth
5. occurrance
6. mispell
7. preceed
8. procede
9. compatible
10. chastise

11. evidentally
12. larnyx
13. seperate
14. column
15. incidently
16. reciept
17. accidently
18. develope
19. sieze
20. hurriedly

Grammar

8

Editing for Grammar

48

The principles of grammar are means to an end: effective communication. They express the conventional practices followed by experienced speakers and writers of Standard English. Not following these conventions often results in writing that is not only technically incorrect but also confusing or misleading. Most of the time we follow the conventions of English without thinking about them. However, some errors are almost inevitable, and knowing the rules makes correcting those errors much easier.

If you find that you need to review any of the parts of speech discussed here, see Chapter 12.

frag

48 Use grammatically complete sentences.

A group of words that is punctuated as a sentence but that is not a grammatically complete sentence is called a *fragment* or *sentence fragment.* Although experienced writers sometimes use fragments intentionally, fragments are usually unacceptable in college writing. Unintentional fragments can create misunderstanding and distract your readers. A fragment is usually either a *phrase* or a *dependent clause.*

Complete sentence:	David is a talented artist. (independent clause)
Fragment:	Because David is a talented artist. (dependent clause)
Fragment:	Like a talented artist. (prepositional phrase)

Most fragments result from chopping a phrase or clause from the end of an adjoining sentence. It is usually a simple matter to correct fragments. You can reconnect the fragment to the previous or following sentence, or you can add the necessary elements to make the fragment a grammatically complete sentence.

Subordinating conjunctions such as *although, because, if,* and *when* (see the list on page 295) introduce subordinate (dependent) clauses, and such clauses cannot stand alone as sentences. The following examples show the most common types of clauses or phrases used incorrectly as fragments:

Incorrect:	Although being left-handed has sometimes been seen as a minor misfortune. Many great athletes, artists, and political leaders have succeeded in adjusting to a right-handed world. (Subordinate clause introduced by *although* is not a sentence.)
Correct:	Although being left-handed has sometimes been seen as a minor misfortune, many great athletes, artists, and political figures have succeeded in adjusting to a right-handed world. (subordinate clause connected to independent clause)

Incorrect:	Science owes its system of plant classification and its double Latin names for plants and animals to Linnaeus. The eighteenth-century Swedish botanist. (final noun phrase not a sentence)
Correct:	Science owes its system of plant classification and its double Latin names for plants and animals to Linnaeus, the eighteenth-century Swedish botanist. (noun phrase as an appositive connected to preceding sentence)
Incorrect:	The Rattlers were disappointed once more. Having finished second in the city baseball tournament for the fifth year in a row. (participial phrase as fragment)
Correct:	The Rattlers were disappointed once more, having finished second in the city baseball tournament for the fifth year in a row. (phrase connected to preceding sentence)
Correct:	The Rattlers were disappointed once more. This was the fifth year in a row that they had finished second in the city baseball tournament. (phrase expanded to independent clause)
Incorrect:	Collectively, they vowed to combine their efforts toward one goal. To win first place next year. (infinitive phrase as fragment)
Correct:	Collectively, they vowed to combine their efforts toward one goal: to win first place next year. (infinitive phrase connected to previous sentence)
Incorrect:	Practice sessions will begin immediately and will be held during the whole year. On the second Saturday of each month. (prepositional phrase as fragment)
Correct:	Practice sessions will begin immediately and will be held on the second Saturday of each month during the whole year. (prepositional phrase inserted in previous sentence)

Exercise

A. Mark with *S* any word group that is a grammatical sentence; mark with *X* those that are sentence fragments. Explain why those marked *X* are fragments.

   1. Maria's friend Jeff Reynolds who joined the football team.

   2. Because the coach urged him to do so.

   3. Good hands combined with better than average speed.

   4. Jeff became a wide receiver, an assignment that he welcomed.

   5. Although the quarterback and the running backs get the most publicity.

49

6. Because they are the ones who score most of the points.

7. Although Jeff was a sophomore, he started every game for Mippallaupa High.

8. Scoring five touchdowns on twenty-seven receptions.

9. Coach O'Reilly's philosophy of using rushing to set up the pass.

10. Coach O'Reilly believed in a balanced attack.

11. Hoping to keep the opponents on their toes.

12. Although, some teams handled the Mippallaupa Rattlers fairly easily.

13. Lake Parson High beating Mippallaupa four years in a row.

14. Absolutely Mippallaupa's most feared rival.

15. Gidneyville Consolidated, however, being something less of a challenge, losing to Mippallaupa 73–6.

B. Rewrite as sentences the fragments that you identified above.

Separate two independent clauses with a period, semicolon, or comma and coordinating conjunction.

fs cs

49

If you fail to separate independent clauses properly, you will create one of two structural problems: a *fused sentence* (or *run-on*) or a *comma splice.*

An independent clause is a group of words that can be punctuated as a complete sentence. Whenever a sentence contains two independent clauses, those clauses must be separated by a semicolon or by one of the coordinating conjunctions *(and, or, nor, for, but, yet,* or *so)* plus a comma. A comma alone is not adequate punctuation, even if it is followed by a conjunctive adverb such as *furthermore, however,* or *moreover.*

Fused sentence:	The arresting officer did not attend the trial the case was dismissed.
Comma splice:	The arresting officer did not attend the trial, the case was dismissed.

Once you learn to identify fused sentences and comma splices, you can easily avoid them. Some of the most common ways are shown here:

1. Make each clause a separate sentence:

The arresting officer did not attend the trial. The case was dismissed.

2. Place a semicolon between the clauses:

The arresting officer did not attend the trial; the case was dismissed.

3. Insert a conjunctive adverb between the clauses. The adverb should be preceded by a semicolon and followed by a comma:

The arresting officer did not attend the trial; therefore, the case was dismissed.

4. Place a comma and coordinating conjunction between the clauses:

The arresting officer did not attend the trial, **so** the case was dismissed.

5. Convert one clause into a dependent clause by beginning it with a relative pronoun (*whoever, whomever, whichever, whatever,* for example) or with a subordinating conjunction such as *because, after,* or *since:*

Because the arresting officer did not attend the trial, the case was dismissed.

6. Rearrange the entire sentence into another pattern:

The case was dismissed because of the absence of the arresting officer.

All of these revisions are grammatically correct. You will find that choosing the best correction is a matter of style. Note that each of the following fused sentences and comma splices can be corrected in ways other than the one shown:

Faulty:	My old car has become too unreliable, I'm going to have to start looking for another one soon. (comma splice)
Corrected:	My old car has become too unreliable; I'm going to have to start looking for another one soon. (semicolon)
Faulty:	The old rancher perceived that a storm was imminent he turned his horse around and headed home. (fused sentence)
Corrected:	The old rancher perceived that a storm was imminent, so he turned his horse around and headed home. (comma plus coordinating conjunction)
Faulty:	There is one major problem with exercise, it is addictive. (comma splice)
Corrected:	There is one major problem with exercise; it is addictive. (semicolon)
Faulty:	Jack wanted to buy a camouflage outfit, he couldn't find one. (comma splice)
Corrected:	Jack wanted to buy a camouflage outfit, but he couldn't find one. (comma plus coordinating conjunction)

49

Faulty:	Many Americans believe that they are victims of the tax laws this attitude causes income tax returns to be highly creative. (fused sentence)
Corrected:	Many Americans believe that they are victims of the tax laws, a belief that causes income tax returns to be highly creative. (sentence rearranged)

Note that in specialized contexts, a colon may sometimes be used in place of a semicolon. If the first independent clause is the "cause" of the second independent clause, the use of a colon is appropriate:

Correct:	Juan apologized for being late: his car had broken down three miles from work.

Use this method sparingly; it won't work in general contexts. (See also **37a.**)

Exercise

In the following sentences, mark *C* for those that are correct and *X* for those that are fused sentences or comma splices. Then correct those marked *X*.

1. The district football tournament was held at Xanadu High the stadium was called the Pleasure Dome.

2. In the first round, Mippallaupa beat Gidneyville, Xanadu beat Lake Parson.

3. Maria attended the game with her parents, and they all sat in the visitors' section.

4. The Xanadu Kublas hadn't lost a game all season, however, their star running back was out with a broken ankle.

5. Maria could hear the chant of the Xanadu cheerleaders: "Beware! Beware! His flashing eyes, his floating hair!"

6. The game was tied at fourteen at the end of the third quarter, nevertheless Xanadu had a first down and goal to go at the Mippallaupa seven-yard line.

7. The Mippallaupa defense dug in, Xanadu scored two plays later.

8. The Kublas missed the extra point, with a Rattler linebacker coming through to block the kick.

9. Jeff Reynolds caught three passes in the Rattlers' final drive he would have scored a touchdown if he had not been caught by the free safety after the third catch.

10. The Rattlers were stopped, however, by an interception.

s/v agr Make each verb and its subject agree
50 in number.

Use the singular form of a verb with a singular subject and the plural form of a verb with a plural subject:

Singular	Plural
She *watches.*	They *watch.*
The watch *runs* fast.	The watches *run* fast.
The team *is* playing.	The teams *are* playing.
The plan *has* changed.	The plans *have* changed.
He *was* especially kind.	They *were* especially kind.

Notice that the *-s* or *-es* ending usually makes nouns plural but makes present-tense verbs singular, except in the first and second person:

She goes.

I go.

You go.

Making subjects and verbs agree is usually easy in short sentences, but it can be more difficult in longer, more complicated sentences. Make sure that you do not let a prepositional phrase or other modifier influence your decision. Be careful to identify the subject so that your verb agrees with the correct word or words:

Incorrect: Ms. Gabriel's attention to time, efficiency, and savings deserve favorable consideration.

Correct: Ms. Gabriel's attention [subject] to time, efficiency, and savings *deserves* favorable consideration.

Incorrect: My supervisor's first priority in cutting departmental expenses are reducing overtime and sick pay.

Correct: My supervisor's first priority [subject] in cutting departmental expenses *is* reducing overtime and sick pay.

50

In a sentence beginning with *there,* the subject follows the verb:

Correct: There *is* an extra *pair* [subject] of shoes in the hall closet.

Correct: There *are* no good *concerts* [subject] at the Civic Center anymore.

Forms of the verb *be* and other linking verbs (see **54**) agree with the subject of the sentence, not the complement, even when the subject is plural and the complement is singular, or vice versa:

Correct: Unsafe working conditions [subject] *were* the primary cause [complement] of the government investigation.

Correct: Mr. Jefferson's reason [subject] for early retirement *was* his health problem [complement].

Correct: Shopping [subject] on the Internet *is* her only reason [complement] for wanting a new computer.

50a With compound subjects joined by and, use a plural verb.

Incorrect: The movement of the tropical fish and the bubbles from the filter fascinates the young cat.

Correct: The movement of the tropical fish and the bubbles from the filter *fascinate* the young cat.

However, when *each* or *every* precedes the compound subject, use a singular verb:

Incorrect: Every boy and girl are required to have parental permission to go on the spring break trip.

Correct: Every boy and girl *is* required to have parental permission to go on the spring break trip.

Note: The phrase *as well as* is used as a preposition, not as a conjunction. It does not create a compound subject.

The Indian diplomat as well as the Pakistani *was* upset by the U.N. vote.

50b With compound subjects joined by *or* or *nor,* make the verb agree with the subject nearer to the verb.

Use a singular verb when two singular subjects are joined by *or* or *nor:*

Incorrect: Either *Hamlet* or *Othello,* rather than the usual *Macbeth,* are going to be performed this year.

Correct: Either *Hamlet* or *Othello*, rather than the usual *Macbeth*, *is* going to be performed this year.

Use a plural verb when two plural subjects are joined by *or* or *nor:*

Incorrect: Neither Stephen King's novels nor Lawrence Block's novels seems to lose popularity.

Correct: Neither Stephen King's novels nor Lawrence Block's novels *seem* to lose popularity.

When *or* or *nor* joins a singular subject and a plural subject, the verb agrees with the subject nearer to the verb:

Incorrect: Gail could not decide whether her math class or her two science classes was harder.

Correct: Gail could not decide whether her two science classes or her math class *was* harder.

Also correct: Gail could not decide whether her math class or her two science classes *were* harder.

Incorrect: Neither the clerks nor the assistant manager were watching the register.

Correct: Neither the clerks nor the assistant manager *was* watching the register.

Also correct: Neither the assistant manager nor the clerks *were* watching the register.

In the last two examples, note that of the two correct sentences shown, the second sentence sounds much better. In this type of situation, placing the plural nearer the verb will produce a more natural-sounding sentence.

50c *Each, either, neither, one, everybody, somebody, nobody,* and *anyone* require singular verbs.

Incorrect: Each of the development team's twelve members were given a portion of the bonus money.

Correct: Each of the development team's twelve members *was* given a portion of the bonus money.

Incorrect: Nobody from inside the company are ever given serious consideration for the top positions.

Correct: Nobody from inside the company *is* ever given serious consideration for the top positions.

50d Quantitative words such as *some, half, all, part, most,* and *more* are singular or plural depending on the nouns to which they refer.

Correct: All of the members *were* notified, and most *have* arrived.

Correct: All of the cake *has* been eaten.

Correct: Most of the committee's time *was* wasted in senseless wrangling.

Correct: One third of all meals eaten in this country *are* purchased in restaurants.

Correct: Two thirds of his diet *is* starch.

None usually obeys the same rule, although some writers consider the word's origin ("not one") and treat it consistently as singular:

Correct: I left messages for all of the members, but none *has* returned my call.

Also correct: I left messages for all of the members, but none *have* returned my call.

50e A collective noun that refers to a group as a unit takes a singular verb.

Nouns such as *class, committee, team, family, crew, jury, faculty, majority,* and *company* take singular verbs when they refer to a group acting as a unit:

Correct: The company *has* tried to diversify its investments.

Correct: If a majority *votes* in favor of adjournment, no further motions are allowed.

Occasionally you may need a plural verb to show that members of a group are acting as individuals:

Incorrect: If a majority votes according to their consciences, these amendments will be defeated.

Correct: If a majority *vote* according to their consciences, these amendments will be defeated.

In the incorrect sentence, the writer has been forced to shift from a singular verb *(votes)* to a plural pronoun *(their)*. Once you have decided whether a collective noun is singular or plural, treat it consistently within the sentence as one or the other. Another example:

Correct: The jury *votes* by secret ballot, with twelve votes required for indictment. *(jury* treated as a whole)

Correct: The jury *have* taken their seats. *(jury* treated as individuals)

Incorrect: The jury has taken their seats.

Many writers of American English avoid using collective nouns in the plural. They say "members of the jury" when they treat the jury as individuals acting separately, or they use the singular: "The jury *is* seated."

50f Some singular subjects may look like plurals.

Certain nouns look like plurals but function as singulars and require singular verbs. *News, economics, politics, physics,* and *mathematics* are common examples of words that cannot be made singular because they already are.

> **Correct:**   Politics, unfortunately, often *affects* hiring decisions. (not plural verb *affect*)

Exercise

A. Study the sentences below for subject-verb agreement. Mark those that are correct with *C* and those that have faulty agreement with *X*.

1. In her junior year, Maria found that physics were a very difficult subject.

2. Neither her mother nor her father were able to help her.

3. All of the students in the class was having trouble.

4. Maria, along with April and Jeff, were planning to form a study group.

5. The group were composed of those three and April's friend Liam, who was making the best grades in the class.

6. Every one of them were responsible for checking the day's assignment on the class website.

7. Mr. Sterne, who had taught physics and chemistry for more than thirty years, were feared by generations of Mippallaupa students.

8. Liam believed that at least one of the study group members were going to fail.

9. A wide variety of problems was expected on the final exam.

10. However, most of the problems were based on those in earlier tests.

B. Correct the sentences above that you marked with *X*.

51 pn agr **51** Use singular pronouns to refer to singular nouns and plural pronouns to refer to plural nouns.

Make each pronoun agree in number—singular or plural—with the noun or pronoun to which it refers. (This noun or pronoun is called the **antecedent.**)

Correct:	The flight instructor [singular antecedent] finished her [singular pronoun] lecture, but the pilots [plural antecedent] remained in their [plural pronoun] seats.

It is usually easy to recognize an antecedent as singular or plural and to decide whether the pronoun should be singular or plural, but some sentences are complicated. The antecedent may be compound, or it may be a collective noun or an indefinite pronoun.

51a Collective nouns such as *team, committee, chorus,* and *class* can be either singular or plural depending on how they are used.

Avoid treating a collective noun as both singular and plural:

Incorrect:	The interview committee *is* going to finish *their* deliberations tomorrow.
Correct:	The interview committee *is* going to finish *its* deliberations tomorrow.

Incorrect:	Our soccer team *has* not won yet, but Saturday *they* will be doing *their* best.
Correct:	Our soccer team *has* not won yet, but Saturday *it* will be doing *its* best.

See **50e** for a fuller discussion of collective nouns.

51b Indefinite antecedents such as *a person, each, neither, either, someone, anyone, no one, one,* and *everybody* almost always take singular pronouns.

Incorrect:	There are too many issues raised by this petition for the officials to give each one the attention they deserve.
Correct:	There are too many issues raised by this petition for the officials to give each one the attention *it* deserves.

Incorrect: When a student first registers for classes, they risk making embarrassing errors.

Correct: When a student first registers for classes, *he* or *she* risks making embarrassing errors.

Correct: When *students* first register for classes, *they* risk making embarrassing errors.

Avoid using *he, him,* or *his* with an indefinite pronoun unless the pronoun refers to an exclusively male group. Use *he or she, him or her,* or *his or her* instead, or rewrite the sentence so that the plural *they, them,* or *their* is appropriate. See **64a** for more on sexist language. See **50c** and **50d** for more on indefinite pronouns.

51c Compound antecedents with *and* take plural pronouns.

Correct: Beth and Eileen won *their* awards in tennis and swimming. (The pronoun *their* refers to Beth and Eileen, a compound or double antecedent.)

51d If a compound antecedent is joined by *or* or *nor*, the pronoun agrees with the antecedent nearer to the pronoun.

If both antecedents are singular, use a singular pronoun:

Incorrect: Neither the television station nor its radio affiliate had their license revoked because of the charges of corruption.

Correct: Neither the television station nor its radio affiliate had *its* license revoked because of the charges of corruption.

If both antecedents are plural, use a plural pronoun:

Correct: It was impossible to blame either the reporters or the editors. *They* did all *they* could to verify the story.

If one antecedent is singular and one plural, make the pronoun agree with the antecedent nearer to the pronoun:

Correct: Either the instructor or the students are responsible for turning off *their* classroom lights and projection equipment.

51 Avoid wasting time puzzling over intricate agreement problems with subjects or antecedents joined by *or* or *nor.* If following the rules in this section and in **50b** results in an absurd or awkward sentence, simply rewrite it. You may be able to join the subjects or antecedents with *and:*

> **Awkward:**   Neither Amanda nor Bob will be in [his? her? their?] office this afternoon.
>
> **Rewritten:**   Both Amanda and Bob will be out of *their* offices this afternoon.

Exercise

A. Mark with *X* those sentences with pronoun agreement errors. If the sentence is correct, mark it *C*.

1. Mr. Rodriguez announced plans to learn how to cook: "Every man should know their way around a kitchen."

2. After some reading, he found that each cookbook has a style of its own.

3. He soon discovered that one cookbook publisher aimed their books at men who were just learning.

4. He realized that an expert chef wouldn't waste their time on such a book.

5. Either Mr. Rodriguez or Mrs. Rodriguez cooked each night for his family.

6. In May, the Clickville Bakeoff was going to be held, and their entry rules were published in the *Clarion.*

7. Mrs. Rodriguez urged her husband to submit his recipe for Rutabaga Surprise.

8. "Anyone who submits their entry has a chance," Mrs. Rodriguez argued.

9. Neither Mr. Rodriguez nor Mrs. Rodriguez expected their recipe to win, however.

10. Both of them were pleased when a letter arrived in his mailbox stating that his recipe had gained second place, losing only to Rutabaga Milano.

B. Correct the sentences above that you marked with *X.*

^{ref} Make each pronoun refer clearly
52 to one antecedent.

Because a pronoun takes the place of its antecedent, a pronoun's meaning is clear only when it points clearly to that antecedent. Two or more plausible antecedents will confuse your reader:

Ambiguous:	Alex told Rafael that he should be earning more money.
Clear:	Alex told Rafael, "You should be earning more money."
Or:	Alex told Rafael, "I should be earning more money."
Or:	Alex complained to Rafael about being underpaid.

Ambiguous:	As soon as Dr. Angela Kennedy treated the porpoise, she was set free in the ocean.
Clear:	As soon as Dr. Angela Kennedy treated her, the porpoise was set free in the ocean.

In the second pair of examples, sensible readers will know that the porpoise, not Dr. Kennedy, was set free, but because they will notice the comical ambiguity, the sentence is still ineffective.

52a Make each pronoun refer to a noun or to an earlier pronoun.

To keep references clear, make each pronoun refer to a noun used as a subject, object, or complement, not as a modifier or a possessive:

Ineffective:	Mrs. Valdez questioned the investigator's honesty even though he had helped her.
Effective:	Even though the investigator had helped her, Mrs. Valdez questioned his honesty.

Ineffective:	At Sybil's office, she is the manager.
Effective:	Sybil is the manager of her office.

Also be sure that a pronoun can logically refer to its antecedent:

Ineffective:	I had tonsillitis when I was eight, so my doctor removed them.
Effective:	I had tonsillitis when I was eight, so my doctor removed my tonsils.
Or:	When I was eight, my doctor removed my tonsils because they were continually inflamed.

52

52b Make each pronoun refer to one word or to a specific group of words rather than to an implied idea.

Except in informal writing, use *you* when referring directly to your reader, not when referring to any person in general. Substitute *one* or an appropriate noun:

Ineffective:	Many people believe that college should help you earn a better living.
Effective:	Many people believe that college should help a person earn a better living.
Or:	Many people believe that college should help one earn a better living.

Except in idiomatic expressions such as "It is cold," use *it* and *they* only to refer to specific nouns:

Ineffective:	On page 381 of our text, it says that Henry Clay was "the great compromiser."
Effective:	On page 381 of our text, the author writes that Henry Clay was "the great compromiser."
Or:	On page 381, our text points out that Henry Clay was "the great compromiser."

Ineffective:	They do not have many Catholics in Iran.
Effective:	Iran does not have many Catholics.
Or:	There are few Catholics in Iran.

52c Insert nouns to clarify the antecedents of *this, that,* and *which.*

This, that, and *which* are often vague when they refer broadly to an idea expressed or implied in a preceding clause. To avoid confusion, change the pronoun to a noun or add a noun.

Vague:	The young residents did the actual cutting even though the surgeon received credit and payment for the operation. This is common in many hospitals.
Clear:	The young residents did the actual cutting even though the surgeon received credit and payment for the operation. This practice is common in many hospitals.

Vague:	The CPA reviewed the tax returns after her interns prepared them, which is quite common.
Clear:	The CPA reviewed the tax returns after her interns prepared them, a common arrangement.

Exercise

Underline all pronouns used inappropriately in the following sentences.

1. Maria enjoyed studying sociology, which led her to consider it as her major in college.

2. "It says in the newspaper that a degree in sociology can be used in many ways," Maria commented.

3. Maria told April that she could choose a major if she weren't so busy.

4. When Maria's father brought home a book that evaluated U.S. colleges, she read it eagerly.

5. "They charge more for tuition in the North than they do in the South," Maria said.

6. One of the reasons Maria liked choosing sociology was that it would gain the approval of her parents.

7. She might need to go through graduate school to finish her education, but she didn't mind this.

8. After Maria finished reading the book on U.S. colleges, she gave it to April.

9. April was in no hurry to plan her career; this is common in young people.

10. Maria and April agreed that she was not getting any younger.

ca 53 Determine the correct case of a pronoun by the word's function in the sentence.

The personal pronouns *(I, we, you, he, she, it, they)* appear in different case forms depending on their function in the sentence: *I* liked *her,* but *she* hated *me.*

	Nominative	Objective	Possessive*
First Person	I, we	me, us our, ours	my, mine
Second Person	you	you	your, yours
Third Person	he, she, it, they	him, her, it, them	his, her, hers, its, their, theirs

*Note that no apostrophe is used for the possessive pronouns.

53

The **nominative** (also called **subjective**) case forms are used for the subject and predicate nominative functions:

We were turned away. (subject)
This is *she.* (predicate nominative)

The **objective** case forms are used for direct objects, indirect objects, and objects of prepositions:

The cloud link gave *us* trouble all night. (indirect object)
The Cougars beat *us* badly in both games. (direct object)
Next year we will be ready for *them.* (object of preposition)

The **possessive** case forms are used to show possession:

Their product was no better than *ours.* (possessives)

Be especially careful of the pronoun case in compound structures. Note the following:

Incorrect:	Me and Diane went on a cruise last year.
Correct:	*Diane and I* went on a cruise last year. (compound subject. No one would say, "Me went on a cruise." Also, put the other person's name first.)
Incorrect:	Mr. Edwards may try to get you and I in trouble.
Correct:	Mr. Edwards may try to get you and *me* in trouble. (object of *get*)
Incorrect:	The judge was unsympathetic to my mother and I.
Correct:	The judge was unsympathetic to my mother and *me.* (object of *to*)

A pronoun used as an appositive (an explanatory word, phrase, or clause that clarifies a noun) should be in the same case as the noun or pronoun it refers to:

Correct:	The culprits, Alice and *I,* were caught at midnight.
Correct:	The police quickly apprehended the culprits, Alice and *me.*
Incorrect:	Three contestants won prizes at the finale: Karen Turner, Kris Butler, and me.
Correct:	Three contestants won prizes at the finale: Karen Turner, Kris Butler, and *I.*

Use the possessive form immediately before a gerund:

Incorrect: My parents are concerned about me working while carrying fifteen credit hours.

Correct: My parents are concerned about *my working* while carrying fifteen credit hours.

However, you can normally use a nonpossessive common noun before a gerund, especially if the noun is plural:

Correct: The officials attributed the rise in unemployment to *women entering* the job market.

Use the nominative case for the subject of an implied verb form:

Incorrect: No one on their team is as tall as me.

Correct: No one on their team is as tall as *I.* (understood: "am tall")

Use the nominative form as the subject of a clause regardless of the function of the clause:

Incorrect: Most Americans still show great respect for whomever is President.

Correct: Most Americans still show great respect for *whoever* is President. (*Whoever* is the subject of *is* in the final clause.)

In formal writing, such as research papers and theses, always use *whom* as you would *me* or any other objective form. Many people have stopped using *whom,* especially in speech and informal writing, but in most college writing it is best to use *whom* whenever it is called for.

Incorrect: Whom did you say was calling?

Correct: Who did you say was calling? (*Who* is the subject of *was.)*

Correct: Whom did you call? (*Whom* is the object of *call.)*

Correct: To whom was that call made? (*Whom* is the object of the preposition *to.)*

A quick way to determine the case is to rephrase such questions as statements—for example, "You did call whom."

As a relative pronoun, *whom* is often dropped from the sentence:

Correct: Commissioner Jackson is the only one [*whom*] we should reelect. (*Whom* is the direct object of *reelect.*)

Exercise

54

A. Study the following sentences. Mark *X* for those with improper pronoun case and *C* for those that are correct.

1. Maria believed that, out of her senior class, no one else wanted to go to college as much as her.

2. Few of the other students were as conscientious as she.

3. However, Bob and Marge Walker, the parents of April, believed that their daughter going to college was in doubt.

4. The school counselor was the person to whom they inquired.

5. The counselor could not find a record of April taking a college preparatory test.

6. "Who do you think is responsible for this problem?" Mrs. Walker asked.

7. "Her parents, Bob and me, would like to know."

8. The counselor replied that he would look through the online records again and would call Marge and Bob to inform her and him about anything that turned up.

9. "Whom will we talk to if you don't succeed?" Mrs. Walker asked.

10. The counselor replied that him losing anything that came into his office would be a rare event.

B. Correct the sentences above that you marked with *X.*

---

adj/adv

54

Use adjectives to modify nouns and pronouns, and use adverbs to modify verbs, adjectives, or other adverbs.

Both adjectives and adverbs are modifiers; they limit or describe other words.

Adjectives: The *radical* changes of personnel were *unpleasant* but *necessary.*

Adverbs: The *highly* complex steering mechanism turned the glider *smoothly.*

Adverbs are usually distinguished by their *-ly* endings *(rapidly, formally),* but many adjectives, such as *ghastly* and *heavenly,* also end in *-ly,* and many adverbs, such as *often* and *well,* do not. If you are in doubt whether a word is an adjective or adverb, check a dictionary.

In very informal writing and speaking, certain adjectives—such as *sure, real,* and *good*—are often used in place of the adverbs *surely, really,* and *well.* In more formal writing, however, the safer practice is to use the adverb forms to modify verbs, adjectives, and other adverbs and to use adjectives to modify only nouns or pronouns:

54

Very informal:	I did so *bad* on my first calculus test that I thought about dropping the class.
More formal:	I did so *badly* on my first calculus test that I thought about dropping the class.

Use adjectives for complements after verbs such as *feel, look, smell, sound,* and *taste,* which function like forms of the verb *be;* use adverbs to modify these verbs. A quick test to make sure that the complement is correct is to substitute *is, was,* or other appropriate forms of the verb *be.*

Complement:	I must have been sick, but I did not feel bad. ("To feel badly" would mean to have a poor sense of touch, so using the adjective *bad* is the correct complement.)
Adverb modifying verb:	He looked *angrily* at us, then stalked off.
Complement:	I felt *nervous* as I approached the dark building. (Substitute *was* for *felt.*)
Adverb modifying verb:	I felt *nervously* in my pocket for a match.

54a Use the correct comparative and superlative forms of adverbs and adjectives.

Most short adjectives add *-er* for the comparative and *-est* for the superlative. Longer adjectives and most adverbs use *more* and *most.* A few have irregular comparative and superlative forms. Check a dictionary when you are in doubt.

Positive	**Comparative**	**Superlative**
strong	stronger	strongest
happy	happier	happiest
surprising	more surprising	most surprising
happily	more happily	most happily
good	better	best
well	better	best
bad	worse	worst

54

Use the comparative form when comparing two items, and use the superlative for three or more:

> **Incorrect:**   Bill and Kathy are both excellent website designers, but Kathy has the most even temperament.
>
> **Correct:**   Bill and Kathy are both excellent website designers, but Kathy has the *more* even temperament.

> **Incorrect:**   Diamonds are the better sellers among the three stones most often picked for engagement rings.
>
> **Correct:**   Diamonds are the *best* sellers among the three stones most often picked for engagement rings.

Exercise

A. Mark the following sentences with *C* if they are correct; mark with *X* those containing incorrectly used adjective or adverb forms.

   1. Maria sent applications to two schools, Harvard University and Click Memorial Union; Harvard was a great school, but C.M.U. was the closest of the two.

   2. She felt pretty good about her chances of getting in either one.

   3. However, the letter she got back from C.M.U. was worded very strange.

   4. "Click Memorial Union accepts only the better students out of those who apply."

   5. "Applicants who do good on their preparatory exams have the best chance of acceptance."

   6. "We eagerly await further evidence of your skills."

   7. Maria had the sudden thought that of her choices of attending Harvard, attending Click, or staying home, the last was not the worse option.

   8. However, she knew that C.M.U. had to be better than what it first seemed.

   9. She felt nervously about her choice of C.M.U.

   10. But her parents were nervous about her going all the way to Massachusetts, so Maria chose C.M.U.

B. Correct those sentences above marked *X*.

t 55 Use the verb tense appropriate to the time of an action or situation.

Although English relies heavily on adverbs and adverbial phrases and clauses to refer to time *(now, tomorrow, yesterday morning, after the play had already started),* English also indicates time by changes in the verb. By using verb tenses accurately, you can help your reader keep track of time relationships in your writing.

English verbs have only two primary tenses—present and past—but by using auxiliary verbs we can create complex verb forms. Thus, we can list three simple tenses, three perfect tenses, and progressive forms for all six tenses.

Simple tenses The **simple present tense** is far from simple in the ways that it is used:

Present time:	I *hear* you calling. He *looks* anxious.
Habitual time:	I *hear* the train go by every morning. He *repairs* his old Volkswagen himself.
Historical present:	Brutus *hears* the mob hailing Caesar.
Literary present:	In "The Man That Corrupted Hadleyburg," Twain *exposes* the ability of money to corrupt us.
Future action:	The case *goes* to court next week. When the defense attorney *finishes* her remarks, the jury will retire to discuss the case.

In the present tense, verbs of third-person singular subjects require an *–s* ending.

The **past tense** is formed by adding *-ed* to regular verbs or by changing the spelling of most irregular verbs. The **future tense** uses the auxiliary *shall* or *will.* Traditionally, *shall* has been reserved for use with first-person subjects *(I shall go),* and *will* is used with second- and third-person subjects *(you will go; she will go),* except when the writer reverses the usage to show strong emphasis: "I *will* win; you *shall* obey me." Today, only the most formal writing observes that distinction, and *will* is regularly used with all persons.

The following box shows the forms for a regular verb *(play)* and for the most irregular and most often used English verb, *be.*

55

	Regular Verb *Play*	Irregular Verb *Be*
Present:	I play	I am
	you play	you are
	he, she, it plays	he, she, it is
	we, you, they play	we, you, they are
Past:	I played	I was
	you played	you were
	he, she, it played	he, she, it was
	we, you, they played	we, you, they were
Future:	I will [shall] play	I will [shall] be
	you will play	you will be
	he, she, it will play	he, she, it will be
	we, you, they will play	we, you, they will be

Perfect tenses The perfect tenses indicate a relationship between two times. The **present perfect** refers to an indefinite time in the recent past or to a time beginning in the past and continuing to the present:

> Representative Green *has voted* with the conservatives more often than with the liberals.
> This five-dollar watch *has kept* perfect time for two years.

The **past perfect** indicates a time before some other specified or implied time in the past:

> The teams *had met* twice before the playoffs.

Similarly, the **future perfect** may be used to indicate a time before some other stated or implied time in the future:

> Before they return, the astronauts *will have broken* the record for time spent in space.

Note that *return* in the previous example is a typical case of the present used for future time. This use of the present is very common in dependent clauses.

The perfect tenses combine a form of the auxiliary *have* with the past participle of the main verb, as shown in the following box.

55

	Regular Verb *Play*	Irregular Verb *Be*
Present perfect:	I have played	I have been
	you have played	you have been
	he, she, it has played	he, she, it has been
	we, you, they have played	we, you, they have been
Past perfect:	I had played	I had been
	you had played	you had been
	he, she, it had played	he, she, it had been
	we, you, they had played	we, you, they had been
Future perfect:	I will [shall] have played	I will [shall] have been
	you will have played	you will have been
	he, she, it will have played	he, she, it will have been
	we, you, they will have played	we, you, they will have been

Progressive tenses Progressive forms of verbs indicate continuous actions:

The candidates *are waiting* for the results of the election.

I *was running* toward the corner when my knee gave way.

I *shall be working* on my tax return all day tomorrow.

Mr. Velkoff told me last week that I *had been using* the wrong database for at least six months.

There are progressive forms for all six tenses, as shown in the box.

Present progressive:	I am playing
	he, she, it is playing
	we, you, they are playing
Past progressive:	I was playing
	he, she, it was playing
	we, you, they were playing
Future progressive:	I, he, she, it will [shall] be playing
	we, you, they will [shall] be playing

55

Present perfect progressive:	I have been playing
	he, she, it has been playing
	we, you, they have been playing
Past perfect progressive:	I, he, she, it had been playing
	we, you, they had been playing
Future perfect progressive:	I, he, she, it will [shall] have been playing
	we, you, they will [shall] have been playing

Tenses of verbals Verbals (infinitives, gerunds, and participles) have present and present-perfect forms. Each participle also has a past form:

Present infinitive: to sink, to be sinking
Perfect infinitive: to have sunk
Present gerund: sinking
Perfect gerund: having sunk
Present participle: sinking
Perfect participle: having sunk, having been sinking
Past participle:sunk

Use the past or perfect form of a verbal to indicate a time before the main verb in the clause:

Amelia would like [now] *to have seen* last night's fireworks.

He could not get over *having failed* his teammates.

Having signed all the letters, she went home early.

But: The woman *addressing* the assembly will retire next month. (The present participle here indicates the same time as the speaking or writing of the sentence.)

Use the past participle to indicate a time before that of the main verb or to describe a condition that began before the time of the main verb:

Angered by the story, the apartment owner sued both the newspaper and the reporter.

In most other cases, use the present forms of verbals:

Emily decided to *play* selections from Sondheim. (The playing follows the deciding.)

Emily enjoys *playing* selections from Sondheim. (The playing and the enjoying take place at the same time.)

Writing about the film Pacific Rim, Anthony Lane remarked. . . . (The writing and the remarking take place together.)

Voice English verbs show active voice (the butler committed the crime) or passive voice (the crime was committed by the butler). The forms presented in this section have all been in the active voice. Verbs in the passive voice combine a form of *be* with the past participle of the main verb, as shown in the box.

	Active	**Passive**
Present:	I know	I am known
Past:	I knew	I was known
Future:	I will know	I will be known
Present perfect:	I have known	I have been known
Past perfect:	I had known	I had been known
Future perfect:	I will have known	I will have been known

Progressive verbs are sometimes used in the passive voice: "I *am being followed.*" Careful writers generally avoid the passive voice because it is wordy, indirect, and less natural than the active. For a thorough discussion of voice and style, see **23e.**

Exercise

A. Mark these sentences with *C* if they are correct and with *X* if they contain errors in verb tense.

1. In 2014 Click Memorial Union will have been operating for seventy years.

2. In 1974 the university was being celebrated as one of the South's leaders in the study of sociology.

3. C.M.U. invested a great deal of money in the sociology program when it had been described as lagging behind the other departments in Arts and Sciences.

4. When Maria took her first sociology class, she felt that she won't understand the instructor.

5. Edwin Click, a grand-nephew of Ezekiel, received his doctorate in 1985 and had started teaching at C.M.U. the next year.

6. Now Click puts his emphasis on teaching and decided to let his research wait a few years.

7. However, he still used a very abstract approach to sociology, and Maria had decided that he was hard to understand.

8. "My major problem at this point," she thought, "will be translating Clickese into English."

9. Professor Click had told the class that he will meet with students who had questions.

10. Having taken the midterm, Maria then faced the research paper.

B. Correct the sentences marked *X.*

vb
56 Use the correct principal parts of irregular verbs.

You must know the principal parts of verbs in order to form all the tenses correctly. English verbs have three principal parts: the infinitive (or present stem), the past tense, and the past participle. For regular verbs, the past tense and past participle are formed by adding -*d* or -*ed* to the infinitive: *walk, walked, walked; move, moved, moved.* Other verbs—the irregular verbs—form the past tense and past participle by various means, usually by changing a vowel in the infinitive *(win, won).* The list below includes the principal parts of the most common irregular verbs and a few regular verbs often mistakenly treated as irregular. Your college-level dictionary also gives the principal parts of irregular verbs. If your dictionary does not list the past tense and past participle forms, you can assume that the verb is regular.

Infinitive	Past Tense	Past Participle
awake	awaked (awoke)	awaked (awoke)
beat	beat	beaten
become	became	become

56

Infinitive	Past Tense	Past Participle
begin	began	begun
bend	bent	bent
bite	bit	bitten
bleed	bled	bled
blow	blew	blown
break	broke	broken
bring	brought	brought
build	built	built
burst	burst	burst
buy	bought	bought
catch	caught	caught
choose	chose	chosen
come	came	come
cut	cut	cut
deal	dealt	dealt
dig	dug	dug
dive	dived (dove)	dived
do	did	done
drag	dragged	dragged
draw	drew	drawn
drink	drank	drunk
drive	drove	driven
drown	drowned	drowned
eat	ate	eaten
fall	fell	fallen
fight	fought	fought
fly	flew	flown
forget	forgot	forgotten (forgot)
freeze	froze	frozen
get	got	gotten (got)
give	gave	given
go	went	gone
grow	grew	grown
have	had	had
hide	hid	hidden
hold	held	held

56

Infinitive	Past Tense	Past Participle
keep	kept	kept
know	knew	known
lead	led	led
leave	left	left
lend	lent	lent
let	let	let
lose	lost	lost
mean	meant	meant
prove	proved	proven (proved)
read	read	read
ride	rode	ridden
ring	rang	rung
rise	rose	risen
run	ran	run
say	said	said
see	saw	seen
sell	sold	sold
send	sent	sent
sew	sewed	sewn (sewed)
shake	shook	shaken
shave	shaved	shaved (shaven)
shrink	shrank (shrunk)	shrunk (shrunken)
show	showed	shown (showed)
sink	sank (sunk)	sunk
speak	spoke	spoken
swear	swore	sworn
swim	swam	swum
take	took	taken
teach	taught	taught
tell	told	told
think	thought	thought
throw	threw	thrown
wear	wore	worn
win	won	won
write	wrote	written

A few verbs with two distinct meanings have different principal parts in each meaning:

56

bid (a price)	bid	bid
bid (an order)	bade (bid)	bidden (bid)
hang (execute)	hanged	hanged
hang (suspend)	hung	hung
shine (emit light)	shone	shone
shine (polish)	shined	shined

Three pairs of verbs are easily confused, especially in their past-tense and past-participle forms. The key distinction is that one of each pair is transitive (it takes an object) but the other is intransitive (no object).

Transitive

lay (place)	laid	laid
set (place)	set	set
raise (lift)	raised	raised

Intransitive

lie (recline)	lay	lain
lie (falsehood)	lied	lied
sit (be seated)	sat	sat
rise (rise up)	rose	risen

He *laid* his head on a rock and *lay* in the sun for an hour.
She *set* her pen on the desk and *sat* waiting for others to finish.
He *rose* from the bed and *raised* the window.

Exercise

Underline the correct verb forms in the following sentences.

1. Maria decided that the best topic for her paper (lay, laid) in the work of Émile Durkheim.

2. Durkheim (lead, led) the intellectuals of the twentieth century to (see, seen) the importance of sociology.

3. Today, many people have (forgot, forgotten) that Durkheim (set, sat) up the study of deviance as a primary field of sociological inquiry.

57

4. Maria had (dived, dove) into her research with a vengeance.

5. She had (wore, worn) out two pencils while taking notes in the library.

6. Her efforts that semester (lend, lent) credence to her parents' theories about the value of hard work.

7. When she received an A on the assignment, her face (shined, shone) with pleasure.

8. She (hanged, hung) the paper on her bulletin board.

9. The memory of Professor Click's difficult lectures (shrank, shrunk) with time.

10. Maria realized that by the time she finished school, she would have (wrote, written) many more essays.

mo

57 Use the mood required by your sentence.

English has three moods: **indicative** for statements of fact and questions about facts, **imperative** for commands, and **subjunctive** for wishes and demands or for statements that are contrary to fact.

Indicative:	I *know* who he is.
Imperative:	*Be* yourself.
Subjunctive:	If I *were* you, I would avoid that subject.

The subjunctive is used far less now than earlier in the history of the language, but there are some situations in which the subjunctive is still the only choice:

Correct:	She demanded that Thomas *finish* the work. (Desired action. Less formally, this might be expressed, "She told Thomas to finish the work.")
Correct:	It is essential that I *be seen* at the boss's party.
Correct:	Eddie drank as if Prohibition *were* being reintroduced. (contrary to fact)
Correct:	Eve wishes that she *were* more talented. (contrary to fact)

Only a few forms of the subjunctive are different from the indicative forms given in **55**. Those forms are shown here in bold type:

58

Present:	that I walk	that I **be**
	that he, she, it **walk** (no -s)	that he, she, it **be**
	that we, you, they walk	that we, you, they **be**
Past:	that I walked	that I **were**
	that he, she, it walked	that he, she, it **were**
	that we, you, they walked	that we, you, they were
Present perfect:	that I have walked	that I have been
	that he, she, it **have** walked	that he, she, it **have** been
	that we, you, they have walked	that we, you, they have been

Exercise

Study the sentences below. Mark with *C* those that are correct and with *X* those that have errors in mood. Correct the sentences marked *X*.

1. Maria looked at her humanities class as though it was a harmless diversion.

2. However, the instructor, Mr. Santellini, insisted that humanities be seen as the "cultural repository of human memory."

3. If Maria were not interested at first, Mr. Santellini changed her mind.

4. He said, "If I was in your situation, I would explore the link between humanities and sociology."

5. He insisted that this connection be the topic of her research paper.

shift 58 Be consistent when using verbs and pronouns.

To present your information smoothly and clearly, be consistent in the tense, voice, and mood of verbs and in the person and number of nouns and pronouns. Unnecessary shifts—from past to present or from singular to plural, for instance—make awkward reading and can confuse your reader. Some shifts are necessary—to indicate passing time, for example—but it is best to make such shifts only when you have no other choice.

58

58a Avoid unnecessary shifts in tense, voice, and mood.

A change in **tense** usually signals a change in time, so be sure not to give your reader a false signal by switching tenses unnecessarily. A shift such as the following is often just the result of carelessness:

Shift in tense:	As he *turned* the corner, he *became* aware that someone *is* following him.
Corrected:	As he *turned* the corner, he *became* aware that someone *was* following him.

Be careful not to shift time when you are using one of the perfect tenses:

Shift in tense:	We had paid our dues and are ready to begin attending meetings. (past perfect with present)
Corrected:	We have paid our dues and are ready to begin attending meetings. (present perfect with present)
Or:	We had paid our dues and were ready to begin attending meetings. (past perfect with past)

See **55** for a discussion of verb tenses. Active and passive **voice** can be mixed in one sentence (she *ran* for senator twice and *was defeated* twice), but an unnecessary shift in voice can spoil the focus of a sentence:

Shift in voice:	Electrolysis is used by Dr. Lambiase, and he also performs minor surgery.
Improved:	Dr. Lambiase uses electrolysis and also performs minor surgery.

Shift in voice:	The report showed that white-collar criminals almost never serve hard time, whereas long sentences are served by petty burglars.
Improved:	The report showed that white-collar criminals almost never serve hard time, whereas petty burglars serve long sentences.

Active voice is usually more direct and natural than passive voice (see **23e**).

A change in mood should reflect a change in the way the writer views the action or situation being described: "If I *were* willing to lie, I *would tell* you I enjoyed the story, but I *am* not willing to lie." Unmotivated shifts are distracting:

58

Shift in mood:	If I were the President, I would take action, not act as if I was still in Congress.
Corrected:	If I were the President, I would take action, not act as if I were still in Congress.

See **57**.

58b Be consistent in the number and person of your nouns and pronouns.

Shift the number of nouns and pronouns (singular or plural) only to show a valid change: "I wanted to go to Europe, but *we* could not afford the trip."

Faulty:	The class of 2012 was academically outstanding, but *they were* unusual.
Improved:	The class of 2012 was academically outstanding, but *it was* unusual.

Faulty:	The jury was given instructions by the judge before *they were* asked to start *their* deliberations.
Improved:	The jury was given instructions by the judge before *it was* asked to start *its* deliberations.

Similarly, keep the person of your pronouns consistent. Be especially careful to avoid slipping into the universal *you* (second person) when you are writing in the third person *(she, he, it):*

Faulty:	Deer hunters in the Ocala National Forest must wear bright clothing so you will not get shot.
Improved:	Deer hunters in the Ocala National Forest must wear bright clothing so they will not get shot.

Faulty:	Often, other hunters will shoot at you if they see movement in the brush.
Improved:	Often, other hunters will shoot carelessly if they see movement in the brush.

Exercise

A. Mark *C* for sentences without awkward shifts and *X* for those with awkward shifts.

1. Maria was leery about her instructor for Sociology II, Ms. Chan, because students always have trouble with her class.

2. If a student had trouble early on in Chan's class, he or she is on a downhill path.

3. The class met in a building that was known by students as "Afterthoughts," and it is located near the Student Center.

4. The building had no air conditioning or any other amenity that invites attendance at classes.

5. Maria decided that if the class was held in any other campus building, the students would have a less difficult time.

6. Ms. Chan was feared by many of the students, but Maria excelled in Sociology II.

7. Each of her friends in the class struggled, but they were all passing at midterm.

8. The third exam was failed by seven students, but Maria received an A.

9. After the third exam had been successfully undertaken, Maria was ready for her next research paper.

10. If she had been allowed to choose her topic, Maria would have selected the work of Erving Goffman, but Ms. Chan insisted that Maria work on the early writings of Max Weber.

B. Reword those sentences above marked *X.*

Diction

Using the Right Words

Getting the right words in the right place to say just what you intend is never easy. As you develop your skills as a writer, you will develop a respect for words, an awareness of their various uses and the various effects they can have on readers. You want to choose words that are specific and concrete, precise and forceful, vivid and clear. As you become more sensitive to words—to their ability to clarify or obscure and to their suitability for your purposes and audiences—you will use them with increasing confidence.

Words are "right" only when they have an appropriate effect in your sentence, so choosing words always means considering the context in which they are used. We speak and write in various "languages": one for friends, one for family members, one for employers and instructors. Although you may say that you're *pissed off*, you will generally write *angry* unless your reader would expect you to sound informal, as in a story. In writing on the job, you would *submit* a report (not *hand it in*) to your supervisor; in writing an assigned paper, you would provide *abundant* (not *a lot of*) facts.

A college-level dictionary will help you decide whether the word that you think is the right one actually expresses what you intend. It will also warn you if a word is considered slang, obsolete, or in some other way inappropriate for college writing. The following sections will help you use your dictionary more efficiently and will offer other advice about choosing words wisely.

lev 59 Write at a level appropriate to your subject and audience.

Your choice of words involves some basic questions of style: How should you sound? Does your subject require a relaxed tone or a dignified tone? Should you talk directly to the reader? You can achieve an effective style by avoiding stilted, impersonal language and by using the appropriate person (see **58b**), using the active voice whenever possible (see **23e**), and using sentences that are properly emphatic (see **23**). In addition, effective writers are aware of various levels of usage when considering what their readers expect.

Dictionaries typically classify words according to four types—formal, standard, informal, or slang:

Formal or learned words are more common in reading than in speaking and are serious and scholarly in tone. Some examples are *prevaricate* (to lie), *ameliorate* (to improve), and *altercation* (quarrel).

Standard or popular words are familiar to the widest group of educated speakers and writers. For instance, *truth* is the standard counterpart of the more formal *veracity*.

Informal or **colloquial** words are appropriate to spoken language and to writing that aims for a conversational effect. Many good writers use colloquial terms for humor or for a casual, relaxed tone.

Informal	Standard
guys	people
cheesy	inferior
mad	angry
TV show	television program
to kid	to tease
to cook up	to invent, concoct

Slang is highly informal language that is used to add color and novelty to speech. Because it often does not last long enough to have a clearly established meaning, slang is inappropriate in most college writing.

Slang	Standard
cool	admirable
neat	wonderful
geek	a technology-obsessed person
chill	relax

The English language includes many dialects—different ways of communicating in particular geographic areas or among particular groups of people. The predominant dialect used by educated writers and speakers of American English is called Standard English. It is the variety of English expected in college essays, business reports, and books like this one. Most dictionaries mark the words not usually used in Standard English as *nonstandard, substandard,* or *dialect. Nowheres,* for example, is labeled "nonstandard" in the *Random House Webster's College Dictionary.* (*Note:* Some words may be standard in one sense but not in another. *Learn* is nonstandard when used to mean "teach.") The abbreviations for these labels vary; your dictionary will have a section at the front or back explaining its labels and abbreviations.

Standard English is written and spoken in many styles, which we can arbitrarily divide into three "levels": formal, informal, and general. Each level is appropriate in some situations but not in others.

Formal English is found in technical reports, scholarly books and articles, and many types of professional or academic writing. It uses an extensive, elevated vocabulary and sentences more complex than those found in other levels of writing. It avoids contractions and colloquial expressions and therefore sounds different from the way people speak:

59

> Money and the habitual resort to its use are conceived to be simply the ways and means by which consumable goods are acquired, and therefore simply a convenient method by which to procure the pleasurable sensations of consumption; these latter being in hedonistic theory the sole and overt end of all economic endeavor. Money values have therefore no other significance than that of purchasing power over consumable goods, and money is simply an expedient of computation.
>
> —*Thorstein Veblen*

Informal English, on other hand, has a more conversational tone. Writers of Informal English regularly use contractions, colloquial expressions (*a couple of* instead of *two, really* instead of *very*), and slang. They usually write in loose sentences with more *and's* and fewer subordinate clauses than are used in other levels of writing. Informal English is popular in journalism but is usually inappropriate in most college writing:

> Tattoos may not be good for your mainstream image, but they can make you feel a lot better about yourself. You might think that people get tattooed because they like the way it looks or the way it feels, and that's true, but what really happens, at least for many people, is that the pain and the permanence of the tattoo are like a test of your willingness to face where you've been and where you're going. Fake tattoos that go on with water and come off with alcohol just don't cut it.

General English follows a middle course between formal and informal. Most of its sentences are less complex than those of Formal English but tighter than those of Informal English. In the right circumstances, General English might use such relatively formal words as *haughty* and *vilify* or informal words such as *stuck-up* and *slander,* but most of the time it uses such words as *proud* and *trash.* General English is usually the best choice for college or business writing.

> The life of the great composer Johann Sebastian Bach was surprisingly uneventful. A family man, he lived all his life in small German towns and seldom traveled; he never went abroad. He had no famous friends, nor was he part of the cultural elite of his times. He had only a few notable public achievements, such as acclaimed appearances as an organist in major German cities. Bach led a private life, about which little is known, devoting himself to perfecting his considerable musical talent. So writing a biography of this man, one of the greatest artistic figures in history, is a challenge.

Reminder: Do you have a recent college dictionary? If not, you can access the free online Merriam-Webster's dictionary, with links to more complete versions, at *www.m-w.com.*

Exercise

A. Label each of the following paragraphs *F* for Formal, *I* for Informal, or *G* for General English. Be prepared to discuss the circumstances in which each paragraph would be appropriate.

1. It is the contention of some philosophers that the aforementioned moral scheme was the historical antecedent of the idea of virtue as it is defined here, the same moral scheme which, in a variety of diverse forms and with numerous rival theories, came to dominate the thinking of the European Middle Ages, at least from the twelfth century onwards, a scheme which included both classical and theistic elements.

2. It used to be you started college with a portable typewriter and maybe even a tape recorder, and you thought you were ready for a run at the dean's list. But if you look at today's college students, who grew up around computers, you find gadgets and gizmos that their parents' generation would connect to *Star Trek* but that, in fact, are absolutely needed for the high-tech learning that goes on.

3. Not too long ago, *multimedia* meant looking at a filmstrip, accompanied by a scratchy record explaining the wonders of nature. More recently, computer technology has given a whole new meaning to the word *multimedia.* Now text, music, and spoken words, once stored separately, are in digital form, allowing them to be interwoven and recombined in a new format that allows students to interact with information in all its various guises.

B. Complete the following exercises by using a college-level dictionary.

1. Check your dictionary to see if the following words are considered slang, colloquial (informal), or standard: *crook, wonk, exam, kid, jock, hacker, klutzy, nutty, sleaze, spin.*

2. Look up the word *gimmick* in your dictionary to see how it can be both colloquial (informal) and slang. Find another such example.

3. Determine which of these words is considered formal, informal (colloquial), slang, or standard: *hassle* (noun), *hassle* (verb), *hang-up, altercation, argument.* How do the meanings differ? Under what circumstances would each be appropriate?

4. List five slang terms, and write short, original definitions for each. Then compare your definitions with those in your dictionary.

d

60

60 Keep your level of usage consistent.

Appropriate diction requires a consistent style. Mixing formal and informal language can produce distracting and absurd results:

> The governor's address to the legislature was politically significant, not a speech he could screw up.

Here the slangy conclusion clashes with the standard level of the rest of the sentence. Just as you would not wear shorts with a dinner jacket, you do not want to call attention to yourself by inappropriately mixing styles of writing.

Inappropriate:	The *New York Times* has this quote that goes, "All the news that's fit to print."
Appropriate:	The *New York Times* has a motto: "All the news that's fit to print."

Keep in mind that *quote* is a verb, not a noun. The noun form is *quotation,* and this word refers to quoted text, not primary text.

Exercise

Study the levels of usage in the following sentences. Rewrite in General English any sentences that are too informal for college writing or that combine slang with more formal usage. If a sentence is correct, mark it *C*.

1. The museum director gave a totally cool presentation.

2. The English language, Orwell observed, is unquestionably hard up.

3. At the recent stockholders' meeting, the president made several off-the-wall remarks.

4. Studying history has never turned Jan on that much.

5. Many television viewers, disgusted with commercials, opt for public television channels.

6. The library's database search produced results in like 0.25 seconds.

7. Even after a whole year of studying Shakespeare, Jeff still finds the plays tough to relate to.

8. Two candidates withdrew from the current presidential primary when they were accused of not being sufficiently hard-nosed about crime.

9. The dean advised the faculty to chill out after submitting their grades.

10. The computer science final exam is not one that you can expect to ace.

idiom

61 Use the idiom of written English.

An **idiom** is a customary expression peculiar to a language. For example, native speakers of English will say "with the naked eye," not "with a bare eye," though it is impossible to explain why. You may have difficulty with some of the idiomatic uses of certain prepositions: When do you say *differ from* instead of *differ with?* Do you say *to the contrary* or *on the contrary?* If your ear cannot guide you, a college-level dictionary usually can. Here are some troublesome phrases:

Unidiomatic	Idiomatic
absolve of	absolve from
accept to	accept by
accuse with	accuse of
accustom with	accustom to
adhere in (*or* by)	adhere to
adjacent of	adjacent to
agree in	agree to (a proposal)
	agree on (a course of action)
angry at (a person)	angry with (a person)
apologize about	apologize for
bored of	bored with (*or* by)
comply to	comply with
concur about	concur with (a person)
	concur in (a decision or action)
conform in	conform to (*or* with)
derived of	derived from
different than	different from
in accordance to	in accordance with
in search for	in search of
intend on doing	intend to do
interfere about	interfere with (= prevent)
	interfere in (= meddle)

62

Unidiomatic	Idiomatic
oblivious about	oblivious of (or to)
plan on doing	plan to do
preferable than	preferable to
similar with	similar to
superior than	superior to

Exercise

Reword any of the following sentences that contain unidiomatic expressions. If a sentence is correct, mark it *C*.

1. The mayor was not concerned for the ownership of the land.

2. Jason believes that all imported wines are superior to domestic ones.

3. Our new neighbors are trying hard to be different than everyone else on the street.

4. Sara was too angry at him to apologize about her own rudeness.

5. Nick graduated high school at sixteen, benefiting by an accelerated program.

6. Some people find themselves caught in a vicious cycle in which they cannot escape.

7. Women are more capable to hold high-stress military jobs than many people think.

8. Laura did not concur with the majority decision.

9. The story contains a warning on amassing wealth and being obsessed over power.

10. Because of today's attitudes of money, a desire for upward mobility is prevalent with many Americans.

vague

62 **Use specific and concrete words.**

Consider the following sentences:

> We protected all of the plants in the yard.
> We mulched the shrubs, mounded around the rose bushes, and covered the eucalyptus tree.

The second sentence is more specific; it identifies the plants and the ways of protecting them. It is longer, but the extra words give the reader a clearer picture.

62

Specific terms give more information than general ones. For example, *surgeon* implies *doctor,* but *doctor* does not identify a person as a surgeon. If you find yourself writing *people* when you mean *U.S. citizens* or *college students,* you are not asking yourself this important question: Am I identifying what I am referring to as specifically as I should? The following list shows how little effort it takes to become more specific:

General	Specific	More Specific
vehicle	car	Toyota Corolla
go	run	sprint
go	walk	shuffle
religion	Christianity	Roman Catholicism
officer	Cabinet officer	Secretary of State

The best choice is usually the most specific expression that says what you mean. In the following examples, notice how the specific sentences clarify the general ones:

General: The vegetables were prepared.

Specific: We chopped the celery, diced the carrots, and sliced the onions.

Specific: We steamed the carrots and baked the Idaho potatoes.

General: Jan worked.

Specific: Jan sold paint at her uncle's hardware store for two years.

Specific: Jan spent last weekend cleaning the windows, floors, and walls of her apartment.

Abstract terms often combine with general terms in dull writing. An abstract term names something intangible, such as an idea or a quality: *democracy, finance, linguistics.* A concrete term, on the other hand, points to something physically real: *desk, checkbook, motorcycle.* We could not communicate complex ideas without using abstract terms, but dull writing tends to be unnecessarily abstract. Sentences filled with *aspects, cases, factors, circumstances,* and *instances* will weaken your writing. Many writers mistakenly convert verbs *(explain, prefer)* into abstract nouns *(explanation, preference)* and use those nouns with such vague verbs as *be, have,* or *make:*

Jonathan offered no explanation for his preference for California wines.

62

We can improve the sentence by changing the abstract nouns *(explanation, preference)* back to verbs:

Jonathan did not explain why he preferred California wines.

Notice how the following abstract sentence, taken from a newspaper report, is improved by avoiding the abstract nouns *decline* and *use:*

Abstract: The U.S. Department of Agriculture statistics show a decline in the annual per capita use of eggs during the period 1994 to 2004.

More concrete: According to U.S. Department of Agriculture statistics, the average American ate fewer eggs in 2004 than in 1994.

Often you may not be able to make your writing more concrete simply by changing a few words. If your sentences are filled with abstract and general terms, you may find that you need to add specific examples. Vague language often indicates vague or incomplete thinking.

Vague: The government official visited the new company headquarters.

Specific: Joan Wood Branham, the Secretary of Commerce, visited the new Southwestern Bell headquarters in suburban St. Louis.

Exercise

A. Mark specific or concrete sentences with *S* and those that are vaguely worded with *X*. Rewrite those marked *X* with specific, concrete words.

Example: Plants can combat indoor air pollution.

Some common houseplants can scour the air of carbon monoxide, benzene, and other harmful chemical fumes.

1. The media are often blamed for too many things.

2. New paint will brighten this old building.

3. For many people, music is a major source of spirituality.

4. Married couples need many resources.

5. The space program continues to make a significant contribution to our society.

6. In many cases, consumers are misled by advertising.

63

7. Toy commercials on television easily manipulate young children's minds.

8. Alternative medicine has undergone considerable growth.

9. The latest video technology offers the possibility of many interesting scenarios.

10. Hip-hop has had a major influence on musical experiments in jazz, rock, and the blues.

ww 63 Make sure that you understand the meanings of words.

A well-chosen word, Eric Sevareid once said, is worth a thousand pictures. If you are to select the word that expresses precisely what you intend to say, you must understand its denotation—what it literally means. If you write *notorious* when you mean *famous,* or *erotic* when you mean *erratic,* you will confuse your readers and cause them to doubt your competence as a writer. The Glossary of Usage (page G-5) lists a number of easily confused words.

Imprecise:	Many English classes require at least one *analyzation* of a poem or story.
Precise:	Many English classes require at least one *analysis* of a poem or story.

Imprecise:	The 2003 article by Olsen *quotes* that "computer-aided literature studies have not yet had the impact many scholars expected."
Precise:	The 2003 article by Olsen *states* that "computer-aided literature studies have not yet had the impact many scholars expected."

Exercise

A. Determine the difference between these paired words:

1. apprehend—comprehend
2. simple—simplistic
3. notable—notorious
4. exceedingly—excessively
5. disinterested—uninterested
6. fortunate—fortuitous
7. feasible—possible
8. forceful—forcible
9. illusion—allusion
10. imply—infer

64

B. Is the italicized word in each of the following sentences correct? If not, supply the correct word.

1. Louise sees things from a unique *vintage* point.

2. Chemical research *includes* effort, time, and efficiency.

3. At the *onset* of the class, the instructor gave a pop quiz.

4. Bob did not wish to be *involved* in his ex-wife's problems.

5. In our *distraughtness* after the accident, we forgot to call our families.

6. Good teachers usually try to *elicit* involvement from students.

7. Always a private person, Mrs. Wilberforce was generous to many charities but wanted to remain *magnanimous*.

8. Medieval Christianity played an important *factor* in the lives of every European.

9. The author goes on to *express* that Lawrence is a powerful writer.

10. The guilty students, in their defense, pleaded *exterminating* circumstances.

ᵂᵂ **64** Make sure that the connotations of your words are appropriate.

We choose words for their literal as well as for their implied meanings. Whereas **denotations** (literal dictionary definitions) are neutral, **connotations**—the suggested or implied meanings of words—convey feelings and attitudes and include emotional overtones. For example, a dictionary will define *politician* as one who actively engages in politics. But if you describe a fellow student as a "real politician," you call up not the literal meaning of *politician,* its denotation, but its connotations: your fellow student is a smooth operator. Consider the differences in tone in each of these sentences:

The faculty senate *discussed* the proposed grading system.
The faculty senate *debated* the proposed grading system.
The faculty senate *argued about* the proposed grading system.
The faculty senate *quarreled over* the proposed grading system.

After three hours of *questioning*, the detained protesters were released.
After three hours of *grilling*, the political prisoners were liberated.

The dictionary can help you distinguish among various synonyms whose meanings overlap yet remain distinct. You might look up *rare* and see how your dictionary distinguishes the meaning of this word from *uncommon, infrequent,* and *unusual.*

Many words have powerful social and political overtones. Because these words may evoke personal, emotional responses in those who hear or read them, you must be conscious of their connotations. *Loaded words,* used especially by propagandists and advertisers, appeal to emotion rather than to reason. These words are imprecise and biased. Words such as *un-American, radical, leftist, subversive,* and *reactionary* indicate prejudicial political stereotyping. Political commentators sometimes refer to liberals as "bleeding hearts" or to welfare payments as "government handouts."

64a Avoid sexist language.

Today's writers try to avoid sexist language and are conscious of the need to use less offensive, more inclusive terminology. Much of this terminology was once exclusively male, but the language preferred today is designed to include women. Good examples are the changes in job titles from *salesman* to *salesperson* and the change from the generic use of *man* or *mankind,* in referring to both men and women, to *human beings* or *humankind.* Other gender-neutral terms that prevent sex-role stereotyping are the following:

chairperson, chair	*rather than:*	chairman
member of the clergy		clergyman
firefighter		fireman
personnel		manpower
member of Congress, legislator		congressman
worker		workman
server		waitress, waiter
technician		repairman

You should also avoid using singular masculine pronouns *(he, him, his)* to refer to both men and women when you are unsure of the gender of the antecedent or when both sexes are involved (see **51b**). That is, you can change:

Every writer has *his* own story to tell.

to:

Every writer has *his or her* own story to tell.

64

Even better, because the use of *his or her* can become awkward, you can just use the plural:

> *Writers* have *their* own stories to tell.

You can also rewrite sentences so that the issue of gender does not arise:

> Before starting *his* practice, a physician must put in many long, hard years of work.
> Before starting *a* practice, a physician must put in many long, hard years of work.

In some instances, the plural cannot be used, so you will have to write *he or she, him or her,* or *his or her.* But doing so indicates to your reader that you are aware of the problem of sexist language and are trying to avoid it.

Exercise

A. Complete the following sentences by selecting the most-appropriate words.

1. Under the circumstances, the cashier's attitude toward the robber was surprisingly _____ (lenient, reasonable, temperate).

2. Beginning drivers are often a bit too _____ (wary, cautious, discreet).

3. Because of some low grades, my plans to attend law school do not seem _____ (feasible, possible, practicable, probable).

4. Paloma attended only one of our _____ (scarce, rare, infrequent, unusual) meetings.

5. The new model-Z car is an unbeatable combination of European _____ (skill, genius, artistry, craftsmanship) and the traditionally _____ (courageous, bold, intrepid) American design. This accounts for its _____ (peculiar, distinctive, special) style.

B. Rewrite these sentences, eliminating sexist language.

1. The Western civilization course concerns the history of man's ingenuity and persistence.

2. Man-made lakes are created for the pleasure of boaters and fishermen.

3. The mayor requested two additional policemen to man the polling place.

4. Success for a law school student depends on his command of language skills.

5. A man alone is in bad company.

C. How do the connotations of these paired words differ?

1. cheap—inexpensive

2. design—shape

3. tough—durable

4. invincible—unbeatable

5. distinguished—distinctive

6. startled—shocked

7. spinster—bachelor

8. childish—childlike

9. brilliance—ingenuity

10. smart—elegant

fig 65 Use figures of speech to create vivid images.

Figurative language, or imagery, is not limited to poetry. Comparisons between the familiar and the less familiar are a basic part of everyday communication. When we talk about a politician playing hardball, we are not speaking literally about sports, but figuratively: we are comparing two unlike things that are similar in some often unexpected way. Figures of speech can clarify a point and make writing come alive by creating vivid pictures for your reader. The most commonly used figures are similes and metaphors.

Similes are direct, explicit comparisons, using *like* or *as:*

Jake was as mean as a ferret with a hangover.
Her laugh was loud and piercing, like hail on a copper roof.

Metaphors are indirect, implied comparisons, without *like* or *as:*

"Churchill mobilized the English language and took it to war."
—*John F. Kennedy*

Memories are hard to control because the mind seldom stays on its leash but dashes randomly off into the past, digging up and retrieving old bones.

65

Personification is a type of metaphor that gives human qualities to inanimate objects or abstractions:

"The bridge wears a necklace of twinkling lights."

—student

Compare these statements to see how a dull literal statement can be made more lively by using imagery:

Dull: His jaw was rigid.

Vivid: "His jaw was as rigid as a horseshoe."

—Flannery O'Connor

Dull: This movie is empty and pretentious.

Vivid: "This movie is a toupee made up to look like honest baldness."

—Pauline Kael

If, however, you cannot create a fresh metaphor that fits your subject, rely on an accurate literal statement. A dull, overused metaphor (see **67**) will demonstrate only that you are not original; a wildly inappropriate or strained metaphor will spoil what you have to say.

Strained: Each wave rolled in like a giant wall of emerald ice cream topped with whipped cream.

Strained: The rising sun, pushing aside the darkness, spit out a glowing welcome sign over the horizon.

Exercise

A. Complete each of the following with an original metaphor or simile.

1. The news of the divorce spread through the town like

   _____.

2. The old woman's hair was so thin that _____.

3. The usually cool detective was shaking like _____.

4. The judge listened, as impartial as _____.

5. After driving nonstop for seven hours, Kim was so exhausted that he _____.

B. List as many figures of speech as you can that are derived from baseball, such as *ballpark figure.*

C. Revise the following strained images so that they create clear and consistent pictures.

66

1. The photographer's lens is riveted to life's passing parade.

2. The prosecutor hammered away at the witness, much like a butcher hacking away at a carcass.

3. The economy must not be nailed to the cross of the stock market.

4. The empty spaces on the library shelves grinned broadly, like a gap-toothed crone.

5. A bad law is like chewing gum stuck to the sole of a shoe.

fig 66 Make your figures of speech consistent with each other and with your subject.

Metaphorical language is so common that writers may be unaware of the comparisons that their words evoke. For example, when you speak of "grasping" or "catching" rather than "understanding" what a writer is saying, you are making a simple comparison between the mind and hands. If you speak of being "flooded with memories," you are using another metaphor: the mind is the land, the memories the floodwaters. But if you were to say "When I grasped what he was saying, it flooded me with memories," you would have a **mixed metaphor,** two images that conflict with each other. Mixed metaphors are a sure sign that you are not thinking about the pictures that your words create:

Mixed: The idea blossomed, then quickly crept away like a thief in the night.

Mixed: The theater of life is often a valley of tears.

Revise trite figures of speech whether they conflict with other images or not (see **67**), and make sure that your images call up pictures that fit your subject.

Exercise

Explain why the figures of speech in the following sentences are ineffective.

1. The avalanche of statistics is hard for voters to swallow.

2. If differences can be ironed out between Congress and the President, the economy will receive a needed shot in the arm.

3. Our language seems to be coming apart at the seams because writers burn themselves out on a diet of clichés.

67

4. The bottom line on inflation boils down to some tough decisions that Congress may find hard to swallow.

5. Evelyn didn't have a leg to stand on after the judge warned her that she was skating on thin ice.

trite Avoid trite expressions and unwarranted
67 euphemisms.

In conversation, we often use stale expressions without thinking about what they mean. But as a writer, you have time to think, so try to make the most out of your words.

Clichés Many of the figures of speech that come most readily to mind were once fresh images. But, through overuse, they have lost their effectiveness. We too easily use these trite expressions, or **clichés**, in place of original thought. No reader will be impressed by such hackneyed images as *fresh as a daisy* or *dead as a doornail*. Here is a brief list of clichés that have lost their value as figures of speech:

frosting on the cake	playing with fire
beat around the bush	in a nutshell
by leaps and bounds	nipped in the bud
bit the dust	light as a feather
crystal clear	no stone unturned

Fillers Also common are useless phrases such as *all in all, so to speak, as it were, needless to say, it goes without saying,* and *as a matter of fact.* These phrases add words but no meaning. Here are some others to avoid:

better late than never	last but not least
each and every	point with pride
easier said than done	rain or shine
few and far between	short and sweet
first and foremost	safe and sound
golden opportunity	without rhyme or reason

Using an original metaphor, Richard Altick sums up the point: A writer should provide "traction for the readers' minds rather than allow them to slide and skid on a slippery surface paved with well-worn phrases."

Euphemisms A **euphemism** refers indirectly to something unpleasant or embarrassing. For example, many people use *pass away* or *expire* to mean "die." A euphemism is sometimes the best way to avoid hurting someone's feelings; however, many euphemisms are trite, many are wordy, and many conceal truths that should be made plain.

67

Members of Congress seldom mention *bribes, graft,* and *expense-paid vacations;* they do mention *honorariums, campaign contributions,* and *travel reimbursement.* The result of such language is a dangerous double-talk that misleads readers and distorts truth.

Trite and wordy:	under the influence (drunk)
	stretch the truth (lie)
	kick the bucket (die)
Misleading:	involuntary force reduction (layoff)
	protective reaction strike (bombing)
	inoperative statement (false, retracted statement)
	revenue enhancement (tax increase)

Exercise

A. To see how easily clichés come to mind, complete the trite expressions in the following "speech":

"First and _____, as you travel down the _____ to success, you will face many challenges _____ and beyond the call of _____. If you persevere, you will pass life's greatest tests with _____ colors; and you can then point with _____ to your achievement. For you will then be truly in a class _____ _____. In the _____ analysis, when all is _____ and _____, it goes without _____ that each and _____ _____ of you can succeed only if you _____ the line and keep your _____ to the wheel as well as your _____ to the grindstone. Last but not _____, I must remind you that all of this is _____ said than _____."

68

B. Find a euphemism for each of the following:

1. bossy
2. cheap
3. steal
4. spy
5. ugly

C. Find equivalents for the following clichés and euphemisms:

1. knowing the ropes	6. skating on thin ice
2. lap of luxury	7. bite the dust
3. bottom line	8. nipped in the bud
4. severe nutritional deficiency	9. wedded bliss
5. electronic surveillance	10. uphill fight

flowery **68** Avoid pretentious and unfamiliar words.

In general, write in plain English. Although you should try to build a rich vocabulary, strive to use it precisely, not just to show it off. "Pomposity," "flowery diction," and "overwriting" are just some of the terms used to describe the common mistake of using big words when familiar words would be more appropriate to the audience and subject. Use a long, formal word only when it expresses your meaning exactly, and avoid falsely poetic, foreign, and artificially formal terms:

Pretentious: It is requested that superfluous illumination be extinguished upon exiting the premises.

Improved: Turn off the lights when you leave the room.

Pretentious: The unauthorized ignition of tobacco-containing substances on this site constitutes felonious behavior.

Improved: Smoking in this area is a felony.

Exercise

Translate the following pretentious sentences into more direct English.

1. Individuals who inhabit domiciles composed of frangible substances containing silicon compounds should be wary of casting hard, nonmetallic mineral matter.

2. The sky's stellar sentinels signaled the termination of the day.

3. Percipient weather prognosticators indicate that significant amounts of precipitation are anticipated in these United States.

4. Harvey, albeit inebriated, was not guilty of prevarication when he asserted that his position had been terminated.

5. A not unimportant date to be borne in the national memory in perpetuity is September 11, 2001.

jargon When writing for the general reader, avoid jargon and highly technical language.
69

Nearly every specialized field develops its own specialized language: psychologists speak of *syndromes* and *psychoses,* computer programmers discuss *core capacity* and *interface,* and art critics refer to *texture* and *value contrast.* Among specialists, a specialized vocabulary can convey exact meanings. Among nonspecialists, however, the same vocabulary is only jargon, usually pretentious and confusing. If you want to use a technical term, ask yourself two questions: Do I really need the term? Will my readers understand it? If you do need the term and your readers might not understand it, be sure to define it.

Jargon also refers to the many unnecessarily technical expressions that develop in most fields. Some of these expressions are euphemisms (see **67**), some just inflated language. Here are a few examples of educational jargon:

learning facilitator (= teacher)
exceptional student (= slow or fast learner)
underachiever (= slow student)
disadvantaged (= poor)
empower (= help)

69

Big words such as the following are often misused to give a technical flavor to nontechnical writing:

ameliorate (improve)	exhibit (show)
endeavor (try)	factor (item, point, cause)
inaugurate (begin)	per se (in itself)
individual (person)	peruse (read)
initiate (begin)	presently (now)
maximum (most)	utilize (use)
optimum (best)	viable (workable)
finalize (finish)	conceptualize (understand)

Here is President Kennedy's famous statement, "Ask not what your country can do for you; ask what you can do for your country," translated into modern jargon:

It is not deemed appropriate to make inquiry as to those initiatives to be actualized by this nation on behalf of individuals but, contrariwise, to ascertain the methodologies by which said individuals can maximize their optimum contributions to said nation.

Such bloated language prevents communication.

Exercise

Rewrite the following sentences, eliminating jargon.

1. A vast majority of the specimens presently under examination exhibit deteriorative tendencies suggestive of a virus as the causal factor.

2. Within the parameters of the social sciences, the thrust of much research is focused on ameliorating conditions which militate against the optimum adjustment of partners in a marital situation.

3. Commencing in the new year, I will endeavor to prioritize my debts.

4. The library's growth necessitates maximizing present resources to the optimum advantage.

5. The staff must initiate a program to utilize every viable mode of aerobic exercise for the employees.

wdy rep 70 Avoid needless repetition and wordiness.

As you revise, look for ways to eliminate anything that does not add to your meaning. Writers often pad sentences with clichés (see **67**) and jargon (see **69**):

Wordy: As to the reason for the delay, it was not because of the absence of the governor.

Improved: The reason for the delay was not the governor's absence.

Wordy: It is our belief that the safety device in question possesses the capability of being used by the airlines.

Improved: We believe that airlines can use this safety device.

Note that verb phrases using *is, are, was,* and *were* can lead to wordiness; the same is true of sentences starting with *there is, there are,* etc.

Wordy: Jon is capable of cooking more than pasta.

Improved: Jon can cook more than pasta.

Wordy: There are some countries that limit or outlaw explicit and violent movies.

Improved: Some countries limit or outlaw explicit and violent movies.

Wordy: It is important for motorists to avoid the right-hand lane unless they want to turn right.

Improved: Motorists must avoid the right-hand lane unless they want to turn right.

Avoid long verb phrases (*give consideration to* or *come to a conclusion*); instead, use simple, concrete verbs (*consider* or *conclude*). Avoid unneeded intensives *(indeed, really, quite frankly)*, windy openers *(it is, there are)*, and stock phrases such as these:

due to the fact that (= because)
in all probability (= probably)
in excess of (= more than)
in many instances (= often)
in a similar fashion (= similarly)
in the neighborhood of (= about)
on a daily basis (= daily)
in the event that (= if)

70

on the part of (= by *or* among)
a large number of (= many)
a small number of (= few)
during the time that (= while)
small-sized (= small)

Exercise

A. Reduce each phrase to one word:

outside of	in the near future
plan ahead	advance forward
can possibly	future plans
recur again	possible likelihood
question as to whether	disappear from view
rectangular in shape	red in color
quite exact	absolutely essential
cease and desist	most unique
contain within	complete monopoly
visible to the eye	

B. Replace each of these phrases with a single verb:

conduct an investigation
undertake the removal of
result in damage to
have a necessity for
take a measurement
place a call to

70a Eliminate meaningless intensives.

We tend to fill our speech with words such as *very, so, certainly, quite, really,* and *totally.* They can add color and emphasis, but in writing you seldom need such words. Clear thoughts do not usually need modifiers such as *very (clear), quite (clear),* or *really (clear).* Watch, too, such imprecise, extravagant modifiers as *incredible, fantastic, terribly,* and *awfully.* What does an *incredible* performance really mean?

70b Eliminate obvious repetition and redundancy.

Other forms of wordiness include obvious repetition, redundancy (express-ing the same idea in different ways, as in *basic essentials* or *the reason is because*), and unnecessary negatives *(not unlikely)*. See the Glossary of Usage (page G-5) for some common redundant expressions and **24a** for rep-etition in sentences.

Obvious repetition:	When any two items are compared, one must consider many aspects. Some of these aspects are readily discernible. These aspects involve similarities and differences.
Improved:	Any comparison must consider both similarities and differences.
Redundant:	Throughout the entire story, the young girl faces many dangers.
Improved:	Throughout the story, the young girl faces many dangers.
Needless negatives:	Not a few modern airports are not well equipped for large numbers of passengers.
Improved:	Many modern airports are not well equipped for large numbers of passengers.

Exercise

A. Improve the following sentences by eliminating unnecessary words. Reword the sentences if necessary.

1. What Gail does is edit an electronic journal.

2. In my opinion, the artist employs the use of color and light very effectively.

3. The LGBT community that lives in places such as South Florida, for example, tends to be politically liberal.

4. In that time period, it was not uncommon to find husbands and wives in business partnership together.

5. The reason why we are gathered together here is because we are celebrating a special birthday.

6. In the first two paragraphs of the story, it indicates who the likely suspect is.

7. *The Zoo Story* is a play by Edward Albee. It is a play that is dealing with the subject of alienation.

8. There is truth to the contention that the causes of the Civil War were in a very real sense economic.

9. This particular device is hexagonal in shape.

10. One reason for the economic decline is because of the past history of the deficit.

B. Explain the redundancy in each of the following.

1. present incumbent

2. personal friendship

3. advance planning

4. past experience/history

5. throughout the entire period of time

A Practical Guide to Writing

III

A Practical Guide to Writing

Writing a Research Paper

71

The research paper is a documented essay containing citations to the sources you have consulted. It combines your own ideas, experiences, and attitudes with supporting information provided by other sources. These sources allow you to develop your topic with informed opinions, which you support with the evidence you have gathered. Using sources properly will help you write more authoritatively.

The process of research involves these principal activities:

1. Searching for a topic and for sources
2. Reading to select an appropriate topic and to gather information
3. Evaluating information and ideas
4. Organizing and writing the paper

The process might be more fully outlined as follows:

Step 1.	Beginning the research
	Choosing an interesting subject
	Selecting a limited topic
	Developing a working thesis
Step 2.	Locating and skimming sources
	Searching for information relevant to your working thesis
	Eliminating irrelevant information
	Reexamining your working thesis
Step 3.	Reading sources and drawing conclusions
	Reading selected sources carefully
	Taking detailed notes
	Analyzing the information
	Developing a thesis statement
Step 4.	Writing the paper
	Composing the first draft
	Revising the paper
	Adding documentation
	Formatting, keying, and editing the final draft
	Preparing the Works Cited or References page
	Proofreading and submitting the paper

Taking the research paper assignment step by step, as outlined in this chapter, and giving yourself adequate time for each step in the process will make the task more profitable and manageable.

71 Select an interesting, manageable topic.   71

Research papers too often become long recitations of facts and opinions copied from sources. The best way to avoid producing anything so un-original and to eliminate needless drudgery is to choose a subject that you already know something about and want to learn more about. As you read general reference books or consult their online equivalents, consider aspects of the broad subject that experts differ on. And look for a topic that can be covered within the limits of your assignment. Then your research will not only satisfy your curiosity but will also allow you to write with authority about a topic that means something to you. By examining facts, sifting evidence, and comparing opinions, you will be able to arrive at your own conclusions and keep your own contribution at the heart of your paper.

If you are free to choose your own subject, do not try to read everything you can find on politics, nature, art, or whatever general field that most interests you. You must focus on one small corner of that field: not politics but the problem of revenue sharing and social-welfare programs, not nature but the causes of weed pollution in local lakes, not art but the influence of Cézanne on Cubist painting. An argumentation topic—one that has at least two sides—or one involving a problem will let you approach the question in an interesting way. Your instruc-tor may propose a general subject, such as "television advertising," and chal-lenge you to develop your own topic. Out of that you might develop these:

Types of deception used in television commercials

Sexual stereotyping in television commercials

Government regulation of television advertising

Methods that advertisers use to influence programming

You can save yourself time if you avoid certain predictable kinds of unsuit-able topics:

- Topics too complex or controversial to be handled in anything less than a book: "influenza research"

- Topics so limited or obscure that you can find only a few brief sources: "developing Ektachrome prints"

- Topics so new that little has yet been published on them

- Topics so cut-and-dried that you can do little more than summarize your sources in a report on your reading: "the life of Abraham Lincoln"

- Topics about which you can write little that is not already known to most people: "drunk driving is harmful"
- Topics about which you have such strong feelings that you might not be able to evaluate what you read objectively, such as the question of abortion's morality

72 Explore available resources.

Before you settle on a topic, be sure that you can find enough material to develop that topic. First, decide on a research plan that suits the available resources, your topic, and your available time. A typical procedure is to read general reference books such as encyclopedias (or their online equivalents) to get an overview of the subject and to help you narrow the focus to a manageable topic. You might then search for books (through your school's library catalog) and magazine and journal articles (through your school library's periodical indexes and online subscription services) that you can skim to see how relevant they are for your purposes.

As you develop a basic bibliography—a list of books, articles, and other sources that you will investigate—write on a 3″ by 5″ card the call number (or URL, for online sources), author's full name, full title, and other pertinent information for each source. Another option is to use a laptop computer or a smartphone for this step, saving your source material in its own file or area. The point is to use whichever method works best for you—being complete and using correct form (see **77b** and **78b**) will save you time later when you prepare your final paper.

Bibliography Card: Book

Rabin, Robert L., and Stephen D. Sugarman, eds. Regulating Tobacco. New York: Oxford UP, 2001.

HD9136.R43

Bibliography Card: Article

Viscusi, W. Kip. "Promoting Smokers' Welfare with
Responsible Taxation." National Tax Journal 47
(1994): 547-58.

HJ2240.N315

72a Locating Information

Today, you can find research sources in three formats: (1) sources that do not appear on the Internet, (2) sources that appear on the Internet only, and (3) sources that appear in a traditional format and have been digitized and posted on the Internet as well. Let's look at how these three categories work.

Traditional research leads you to books and to articles published in journals, magazine, and newspapers. Your school library is the best place to begin.

The library catalog The physical card catalog—wooden boxes containing a card for each holding—has all but disappeared from most college libraries. Most library catalogs are now accessed through dedicated Internet connections. This approach usually adds a very handy feature: you can search for books *and* articles. (A traditional, physical card catalogue listed the library's books only.) Modern library databases allow you to search by title, by author, by subject, or by key word(s). Although these search options tend to be standard, don't hesitate to ask your research librarian for help as you learn how to use the online catalog.

Periodical indexes Because some of the most current information is available in magazine and journal articles, using the various indexes to periodical literature is essential in almost every library research project. The periodical guides are the keys to articles. Do not limit yourself to the best-known and most general of these indexes, the *Readers' Guide to Periodical Literature*.

72

Note that many of the periodical indexes listed below are also available as online databases, allowing you to search for articles electronically by entering key words, words that would logically appear in titles of articles in a given area. Also note that there is a national network of research files. These include PAIS (Public Affairs Information Service), Newsearch (a daily index of news articles from 1,400 newspapers and periodicals), ERIC (Educational Resources Information Center), and many other specialized databases.

General indexes:

> *Humanities Index* (1974–)—formerly the *Social Sciences and Humanities Index* (1965–73) and the *International Index* (1907–65)
>
> *New York Times Index* (1913–)
>
> *National Newspaper Index* (1979–)
>
> *Readers' Guide to Periodical Literature* (1900–)
>
> *Social Sciences Index* (1974–)—formerly the *Social Sciences and Humanities Index* (1965–73) and the *International Index* (1907–65)

Specialized indexes:

> *Applied Science and Technology Index* (1958–)
>
> *Biography Index* (1946–)
>
> *Biological and Agricultural Index* (1964–)
>
> *Business Periodicals Index* (1958–)
>
> *Central Index to Journals of Education* (1969–)
>
> *Education Index* (1929–)
>
> *General Science Index* (1978–)
>
> *Index to Legal Periodicals* (1908–)
>
> *MLA International Bibliography* [literature, language] (1921–)
>
> *Public Affairs Information Service Bulletin* (1915–)

See also the various abstracts, such as *Chemical Abstracts* (1907–) and *Psychological Abstracts* (1927–).

Reference books Also cited in the library's electronic catalog are the library's encyclopedias, dictionaries, atlases, and many other basic reference tools. Here are a few:

Special encyclopedias:

> *International Encyclopedia of the Social Sciences.* 17 vols.
>
> *The New Catholic Encyclopedia.* 15 vols.
>
> *Van Nostrand's Scientific Encyclopedia*

Other:

Current Biography (1940–)
Facts on File (1941–)
Statistical Abstract of the United States (1878–)
World Almanac and Book of Facts (1868–)

Libraries also contain pamphlets, government documents, films on DVD and videotape, filmstrips, audiotapes, music CDs and records, and other non-print sources.

The Internet Today, the Internet contains sources of all levels of quality—from the biased and harmful to the too-general and relatively useless to the specific, expert, and extremely valuable. Documents that are first published on the Internet are tempting for the student researcher because of their convenience. However, real problems occur for students who want to rely on Internet research:

1. Is the source reliable? If you are looking for sources about current events and find yourself reading articles on the website of the *New York Times* or the *Wall Street Journal,* you can trust this online publication at the same level that you trust the traditional publication of the company. However, many groups with strong agendas have their own websites containing articles written for—or by—the organization. Are these unbiased? Probably not. Are they useful for your research? Possibly. You will need to be very careful if you plan to include such sources in your research paper. The worst case is the handsome, well-designed website of some hate group or other representative of the lunatic fringe. Keep in mind that North America has a surfeit of Web designers; it's not difficult to make any website look good, regardless of its content. A basic rule of thumb is that a source whose URL ends in "edu" or "org" is probably better than a source whose URL ends in "com." However, the key word here is "probably." As well, sources that appear in PDF format are more likely to come from reputable sources—but not always.

2. Are you relying too much on basic search-engine research and ignoring true academic research? During the past fifteen years we have seen some weak papers caused by the student's reliance upon "easy" research. The essay might include a definition from an online commercial encyclopedia (one source), a posting to a discussion group (one more source), and information from the home page of a major company (and so on). Do you see the problem here? The student is trying to use the Internet to *avoid* doing true academic research. Always remember that the Internet is a tool, not a crutch.

73

However, modern library technology does offer an extremely convenient use of the Internet for academic research. Most college libraries now subscribe to search databases such as EBSCOhost and JSTOR. These services will link you to full-text articles that were originally published in print form but are now also available digitally. Moreover, these services will link you to articles in journals that your library might not carry. Finally, many college libraries allow you to log in from a remote location by using your college ID number. Then you can access the digital subscription service. This is a true convenience. Check with a research librarian at your school to find out which services are available and to get help in learning how to use them.

73 Evaluate your sources of information.

Analyzing the material you find is always important. We discussed the problems of Internet sources in the previous section, but we also need to point out that not everything in print is reliable and that some sources carry more weight than others. A short article in a popular magazine will seldom be as authoritative as a book or journal article, but even a book may represent an extreme approach to a subject. Always be careful to distinguish between facts and opinions. As you examine any source, ask yourself these questions:

- Is the writer a recognized authority on the subject, one whose work is cited by other writers?

- Does the work seem to be biased? Does the author give sufficient attention to other points of view?

- Is the work recent enough to provide up-to-date information?

Aim for a balanced bibliography that reflects as many viewpoints as possible and that includes journal articles as well as books and magazine articles. In most cases, if half of your sources consist of articles from one periodical, search further. Scholarly journals provide more thoroughly documented material than do magazines, which might be general, exaggerated, or slanted to reflect a particular bias. For a paper on acid rain, for example, you would not depend on a newspaper article but would instead consult a journal such as *Nature* or *Science.* Interviews, if they provide information not easily found in published sources, can be useful as long as those interviewed are knowledgeable and objective. Corporations, museums, government agencies, specialized organizations (the Red Cross, for example), as well as your class notes can also provide information not found in libraries.

Primary and secondary sources Primary sources are the actual texts of reports, novels, and documents, as well as interviews, questionnaires, recordings, and other original material. Secondary sources are the critical and historical accounts based on primary materials. For a documented essay on the end of the space shuttle program, for example, your primary sources might include reports from NASA as well as interviews with or letters from space officials. For a paper on educational television for children, reports of experiments in childhood learning as well as the programs themselves would be your primary sources. Clearly, watching the programs would be essential to understanding the topic; you would not want to get most of your information secondhand. Whatever your topic, locate and use as many primary sources as possible.

Secondary sources may help you find additional primary sources, and they can point out ways of interpreting those sources. By examining a number of secondary sources, you can determine which ones offer the most convincing interpretation of the facts. Because you will probably not have time to read all the available secondary sources in their entirety, check their indexes and tables of contents, and skim chapters that you think might help you. Also check each secondary source for a bibliography that might direct you to other sources; this can be a very fruitful approach.

74 Prepare a preliminary thesis statement and working outline.

As early as possible in your research, formulate a tentative statement of the main point you expect to make in your paper (see 6). You will need to change this preliminary thesis statement if further research gives you a new perspective, but deciding on your thesis will help you concentrate your note taking on material that supports, contradicts, or in some other way bears directly on your main point.

Next, consider the subpoints you will need to support your thesis, and arrange these into a rough outline (see 7). For example, if you are working on the future of the Olympic movement, your preliminary thesis and rough (working) outline might look like this:

> **Thesis:**   The Olympic Games will surrender to commercialism unless reforms are made.
>
> I.   Most competitors are now professionals.
> II. Corporate sponsors are much too visible.
> III. Product merchandising should be curbed.

As you develop the topic further, you will find ways to develop each of the subtopics: When did the shift occur from amateur status to professional status? Why are corporate sponsors a problem? Is there a practical, equitable way to limit product merchandising? You may also find new subtopics or discover that you have to change some of the ones you have. You might also find that you need to sharpen your thesis statement. For example, you could specify how changes in the Olympics would solve the recent problems:

> The Olympics can regain some of its lost luster by emphasizing the importance of amateur athletics, curbing corporate sponsors, and limiting product merchandising.

Think of your working outline as a flexible guide in your search for pertinent information. If you code your note cards or digital research files to the sections of your rough outline, you will be able to see if you are finding enough information for each section and if you are turning up new information that calls for changes in your outline.

75 Take thorough, accurate notes on your sources.

Your aim in taking notes is to record accurately and concisely the important facts from your sources. A 4″ by 6″ note card will provide room for substantial notes as well as for a subject heading and a key to the corresponding bibliography card. Use one card for each idea so that you can later sort the cards as you refine your organization. Each card should contain the following information:

1. *Subject.* In a few words at the top of the card, identify the information that the card contains.

2. *Source.* List the author's name or an abbreviated title.

3. *Page number.* If a quotation runs from one page to the next, use a slash to indicate the page break. You may later want to use just part of the quotation.

The note itself may be a quotation, a paraphrase (rewording) of the original material, or a summary.

An alternative to using note cards is to record the data digitally. You can set up a separate file for notes or combine this information with the bibliographic information we discussed on page 208. For safety's sake, remember to back up research files to another storage area.

Quotation Although most note taking should not be word-for-word copying, quote your source directly whenever you think you might want to use the exact wording. When quoting, follow these guidelines:

1. On your note card or in your digital file, place quotation marks around all direct quotations to remind yourself that the wording is not yours. This distinction is essential.

2. Copy your source exactly, including punctuation marks. If an error appears in the original, put [*sic*], meaning *thus* or *so* ("this is the way I found it"), in your notes.

3. Use an ellipsis mark of three spaced periods (. . .) to indicate omitted material within a quoted sentence. Avoid using ellipses before quotations of only parts of sentences (see **40d**).

4. Use square brackets for your own insertions in a quotation: "Last year [2016], Americans spent more than $10 billion on pet foods alone."

Paraphrase Direct quotation is not the only way to record the material you will use. You can reword passages from your sources, but be careful to capture the ideas of an author without copying his or her sentence structure or word choice. You do not have to change every word in your source; simply write in your own style, and note the exact location of the ideas you are rephrasing. When your source contains phrases that you think deserve direct quotation, you can combine paraphrase and quotation, but be sure to distinguish carefully between your words and those of your source.

Summary Instead of copying or carefully paraphrasing background information or other material that you do not plan on presenting in detail, write a brief summary. Record the important facts; skip unimportant details. Early in your note taking, you may want to take summary notes on sources that you expect to investigate more carefully later. Rough summary notes can include abbreviations and incomplete sentences. Such notes give a quick sketch of material you may use and will be more fluently worded in your paper.

The following examples illustrate each of these three note-taking methods. Be sure to include source information (author and page number, if applicable) on all note cards and in all digital research files.

Note Card: Original Material

75

> Storytelling
>
> "The humorous story is told gravely; the teller does his best to conceal the fact that he even dimly suspects that there is anything funny about it; but the teller of the comic story tells you beforehand that it is one of the funniest things he has ever heard, then tells it with eager delight, and is the first person to laugh when he gets through. And sometimes, if he has had good success, he is so glad and happy that he will repeat the 'nub' of it and glance around from face to face, collecting applause, and then repeat it again. It is a pathetic thing to see."
>
> (Mark Twain [Samuel Clemens]), "How to Tell a Story." How to Tell a Story and Other Essays <www.gutenberg.org/files/3250/3250.txt>)

Note Card: Paraphrase

Twain (Clemens)   Storytelling
Twain distinguishes the "humorous" story from the "comic" story. The teller of the humorous story tries to tell the tale "gravely" in order to heighten its humorous effect, but the teller of the comic story is extremely conscious of its potential for humor, which he or she exploits beyond all reason, being all too ready to laugh at his or her effort and repeating the punch line after the story is done. According to Clemens, the effect is "pathetic."

Note Card: Summary

> *Twain (Clemens)*   *Storytelling*
> *Twain contrasts a skillful storyteller, who is playing*
> *a role that requires a deadpan delivery, with a*
> *"comic" storyteller, who exploits his material to the*
> *point that the audience is disgusted.*

Careful note taking can help you avoid plagiarism (see page 219) in your finished paper. It should also indicate your solid understanding of what you have read. For this reason, summaries and paraphrases are preferable to word-for-word copying. Some of the following examples are too close to the original wording to be effective paraphrases:

Original sentence:	"*Gender* is a term that has psychological or cultural rather than biological connotations."
Poor paraphrase:	*Gender* has psychological or cultural, not biological, implications.
Effective paraphrase:	The word *gender* refers to behavior or culture, not biology.
Original sentence:	"The ideal of strict objectivity is absurd."
Poor paraphrase:	Complete objectivity is an absurd ideal.
Effective paraphrase:	No one should strive to be completely objective.
Original quotation:	One of the problems with traveling alone involves the critical issue of choices. When two people travel together, the questions of where to stay, what to eat, and what to do are made simpler: on any single issue, at least one of the pair will have an opinion. Unless the other has her own, radically different opinion, she can default to her companion's suggestion. The companion is on the hook, so to speak, for the responsibility of making a good choice. The other doesn't have to come up with anything.
	However, the solitary traveler is left without this crutch. The first time that I took an extended vacation after my split, the volume of choices was overwhelming. However, the next time out I

75

realized that the alternative—a rigidly planned "itinerary"—was unspeakable.

—From Alexandra Valdez, "On My Own Again" (*Maritime Vistas*, October 2005), 38–39.

Compare this with the following student note cards:

Note Card A (unacceptable)

> *A problem with traveling alone is choices. Two people traveling together can come up with answers on where to stay, eat, and do. If one person suggests a choice, the other can agree and make the first person responsible for the choice. The second person doesn't have to make a suggestion.*
>
> *But someone traveling alone doesn't have this crutch. When Valdez took a trip after her split, she was faced with an overwhelming range of choices. However, she soon found that a rigidly planned itinerary was even worse.*

This note is unacceptable because all its sentences closely follow the original wording. It will be difficult to determine later if these notes are quoted or paraphrased.

Note Card B (acceptable)

> *Solitary traveling requires a formidable array of choices, according to Alexandra Valdez, that people traveling in pairs do not face. In the latter situation, one person can logically be expected to have an opinion, and the other can simply accede, putting the responsibility on the companion. The solitary traveler faces something different: too many choices. But, as Valdez points out, taking a trip with every choice made beforehand is "unspeakable" (38).*

This note is acceptable because no plagiarism (see below) will result; the source is clearly introduced and acknowledged while the expert's key terms are assimilated into the student's own writing.

As you read and take notes, consider possible subtopics to complete the ideas in your rough outline (see **74**). These subtopics will help guide your reading and note taking, and your reading will then provide ideas for more subtopics. You will be organizing the paper as you prepare to write it. If you are investigating ways to restore the tarnished image of the Olympic Games, you might develop these subtopics:

> small countries with amateur athletes/large countries with professional athletes
>
> corporations as official providers of absurd or tangential services
>
> why souvenirs are valuable

The order of the subtopics, as well as the subtopics themselves, will doubtless change as you find material and as your ideas develop.

Plagiarism Plagiarism—presenting the words or ideas of others without giving proper credit—is both unethical and illegal. When you put your name on a piece of writing, the reader assumes that you are responsible for the information, wording, and organization and that you will acknowledge the source of any fact or idea that is not your own—including information taken from Internet sources, a prime source of deliberately plagiarized material these days.

A writer cannot copy direct quotations without using quotation marks and without acknowledging the source. Paraphrasing material or using an original idea that is not properly introduced and documented is another common type of plagiarism. Sloppy note taking, in which the writer has not distinguished between his or her thoughts and those of the sources, is a frequent culprit. To avoid plagiarism, follow these guidelines:

1. Introduce every quotation and paraphrase by citing in the text of your paper the name of the source of the material used.
2. Place quotation marks around all directly quoted material.
3. Rewrite paraphrased material so that it is faithful to the original ideas; rearranging sentences is not enough.
4. Document all source material used.
5. Include on the Works Cited or References page every source referred to in your paper.

The penalties for plagiarism can be severe; it is a serious offense. A student who has been caught plagiarizing can expect, at the least, to receive no credit for the assignment, and at some schools, expulsion is the mandated result.

76 Organize, write, and revise the rough draft.

If you revise your outline as you collect information, you should be nearly ready to write your rough draft by the time you finish taking notes. But first review and refine the organization. Start with your thesis statement: Does it clearly express what you now see as the central, unifying idea of the paper? (See **6.**) If, for example, your initial thesis was "Library censorship is dangerous to our schools," your research might lead you to a more limited, precisely focused thesis: "Censorship in high school libraries denies students their constitutional right to the free exchange of ideas."

A *sentence outline* can be especially useful at this point. Write a sentence stating each of the main ideas supporting your thesis. Then complete the outline with sentences that represent the subdivisions of your main points. You will be able to see how well the parts of your paper fit together, and you may be able to use many of the sentences as topic sentences for your main subsections.

To help make the organization of your material clear and logical, follow these conventions when outlining:

1. Make sure that *all* the divisions and subdivisions are complete sentences; do not mix phrases with sentences.

2. Type your thesis statement at the head of the outline, followed by capitalized Roman numerals for the main headings; then A, B, etc., for main subheadings; then 1, 2, etc.; then a, b, etc.

3. Always use at least two subdivisions. If you have "I. A.," you must logically have "I. B." As a general rule, subdivisions stand for blocks of material in the essay, not for single sentences.

4. Make the subdivisions logically consistent. If your first main division is "I. Students in four-year colleges" and your first two subdivisions are "A. Freshmen" and "B. Sophomores," then you must continue with "C. Juniors" and "D. Seniors," not "C. History majors" or "D. Student athletes."

The following sentence outline was written for a research paper on year-round schools:

Thesis: The time for year-round schools has arrived, for they can solve many of the mounting problems, such as overcrowding and inefficiency, that our educational system faces.

  I. Year-round schools are largely misunderstood.

     A. Parents' and students' misunderstandings are based on preconceived notions of how year-round schools operate.

    B. A wide variety of plans allows flexibility in implementing a year-round school system.

II. Year-round schools offer advantages to those directly involved in education as well as to the community at large.

    A. Parents' and students' apprehensions about year-round schools are often dispelled after they have experienced such a system.

        1. Year-round schools offer greater flexibility in vacation planning.

        2. Students often retain knowledge more easily in a year-round plan.

        3. Both marginal and gifted students benefit from a year-round school system.

    B. Year-round schools provide economic benefits to school systems.

        1. School facilities are used more efficiently.

        2. Year-round schools relieve overcrowding.

    C. Teachers also benefit from year-round plans.

        1. Smaller class sizes make for less stressful situations.

        2. Teachers have more time to plan curricula.

III. Although some teachers point out drawbacks to year-round school plans, students' experience is more positive.

IV. Although year-round schools may not be the answer to every school system's problems, many communities are finding that the advantages of year-round schools far outweigh their disadvantages.

Handling source material Identify your sources so that readers can make their own judgment about content and reliability. Make sure that material from your sources supports the points you wish to make and that your own voice is not drowned out by excessive quotations. If all the quoted and paraphrased passages were to be removed from the paper, it should still make sense. These guidelines will help you achieve that goal:

1. Write a topic sentence in your own words for each of your main paragraphs. Even if you later incorporate a quotation into a topic sentence or drop the topic sentence altogether, writing it in your own words will help you make sure that the paragraph expresses your thoughts. (See **16.**)

2. Use direct quotations only to emphasize significant points or to show your reader how your source expressed a key idea.

3. Avoid long paragraphs of quotations.

4. Make short quotations part of your own sentences:

> Frances FitzGerald writes that history textbooks have changed so much that "many an adult would find them unrecognizable" (21).

5. Introduce quoted and paraphrased material so that your reader will know whose work you are citing:

> As B. F. Skinner wrote, "The goal of science is the destruction of mystery" (59).

6. After each paraphrase or quotation, place the page number in parentheses.

Revising the rough draft You will probably need to revise your paper several times to make it read smoothly and say exactly what you want it to say. Check especially to see that your paragraphs are unified and sufficiently developed (see **17** and **19**) and that you have supplied transitions to guide your reader through the paper (see **18**).

Make sure that your final draft is free of errors (spelling, mechanics, grammar, punctuation) and that its sentences are logical and its diction clear. Compare the final draft with your outline to make sure that they are consistent. (If not, decide which needs to be changed.) Type from your bibliography cards or digital research file a Works Cited or References page for those materials you have cited in the paper. Eliminate sources you have not used, but include each source that appears in your essay. Arrange the cards in alphabetical order by author (or title if there is no author), and type one continuous list according to the format outlined in **77b** and **78b**.

Format Choose a roman, serif font—twelve-point type is today's standard. Never use italic, script, or all-capital letters for your text font. (Italic is used for emphasis, for foreign words, and for titles as appropriate—see **41**.) A serif font is easier to read than a sanserif font because the characters are more distinctive:

Research is a worthy process. (Times New Roman: serif)
Research is a worthy process. (Arial: sanserif)

If you would like to use a different font for heads (the title of your paper, Works Cited or References, etc.), a sanserif font is a good choice.

Research Paper Formats

This chapter illustrates guidelines from two academic organizations: the Modern Language Association (MLA) and the American Psychological Association (APA). Their documentation formats are similar in that both use parenthetical notes rather than relying on footnotes or endnotes. However, the two systems have substantial differences, so both are discussed here. MLA guidelines tend to be used in English, foreign language, and humanities research papers, and APA guidelines are generally used in social sciences, education, and technical writing.

77 Guidelines for MLA-Style Research Paper

77a Document sources accurately.

Documentation means including notes within your paper to tell readers where you found specific ideas and information and also including a list of your sources at the end of the paper. Documentation has two important functions: to give credit to the sources you have consulted and to enable your readers to look up the original material. Documenting also protects you against possible plagiarism (see page 219): it distinguishes your thoughts and words from those of your sources.

According to MLA style, you document by using in-text citations of author and page, in parentheses, at the end of every sentence containing a quotation or paraphrase. For example:

```
American children need to learn traditional information
at an early age (Hirsch 31).
```

On your Works Cited page at the end of the paper, you will provide in an alphabetical list the complete information about each source; your in-text citation specifies the page from which the quotation or paraphrase is taken.

What must you document? Because you have read extensively to prepare your research paper, you may think at first that nearly every sentence in the paper will have to be documented. But readers are interested in what *you* have to say, in how you have used your reading. Information that is common knowledge, short dictionary definitions, and well-known quotations do not require documentation. But every sentence taken from a source requires a citation so that the reader knows who says what—and with a minimum of disruption. Whenever possible, introduce each quotation and paraphrase with the name of the authority.

77

You must document the following:

1. All directly quoted material:

> Roger Rosenblatt writes that "Americans have never
> hated big government as much as they have loved its
> services" (33).

If you did not use the author's name to introduce the quotation, cite it along with the page:

> (Rosenblatt 33).

If the source is a one-page article (common in popular magazines), citing the page number is optional—you may cite the author (or the title, if there is no author) without the page number.

2. All paraphrased and summarized material:

> The prestige of a college education, John W. Gardner
> says, has led many people to assume (falsely) that there
> is no other type of learning after high school (103).

or:

> According to John W. Gardner (103), the prestige of a
> college education has led many people to assume (falsely)
> that there is no other type of learning after high school.

3. Facts and data that are not common knowledge:

> The average American's life expectancy has increased
> from 47 years, when the twentieth century began, to 77
> years today (Norman 36).

When two or more works by one author are listed in the Works Cited, provide a shortened version of the title to prevent confusion. Here the complete title—*The Presence of the Word*—is cited in shortened form at the end of the paper:

> Speech as sound, Ong says, is "irrevocably committed to
> time" (*Presence* 40).

For repeated references to a primary source (such as a play or poem), simple citations (such as to act, scene, and line) will suffice once you have established the title of the work (for more on this subject, see 79h):

> Lear's dying words are "Look there, look there!"
> (5.3.316).

When several items are taken from the same source, such as four sentences in a paragraph giving statistics derived from a single book, use one citation at the end of the paragraph: doing so will indicate that all the data in the paragraph come from that book. In such cases, especially, introducing your sources is important. And strive for some variety in introducing quotations and paraphrases and in incorporating them into your sentences fluently. Some possibilities:

> In his famous study of the Third Reich, William L. Shirer describes the Nazi war machine (399).

> Others, such as Koehl (360) and Bloch (36-37), present a different view.

> From 1939 on, Johnson writes, Hitler became a militarist, ceasing "to play the politician, the orator, the demagogue" (356).

> As Bruce Pauley (102) has observed, . . .

> Yet, according to one scholar (Fussell 245), the issue in 1939 was . . .

> Other historians disagree with this interpretation (for example, O'Neill 52-59 and Binion 78-82).

> Istvan Deak is surely right in agreeing with Koehl that not even the SS in Nazi Germany was totally committed (42).

Although you will most often use short quotations, occasionally you will need to use a longer quotation to present an especially important point. If a quotation will take up more than four lines in your paper, indent the quotation one-half inch from the left margin (use your word processing program's "format paragraph" option) and do not add quotation marks. Double-space the quotation. Introduce the quoted material, using a colon to connect the introduction with the quotation, as in this example:

> In the past, the travel and tourism industry presupposed either the solitary business traveler or the family traveling together. Today's increasingly fragmented and diverse society presents other issues, as Alexandra Valdez comments:
>
> > One of the problems with traveling alone involves the critical issue of choices. When two people travel together, the questions of where to stay, what to eat, and what to do are made simpler: on any single issue, at least one of the pair will have an opinion. Unless the other has her own, radically different opinion, she can default to her companion's suggestion. The companion is on the hook, so to speak, for the responsibility of making a good choice. The other doesn't have to come up with anything. (38)

Note that in a long quotation, the parenthetical citation *follows* the period.

For subsequent citations to the same page in a source just cited, simply repeat the page. (*Ibid.* and other Latin abbreviations are no longer used.)

```
Another writer argues that "it may turn out that apes
do have a dim awareness of syntax" (Gardner 6). He
also points out, however, that such a discovery may
not be major (6).
```

Content endnotes Certain types of information cannot appropriately be included in the body of your paper. Such items include comments on your research process or on the sources you used, or acknowledgment of assistance you received. This information should be placed on a separate page labeled "Notes," following the last page of your text and preceding the Works Cited. The accepted format for such notes is as follows:

```
¹On this point see also Kennedy (12) and Garrett (119).
²All citations to Shakespeare are to the Bevington
edition.
³The data for this study were collected between 20
January 2016 and 7 August 2016 in Miami, Orlando, and
Tampa, Florida.
⁴This study has benefited from the research assistance of
Brenda Gordon, graduate assistant, Department of English.
```

Include bibliographical information in the Works Cited, *not* in content endnotes. Place the consecutive note numbers in the text immediately following the relevant sentence. The note number is a superscript, as shown in this example:

```
during the war.²
```

77b Construct your list of Works Cited.

End the paper with an alphabetical list of the books, articles, and other sources that you cite. This bibliography is titled "Works Cited." Although some instructors may require you to list all the works you consulted in preparing your research paper, the most common practice is to list only those sources you have used and cited. Copy on your bibliography cards or in your digital research file the complete information for each such source, and keep these entries in alphabetical order by author's last name (or title if there is no author).

The following bibliography format is that of the Modern Language Association (MLA). In 2016 the MLA issued its eighth edition of the *MLA*

Handbook, which includes major changes in how to document sources, especially in its Works Cited style.*

The new MLA seeks to be more streamlined, deleting extraneous information. For example, when writing a bibliographic entry for a book, you no longer need to include the city where the book was published, information that was traditionally required. The new MLA is also based on a "container" concept that is intended to make it easier to decide how to format an entry. For example, suppose that you want to use in a research paper an article found in a magazine that is not also published online. You go to a bookstore and ask to buy the article. "No," the clerk says, "you have to buy the whole magazine." The magazine is the main part of the *container* (with its title listed in your Works Cited in italics); the article is the main part of the *source* (with its title listed in quotation marks, no italics). Or suppose that you want to cite one episode of a television series. The episode title is the main part of the source (use quotation marks); the series title is the main part of the container (use italics).

In the next several pages we will show you how to use the new MLA style and also show how it differs from the previous edition of the *MLA Handbook*. Regarding works cited,

1. Because the list is alphabetical, place authors' last names first. (If no author or editor is given, alphabetize by title, not taking into consideration *a, an,* or *the.*)

2. Then list the full title. Use italics for titles of books and periodicals; use quotation marks for articles, poems, essays, and parts of books.

3. Separate the items within the entry with periods.

4. For books, cite the publisher's name and the year of publication: Scribner's, 2005. If more than one copyright date is listed, use the most recent one.

5. For journals, cite the volume, year, and full pages: *Cithara*, vol. 50, no. 2, 2011, pp. 14–22. For magazines, cite the date and full pages: *Esquire*, Feb. 2004, pp. 60–62. (If pages are not continuous, use pp. 60+.)

6. Double-space the lines of each entry, and indent the second and following lines one-half inch (use your word processing program's "format paragraph" function to establish a hanging indent).

7. In listing two or more works by the same author, use three hyphens followed by a period instead of repeating the author's name. Alphabetize by title:

Schama, Simon. *The Embarrassment of Riches*. Knopf, 1995.
---. *Landscape and Memory*. U of California P, 1988.

---

*For full information, see *MLA Handbook*, 8th ed. (New York: Modern Language Association, 2016).

77

"U of California P" is the shortened version of the University of California Press. Follow this format as you list university presses.

MLA Works Cited Format

Note that almost all of the following examples compare the new *MLA Handbook* (eighth edition) style to the seventh edition style. Use the eighth edition format unless your instructor indicates otherwise.

Works Cited Format: Books

Single author:

MLA 7th edition: Boyd, William. *Waiting for Sunrise.* New York: Harper, 2012. Print.

MLA 8th edition: Boyd, William. *Waiting for Sunrise.* Harper, 2012.

MLA 7th edition: Strong, Roy. *Feast: A History of Grand Eating.* Orlando: Harcourt, 2002. Print.

MLA 8th edition: Strong, Roy. *Feast: A History of Grand Eating.* Harcourt, 2002.

Two authors:

MLA 7th edition: Green, Michael, and James D. Brown. *War Stories of D-Day.* Minneapolis: Zenith, 2009. Print.

MLA 8th edition: Green, Michael, and James D. Brown. *War Stories of D-Day.* Zenith, 2009.

MLA 7th edition: Kimmel, Michael S., and Michael A. Messner. *Men's Lives.* 4th ed. Boston: Allyn and Bacon, 1998. Print.

MLA 8th edition: Kimmel, Michael S., and Michael A. Messner. *Men's Lives.* 4th ed., Allyn and Bacon, 1998.

In the Kimmel and Messner entry, look at how the edition is noted. Never indicate a first edition, but indicate later editions as follows: 2nd, 3rd, 4th, and so on.

Three or more authors:

MLA 7th edition: Poole, Debra, Amye Warren, and Narina Nuñez. *The Story of Human Development.* Upper Saddle River: Prentice Hall-Pearson, 2007. Print.

MLA 8th edition: Poole, Debra, et al. *The Story of Human Development.* Prentice Hall-Pearson, 2007.

Translated and edited books:

MLA 7th edition: Alighieri, Dante. *Inferno.* Trans. Robert Hollander and Jean Hollander. New York: Anchor, 2002. Print.

MLA 8th edition: Alighieri, Dante. *Inferno.* Translated by Robert Hollander and Jean Hollander, Anchor, 2002.

MLA 7th edition: Heft, James L., ed. *Believing Scholars.* New York: Fordham UP, 2005. Print.

MLA 8th edition: Heft, James L., editor. *Believing Scholars.* Fordham UP, 2005.

MLA 7th edition: Merton, Thomas. *The Hidden Ground of Love.* Ed. William H. Shannon. New York: Farrar, 1985. Print.

MLA 8th edition: Merton, Thomas. *The Hidden Ground of Love.* Edited by William H. Shannon, Farrar, 1985.

MLA 7th edition: Virgil. *The Aeneid.* Trans. Robert Fitzgerald. New York: Random, 1983. Print.

MLA 8th edition: Virgil. *The Aeneid.* Translated by Robert Fitzgerald, Random, 1983.

A work in an anthology:

MLA 7th edition: Kinney, Arthur F. "Imagination and Ideology in *Macbeth*." *The Witness of Times.* Ed. Katherine Z. Keller and Gerald J. Schiffhorst. Pittsburgh: Duquesne UP, 1993. 148-73. Print.

MLA 8th edition: Kinney, Arthur F. "Imagination and Ideology in *Macbeth*." *The Witness of Times,* edited by Katherine Z. Keller and Gerald J. Schiffhorst, Duquesne UP, 1993, pp. 148-73.

Encyclopedias and Dictionaries:

MLA 7th edition: "Melodeon." *Merriam-Webster's Collegiate Dictionary.* 2003 ed. Print.

MLA 8th edition: "Melodeon." *Merriam-Webster's Collegiate Dictionary.* 11th ed., Merriam-Webster, 2003.

Reprinted and revised editions:

MLA 7th edition: Fitzgerald, F. Scott. *The Great Gatsby.* 1925. New York: Scribner's, 1953. Print.

MLA 8th edition: Fitzgerald, F. Scott. *The Great Gatsby.* 1925. Scribner's, 1953.

77

Here the date of the original edition is included after the title of a reprinted book. If an edition is other than the first, cite *Rev. ed.* or *4th ed.* after the title:

MLA 8th edition: Kendall, Diana. *Sociology in Our Times.* 10th ed., Cengage Learning, 2015.

Multivolume work:

MLA 7th edition: Parrington, Vernon L. *Main Currents in American Thought.* 3 vols. New York: Harcourt, 1927-32. Print.

MLA 8th edition: Parrington, Vernon L. *Main Currents in American Thought.* Harcourt, 1927-32. 3 vols.

MLA 7th edition: Churchill, Winston S. *The Age of Revolution.* New York: Dodd, 1957. Vol. 3 of *A History of the English-Speaking Peoples.* 4 vols. 1956-58. Print.

MLA 8th edition: Churchill, Winston S. *The Age of Revolution. A History of the English-Speaking Peoples,* vol. 3, Dodd, 1956-58.

Corporate author:

MLA 7th edition: Committee on Guidelines for Human Embryonic Stem Cell Research. *Guidelines for Human Embryonic Stem Cell Research.* Washington: National Academy of Sciences, National Research Council, 2005. Print.

MLA 8th edition: Committee on Guidelines for Human Embryonic Stem Cell Research. *Guidelines for Human Embryonic Stem Cell Research.* National Academy of Sciences, National Research Council, 2005.

Government publication:

MLA 7th edition: United States. Dept. of Labor. Bureau of Labor Statistics. *Occupational Outlook Handbook.* 2006-07 ed. Washington: GPO, 2007. Print.

MLA 8th edition: United States, Department of Labor, Bureau of Labor Statistics. *Occupational Outlook Handbook.* Government Printing Office, 2007.

Works Cited Format: Periodicals
Article in journal (paged by volume):

MLA 7th edition: Ridge, Michael. "Saving the Ethical Appearances." *Mind* 115 (2006): 633-49. Print.

MLA 8th edition: Ridge, Michael. "Saving the Ethical Appearances." *Mind,* no. 115, 2006, pp. 633-49.

MLA 7th edition: Tolan, John. "The Friar and the Sultan." *European Review* 16 (2008): 115-26. Print.

MLA 8th edition: Tolan, John. "The Friar and the Sultan." *European Review,* no. 16, 2008, pp. 115-26.

MLA 7th edition: Weiss, Timothy. "Translation in a Borderless World." *Technical Communication Quarterly* 4 (1995): 407-23. Print.

MLA 8th edition: Weiss, Timothy. "Translation in a Borderless World." *Technical Communication Quarterly,* no. 4, 1995, pp. 407-23.

A journal paged by volume starts the first issue of each year on page 1 and then numbers consecutively throughout the year.

Article in journal (paged by issue):

MLA 7th edition: Hynes, Joseph. "Morality and Fiction: The Example of Henry James." *South Atlantic Review* 60.4 (1995): 27-34. Print.

MLA 8th edition: Hynes, Joseph. "Morality and Fiction: The Example of Henry James." *South Atlantic Review,* vol. 60, no. 4, 1995, pp. 27-34.

MLA 7th edition: Pulju, Rebecca. "Consumers for the Nation." *Journal of Women's History* 18:3 (2006): 68-90. Print.

MLA 8th edition: Pulju, Rebecca. "Consumers for the Nation." *Journal of Women's History,* vol. 18, no. 3, 2006, pp. 68-90.

MLA 7th edition: Wolf, Howard R. "Ernest Hemingway: 'After Such Knowledge.'" *Cithara* 50.2 (2011): 14-22. Print.

MLA 8th edition: Wolf, Howard R. "Ernest Hemingway: 'After Such Knowledge.'" *Cithara,* vol. 50, no. 2, 2011, pp. 14-22.

A journal paged by issue starts each issue on page 1.

77

Article in monthly magazine:

MLA 7th edition: Simons, Lewis M. "Genocide and the
  Science of Proof." *National Geographic* Jan. 2006:
  28-35. Print.

MLA 8th edition: Simons, Lewis M. "Genocide and the
  Science of Proof." *National Geographic,* Jan. 2006,
  pp. 28-35.

When listing articles from monthly or weekly magazines, as well as from newspapers, abbreviate all months except May, June, and July.

Article in weekly magazine:

MLA 7th edition: Nussbaum, Emily. "Beaches." *New Yorker*
  6 Mar. 2017: 82-83. Print.

MLA 8th edition: Nussbaum, Emily. "Beaches." *The New
  Yorker,* 6 Mar. 2017, pp. 82–83.

MLA 7th edition: Bruck, Connie. "Jerry's Deal." *New Yorker*
  19 Feb. 1996: 54+. Print.

MLA 8th edition: Bruck, Connie. "Jerry's Deal." *The New
  Yorker,* 19 Feb. 1996, pp. 54+.

MLA 7th edition: Luscome, Belinda. "Confidence Woman."
  Time 19 Mar. 2013: 36+. Print.

MLA 8th edition: Luscome, Belinda. "Confidence Woman."
  Time, 19 Mar. 2013, pp. 36+.

When the pages of an article are not continuous (see the Bruck entry and the Luscome entry), list the first page followed by a plus sign. Otherwise, always list the inclusive pages.

Article in newspaper:

MLA 7th edition: Fackler, Martin. "Nuclear Plant in Japan
  Leaks Toxic Water." *New York Times* 7 Apr. 2013,
  national ed.: A11. Print.

MLA 8th edition: Fackler, Martin. "Nuclear Plant in Japan
  Leaks Toxic Water." *The New York Times,* 7 Apr. 2013,
  national ed., p. A11.

Most daily newspapers have section numbers that precede the page.

Book review:

MLA 7th edition: Anderson, Jarvis. "Life with Father: Duke
  Ellington." Rev. of *Duke Ellington in Person,* by Mercer
  Ellington. *New York Times Book Review* 28 May 1978: 8.
  Print.

MLA 8th edition: Anderson, Jarvis. "Life with Father: Duke Ellington." Review of *Duke Ellington in Person,* by Mercer Ellington. *New York Times Book Review,* 28 May 1978, p. 8.

MLA 7th edition: Goddard, Hugh. Rev. of *St. Francis and the Sultan,* by John Tolan. *Speculum* 86.2 (2001): 560-62. Print.

MLA 8th edition: Goddard, Hugh. Review of *St. Francis and the Sultan,* by John Tolan. *Speculum,* vol. 86, no. 2, 2001, pp. 560-62.

MLA 7th edition: Robinson, Marilynne. "Hysterical Scientism: The Ecstasy of Richard Dawkins." Rev. of *The God Delusion,* by Richard Dawkins. *Harper's* Nov. 2006: 83+. Print.

MLA 8th edition: Robinson, Marilynne. "Hysterical Scientism: The Ecstasy of Richard Dawkins." Review of *The God Delusion,* by Richard Dawkins. *Harper's,* Nov. 2006, pp. 83+.

Pamphlet:

Follow the format for books.

Works Cited Format: Electronic Media

Online documents:

In citing online documents, include the following:

1. The author's name (if given).
2. The title of the document.
3. The title of the database or website (italicized).
4. The date of the document's posting (if available).
5. The address (URL) where the document was found—unless your instructor indicates that this element is not necessary.
6. The date that you accessed the document.

Note how these guidelines apply in the following cases:

a. Article from a Website

MLA 7th edition: "ACLU Urges Supreme Court Not to Abandon Landmark Student Free Speech Ruling." *ACLU.org.* American Civil Liberties Union, 19 Mar. 2007. Web. 25 Mar. 2016.

77

MLA 8th edition: "ACLU Urges Supreme Court Not to Abandon Landmark Student Free Speech Ruling." *ACLU.org,* 19 Mar. 2007, www.aclu.org/news/aclu-urges-supreme-court-not-abandon-landmark-student-free-speech-ruling. Accessed 25 Mar. 2016.

MLA 7th edition: McMurtry, Larry. "What Woody Wrote." Rev. of *House of Earth,* by Woody Guthrie, ed. Douglas Brinkley and Johnny Depp. *New York Review of Books,* 25 Apr. 2013. Web. 7 July 2013.

MLA 8th edition: McMurtry, Larry. "What Woody Wrote." Review of *House of Earth,* by Woody Guthrie. Edited by Douglas Brinkley and Johnny Depp, *The New York Review of Books,* 25 Apr. 2013, www.nybooks.com/articles/2013/04/25/what-woody-guthrie-wrote. Accessed 7 July 2013.

b. Article from an Online Scholarly Journal

MLA 7th edition: Price, Bronwen. "Verse, Voice, and Body: The Retirement Mode and Women's Poetry 1680-1723." *Early Modern Literary Studies* 12.3 (2007). Web. 24 Feb. 2007.

MLA 8th edition: Price, Bronwen. "Verse, Voice, and Body: The Retirement Mode and Women's Poetry 1680-1723." *Early Modern Literary Studies,* vol. 12, no. 3, www.extra.shu.ac.uk/emls/12-3/priceve2.htm. Accessed 24 Feb. 2007.

c. Article from an Online Weekly or Monthly Magazine

MLA 7th edition: Baldor, Lolita C., and Scott Lindlaw. "Officers Blamed for Tillman Errors." *Time.com,* Time 24 Mar. 2007. Web. 25 Mar. 2007.

MLA 8th edition: Baldor, Lolita C., and Scott Lindlaw. "Officers Blamed for Tillman Errors." *Time,* 24 Mar. 2007, www.time.com/time/nation/article/0,8599,1602701,00.html. Accessed 25 Mar. 2007.

d. Article from an Online Newspaper

MLA 7th edition: Krugman, Paul. "Insurance and Freedom." *New York Times.* New York Times, 7 Apr. 2013. Web. 9 Sept. 2013.

MLA 8th edition: Krugman, Paul. "Insurance and Freedom." *The New York Times,* 7 Apr. 2013, www.nytimes.com/2013/04/08/opinion/krugman-insurance-and-freedom.html. Accessed 9 Sept. 2013.

MLA 7th edition: Salinero, Mike. "Shed No Tears for the Crocodile." *Tampa Tribune.* Tampa Tribune, 21 Mar. 2007. Web. 27 Mar. 2007.

MLA 8th edition: Salinero, Mike. "Shed No Tears for the Crocodile." *The Tampa Tribune,* 21 Mar. 2007, www.tbo.com/news/metro/MGB55H99JZE.html. Accessed 27 Mar. 2007.

e. Online Book

MLA 7th edition: Hawthorne, Nathaniel. *The House of the Seven Gables.* N. pag. *Project Gutenberg.* Web. 4 Dec. 2006.

MLA 8th edition: Hawthorne, Nathaniel. *The House of the Seven Gables. Project Gutenberg,* www.gutenberg.org/etext/77. Accessed 4 Dec. 2006.

f. Document Accessed from a Library Online Subscription Service

MLA 7th edition: Wheida, E., and R. Verhoeven. "The Role of 'Virtual Water' in the Water Resources Management of the Libyan Jamahiriya." *Desalination* 205 (2007): 312–16. *EBSCO Academic Search Premier.* Web. 4 Mar. 2007.

MLA 8th edition: Wheida, E., and R. Verhoeven. "The Role of 'Virtual Water' in the Water Resources Management of the Libyan Jamahiriya." *Desalination,* vol. 205, 2007, pp. 312–16. *EBSCO Academic Search Premier,* www.ebscohost.com/academic/academic-search-premier. Accessed 4 Mar. 2007.

If you have used a subscription service to access a previously published article, make sure that you use this format when preparing your works cited entry.

Electronic mail:

E-mail citations should include the writer, a description of the document and the recipient, and the date, as in this example:

MLA 7th edition: Bayston, Tom. "Status Report." Message to Brook Sizemore. 20 July 2006. E-mail.

MLA 8th edition: Bayston, Tom. "Re: Status Report." Received by Brook Sizemore, 20 July 2006.

In all instances of electronic media, if you cannot locate complete information, cite what is available.

77

Works Cited Format: Miscellaneous Elements

Interview or letter:

MLA 8th edition: Fernandez, Luis. Telephone interview.
4 May 2016.

MLA 8th edition: Willis, Dr. Susan L. Personal interview.
7 Feb. 2015.

TV program or film:

MLA 8th edition: "Mountain Wedding." *The Andy Griffith
Show,* created by Sheldon Leonard, performances by
Andy Griffith, Don Knotts, Howard Morris, and Denver
Pyle, season 3, episode 94, Danny Thomas
Enterprises, 1963.

MLA 7th edition: *Downton Abbey.* Perf. Hugh Bonneville and
Elizabeth McGovern. *Masterpiece Classic.* BBC.
27 Sept. 2015. Television.

MLA 8th edition: *Downton Abbey,* created by Julian Fellowes,
performances by Hugh Bonneville and Elizabeth
McGovern, season 6, episode 2, Carnival Films and
Masterpiece, 2015.

Note that *The Andy Griffith Show* has episode titles but that *Downton Abbey*
does not.

MLA 7th edition: *To the Wonder.* Dir. Terrence Malick. Perf.
Ben Affleck and Olga Kurylenko. Redbud, 2013. Film.

MLA 8th edition: *To the Wonder.* Directed by Terrence
Malick, performances by Ben Affleck and Olga Kurylenko,
Redbud, 2013.

MLA 7th edition: *Volver.* Dir. Pedro Almodóvar. Perf.
Penélope Cruz and Carmen Maura. Canal+España, 2006.
Film.

MLA 8th edition: *Volver.* Directed by Pedro Almodóvar,
performances by Penélope Cruz and Carmen Maura,
Canal+España, 2006.

77c Formatting the Research Paper

The following sample paper should answer most of your questions about
the format of the research paper. It should be typed on white 8 1/2″ by 11″
bond paper, double-spaced. Leave one-inch margins on all four sides of the
page. Indent the first word of each paragraph one-half inch from the left
margin, and indent long quotations (more than four typed lines) one-half

inch from the left margin. Such quotations, like the body and the list of works cited, are double-spaced. (Note that for practical reasons, the sample paper that follows is not double-spaced.)

Many instructors prefer a separate title page with an accompanying outline as a guide for the reader, but these are not required by MLA style. Instead, on the first page you should type your name, the instructor's name, the course number, and the date on separate lines, double-spaced, starting one inch from the top of the page and flush with the left margin; this first page may also be numbered. Note that the title is not underlined, fully capitalized, enclosed in quotation marks, or ended with a period. Capitalize the first and last words of the title and all other words except articles *(a, an, the—*unless they are the first word of the title and/or the subtitle) and prepositions and conjunctions (unless they are the first word of the title and/or the subtitle). Double-space between the title and the first line of text.

Number your pages consecutively throughout the paper in the upper-right-hand corner. Use your last name, followed by the page number, positioned flush against the right margin. Double-space between this head and the text.

77

1" ½"
                                                    Mickelson 1

V. K. Mickelson
Dr. Pharr
ENC 1102
18 December 2016

2 spaces

The Need for Additional Cigarette Taxation

2 spaces

1"

Gone are the days when actresses lounged in door frames, a lighted cigarette between their elegant fingers emphasizing the sensuous lines of their silhouettes. No longer do images of "tough guys" include, of necessity, a cigarette dangling from the corner of their mouth. Once, the movie industry portrayed smoking as a "glamorous" and "sophisticated" mode of expression, perhaps reflecting the American fascination with this seductive vice. But today that fascination has waned, and smoking now is viewed in a very different and increasingly negative light.

Several introductory paragraphs provide context for complex topic.

In those early days, the cigarette was ubiquitous, dominating restaurants, schools, airplanes, and even doctors' offices. Today, however, smokers have been sent outdoors, forced to stand by entranceways and in parking lots if they choose to indulge in the dubious pleasure of inhaling superheated carbon particles and vaporous forms of tar and nicotine. Only in bars, gambling establishments, and parts of some restaurants is indoor smoking common. Medical science has proven what many had long suspected: cigarette smoking is lethal.

In addition to the obvious health risks facing smokers, cigarettes present a commonly overlooked danger known as secondhand smoke. Whereas the gases that make up cigarette smoke can cause emphysema, heart disease, and various cancers of the lips, mouth, esophagus, and lungs when inhaled directly, secondhand smoke also poses a significant threat of

1"

cancer to anyone in relatively close proximity to this exhalation, even if he or she has never smoked a cigarette in his or her life.

The costs of treating people who are victims of cigarette smoke are enormous, totaling $22 billion per year in 1992 ("Wages of Sin" 26). By 1998, the figure had increased to $75.5 billion ("CDC Report"). The American Lung Association estimates that in 2004, the total cost to society caused by smoking had reached $193 billion ("Smoking"). By 2012, however, the American Cancer Society reported that the figure had stabilized at $133 billion ("Tobacco: The True Cost"). Yet cigarettes have managed to retain considerable popularity, and now the question is clear: What must be done to cope with what is, in essence, a national nightmare? An additional tax on cigarettes is the most practical answer.

The federal government takes a peculiar, contradictory stand on this issue. Motivated by pressure from powerful, long-established senators from the tobacco-producing states, the government subsidizes farmers, controls the amount of tobacco they may grow, and generally helps to support the profitability of the industry.[1] However, the government also forces cigarette manufacturers to print labels on packaging to warn the user of the dire health consequences that can ensue. Meanwhile, although the number of American smokers drops appreciably every year, people in their fifties, sixties, and beyond still run up huge medical bills to try to repair the damages caused by a lifetime of smoking. Accordingly, the debate over the government's role in dealing with tobacco has shifted from the health-related legislation and public advisories of the 1960s and 1970s to a concentration on financial and economic ramifications.

Many people who face major smoking-related illnesses in middle age have health insurance. However, as Werner and Sharon Hoeger point out, "heavy smokers use the healthcare system, especially hospitals, twice as much as nonsmokers

Superscript alerts reader to endnote.

Mickelson 3

The page number suffices because the source (the Hoegers) is cited in the sentence.

do" (243). Needless to say, the cost of this medical care is enormous, and because almost all health plans are capped, normally at about a million dollars, eventually that cap is reached. For instance, the cost of treating lung cancer alone can easily exceed this figure, at which point the "insured" find themselves in the same position as those with no insurance to start with: at the mercy of hospitals and in some cases dependent on Medicare/Medicaid. Three results issue from the preceding scenario: everybody's health insurance premiums go up to account for smokers' medical expenditures, hospitals pass along their costs for providing what is supposedly pro bono care for the uninsured and/or indigent, and the government—meaning the taxpayers, you and I—pay the rest.

Thesis is restated, followed by block quotation that indicts the tobacco industry emphatically.

The situation is intolerable. As Charles Scriven has asked,

> Can you name a respectable American industry that:
> - kills more than a third of its long-time customers;
> - kills, every year, another 53,000 *involuntary* users of its product;
> - paves the way to marijuana and cocaine addiction;
> - gets 90 percent of its new customers from the ranks of children;
> - spends $500,000 an hour hawking its deadly merchandise?
>
> The answer, by now well known, is the tobacco industry. (21)

Page reference follows end of block quotation.

Although Scriven's statement about "marijuana and cocaine addiction" is somewhat forced, the rest of his list reflects facts that the American public has grown weary of. During former President Clinton's first year of office, various public-interest groups suggested adding a two-dollar-per-pack tax so that smokers could, in essence, pay as they use. In 1993, Scriven pointed out that "Among developed nations, U.S. cigarette taxes are, along with Spain's, the lowest of all" (21). This situation is still generally true today, and any funds generated by a federal tax increase could be placed in a fund reserved for the payment of necessary medical care for smokers who persist in their habit. However, the debate over adding a hefty additional federal tax to each pack of cigarettes has continued for more than two decades now, and although there are some problems with this idea, I believe that such an additional tax is the best solution to what has become a national nightmare.

The American ideal is self-reliance, and a sense of responsibility is a major part of that ideal, if not the reality. Americans, on principle, dislike the idea that a person would choose a harmful lifestyle and then expect insurers, their other clients, the federal government, and its other clients (us) to pay for the results. Even the occasional "libertarian," such as Daniel Seligman, does not dislike the idea (138). I believe that most Americans would be perfectly willing to put up with smokers (outdoors, of course) if smokers were forced to be financially responsible for their own behavior.

To be impartial, the writer mentions objections to the proposal, then counters them.

As mentioned above, there are a few legitimate objections to this proposal. One is a change in the way that convenience stores—and to a lesser extent, grocery stores and drugstores—would do business. A two-dollar-per-pack tax increase would drive the retail price of a carton of cigarettes to almost ninety dollars, and in the case of convenience stores, a carton would become the most expensive item in the store. Given that most quick stops avoid keeping spare cash in the register, it is easy to visualize thieves who steal not money but, say, twenty cartons of cigarettes, an easily transportable

77

number. However, it is possible that convenience stores would either stop selling cigarettes altogether or, more likely, decrease the number and variety they carry. Perhaps specialty shops would emerge, similar to liquor stores, but with far greater security than the average quick stop. Then buying cigarettes would become more of a conscious choice, no longer just a last-minute, casual impulse.

Another objection is that smokers already pay enough because many of them die in their mid-fifties. According to this view, then it is entirely possible that all the contributions made by a smoker will remain the property of the federal government, never to be paid out (Huber 172). In effect, any worker (whether a smoker or not) is forced to gamble that he or she will live to receive Social Security payments, and in the case of smokers, the risks are obviously much greater that this will not happen, that the smoker will die at "a tax-efficient 60 or so" ("Wages of Sin" 27). Richard Aherne adds that, in 1979 dollars, the dead smoker misses out on benefits worth "a conservative $5000 per year per person" (qtd. in Troyer and Markle vi), and this figure would be much higher today. However, tissue plasmogen activator, a drug now used to prevent permanent damage after a heart attack, is already changing even this likelihood (Falla interview).

Paraphrase must be documented.

The source of the quotation is Troyer and Markle.

In any case, the proposal to tax cigarettes in proportion to the harm they cause has two goals: to convince people not to smoke and to create an ongoing fund to pay for the health care of those who persist. Cost may be a significant obstacle to many smokers, causing them to at least sharply curtail their intake if not actually quit. As Viscusi points out, "one can view taxes as a mechanism for selecting the optimum degree of discouragement of smoking" (547). A person who smokes one and 1.5 packs per day spends around $4,000 per year. If

77

that dollar figure were doubled, it is logical to assume that financial pressures would seriously affect most smokers' perception of their habit. It would, at least, get their attention; Viscusi believes that smokers are short-sighted regarding their future and that additional costs would make them reconsider their choice to smoke (549). Also, the probability is that anyone willing to undergo such a large financial drain in order to obtain a deadly substance would be viewed as a pathetic addict, and this external perception could be a powerful motivator in smokers' thoughts about quitting. Finally, Grossman, Sindelar, Mullahy, and Anderson stress the following:

> It is important to focus on teenagers and young adults, because cigarette smoking and alcohol abuse are addictive behaviors that generally begin early in life. Thus, policies to prevent their onset might be the most effective means to reduce them in all segments of the population. (215)

Note the use of the colon to introduce the long quotation.

In terms of the second goal, large sums of money would flow into the federal coffers. The money could reasonably be expected to grow at the prevailing interest rates. It seems doubtful that the money generated would pay for all the health care costs that would be applicable, but at least this funding would come from a focused, prepaid source, instead of from general revenues as it does today.

Canada has tried a proposal similar to the one described here, raising by way of taxation the average price of cigarettes to about $6.50 Canadian in 1993 (Fennell, "Up in Smoke" 14), a price that has gone up steadily since then. However, a significant problem soon developed: the smuggling of cigarettes from the United States through the vast, poorly patrolled border (Viscusi 555). Provincial governments and the national government obviously lose badly in such a situation: they receive no tax revenues at all, and in the case of Ontario's Cornwall, a popular tourist location, the battle between smugglers and police threatened the area's viability as an attraction (Fennell, "Up Smugglers' Alley" 46).

In the late 1990s, Canada "had to lower its punitive cigarette taxes" ("Senate's Tobacco Wad" 1) in order to curtail the smuggling problem. The intervening years had seen some bizarre incidents. Accompanying the smuggling issue was the Canadian government's charge that a large multinational tobacco company was involved in the illegal activity (Louis 1). As a letter to the editor of the *Toronto Star* pointed out in 2004, "High taxation doesn't deter smoking, it just makes criminals rich" (Stewart A23).

But if the United States were to institute higher cigarette taxes that were similar to those of its northern neighbor, smuggling would be less of a problem for Canada and little problem for U.S. interests. However, the smuggling issue that the United States would face would be contraband traveling north from Latin America. Nevertheless, in that circumstance it is illogical to believe that smuggling would test the much more stringent security of the southern United States when vastly superior profits can be made from the smuggling of narcotics.

What would happen to the tobacco companies? Obviously, their revenues would decline, but this has been true for years. American cigarette makers have been concentrating on markets in developing countries for some time now. Also, the current perception of tobacco companies in America makes it understandable that they should want to export their product instead of selling it domestically: they are starting to lose the product liability suits brought against them by individual consumers and, increasingly, by state governments tired of paying out health care

The writer speculates on possible secondary effects of the proposal.

benefits made necessary by the nicotine habit
(see Gruber 193-94). Consequently, the
perception of tobacco companies in the United
States has become increasingly sour.

This is a back-and-forth struggle with money
barely in the background. The federal and state
governments want higher taxes for three reasons:

1. As part of their traditional "cut,"
   just as with alcohol sales and legal
   gambling.

2. To dissuade people from smoking.

3. To help pay for the health care of people
   who have suffered from tobacco use.

The tobacco companies have two very different
needs:

1. Increasing profits.

2. Avoiding liability.

In the 2010s a new product arrived on the
market: e-cigarettes. The makers and
distributors of this delivery system claimed
that its users (commonly known as "vapers")
receive only flavored nicotine, with no tar and
none of the other chemicals that end up in
traditional cigarettes. Hence, the product was
supposed to be much safer, secondhand smoke
would not hurt others, and smokers could safely
light up indoors. Some tobacco companies got in
the market; others saw e-cigarettes as a
threat. Many studies argued for either the
safety or the danger of vaping. Some of these
studies seem biased from the start
(Floorwalker), as studies can be more or less
objective according to who is paying for them.

Whether e-cigarettes represent a net gain in
health effects is a subject that has not been
settled. However, most commercial
establishments—stores and restaurants, for
example—that prohibit traditional smoking also

Mickelson 9

prohibit vaping (Floorwalker). Nonsmoking
customers don't like seeing the vapor in the air
and also don't trust what effects it might have.

However, cigarette taxes work, and work very
directly. In Australia the smoking population has
dropped to 15 percent, as a pack of 25 will cost
$40 (Australian) by 2020 after years of
incremental tax increases. It's hard to justify a
habit that costs this much, so Australians are
quitting in droves. In the United States, many
people criticize the federal government for inept
and expensive social engineering, but the
cigarette-tax proposal seems a clear improvement
in terms of efficiency and general results. One
condition, however, would have to be met in order
for the program to succeed: the funds generated by
the tax would have to be kept separate from other
revenues. Americans have seen too much money flow
down the maw of the General Fund to trust
politicians' promises that tax dollars will be
used as intended. If this condition is satisfied,
an extremely valuable piece of social legislation
could be put into effect, perhaps eventually
enhancing the quality of life by decreasing the
incidence of horrible, life-threatening illnesses
caused by a habit unjustifiably considered
acceptable for far too long.

The thesis is restated in the conclusion.

Mickelson 10

Note

1. The senators from North Carolina and Kentucky are also, understandably, opposed to an increased cigarette tax. See Cohn and Hager (51) and "Wages of Sin" (27).

77

Works Cited

Bulman, May. "Australians Will Soon Have to Pay $40 for a Packet of Cigarettes." *The Independent,* 15 Sept. 2016, www.independent.co.uk/news/world/australasia/ australia-cigarettes-price-pack-smoking-tax-hike-how-much-do-they-cost-a7308381.html. Accessed 12 Dec. 2016.

"CDC Report Shows Smoking-Related Health Costs Rose over Last Decade." *U.S. Medicine: The Voice of Federal Medicine.* Oct. 2005, www.usmedicine.com. Accessed 8 Jan. 2007.

Cohn, Bob, and Mary Hager. "The Power of Sin." *Newsweek* 4 Oct. 1993, p. 51.

Falla, Colin. Personal interview. 5 Mar. 1996.

Fennell, Tom. "Up in Smoke." *Maclean's* 6 Dec. 1993, pp. 14-16.

---. "Up Smugglers' Alley." *Maclean's* 4 Oct. 1993, p. 46.

Floorwalker, Mike. "Ten Facts That Everyone Gets Wrong About Vaping." *Listverse,* 12 Nov. 2014, listverse.com/2014/11/12/10-facts-that-everyone-gets-wrong-about-vapin. Accessed 12 Dec. 2016.

Grossman, Michael, Jody L. Sindelar, John Mullahy, and Richard Anderson. "Policy Watch: Alcohol and Cigarette Taxes." *Journal of Economic Perspectives*, vol. 7, 1993, pp. 211-22.

Gruber, Jonathan. "Tobacco at the Crossroads: The Past and Future of Smoking Regulation in the United States." *Journal of Economic Perspectives,* vol. 15, no. 2, 2001, pp. 193-212.

Hoeger, Werner W. K., and Sharon A. Hoeger. *Principles & Labs for Physical Fitness and Wellness.* 3rd ed., Morton, 1994.

77

Mickelson 12

Huber, Peter. "Health, Death, and Economics."
    Forbes 10 May 1993, p. 172.

Louis, Brian. "Canada Determined to Pursue R.J.
    Reynolds in Court." *Knight Ridder Tribune
    Business News* 21 Aug. 2003, p. 1.

Scriven, Charles. "A Tax We Can Live with."
    Christianity Today 8 Mar. 1993, p. 21.

Seligman, Daniel. "Taxing Puffing." *Fortune* 14
    June 1993, p. 138.

"The Senate's Tobacco Wad." *The Wall Street
    Journal,* 20 May 1998, eastern ed., p. 1.

"Smoking." *American Lung Association,*
    www.lung.org. Accessed 11 Aug. 2013.

Stewart, John. Letter. *Toronto Star,* 13 Aug.
    2004, p. A23.

"Tobacco: The True Cost of Smoking." *American
    Cancer Society,* 2016,
    www.cancer.org/research/infographics-
    gallery/tobacco-related-healthcare-
    costs.html. Accessed 12 Dec. 2016.

Troyer, Ronald J., and Gerald E. Markle.
    Cigarettes: The Battle over Smoking. Rutgers
    UP, 1983.

Viscusi, W. Kip. "Promoting Smokers' Welfare
    with Responsible Taxation." *National Tax
    Journal,* 47, 1994, pp. 547-58.

"The Wages of Sin." *Economist,* 20 Mar. 1993,
    pp. 26-27.

78 Guidelines for APA-Style Research Paper

78a Document sources accurately.

Documentation means including notes within your paper to tell readers where you found specific ideas and information and also including a list of your sources at the end of the paper. Documentation has two important functions: to give credit to the sources you have consulted and to enable your readers to look up the original material. Documenting also protects you against possible plagiarism (see page 219): it distinguishes your thoughts and words from those of your sources.

According to APA style, you document by using in-text citations of author, year, and page, in parentheses, at the end of every sentence containing a quotation or paraphrase. For example:

```
The EPA's GIS system will provide various benefits
(Copeland, 1994, p. 44).
```

In your References page at the end of the paper, you will provide in an alphabetical list the complete information about each source; your in-text citation specifies the page from which the quotation or paraphrase is taken.

What must you document? Because you have read extensively to prepare your research paper, you may think at first that nearly every sentence in the paper will have to be documented. But readers are interested in what *you* have to say, in how you have used your reading. Information that is common knowledge and quotations that are well-known do not require documentation. But every sentence taken from a source requires a citation so that the reader knows who says what—and with a minimum of disruption. Whenever possible, introduce each quotation and paraphrase with the name of the authority. You must document the following:

1. All directly quoted material:

```
Aaron Shearer has pointed out that the midrange of a
finger joint is "approximately the middle two-quarters
of the range between the comfortable limits of flexion
and extension" (1990, p. 31).
```

If you did not use the author's name to introduce the quotation, cite it along with the page:

```
(Shearer, 1990, p. 31).
```

2. All paraphrased and summarized material:

    Nikola Tesla's realization about alternating current,
    Stephen Hall explained, came when Tesla was walking
    with a friend in Budapest (1986, p. 125).

or:

    According to Stephen Hall (1986, p. 125), Nikola
    Tesla's realization about alternating current came when
    Tesla was walking with a friend in Budapest.

3. Facts and data that are not common knowledge:

    Flextime scheduling includes a fixed, base period and a
    flexible period in the morning and/or afternoon
    (Thomas, 1986, p. 43).

When you cite two or more works by one author in the same year, add *a, b, c,* and so on to the year to prevent confusion:

    Walkerson pointed out that "age and intelligence
    quotient can be correlated" (1989a, p. 457).

When a work has been written by two authors, document it as follows:

    Baldanza and Mackinnon wrote that Alan Shepard's bout
    with Ménière's disease was probably the reason that
    Shepard became the oldest astronaut to fly in the
    Apollo program (1989, p. 4).

or:

    Alan Shepard's bout with Ménière's disease was probably
    the reason that Shepard became the oldest astronaut
    to fly in the Apollo program (Baldanza & Mackinnon,
    1989, p. 4).

Note the use of the ampersand (&) when the authors' names are listed parenthetically.

If a source has three to five authors, list all of them in your first citation of the source. In following citations, use only the first author's name followed by *et al.:*

First citation:	Brown, Walker, Stein, and Litrola (1994)
	or: (Brown, Walker, Stein, & Litrola, 1994)
Further citations:	Brown et al. (1994)
	or: (Brown et al., 1994)

78

If a source has six or more authors, use *et al.* after the first author's name in each citation, including the first citation.

When several items are taken from the same source, such as four sentences in a paragraph giving statistics derived from a single book, use one citation at the end of the paragraph: doing so will indicate that all the data in the paragraph come from that book. In such cases, especially, introducing your sources is important.

Although you will most often use short quotations, occasionally you will use a longer quotation to present an especially important point. If a quotation has more than forty words, indent the quotation one-half inch from the left margin (use your word processing program's "format paragraph" option) and do not add quotation marks. Double-space the quotation. Introduce the quoted material, using a colon to connect the introduction with the quotation, as in this example:

> In the past, the travel and tourism industry presupposed either the solitary business traveler or the family traveling together. Today's increasingly fragmented and diverse society presents other issues, as Alexandra Valdez commented:
>> One of the problems with traveling alone involves the critical issue of choices. When two people travel together, the questions of where to stay, what to eat, and what to do are made simpler: on any single issue, at least one of the pair will have an opinion. Unless the other has her own, radically different opinion, she can default to her companion's suggestion. The companion is on the hook, so to speak, for the responsibility of making a good choice. The other doesn't have to come up with anything. (2005, p. 38)

Note that in a long quotation, the parenthetical citation *follows* the source.

Content footnotes Certain types of information cannot appropriately be included in the body of your paper. Such items include comments on your research process or on the sources you used, or acknowledgment of assistance you received. This information should be placed in footnotes. The accepted format for such notes is as follows:

> [1]On this point, see also Kennedy (1994, pp. 216-238).
> [2]This study has benefited from the research assistance of Brenda Gordon, graduate assistant, Department of English.

Include bibliographical information on the References page, *not* in footnotes. Format the consecutive note numbers as superscripts, and place them in the text immediately following the relevant sentence, as in this example:

```
during the war.²
```

All footnotes should appear at the bottom of the page where they are referenced. Use your word processing program's "footnotes" option to place them properly.

78b Construct your list of References.

End the paper with an alphabetical list of the books, articles, and other sources you cite. This bibliography is titled "References." Although some instructors may require you to list all the works you consulted in preparing your research paper, the most common practice is to list only those sources you have used and cited. Copy on your bibliography cards or in your digital research file the complete information for each such source, and keep these entries in alphabetical order by author's last name (or title if there is no author).

The following bibliography format is that of the American Psychological Association.*

1. Because the list is alphabetical, place authors' last names first. (If no author or editor is given, alphabetize by title.)

2. Then list the date, in parentheses, and the full title. Use italics for titles of books and periodicals. For periodicals, use normal capitalization; for all other titles, capitalize only the first word of a title or subtitle, proper nouns, and "proper adjectives," such as *Canadian*.

3. Separate the items within the entry with periods.

4. For books, cite the publisher's city and state, and a shortened form of the publisher's name: New York, NY: Scribner's. Use only the first city printed on the title page and the most recent copyright date.

5. For articles in journals and magazines, cite the volume, year, and full range of pages.

6. Double-space the lines of each entry, and indent the second and following lines one-half inch (use your word processing program's "format paragraph" option to establish a hanging indent).

7. In listing two or more works by the same author, place the earliest work first:

---

*For full information, see *Publication Manual of the American Psychological Association,* 6th ed. (Washington, DC: American Psychological Association, 2010).

78

Ong, W. J. (1962). *The barbarian within*. New York, NY:
    Macmillan.

Ong. W. J. (1967). *The presence of the word*. New Haven,
    CT: Yale University Press.

If two (or more) works were published in the same year, add *a, b, c* as needed to
the year and alphabetize by the first important word of each title (see the Menzel
entries on the Reference page of the sample essay, page 269).

Reference Format: Books

Single author:

McMahon, D. M. (2006). *Happiness: A history*. New York, NY:
    Atlantic Monthly Press.

Strong, R. (2002). *Feast: A history of grand eating*.
    Orlando, FL: Harcourt.

Two authors:

Kimmel, M. S., & Messner, M. A. (1998). *Men's lives*
    (4th ed.). Boston, MA: Allyn and Bacon.

In this entry, look at how the edition is noted. Never indicate a first edition,
but indicate later editions as follows: 2nd, 3rd, 4th, and so on.

Three to seven authors:

Poole, D., Warren, A., & Nuñez, N. (2007). *The story of
    human development*. Upper Saddle River, NJ:
    Pearson/Prentice Hall.

If a book has more than seven authors, list the first six in the style indicated
above, but then insert an ellipsis (. . .), followed by the last name in the list.

Translated and edited books:

Virgil. (1983). *The Aeneid*. (R. Fitzgerald, Trans.). New
    York, NY: Random.

Merton, T. (1985). The hidden ground of love. (William H.
    Shannon, Ed.). New York, NY: Farrar.

Heft, J. L. (Ed.). (2005). *Believing scholars*. New York,
    NY: Fordham University Press.

A work in an anthology:

Rubinstein, A. (1986). Children with AIDS and the public
    risk. In V. Gong and N. Rudnick (Eds.), *AIDS: Facts and*

issues (pp. 99–103). New Brunswick, NJ: Rutgers University Press.

The full pages of the article or chapter are cited. If you cite an article or essay in a collection of previously published works, list the earlier publication data:

Lewis, C. S. (1965). Satan. In A. E. Barker (Ed.), *Milton: Modern essays in criticism* (pp. 196–204). New York, NY: Oxford University Press. (Reprinted from *A preface to "Paradise Lost,"* pp. 92–100, by C. S. Lewis, 1942, London, England: Oxford University Press).

Encyclopedia entries:

Melodeon. (1984). In *Encyclopedia Americana* (Vol. 18, p. 669). Danbury, CT: Grolier.

Reprinted and revised editions:

Fitzgerald, F. S. (1953). *The great Gatsby.* New York, NY: Scribner's. (Original work published 1925)

Here the book has been reprinted, and the date of the original edition is included after the title. In text, this book would be cited as Fitzgerald, 1953/1925. If you are using an edition other than the first, cite *Rev. ed.* or *4th ed.* after the title.

Multivolume work:

Parrington, V. L. (1927–1932). *Main currents in American thought* (Vols. 1–3). New York, NY: Harcourt.

In text, this book would be cited as Parrington, 1927–1932.

Corporate author:

Committee on Guidelines for Human Embryonic Stem Cell Research. (2005). *Guidelines for human embryonic stem cell research.* Washington, DC: National Academy of Sciences, National Research Council.

Government publication:

United States Department of Labor, Bureau of Labor Statistics. (2007). *Occupational outlook handbook.* Washington, DC: GPO.

Note that *GPO* stands for "Government Printing Office."

Reference Format: Periodicals

78

Article in journal (paged by volume):

Chang, F., Dell, G., & Bock, K. (2006). Becoming syntactic. *Psychological Review, 113*, 234-272.

Ridge, M. (2006). Saving the ethical appearances. *Mind, 115*, 633-649.

Weiss, T. (1995). Translation in a borderless world. *Technical Communication Quarterly, 4*, 407-423.

A journal paged by volume starts the first issue of each year on page 1 and then numbers consecutively throughout the year.

Article in journal (paged by issue):

Hynes, J. (1995). Morality and fiction: The example of Henry James. *South Atlantic Review 60*(4), 27-34.

Pulju, R. (2006). Consumers for the nation. *Journal of Women's History 18*(3), 68-90.

A journal paged by issue starts each issue on page 1.

Article in monthly magazine:

Simons, L. M. (2006, January). Genocide and the science of proof. *National Geographic, 209,* 28-35.

Article in weekly magazine:

Als, H. (2006, June 19). The cameraman. *The New Yorker, 82,* 46-51.

Bruck, C. (1996, February 19). Jerry's deal. *The New Yorker, 72,* 54-59, 61-66, 68-69.

The pages for the Bruck article are discontinuous. The commas show where the article "jumps."

Article in newspaper:

Erlanger, S. (2007, March 21). Aid to Palestinians rose in '06 despite international embargo. *The New York Times,* pp. A1, A12.

Most daily newspapers have section numbers that precede the page.

Book review:

Anderson, J. (1978, May 28). Life with Father: Duke
    Ellington. [Review of the book *Duke Ellington in*
    person]. *New York Times Book Review,* p. 8.

Robinson, M. (2006, November). Hysterical scientism: The
    ecstasy of Richard Dawkins. [Review of the book
    The God delusion]. *Harper's, 313,* 83–84, 86–88.

Pamphlet:

Follow the format for books. If there is no date of publication, list *n.d.* in
parentheses after the title.

Reference Format: Electronic Media

In citing online documents, include the following:

1. The author's name (if given).
2. The date of the document's posting or publication.
3. The title of the document.
4. The title of the website or online publication (in italics).
5. The date that you accessed the document and the address (URL)
   where you found it.

Article from a Website:

ACLU urges Supreme Court not to abandon landmark student free
    speech ruling. (2007, March 19). *The American Civil Liberties*
    Union. Retrieved March 25, 2007, from www.aclu.org/
    -scotus/2006term/morsev.frederick/29056prs20070319.html

Article from an Online Scholarly Journal:

Price, B. (2007). Verse, voice, and body: The retirement
    mode and women's poetry 1680–1723. *Early Modern*
    Literary Studies, 12(3)5.1–44. Retrieved February 24,
    2007, from extra.shu.ac.uk/emls/12-3/priceve2.htm

Article from an Online Weekly or Monthly Magazine:

Baldor, L. C., & Lindlaw, S. (2007, March 24). Officers
    blamed for Tillman errors. *Time.* Retrieved from
    www.time.com/time/nation/article/0,8599,1602701,00.html

78

Article from an Online Newspaper:

```
Salinero, M. (2007, March 21). Shed no tears for
    the crocodile. The Tampa Tribune. Retrieved March 27, 2007,
    from www.tbo.com/news/metro/MGB55H99JZE.html
```

Online Book:

```
Hawthorne, N. (1993). The house of the seven gables.
    Retrieved from www.gutenberg.org/etext/77
```

In all cases, if you cannot locate full information, cite what is available.

Reference Format: Miscellaneous Elements

Interview, letter, telephone conversation, or e-mail message:

Personal communication is cited in text only—for example, S. L. Willis (personal communication, February 2, 2015).

Film or TV program:

```
Almodóvar, A. (Producer), & Almodóvar, P. (Director).
    (2006). Volver [Motion picture]. Spain: El Deseo.
```

```
Bullock, H. (Writer), & Sweeney, B. (Director). (1963)
    Mountain wedding [Television series episode]. In A.
    Ruben (Producer), The Andy Griffith show. Los Angeles,
    CA: Danny Thomas Enterprises.
```

78c Research Paper Format

The following format is derived from APA guidelines for manuscript preparation. The essay should be typed on white 8.5" by 11" bond paper, double-spaced. Leave one-inch margins on all four sides of the page. Indent the first word of each paragraph one-half inch from the left margin, and indent long quotations (more than forty words) one-half inch from the left margin. Such quotations, like the body and the list of works cited, are double-spaced. (Note that for practical reasons, the sample paper that follows is not double-spaced.)

On the title page, type your name, the instructor's name, the course number, and the date on separate lines, double-spaced, and centered on the page. Note that the title is not underlined, fully capitalized, enclosed in quotation marks, or ended with a period. Capitalize all words except articles (*a, an, the*—unless they begin the title or subtitle) and prepositions and conjunctions (unless they begin the title or subtitle—see the sample paper below).

Number your pages consecutively throughout the paper in the upper right-hand corner, one-half inch from the top. Type a shortened version of your essay title, then a half-inch gap followed by the page number, which should be flush against the right margin. Double-space between this head and the text.

Shortened title is used as header.

78

An Analysis of
Fingerprinting Techniques
Jyll Holzworth
Dr. Pharr
ENC 3241
7 March 2012

78

Abstract

Since the beginning of the twentieth century, fingerprints have been used in criminal investigations to identify someone as having been at the scene of a crime. The reason is that no two people have exactly the same fingerprint pattern. Thus, if a person's fingerprint is found at the scene of a crime, then this person was definitely there at some point in time.

Because fingerprints are so important in solving crimes, it is necessary that they be discovered at the scene. Fingerprints are almost always invisible to the naked eye because they are composed of very little material; therefore, many techniques are used by police investigators to make the latent, or hidden, fingerprint visible. The type of technique used depends on a variety of factors, such as how old the print is and what type of surface it is on. Some techniques are more successful than others in certain situations.

Although there are many different techniques to choose from, the four most popular techniques are dusting, Super Glue fuming, ninhydrin, and lasers. New approaches are also being rapidly developed.

Whenever a crime is committed, the police officers called to the scene of the crime almost always check for latent, or hidden, fingerprints. Why? Because fingerprints are the surest way of proving that someone was at the scene of a crime. They are a unique part of each human: "Fingerprint patterns are formed on the fetus in the womb" (Swofford, 2005, p. 480). No two people have the exact same pattern of ridges on their fingers. In other words, everyone has a unique fingerprint pattern. Even identical twins, who share the same DNA, have different fingerprints (Hanson, 2006, p. 104).

Abstract is provided as brief summary of paper.

Title is repeated on first text page.

Running head: FINGERPRINTING TECHNIQUES   3

An Analysis of Fingerprinting Techniques

Over the years, different techniques have been used to find latent fingerprints. Although there are many techniques available, not all techniques are successful in every situation. The technique used depends on various factors, such as what type of material the fingerprint was left on and how long it has been since the fingerprint was left.

Introductory paragraphs provide context for paper.

There are some situations in which one technique may be unsuccessful while another technique is successful. Again, it depends on the situation. As Nickell and Fischer have pointed out, "Criminals have never been considerate enough to leave rolled impressions of all ten fingers at the scenes of their crimes" (1999, p. 123). Although there are many techniques, the four most commonly used ones are dusting, Super Glue fuming, ninhydrin, and lasers. An analysis of these four techniques shows that they have advantages and disadvantages based on their effectiveness, cost, and possible health hazards. However, new and improved techniques and procedures are also being developed, including ones to procure fingerprints from decomposing corpses (Magers, 2006).

Subheads are boldfaced per APA style.

Fingerprint Residue

To begin with, it is important to understand exactly what a fingerprint is. When someone touches something, a slight residue from the person's finger is left behind. This residue is composed of approximately .0001 grams of material. Approximately 98% to 99% of this material is just water, which evaporates quickly, leaving only .000001 grams of material on the surface that was touched. About one-half of this material is inorganic, whereas the other half is an "organic mixture of amino acids, lipids, vitamins, and other matter" (Menzel, 1989b, p. 89).

Using this knowledge about fingerprint residue, police investigators are able to locate the latent fingerprint through a variety of techniques. The

78

technique used will be determined by factors such as the type of material the print was left on and the length of time that has elapsed since the print was left (Olsen, 1978, p. 6).

Dusting

The technique most commonly used by police investigators is dusting (Wingate, 1992, p. 75). Dusting involves taking a small brush, dipping it into a powder, which is usually black, and then lightly brushing the surface where a latent fingerprint is thought to be (Moenssens, 1969, p. 24). For dark surfaces, "white powders (alumina) and other materials were developed . . ." (Hanson, 2006, p. 105). If the procedure is done correctly, the latent fingerprint will become visible.

Whereas dusting is the preferred method because it is safe, inexpensive, and easy to use, it does have some disadvantages. First, it can be used only while the latent print still contains water, for that is what the powder adheres to. Because the water content of a print evaporates within a couple of days, dusting would be unsuccessful on older prints (Hartsock, 1982, p. G2). Second, dusting works well only on smooth, nonporous surfaces, such as metal or glass (Hartsock, 1982, p. G2). It is unsuccessful on porous surfaces such as vinyl and leather because the powders tend to "paint such surfaces" (Olsen, 1978, p. 223). As a result, the ridge details of any latent prints will be hard to see because the powder covers both the prints and the surface that the print is on. Dusting also does not work well on plastic bags because brushing may rub off any latent print residue (p. 223). In addition, dusting is not a good technique for uncovering latent fingerprints on paper because "brushing disturbs the fibers of the paper to the extent that ridge detail may be destroyed in the developed image" (Olsen, 1978, p. 220).

78

Super Glue Fuming

Introductory sentence links new section to the preceding one.

Other techniques have successfully been used to bring out latent fingerprints on the surfaces where dusting does not work. On vinyl, leather, and plastic bags, for example, a technique called Super Glue fuming is the preferred method for finding latent fingerprints. As the name implies, this technique relies on the use of Super Glue, which costs less than three dollars per bottle (Hartsock, 1982, p. G2). This technique works by putting the item containing the print onto a hard, nonflammable surface. The glue is then poured next to the item. Both are put into a container, which is then sealed shut. The fumes from the Super Glue will bring out any latent prints on the item, forming a "solid cast" (Hanson, 2006, p. 106). The main ingredient in the Super Glue that works to bring out the latent prints is cyanoacrylate ester. When the prints develop, in about two days, they will be white (Wingate, 1992, p. 82).

Super Glue fuming is a cheap and effective method of bringing out latent prints on surfaces where dusting does not work. It is, however, somewhat unsafe because it produces highly toxic fumes, which can be harmful if inhaled (Wingate, 1992, p. 82). Therefore, it is very important that the person opening the container holding the glue not have his or her face right above it when it is opened, or the person will certainly inhale the noxious fumes.

Ninhydrin

Introductory sentence links new section to the preceding one.

Super Glue fuming may work well on porous surfaces such as vinyl and leather, but it is not successful on paper. Because dusting does not work well on paper either, police investigators needed something that would show latent prints on paper. A chemical known as ninhydrin was discovered to be very successful in bringing out latent prints not only on paper but also on cardboard, wood, and wallboard (Menzel, 1989a, p. 557A).

Unlike the dusting procedure, ninhydrin can develop prints that have lost their water content. Thus, prints several years old can be developed with the use of ninhydrin (Hartsock, 1982, G2). Ninhydrin works by reacting with the amino acids in the fingerprint residue to form a bluish-purple product called Ruhemann's Purple (Menzel, 1989a, p. 557A).

Ninhydrin in powder form is white. To be used correctly, it must be dissolved in a suitable solvent. The item to be treated is then either sprayed with or dipped into the ninhydrin solution (Moenssens, 1969, p. 25). The solvent to be used depends on whether the ink on the document must be protected and on the possible health risks (Olsen, 1978, p. 282).

The two most common solvents used today are acetone and amyl acetate. Although both are quite effective in uncovering latent prints on paper, both also have some disadvantages. The use of acetone will cause most inks to run. Also, too much exposure to acetone fumes can "irritate the mucous membranes and cause headaches, fainting, and general poisoning" (Olsen, 1978, p. 285). Amyl acetate, on the other hand, does not cause inks to run, but it is just as likely to cause severe headaches (Wingate, 1992, p. 80). Thus, although ninhydrin is inexpensive, it may damage documents and may cause health problems.

An alternative to ninhydrin is the use of vacuum boxes. This process has a lower level of health risks, and "[t]he processing techniques for this procedure are nondestructive, uncomplicated, and time-efficient" (Ostrowski & Dupre, 2006, p. 357).

Lasers

Today, there is a technique that can be used by itself or in conjunction with the previously mentioned techniques. This technique involves the use of lasers. It was discovered that the organic matter in fingerprint residue is inherently fluorescent (Menzel, 1989b, p. 89). When the appropriate light from a laser beam is shone onto a latent fingerprint, the print will "glow like a firefly in the dark" (Hotz, 1986, p. G5).

Because the fluorescent components in fingerprint residue absorb light in the blue-green range, the Argon laser has become the accepted laser to use for fingerprint detection (Menzel, 1989b, pp. 89-90). The Argon laser is used both in crime labs and at crime scenes, although portable lasers offer less sensitivity because they have less power (Menzel, 1989b, p. 90).

Using lasers to bring out the fluorescence inherent in fingerprint residue is a very simple procedure. The area to be studied is placed in a dark room. Then the laser travels through a fiber optic cable for "convenient illumination of the fingerprint area" (Menzel, 1989b, p. 90). Because of the danger in working with lasers, goggles must be worn to reflect the laser light but allow the fluorescent fingerprint to be seen (p. 90).

The use of lasers to detect fluorescence inherent in fingerprint residue is successful only on smooth or porous surfaces and only if there is almost no background fluorescence. This is necessary because inherent fluorescence is not very strong. Thus, if the background fluorescence is as strong or stronger than the inherent fluorescence, the print will not be seen (Menzel, 1989a, p. 558A). Because many surfaces fluoresce strongly, the use of lasers was at first restricted to specific surfaces (Menzel, 1989b, p. 90).

In order to be able to increase the use of lasers, fingerprints began to be first treated with something that would make them fluoresce

78

more strongly than the background (Menzel, 1989b, p. 90). These treatments make use of the previously mentioned fingerprint techniques. One such treatment is to dust with fluorescent powders. Another is to stain with a fluorescent dye, such as Rhodamine 6G, after Super Glue fuming. The cyanoacrylate ester in the Super Glue combines with the ridges of the fingerprint residue to form a white product. This white product is stable and will not wash away after it is treated with a fluorescent dye. Without Super Glue fuming first, the dye would wash away the latent print (Menzel, 1989a, p. 558A). Still another method involves ninhydrin. A document treated with ninhydrin does not fluoresce, but add the right amount of zinc chloride, and a highly fluorescent orange coordination compound is produced (Menzel, 1989a, p. 559A).

Many police departments now use lasers to detect latent fingerprints. Although laser equipment is very expensive, these departments feel that the "laser is already paying for itself in guilty pleas" (Hotz, 1986, p. G5). Lasers are dangerous to work with, but they are extremely accurate and can be used to check for prints from as far back as forty years ago (p. G5).

Evaluative paragraph states social benefits of laser detection of fingerprints.

Certain rates of crime appear to be declining. In a comparison of homicide rates from 1994 to 1995 among nine major cities in the United States, only Dallas and Phoenix saw an increase in their homicide rate. The other seven cities all had a lower homicide rate than the levels of 1994 (Steckner, 1995, p. C10). Laser technology may be one of the reasons for the decline. The use of lasers could have resulted in more fingerprints being discovered at crime scenes, which would have resulted in more guilty verdicts. If this is so, then there may be many more police departments that are willing to stretch their budget in order to make room for laser technology. In the 2010s, the crime rate has continued to decline. Better technology equals more convictions. Also, criminals and potential criminals watch television just like everyone else, and the proliferation of police dramas centering on forensic analysis may have some valuable, if unintended, social effects.

Distribution

Finding a latent fingerprint is only half the battle. Once a print is found, it must be digitally photographed and then entered into a computer system known as the Automated Fingerprint Identification System, or AFIS. This system narrows the number of suspects from hundreds to about eight or ten in a short period of time. Police officers used to have to do this task manually by comparing the print to hundreds of other prints on file, but with this new computer system, much time is saved, and the police can spend more time solving other crimes as well.

A recent development allows officers in the field, such as those patrolling traffic, to use a portable remote device to fingerprint drivers pulled over for moving violations and suspected of other offenses ("Traffic Police Trial," 2006, p. 53). However, the issue of the rights of a suspect is still very important. As Cole has pointed out, "The principal limitation on fingerprint checks is now legal, not technical" (2001, p. 257). In other words, the courts have to decide when an occasion is appropriate for the police to fingerprint a suspect.

Other technical and legal issues are coming to the fore. For almost a century Americans have been virtually trained to trust forensic analysis. "Send it to the lab!" seemed to settle the issue. However, traditional areas of forensic analysis—such as bullet-to-gun

Final paragraphs discuss social issues involved in using modern technology to retrieve fingerprints to help solve crimes.

78

matching, footprint analysis, and blood-spray patterning—are being critically examined (see, for example, the report from the National Academies: "Badly Fragmented Forensic Science System," 2009). Questions also arise about the so-called gold standard, DNA analysis (see Lander, 2015), but these seem to be dwindling.

In any case, fingerprinting remains a standard part of crime scene analysis. By using the right technique to image a fingerprint, and then putting the print into AFIS, police officers can solve more crimes. This is technology working together to make the world a safer place to live.

78

References

Badly fragmented forensic science system needs overhaul; evidence to support reliability of many techniques is lacking. (2009, February 18). *National Academies*. Retrieved from www8.nationalacademies.org/onpinews/newsitem.aspx?RecordID=12589.

Cole, S. A. (2001). *Suspect identities: A history of fingerprinting and criminal identification*. Cambridge and London, England: Harvard University Press.

Hanson, D. (2006, July). Improved fingerprint acquisition. *Law and Order,* pp. 104-107.

Hartsock, J. (1982, October 27). Glue clue. *Annapolis Evening Capital,* p. G2.

Hotz, R. L. (1986, April 1). Laser method to detect fingerprints enlightening police on crime cases. *Atlanta Journal,* p. G5.

Lander, E. S. (2015, April 21). Fix the flaws in forensic science. *The New York Times*. Retrieved from www.nytimes.com/2015/04/21/opinion/fix-the-flaws-in-forensic-science.html?_r=0

Magers, P. (2007, February 15). New fingerprinting techniques identify the dead. *CBS2.com*. Retrieved from cbs2.com/specialreports/local_story_046195024.html

Menzel, E. R. (1989a). Detection of latent fingerprints by laser-excited luminescence. *Analytical Chemistry, 61,* 557A-561A.

Menzel, E. R. (1989b, November). Ion-laser detection of fingerprints grows more powerful. *Laser Focus World,* pp. 89-92.

Moenssens, A. A. (1969). *Fingerprints and the law*. Philadelphia, PA: Thomas Nelson.

Running head: FINGERPRINTING TECHNIQUES   12

Nickell, J., & Fischer, J. F. (1999). *Crime science: Methods of forensic detection.* Lexington, KY: University Press of Kentucky.

Olsen, R. D. (1978). *Scott's fingerprint mechanics.* Springfield, IL: Charles C Thomas.

Ostrowski, S. H., & Dupre, M. E. (2006). Fingerprint impression development using a vacuum box. *Journal of Forensic Identification, 56,* 356-363.

Steckner, S. (1995, July). Phoenix homicide rate fastest rising in the nation. *Phoenix Gazette,* p. C10.

Swofford, H. J. (2005). Fingerprint patterns: A study on the finger and ethnicity prioritized order of occurrence. *Journal of Forensic Identification, 55,* 480-488.

Traffic police try remote fingerprinting. (2006, December 13). *Professional Engineering,* p. 53.

Wingate, A. (1992). *Scene of the crime: A writer's guide to crime-scene investigations.* Cincinnati, OH: Writer's Digest Books.

Other Types of Writing

11

Other Types of Writing

79
The writing techniques discussed in this book apply to many writing situations outside the composition class, including the four special applications treated in this chapter: the literary analysis, the business letter, the business memorandum and e-mail, and the résumé.

79 Writing literary analyses.

Responding to what you read and putting your responses into words is a basic part of most college courses, which often require you to summarize, analyze, or discuss various texts. Analyzing literature is an excellent way to develop these writing skills and to learn about your own experiences as a reader.

Most college essays that require writing about other writing are analytical: you explain the reasons for an economic downturn, the effects of a disease, or the meaning of a poem. That is, you explain relationships and what they mean. Rather than merely summarizing a work or event, you will most often comment on and interpret it, pointing out why a work or event means what it does. Explaining the reasons for your opinions about a piece of literature requires critical reading and thinking, skills that will be of value in many real-world tasks. All serious thinking is analytical: it is only by mentally taking a subject apart and then reconstructing it that a person can understand how it functions, why it occurred, or what it is.

79a Analysis requires interpretation.

In explaining the reasons for your opinions about a novel, short story, poem, or play (as well as essay, film, song, or advertisement), you learn about yourself, your values, the values of your society, and the values of the author. You read such texts not merely for information but for pleasure and insight as well. Writing a good analysis adds to your original pleasure and deepens your first insights by bringing you closer to the work and to your own thoughts and feelings about it. You analyze a text to explain what it means to you and why it affected you as it did.

Your assignment might be to write a *response statement* that indicates your personal reactions to a work. Or you might be asked to write a *review*. Sometimes you will write a *summary* of the action or plot. But most often you will be expected to write an *analytical essay* that explains how the elements of the work (plot, character, setting, and point of view, among others) add up to some overall meaning or theme. To develop a convincing analysis, you will provide evidence from the text to back up your *interpretation,* your explanation of a meaning that is not readily apparent. You may discover that a work reveals meanings other than what the author intended, that there is no single "right" interpretation. However, an interpretation is not merely a subjective reaction; it is a reasoned evaluation that is supported by examples and quotations from the text. As long as you can support your interpretation and prove your solid understanding of the work, your readers will be satisfied that your opinions are worth considering.

79b Read the work carefully.

Unlike newspapers, which are read quickly for facts, literary texts are meant to be read slowly and carefully, not just for information but for understanding. The first reading serves mainly to help you discover what the work is about. In your second reading, make sure that you have a pencil handy to mark passages that strike you as important, interesting, or revealing. Check your dictionary for the definitions of any unfamiliar words. With each reading, you will be conscious of your reactions to different aspects of a work and to the cultural background; the text's meanings will gradually become clear to you.

79c Choose a limited topic.

As you reread a work, consider possible topics that interest you. Although you will be considering the significance of the whole work, you must choose a limited topic. To write an essay about everything in a novel or even a short story would result in general, superficial comments. A limited topic—on a symbolic color, unusual title, or revealing characterization, for example—will not be trivial or dull; in fact, if developed properly, this kind of topic can shed light on the whole work, helping you and your reader understand it from a specific point of view (see 5).

Literary analysis has a few advantages over many other types of writing. A literary text is filled with human experiences; it provides many subjects for you to analyze. It is also the source of the evidence needed to develop the essay. You can always return to the text for ideas, and many more topics than you can use will occur to you as you read. Selecting the most interesting and appropriate topics, those that mean the most to you and to your readers, may be the most challenging task.

79d Formulate a thesis statement.

Once you have your topic, consider your attitude toward it. This attitude or stance should be expressed in the introduction to give your writing a unifying purpose. If the subject of a poem is death, try to determine what the poet's attitude toward death is—and how it reflects your attitude or differs from it. Be sure to formulate your own thesis so that you will develop *your* views and not rely on those of others. If you are assigned a topic, consider the importance of this topic in relation to the work as a whole. If, for example, your topic is "The Importance of the Town in William Faulkner's 'A Rose for

Emily,'" your thesis statement might be as follows: "The town in Faulkner's 'A Rose for Emily' is one of the principal characters." Once you have your thesis, read the text again, this time with the eye of a detective eager to make a good case. Look for evidence—examples, descriptive details, quotations—that proves the importance of the town as a "character" in Faulkner's story (see **6**).

79e Assume that your reader has read the work.

Unlike the readers of a book report or a review, readers of a literary analysis are familiar with the work and do not require summaries or long quotations. (In explicating a poem, you may need to supply the text of the poem for the readers' convenience.) Summarize only those events of the plot necessary to make your observations clear. In the following two paragraphs, you can see the difference between retelling what happens in a work and analyzing it:

A. Paul Morel in D. H. Lawrence's *Sons and Lovers* is a sensitive, tormented character. As a very young man, he begins a long relationship with the spiritual Miriam that is never fulfilling. Later, he has a more mature, physical relationship with Clara, but this, too, is unsuccessful. Throughout his life, his strong, possessive mother is a dominating presence. It is not until her death that Paul is able to free himself.

B. Paul Morel in D. H. Lawrence's *Sons and Lovers* is a sensitive, tormented character whose failure is linked to his mother's strong presence. He has a relationship with Miriam, whose reserved, spiritual character is an extension of his mother's. Therefore, Paul never sees Miriam as a woman but as an entity who wants to possess him. In his more mature relationship with Clara, Paul finds no genuine satisfaction because he sees in her the physical aspects of his mother, to whom he is forever tied. By failing to relate to either Miriam or Clara, Paul is unable to find himself or the freedom he needs to break away from his mother's domination, which ends only with her death.

Whereas the first paragraph relies on plot summary, the second paragraph develops the *reasons* for its opening sentence by exploring the relationship between the women in Paul's life and his lack of freedom and fulfillment. Literary analysis, then, presents ideas, reflections, and judgments about the work rather than merely facts; it explains *why,* not just *what.*

79f Write an interesting introduction.

Your opening paragraph should capture the reader's interest and clearly state your main point (see **8**). Also, you should identify the full title and author of the work at this point.

79g Develop the body of the essay with evidence.

Rather than follow the structure of the work you are analyzing, arrange your body paragraphs according to major ideas. Each paragraph should support one aspect of your thesis statement (see **7**) and should contain examples or quotations from the work. If, for example, your introduction mentions that two characters in a play have some similarities despite their many differences, you could devote one paragraph to their differences and two paragraphs to their similarities. Or you could have a thesis statement such as the following: "Through his references to darkness, robbing, and animals, Iago establishes the pervasive atmosphere of evil in *Othello.*" You could structure such an essay in terms of the three types of references.

An essay will be convincing to the extent that it contains evidence from the text in support of your main point. The sample paper (pages 278–281) shows how you can combine your comments with supporting quotations. Note that an essay about literature must be written in the present tense: the work is ongoing. Use the past perfect (*had lived,* etc.) for events occurring before the time frame that you are discussing.

Include only your final opinions about the work, and eliminate any sentences that do not advance your thesis. Your purpose is not to congratulate the author, not to discuss his or her life, not to preach to the readers about your philosophy, not to find fault (as a reviewer might), but to express your understanding of the ideas and artistry of the work.

79h Use quotations correctly.

In developing the body of the essay with selected quotations, be sure to copy each quotation exactly from the original. Include the page number (or line number, in the case of poetry) from the original in parentheses at the end of the sentence:

Connie "knew she was pretty and that was everything" (212).

A brief literary analysis usually does not require a bibliographical citation of the primary source, but any secondary (critical) sources should be acknowledged (see **77a**). For repeated references to your primary source, simple citations are acceptable once you have identified the work in your essay. In the following example from a play, the act, scene, and line are cited:

Othello speaks of himself as one "that lov'd not wisely but too well" (5.2.344).

79

When writing about a short story, you will sometimes need to use a long quotation (defined as more than four of your typed lines). (See **78a**.) Indent a long quotation. Set it off ten spaces—one inch—from the left margin by using the paragraph format function of your word processing program. Do not add quotation marks. Incorporate all other quotations into your own sentences. Short passages of poetry (one to three lines) should be included in your text:

> Butler speaks of "a leering company / Of unholy ghosts" (lines 10–11).

But longer quotations of poetry (four or more lines) are set off. Indent ten spaces—one inch—from the left margin by using the paragraph format function of your word processing program. Type the extract line for line, and don't use added quotation marks. Note that in a long quotation involving either prose or poetry, the parenthetical citation is placed after the end punctuation (see **40a**).

79i Develop an effective conclusion.

Conclude your analytical essay by summarizing your main points and by assessing the significance and impact of the work. Do not introduce new ideas, cite critics' views, or provide quotations; instead, emphasize what your analysis has discovered.

Here is a sample student analysis of a poem by Sylvia Plath titled "Daddy."

Sylvia Plath: Resolving Paternal Conflict in "Daddy"
by Karen Crew

To Sylvia Plath, poetry is a method of controlling the emotionally disturbing events of her life. Although her work is not exclusively autobiographical, Plath uses elements from her own experiences as foundations for the thematic elaborations presented in her poems. Through these elaborations, she attempts to put the disturbing events of her life into perspective. One of Plath's later poems, "Daddy," shows a great effort to organize and control the pain resulting from personal experience. The poem exemplifies Plath's attempt to release herself from the conflicts resulting from rage, guilt, and grief. As a basis for the tone of despair and anger in "Daddy," Plath uses personal allusions to the loss of her father, to her failed marriage with Ted Hughes, and to her own suicide attempt. In addition, Plath draws on historical allusions, on the theory of the Electra complex, and on her own archetypal ideas of death and rebirth to extend the initial theme of loss and grief even further. As she extends the theme presented in "Daddy" into a greater, internal conflict, Plath develops and reiterates the meaning through the literary devices of allusion, allegory, diction, and symbolic enactment.

Plath draws on personal experience to develop the speaker (a woman who cannot escape the memory of her father) and the initial conflict (between the woman and her oppressive father) of "Daddy." Explicit allusions to the death of her father, to her suicide attempt (at age twenty), and to her seven-year marriage with Ted Hughes serve as a foundation for the grief-stricken theme of loss and pain in the poem. Plath also relies on many external allusions to elaborate the theme. The first stanza establishes a childlike tone with an allusion to the nursery rhyme of "the little old lady who lived in a shoe" as she compares the constraining memory of her father to a "black shoe / in which I have lived like a foot" (2-3). Historical allusions to the Holocaust serve to heighten the conflict, for the speaker calls her father "panzer-man" (40) and she thinks she "may well be a Jew" (35). Finally, allusions to the Electra complex are found throughout the poem; for example, the speaker declares that "Every woman adores a Fascist" (48), and she marries a man who is "a model" (64) of her father. This allusion to the Electra complex serves to internalize the conflict within the speaker, for she realizes how she has projected her love (and hate) for her father into her marriage and into her life.

As Plath uses allusions to develop the speaker and the conflict, she employs allegories to characterize the father and to dramatize the speaker's rebellion against him. At the time of her father's death, the speaker idealizes him as "God" (8), but as she grows older, she begins to resent him for deserting her. This resentment dominates her imagination as his memory becomes a "Ghastly statue" (9), an effigy that she wishes to destroy. Through allegory, she equates her father with a Nazi, a devil, and a vampire—all of which characterize him as an oppressive, destructive force. Throughout the poem, the speaker attempts to do away with the idealized father, but the allegories demonstrate how difficult that task has become: "Daddy" keeps returning in different guises.

Plath's precise use of diction develops the conflicts of the poem and reveals the tone. Throughout the poem, the speaker characterizes the images of her father as black: "black shoe" (2), "a swastika / so black" (46-47), "black man" (55), and "your fat black heart" (76). These ominous images contrast with the image of the speaker as "poor and white" (4) and show how her father's memory corrupted her as he "bit [her] pretty red heart in two" (56). The repetition of "wars, wars, wars" (18) serves to intensify the external and internal conflicts that result in a suicide attempt as the speaker tries to "get back, back, back" (59) to her father. As the poem progresses, the words become angrier as the innocent tone of an emotionally abused child is sacrificed. The speaker destroys her love for her father and replaces it with hatred as she drives "a stake through [his] fat black heart" (76) and declares, "Daddy, daddy, you bastard, I'm through" (80).

Finally, Plath develops and reiterates the meaning of "Daddy" with a symbolic enactment of the Electra complex and of her own archetypal ideas of death and rebirth. The speaker idealizes her father and is equally oppressed by him, so she must act out the complex before she is free of it. Therefore, she marries a man with "a love of the rack and screw" (66), endures her torture as her mother endured "The boot in the face" (49), and finally drives a stake through the heart of "the vampire" (72) husband. By symbolically killing her husband, the speaker kills her Electra complex. Neither can oppress her anymore: "the voices just can't worm through" (70), and she is "finally through" (68).

The speaker also attempts to release herself from the pain of her father's death (thus extending the theme of loss and grief) by acting out Plath's own archetypal ideas of death and rebirth. Due to the overwhelming sense of loss in her life, Plath believed that death would cleanse her of the grief and pain associated with life; in this sense, she would undergo the purification of "rebirth." Although she hated the death of others because it destroyed her love and left her in a world of "Ghastly statue[s] . . ." (9), she idealized her own death because it enclosed her in a protective, womb-like world. The speaker of "Daddy" realizes that the world of her father is closed to her while she is alive, so she "tried to die" (58) in order to "get back" (59) to him and continue loving him. After she is rescued, she realizes that he is still "alive" in her memory, so she puts him to rest by killing him: "Daddy, you can lie back now. / There's a stake in your fat black heart" (70-71). The speaker realizes that she can bury her love for her father, but the pain of loss will follow her to the grave. This realization is apparent through the anger

of the last stanza: "you bastard, I'm through" (80). The
speaker is through with loving her father, her husband,
and maybe even life, for she has resigned herself to a
life devoid of love.

Through allusion, allegory, and diction, Plath
develops the external and internal conflicts and the
theme of loss in "Daddy." By allowing the speaker
symbolically to enact the Electra complex and her own
archetypal ideas of death, Plath reinforces the meaning
of loss and adds her own methods of dealing with that
loss. Plath uses personal experience as a foundation for
the conflict of the poem, elaborates the conflict through
literary devices and Freudian theory, and uses personal
theories to resolve that conflict.

80 Use conventionally accepted style and form for business letters.

Today, no other type of writing is as stylized as the business letter. Although
conventional practices concerning letter form and tone vary somewhat, you
must follow some standards if you want your reader to accept and respect
your letters. The suggestions below reflect current conventions.

80a Arrange the parts of your letter according to standard form.

The eight parts listed below are required in all business letters. Arrange them
as shown in the sample. Use a conventional font (not one that calls attention
to itself), and use at least 10-point type, but note that 12-point type is much
easier to read than 10-point type. Never use italic or script as your text font.
Single-space within each part, but double-space between parts and between
paragraphs. Use at least one-inch margins at the sides and one and one-half
inches at the top and bottom. However, vertically center a short letter.

Letterhead or return address If no printed letterhead is available, type your
return address starting at the left margin.

Date Type the correct date two lines below the letterhead. If you are using a
return address instead, type the date immediately below the last line of the
address.

80

Inside address Two spaces below the date line, enter the name, title, and mailing address of the person to whom you are writing. The inside address may require several lines, each starting at the left margin.

Salutation Write the salutation flush with the left margin, two spaces below the inside address. If the letter is addressed to an individual, use *Dear Ms. X, Dear Mrs. X,* or *Dear Miss X* for women and *Dear Mr. X* for men. (If you do not know how a female addressee prefers to be called, use *Ms.*) When appropriate, use a title such as *Dr.* or *Professor.* If the letter is addressed to a job title without a specific person's name (such as *Director of Personnel*), use *Dear Sir or Madam.* If the letter is addressed to a group, such as a company or department, use *Dear Members of X Department.* Put a colon (:) at the end of the salutation.

Body Begin the body two lines below the salutation. Start the first line of each paragraph at the left margin. Double-space between paragraphs.

Complimentary close Put the complimentary close two lines below the end of the letter, flush left. Use only standard closings such as *Sincerely yours, Sincerely,* or *Cordially.* Capitalize the first word, and put a comma after the last word.

Signature Type your name four spaces directly below the complimentary close. Women should type *Ms., Mrs.,* or *Miss* before their names to indicate their preference.

Written signature Sign your name in the space between the complimentary close and the typed signature.

In addition to these eight required elements, certain others are sometimes needed:

Identification line When typing someone else's letter, list that person's initials before your own in the following manner:

```
DEF: lf
```

Start the identification line at the left margin, two lines below the typed signature.

Enclosure notation If you enclose anything with the letter, place an enclosure notation two spaces below the identification line or typed signature. Use one of the following forms:

```
Encl. or Encl. 2
```

Copy notation If anyone other than you and the addressee is to receive a copy of the letter, note this fact on the left margin two spaces below the previous notation. Use the following form:

```
cc: Mr. Anthony Canteras
```

Second-page heading If a letter requires more than one page, use plain paper instead of letterhead for the second and subsequent pages. Leave a one-inch margin at the top, type a second-page heading as shown below, skip three spaces, and then continue the letter.

```
Mr. Takaki 2
```

Envelopes Placement of the address is important so that the address can be read by the postal service's optical scanners. The last line should be no more than three inches and no less than one-half inch from the bottom of the envelope. Leave at least one inch from the end of the longest line to the right-hand edge.

80b Use the all-purpose letter pattern.

Nearly any letter that you will have to write can be developed by using a three-phase pattern. Begin by getting to the point within a brief introduction, stating the basic purpose of your letter much as you would the thesis of an essay. Then develop your point by adding specific details and examples as needed in the body of your text. Be concise, and use short paragraphs so that your reader can refer quickly to each specific point you make. Finally, write a brief one- or two-sentence paragraph to close the letter smoothly. Note how the sample letter on page 284 follows this pattern.

Adapt your tone to your reader and the situation, and be cordial but businesslike. Avoid the jargon often associated with business letters: *in reference to, pursuant to, yours of the 12th received,* and so on. You can communicate more clearly and effectively without such phrases (see **69**).

80

5100 Fair Oaks Blvd.
Winter Park, FL 32790
September 25, 2017

Ms. Elena J. Rogers
Advanced Colortech, Inc.
18 Orange Trail
Orlando, FL 32802

Dear Ms. Rogers:

I am writing to apply for the position of Vice President, Graphic Division, as advertised in the *Orlando Sentinel* on September 20. With a B.A. and three years' experience in the field, I believe that I am qualified for the position.

As indicated in the enclosed résumé, I received my B.A. in 2014. While in school, I was responsible for the design and production of three serial documents, including *Crosscurrents*, the student literary magazine recognized in statewide competition during my senior year as the winning design/conception among twenty-four entries. After graduation, I accepted a position at Clovis Magazine Group as a graphic artist. Within a year, I was assigned my own production group and given the responsibility of designing and producing art for Clovis's new four-color fashion magazine, *Else*. During the two years that I have been art director for *Else*, I have had a wide range of duties, from the care and feeding of high-end computers to liaising with printers and separators to attending our weekly executive planning sessions. I am experienced from the bottom to the top of graphic design, and now I would like to move to the next level.

Ms. Rogers, I have known of and admired your organization since I was an undergraduate, and I believe that my background and experience meet your requirements. I am available for an interview at your convenience.

Sincerely,

Ms. Dominique Walker

Encl.

81 Writing memorandums and e-mail

A memorandum is used to communicate within an organization. Memos are frequently short and are always direct, highlighting essential information in clear, easy-to-read form.

Heading

The heading of a memo, clearly separated by white space from the text, is divided into four sections:

TO:	List the name and job title (if applicable) of your recipient.
FROM:	List your name, and list your job title (if you did so in the **TO:** line). Always initial memos to certify that you are the writer.
DATE:	Include either the date that you wrote the memo or the date on which you want it distributed.
SUBJECT:	Write a brief phrase indicating your memo's topic. Be specific; many readers, backlogged by paperwork, will decide at this point whether to continue.

The message that follows the heading is separated by enough white space to clearly distinguish between the heading and the body, which is single-spaced. At the end of the message there is no complimentary close or signature.

Content

Most memos inform readers about a course of action, recommend policies, or announce decisions. Because it is circulated inside an organization, a memo takes for granted a general knowledge concerning the products, practices, or personnel of the organization. Therefore, background information and formal documentation are frequently omitted.

In your first sentence, come directly to the point: "This memo summarizes. . . ," "The practice of ninety-minute lunch breaks violates company policy and must cease immediately," etc. If your memo is very brief, one paragraph will normally suffice. In a longer memo, however, move from a short introduction to the body of your text. Here, be objective, thorough, and clear. In your conclusion, which may well consist of a single sentence, ask your reader for a response or volunteer to answer any questions that might arise.

Style

Because you are writing to people with whom you work, an informal style is appropriate. Avoid long sentences. Abbreviations, contractions, in-house jargon, and technical terms (provided that everyone knows them) are acceptable.

81

MEMO

TO: Dave O'Reilly, Manager of Building
            Services
FROM: Mikhail Savinsky,
            Professor of Sociology **MS**
DATE: November 10, 2017
SUBJECT: Heating/cooling in Office 9-147

The temperature in my office has ranged from 51° to
83° during the last three weeks. Despite my repeated
requests by phone, your technicians can't seem to fix
the problem.

I realize that the weather has been quite
unpredictable lately, but my office (and myself)
would seem to be suffering more than should be
expected. On Monday and Tuesday of last week, for
example, my office was boiling. After my phone call,
a technician came by and then said that he had fixed
the problem. Indeed, on Tuesday afternoon the office
was more comfortable. When the cold front moved
through on Tuesday evening, however, my office got
colder and colder, aided by the fact that the vent
blew cold air—nonstop—for the rest of the week.

Is it possible to reach a "happy medium" here?
Please call me at 2298 if you have any questions.
Thank you.

E-mail Messages

At work, an e-mail message functions as an electronic memo. Its format is
quite similar:

    From:
    Subject:
    Date:
    To:

Use the same rhetorical structure in an e-mail as you would in a memo: a
brief opening, then the body, and then a brief conclusion asking for a
response or offering further clarification.

At work, don't send out an e-mail before you have proofread it thoroughly. The message may be forwarded to individuals whom you had not even considered. If your e-mail messages are filled with mechanical and grammatical errors, this lack of proofreading can come back to haunt you.

82 Prepare a clear, concise résumé to emphasize your strengths.

Few things you ever write will be as important to you as the résumé you submit to prospective employers. The facts about your education and work experience do not speak for themselves; a well-prepared résumé will always help you in a job search.

82a Include the appropriate information in your résumé.

When preparing a résumé, select facts about your background that will present you as positively as possible. Never lie or concoct fictitious credentials, but select those that present the best impression.

Position desired Many applicants name the actual position being sought; others list a broader "objective." Use either if you wish, but your accompanying letter of application should state the position you are seeking; stating that position in your résumé may prevent your being considered for other openings.

Personal data By law, you do not have to furnish personal data to prospective employers, but many people include such information on their résumés. You might choose to include your date of birth, marital status, and number of children (if any). However, consider whether this information will help you. If you are very young (or very old) relative to the other applicants against whom you logically expect to compete, don't include your date of birth. Also, if the position for which you are applying is one that will require you to travel extensively or move every year or so, your being single would be an asset. However, a company that wants its employees to be a part of the community and prefers "settled" people would see a spouse as a good sign. Because personal information can be used against you, make sure that you consider the issue carefully, and note that many résumés avoid this category.

Educational background Begin with the college you are currently attending and work backward. Give dates of attendance or degrees, names of degrees or majors and minors, memberships in organizations and honor societies, and grade point average (if it is impressive).

82

Work experience Begin with your present or most recent job, and work back to your high school graduation date; include significant part-time work. Give your past employers' names and addresses, dates of employment, and job descriptions.

Professional skills If you have relevant experience or training, develop a special section summarizing your skills. The exact skills will vary with your field, but the following suggestions should help: equipment, procedures, computer software, or special techniques used; supervisory positions held; noteworthy promotions or awards; certifications or registrations.

Related skills or activities If you have acquired through elective courses, hobbies, or other means any skills that might be useful in the desired position, include them. You may also mention community activities. Use anything that might give you a slight edge over other candidates. Do not bother listing interests or hobbies merely to give the reader a notion of what you are like; that interaction takes place at a job interview.

References Including references is usually unnecessary, but references can be used to fill out an otherwise very short résumé. If you do include references, give the names, titles, and business addresses of three or four people (except for relatives and clergy members) who know you well and who can be trusted to speak favorably about you. Try to get variety, selecting people who know you in various ways. However, ask their permission before listing them as references.

82b Carefully prepare your résumé in an effective form.

The following checklist will help you prepare an effective résumé:

1. Put your name, address, and telephone number at the top.
2. Use correct grammar. You may use fragments instead of complete sentences, but be sure that you are consistent.
3. Use common abbreviations to save space.
4. Single-space within sections; double-space between sections.
5. State everything as positively as possible.
6. Make the final copy clean and neat.

Rosalie A. Gonzalez

1838 Jackson Highway
Merivale, FL 30000
352/555-9845 (home)
rgonzalez@hernandofluniv.edu

**CAREER
OBJECTIVE**   To obtain a teaching position in
elementary education.

EDUCATION
August 2011–
May 2017:   Hernando University, Merivale, FL.
Bachelor of Arts in elementary
education. GPA: 3.65.
August 2010–
May 2011:   Gulf View Community College,
Merivale, FL. Associate of Arts in
general studies. GPA: 3.27.

EXPERIENCE
November 2015–
present: New Mornings Daycare, Barkerville,
FL. Education Coordinator.
• Responsible for entire curriculum.
• Order educational supplies and
balance budget.
• Supervise three full-time and five
part-time teachers and educational
assistants.

May 2013–
September 2015:   Walmart, Merivale, FL. Cashier.
• Worked part time until May 2011,
then became full time thereafter.
April 2011–
April 2013:   Circle K, Merivale, FL. Store Clerk.
• Worked the first shift full time.
• Became responsible for weekly
supplier orders in September 2007.

82

**CERTIFICATIONS
AND AWARDS**

Spring semester 2017,
fall semester 2016,
and spring semester
2016:   Dean's List, Hernando
University.

May 2017:   Received Florida certification
for elementary education.

October 2017:   Chosen as sole student member
of faculty research group
exploring the use of active
learning with ADD children.
Worked with group to present
findings at the state annual
ADD conference in Gainesville.

**ADDITIONAL
INFORMATION**   Fluent in Spanish.
Extensive experience with MS
Word, MS Excel, and MS
PowerPoint.

REFERENCES   Available upon request.

Grammatical Definitions and ESL Concerns

12

Grammatical Definitions and ESL Concerns

Grammatical Definitions

83 Know the parts of speech and their uses.

The parts of speech are the classifications of English words according to their forms and their uses in sentences: verbs, nouns, pronouns, adjectives, adverbs, prepositions, conjunctions, and interjections. Many words can serve as more than one part of speech. For example, *round* can be a noun (we won the *round*), a verb (they *rounded* the corner), or an adjective (I have a *round* table). Being able to recognize parts of speech will help you analyze and discuss the sentences that you write.

83a Verbs show action, process, or existence.

The **verb** is an essential part of every sentence. Most verbs show some kind of action or process:

Barry *resigned.*   The lady *screamed.*   The water *boiled.*

Other verbs, known as **linking verbs,** express a state or condition. They link the subject with the noun, pronoun, or adjective that describes or identifies it. (The word linked to the subject is the **subject complement.**) Linking verbs include *be (am, is, are, was, were, being, been)* and *become, remain, grow, seem, appear, look, sound, feel, taste,* and *smell:*

Rosa *is* a brilliant attorney.   The meat *smelled* rancid.

Tense Tense refers to the time indicated in the sentence. The form of the verb indicates the time of the action or statement (see **55**):

Sam writes. Sam wrote. Sam will write.

Voice If the subject of the sentence does the action, its verb is in the active voice. If the subject receives the action, the verb is in the passive voice (see **23e** and **57**):

Active voice: The reviewer condemned the film's violence. *(Subject* [reviewer] *acts.)*

Passive voice: The film's violence was condemned by the reviewer. *(Subject* [violence] *receives action.)*

Forms The English verb has a limited number of forms. Verbs may be regular *(walk, walked, walked)* or irregular *(see, saw, seen).*

Infinitive:	to walk, to see
Present:	walk, walks; see, sees
Past:	walked, saw
Past participle:	walked, seen
Present participle:	walking, seeing

The infinitive, the past tense, and the past participle are known as the **principal parts** of a verb. Most verbs are regular: they just add *-ed* to form the past and past participle. Irregular verbs may change spelling: *go, went, gone; see, saw, seen.* The present participle always ends in *-ing.* For the addition of *-s* in the present tense, see **55.**

Predicates The main verb in a sentence is called the **simple predicate.** The main verb with all the words that belong to it or qualify it is called the **complete predicate** because it completes the subject (see **84c**).

Verb phrases A **verb phrase** is made up of a **main verb** preceded by one or more **auxiliary verbs:** I *will have left* by Friday. The most commonly used auxiliaries are *have (has, had), be (am, is, are, was, were, been), do (does, did), will, would, shall, should, can, could, may, might, must,* and *ought.*

The first word in a verb phrase shows tense and agrees with the subject: she *has* gone; she *had* gone; they *have* gone; they *had* gone. In identifying verb phrases, note that other words may come between the first auxiliary verb and the rest of the phrase:

His writing *has* never *made* sense to me.

Most children *have,* at least once in their lives, *dreamed* of riding on a spaceship.

Verbals Forms of the verb may function as nouns, adjectives, or adverbs. When they do, they are called **verbals,** and they may combine with other words in **verbal phrases:**

Waiting for the train every day is not my idea of happiness.

Gerunds are verbals ending in *-ing* that are used as nouns: "*Jogging* is popular." Sometimes a gerund has an object and/or modifiers:

Paying bills promptly is not easy. (The gerund phrase—*paying bills promptly*—also functions as a noun.)

Laughing is good for one's health. (gerund as subject)

I would enjoy *laughing all the way to the bank.* (gerund phrase as direct object)

Present participles have the same form as gerunds but are used as adjectives, not as nouns:

The man *laughing* too loudly annoyed us. (*Laughing* is a present participle modifying *man.*)

83b Nouns name things.

Nouns are the names given to things real or imagined, tangible or intangible:

trees   endurance   Colorado   woman   physics

In sentences, nouns can be used as subjects, objects of active verbs, complements of linking verbs, and appositives:

Subject	Appositive	Object of preposition	
John Nolan,	assistant to the	mayor,	gave

Indirect object		Direct object
reporters	a written	statement.

Nouns can also function as modifiers, as in *brick* wall and *television* news.

Almost all nouns take an *-s* or *-es* ending or change spelling to form plurals (see **47**). They also take an apostrophe and *s* or apostrophe alone to show possession: *women's* rights, *prospectors'* expeditions (see **42**).

83c Pronouns take the place of nouns.

The noun that a pronoun refers to is called the *antecedent:*

The men rushed in. *They* were angry. (The antecedent of *they* is *men.*)

There are six different kinds of pronouns:

Personal pronouns *(I, he, she, it, they, we,* etc.) take different forms according to their function in a sentence. See **51**.

Relative pronouns *(who, whom, whose, which, that)* join a dependent clause to a noun. See **83h**.

Interrogative pronouns *(who, whom, whose, which, what)* are used in questions.

Demonstrative pronouns *(this, that, these, those)* point to nouns: "*This* is better than *that.*" (When used with nouns, they are called demonstrative adjectives: "*This* tablet is cheaper than *that* tablet.")

Indefinite pronouns refer to indefinite persons or things. Examples are *someone, everyone, anything, another.* For verb agreement with indefinite pronouns as subjects, see **50.**

Reflexive pronouns are used when the antecedent takes action toward itself: "The tomcat bathed *himself* after eating the bowl of food."

83d Adjectives and adverbs are modifiers.

To *modify* is to describe, qualify, or limit the meaning of a word. **Adjectives** modify nouns and pronouns; **adverbs** modify verbs, adjectives, and other adverbs:

> The saleswoman approached the *reluctant* customer. (adjective *reluctant* modifying noun *customer*)

> The program progressed *quite rapidly.* (adverb *quite* modifying adverb *rapidly,* which modifies verb *progressed*)

> We faced *extremely* serious problems. (adverb *extremely* modifying adjective *serious*)

Most adjectives and adverbs can be arranged in order of intensity: *happy, happier, happiest; angrily, more angrily, most angrily.* See **54.**

Conjunctive adverbs are words that can introduce independent clauses and join independent clauses to form compound sentences (see **36** and **49**):

> *Therefore,* I move that we vote on the bill today.

> Rain is forecast; *however,* let's go ahead and start the game.

The conjunctive adverb, which indicates transition, can also appear within or at the end of an independent clause:

> He felt, *moreover,* that the job didn't pay enough to warrant moving to another state.

> All things are not equal, *however.*

Conjunctive Adverbs

accordingly	finally	likewise	similarly
also	furthermore	meanwhile	specifically
anyway	hence	moreover	still
besides	however	nevertheless	subsequently
certainly	incidentally	next	then*
consequently	indeed	nonetheless	therefore
conversely	instead	otherwise	thus

Then is the only conjunctive adverb that is not usually followed by a comma.

Note that **transitional phrases** have the same function as conjunctive adverbs and require the same punctuation:

Nina did not like the car; *as a matter of fact,* she hated it. *For example,* she especially disliked the exterior color, the cramped interior, and the diesel engine.

Transitional Phrases

after all	even so	in fact
as a matter of fact	for example	in other words
as a result	for instance	in the first place
at any rate	in addition	on the contrary
at the same time	in conclusion	on the other hand

83e Prepositions and conjunctions are structural words that work with the major parts of speech.

Verbs, nouns, adjectives, and adverbs express most of the information in sentences, but the meaning of a whole sentence also depends on structural words that show relationships among those major words. Two main groups of structural words are prepositions and conjunctions.

Prepositions relate and link one word with another; examples are *of, in, on, into, at, to, for, after, with, with regard to,* and *aside from.* They are followed by nouns and pronouns that form the object of a preposition.

After the long wait, we enjoyed the concert.

    ↑   ↑

Preposition   Object of
                   preposition

A preposition and its object together are called a **prepositional phrase:**

> The old tree *in the center of town* stood *near the condemned building.*

Prepositional phrases can function as adjectives or as adverbs. See **83g.**

Conjunctions connect words or word groups. The **coordinating conjunctions** *and, but, or, nor,* and *yet* join words, phrases, or clauses of the same grammatical type:

> The *camera* and the *lens* must be purchased separately. (*And* joins two nouns.)
>
> He *lied* and *stole.* (*And* joins two verbs.)
>
> The hunter was *old* yet *strong.* (*Yet* joins two adjectives.)
>
> Neither *on land* nor *on sea* did they meet any resistance. (*Nor* joins two prepositional phrases.)
>
> *The mountains were steep,* but *natural passes separated them.* (*But* joins two independent clauses.)

The coordinating conjunctions *for* and *so* are used only between word groups that express complete thoughts:

> He used the wrong film, *so* the pictures did not turn out.

Subordinating conjunctions introduce word groups and make them subordinate, or dependent: they need other word groups for their completion (see **20**).

> **Since** *Jamie moved to Dallas* [subordinate], she has matured.
>
> I feel weak **because** *I have not eaten* [subordinate].

Subordinating Conjunctions

after	if	unless
although	in order that	until
as	rather than	when
as if	since	where
because	so that	whereas
before	that	whether
even though	though	while

83

83f Interjections express emotion.

Interjections such as *oh* and *ah* show emotion. They may be punctuated as sentences *(Oh!)* or included in sentences *(Oh, I wish you would say something)*, but they are not grammatically related to other words in the sentence.

83g A phrase is a group of related words without a complete subject and verb.

The function of a single word can be filled by a group of words. Such a group of words that work together, but lack a subject and verb, is called a **phrase:**

Noun:	I enjoy *art*.
Phrase as noun:	I enjoy *visiting museums*.
Verb:	He *went*.
Verb phrase:	He *should have been going*.
Adjective:	The *tall* man is my uncle.
Phrase as adjective:	The man *towering over the others* is my uncle.
Adverb:	She tried *hard*.
Phrase as adverb:	She tried *with all her strength*.

There are four other common types of phrases:

Prepositional phrase:

Adjective:	The clock *on the mantel* belonged to my grandfather.
Adverb:	He drove the truck *around the block*.

Infinitive phrase:

Noun:	He wants *to fight with everyone*.
Adjective:	There must be another way *to settle this problem*.
Adverb:	The plumber came *to fix the sink*.

Gerund phrase:

Noun:	*Playing on a winning team* adds to the fun of baseball.

Participial phrase:

Adjective:	The smoke *rising from the house* alerted the neighbors.
	A house *built on a rock* will endure.

83h A clause is a group of words with a subject and verb that is used as part of a sentence.

If a clause expresses a complete thought and can stand alone as a sentence, it is called an **independent clause** (or *main clause*). If it does not express a complete thought, it is called a **dependent clause** (or *subordinate clause*) and cannot stand alone as a sentence.

> The mayor spoke last night. (independent clause properly punctuated as a sentence)

> When the mayor spoke last night. (dependent clause improperly punctuated as a sentence)

Dependent clauses are introduced and made dependent or subordinate by subordinating conjunctions (such as *because, when, after, although*—see the list on page 299). Such clauses cannot stand alone; they modify the main part of the sentence.

> *When the mayor spoke last night,* reporters were strangely absent.
> ↑   ↑
>
> **Dependent/subordinate**   **Independent/main**
> **clause**   **clause**

A subordinate clause functions as a noun, adjective, or adverb:

> **Noun:**   They do not know *who wrote the threatening letter.* (clause as object of *know*)
>
> **Adjective:**   People *who exercise* live longer than people *who do not.*
>
> **Adverb:**   I ate the cake *because I was hungry.*

Know the elements of a sentence.

84a Subject

When a noun, pronoun, or verbal is doing something or is being described by a verb in a sentence, it is a **subject:**

> *I* [subject] saw the game Tuesday night.

> Joan's *portrait* [subject] was painted.

> *Walking* [subject] is excellent exercise.

84b Compound Subject

84

When a subject consists of more than one noun, pronoun, or verbal, it is a **compound subject:**

> *Bushes and shrubs* obscure our rusty old back door.

The complete subject includes all the words related to the subject:

> *The first person who comes to the party* [complete subject] never wants to leave.

84c Predicate

The main verb in a sentence is called the **predicate.** It can be one word: "I *saw* the game Tuesday night." More often, the predicate will consist of several words that make up the complete verb:

> He never *wants to leave.*

> She *has always been able to learn languages easily.*

84d Compound Predicate

When a predicate has more than one main verb, it is a **compound predicate:**

> Every fall, we *prune and fertilize* our azalea bushes.

The complete verb or predicate includes all the words related to the predicate:

> The first person who comes to the party *never wants to leave* [complete predicate].

84e Objects

A noun, pronoun, or verbal that directly receives the action of a verb is called a **direct object:**

> Jennifer despises *housekeeping.* (*Housekeeping* is the direct object of *despises:* What does Jennifer despise?)

> The library discarded forty-eight *books.* (*Books* is the direct object of *discarded:* What did the library discard?)

A noun, pronoun, or verbal that is related to the action but that is not the direct receiver of the action is called an **indirect object.** It states to whom (or to what) or for whom (or for what) something is done:

84

> Mystery writers usually give *readers* a few clues. (Writers give clues [direct object] to readers [indirect object.])

> The teacher told *Jay* some sad news about his grades. (The teacher told news [direct object] to Jay [indirect object.])

84f Complements

Whereas action verbs may have direct objects, linking verbs—forms of the verb *be* such as *is, are, was, were, been*—as well as those verbs that describe a condition or position—such as *feel, look, seem, become, taste, smell*—take a **complement.** Subject complements complete the meaning of a subject:

> Cocoa, in its natural state, is *bitter.* (*Bitter* describes *cocoa,* the subject.)

Object complements complete the meaning of verbs such as *call, elect, find, make, name;* they identify or qualify the direct object:

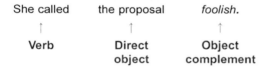

She called   the proposal   *foolish.*

| Verb | Direct object | Object complement |

84g Compound Sentences

When two independent clauses are joined by a coordinating conjunction *(and, but, or, nor, for, so, yet)* or by a semicolon, the result is a **compound sentence:**

> Online writing labs have much to offer a student writer; they are a valuable Internet resource.

> Working while being a full-time student is difficult, **yet** many students manage to do both.

84h Complex Sentences

When a dependent clause is joined to an independent clause, the result is a **complex sentence:**

> When the snow stopped, the ground was white.

Dependent   Independent
clause   clause

84i Compound-Complex Sentences

85

When one or more dependent clauses are joined to two or more independent clauses, the result is a **compound-complex sentence:**

Because the machine parts were defective,	the manager made an angry phone call to the supplier;	in fact, she threatened to sue.
↑ dependent clause	↑ independent clause	↑ independent clause

ESL Concerns

English has a number of features that can cause difficulty for international students. The following guidelines will help to clarify these issues.

85 Use plurals and possessives carefully.

As in most languages, English nouns usually change spelling when they move from singular to plural:

Singular	Plural
boy	boys
chair	chairs
cactus	cactuses
woman	women

However, unlike most languages, English nouns show possession by using the apostrophe and *s* (for singular and some plurals) and the apostrophe only (for most plurals):

boy's	(regular singular possessive)
boys'	(regular plural possessive)
chair's	(regular singular possessive)
chairs'	(regular plural possessive)
cactus's	(regular singular possessive)
cactuses'	(regular plural possessive)
woman's	(regular singular possessive)
women's	(irregular plural possessive)

Make sure that you know whether the word you are spelling is singular or plural and if it is possessive. A possessive is a shortened form:

86

the car of John = John's car

the issues of women = women's issues

Using this distinction can help you when you are dealing with a troublesome word such as *company* (in the sense of a business or firm). There are four possible spellings of this word, according to the singular/plural/possessive context:

company (singular, not possessive)

company's (singular possessive = of the company)

companies (plural—more than one—not possessive)

companies' (plural possessive = of the companies)

See also **47** for spelling plurals and **42** for apostrophe usage.

Make sure that your sentence has a subject.

Some languages use understood subjects, with sentences frequently starting with a verb. However, in English, subjects must be stated in all sentences except imperatives (commands), in which the subject *(you)* is understood:

Start the car.

Close your books before beginning the exam.

Wake up and smell the coffee.

The subjects of all other English sentences must be present:

Incorrect: Is a very effective computer analyst.
Correct: She is a very effective computer analyst.

English sometimes uses *there* and *it* as expletives, words that postpone the subject. Do not omit these:

Incorrect: Is a very nice day.
Correct: It is a very nice day.

Incorrect: Is a troubleshooting manual in my desk.

Correct: There is a troubleshooting manual in my desk.

87 Distinguish between count and noncount nouns for correct article use.

87a The indefinite articles (*a* and *an*) should be used with nouns that refer to persons, places, things, or ideas that can be counted:

a woman	four women
an estate	seven estates
a smartphone	three smartphones
a theory	several theories

Some nouns refer to quantities, collections, or abstractions and are called "noncount":

salt	wisdom
rice	information
furniture	advice

Do not use an article with a noncount noun. These words are either not modified or are preceded by words such as *some, any,* or *more:*

Incorrect: Can I have a rice, please?
Correct: Can I have some rice, please?

Incorrect: Is there a salt left?
Correct: Is there any salt left?

Incorrect: Ralph bought a new furniture yesterday.
Correct: Ralph bought some new furniture yesterday.

Also correct: Ralph bought new furniture yesterday.
Also correct: Ralph bought a new piece of furniture yesterday.

Incorrect: Can I get an information from you?
Correct: Can I get some information from you?

Some English nouns are both count and noncount. Frequently, this situation reflects the noun both as a thing and as a concept:

His writings about world currency gained him the Nobel Prize in Economics. (Here, *currency*—money—is used as a concept and is noncount.)

87

Some of the currencies of that region are extremely colorful. (Here, the reference is to actual pieces of money: things that can be counted.)

87b The definite article *(the)* can be used with most singular nouns. When introducing a new noun, use an indefinite article:

A car broke down in the passing lane of the interstate this morning.

In a subsequent reference to the same noun, switch to the definite article, *the:*

The car blocked traffic for almost an hour.

Similarly, when a noun's context is fixed, *the* should be used:

Incorrect	Correct
a ground beneath my feet	the ground beneath my feet
a nose on her face	the nose on her face
a moon circling the Earth	the moon circling the Earth

Sometimes, elements in the sentence define the context of the noun:

The cat *in the window* is the one that I want.

The problem *on page 428 of my algebra textbook* is very difficult.

Do not use *the* with nouns in the following situations:

Noncount Nouns Reflecting Unmodified Abstractions

Incorrect: The wisdom is a very good thing to attain.

Correct: Wisdom is a very good thing to attain.

But: The wisdom of the ages is a very good thing to attain. (Here, the abstract noun *wisdom* is followed by a modifier, *of the ages.*)

Noncount Nouns Reflecting Quantity

Incorrect: The sugar is a good thing to add to coffee.

Correct: Sugar is a good thing to add to coffee.

But: The sugar *grown in South Florida* has a curious history.

Proper Nouns

88

Incorrect:	I went to the London for the 2012 Summer Olympics.
Correct:	I went to London for the 2012 Summer Olympics.

Incorrect:	I asked the Robert if he had a spare pencil.
Correct:	I asked Robert if he had a spare pencil.

There are numerous exceptions to this rule, most of them involving large geographical areas or features:

the Great Lakes	the Atlantic Ocean
the Great Plains	The Hague
the Adirondack Mountains	the West Coast
the Appalachians	the Bahamas

88 Use cumulative adjectives in a commonly accepted order.

Cumulative adjectives are those in which one adjective modifies the rest of the expression (see **29d**):

a wonderful old house

English requires that these adjectives be ordered according to their type. The normal order is as follows:

Determiner: a, an, the, this, those, my, our, many, two
Evaluation: wonderful, excruciating, interesting, awful
Size: big, small, minute
Shape: round, oblong, trapezoidal
Age: old, new, young, antique
Color: green, teal, brown
National or Geographic Origin: Irish, Scandinavian, Middle Eastern
Religion: Catholic, Methodist, Jewish
Material: wood, iron, paper

Correct:	a wonderful little antique French saucer
Correct:	an excruciating old brown cotton dress

Be careful with complex verb structures.   89

89a With modal verbs and forms of *do*, use the base (infinitive) form.

Incorrect:	The letter carrier *will brings* us good news, I hope.
Correct:	The letter carrier *will bring* us good news, I hope.

Incorrect:	I *can plays* a violin very well.
Correct:	I *can play* a violin very well.

Incorrect:	*Do* you *wants* to go to a movie?
Correct:	*Do* you *want* to go to a movie?

89b Use infinitives or gerunds after verbs according to convention.

Some verbs are followed by infinitives (I choose *to write*), some by gerunds (I enjoy *writing*), and some by either (I like *to write;* I like *writing*).

Verbs That Must Be Followed by Infinitives

agree	decide	mean	refuse
ask	expect	need	venture
beg	fail	offer	wait
bother	plan	want	choose
hope	pretend	wish	claim
manage	promise		

Incorrect:	I need *telling* you something.
Correct:	I need *to tell* you something.

Incorrect:	I promise *taking* good care of your dog.
Correct:	I promise *to take* good care of your dog.

In some instances, a noun or pronoun follows the verb and precedes an infinitive:

She *convinced me to change* my mind.

His sleepless night *caused him to fail* the exam.

89

Have, let, and *make* are special cases that are followed by the verb (but without *to*):

> My uncle *let me drive* his car.

> My wife *made me change* my shirt before dinner.

> The customs officer *had her complete* a new set of forms.

Verbs That Must Be Followed by Gerunds

admit	deny	imagine	recall
appreciate	discuss	keep	resist
avoid	dislike	miss	risk
consider	enjoy	postpone	suggest
delay	finish	practice	tolerate

> **Incorrect:** He recalled *to meet* with me last week.
> **Correct:** He recalled *meeting* with me last week.

> **Incorrect:** I avoided *to take* the class.
> **Correct:** I avoided *taking* the class.

Verbs That Can Be Followed by Either Infinitives or Gerunds

begin	like
continue	love
hate	start

> **Correct:** I began *to sing.*
> **Correct:** I began *singing.*

> **Correct:** Eduardo hates *talking* to Melissa.
> **Correct:** Eduardo hates *to talk* to Melissa.

Note that the meaning is the same in each pair of sentences. With *forget, remember, stop,* and *try,* however, the choice of infinitive or gerund will radically alter the sentence's meaning:

> The old man *stopped to take* his medicine.

> The old man *stopped taking* his medicine.

For a discussion of other problems involving complex verb structures, see **55** and **56.**

89c Use phrasal verbs according to convention.

Phrasal verbs are sometimes called "two-word verbs." Although they can seem redundant *(sit down, stand up)*, phrasal verbs in English often have figurative, idiomatic usages:

> Jim *stood* me *up* on our last date. (Jim didn't arrive for the date.)

> The boss *sat* Mario *down* and explained what he would have to do to succeed in his new job. (The boss may or may not have asked Mario to be seated.)

The two examples are of **separable phrasal verbs**—an object comes between them. In an **inseparable phrasal verb,** however, the two words stay together:

> The car *broke down* sixty miles from the nearest mechanic.

> I *got up* at 5:00 this morning.

> Linda's secretary will *look into* the situation.

Note that phrasal verbs can contain three words, the last being a preposition:

> I have *put up with* his insults for too long.

> You don't expect to *get away with* that plan, I hope.

> Maria was *looking forward to* the end of the semester.

Glossary of

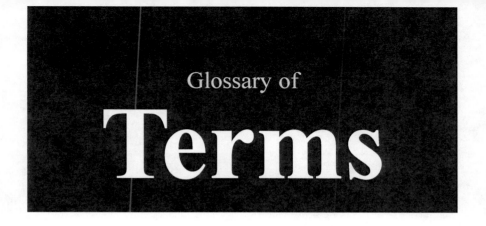

Terms

A

absolute construction A phrase that qualifies a sentence but is not grammatically related to it: *This being true,* she left.

abstract A brief summary of the key ideas in a work.

active voice See *voice.*

adjective A word that describes or limits a noun or pronoun: the *rude* remark.

adverb A word modifying a verb (ran *quickly*), an adjective (*very* grateful), or another adverb (*quite* smoothly).

analogy The use of a comparison to note a resemblance between two otherwise very different things. Analogies often explain complex things by showing how they resemble simpler things.

analysis A type of writing in which you explain a subject by examining the parts that constitute it.

antecedent A noun to which a pronoun refers: The *men* are coming; here they are. (*They* refers to, or stands for, *men,* the antecedent of *they.*)

appositive A noun, noun phrase, or pronoun placed next to a noun to explain it: Sam, *the teller,* was wrong.

argumentation Writing that uses logic and persuasion to prove a point and convince the reader.

auxiliary verb A form of *be, can, could, do, get, have, may, might, must, ought, shall, should, will,* or *would* used in a verb phrase (*had* seen, *will be* going).

C

case The grammatical category of a noun or pronoun that indicates its relationship to other elements in a sentence. The nominative case is used for subjects of verbs (*he* is); the objective case is used for objects of verbs and prepositions (I hit *him*); and the possessive case indicates ownership (*his* arm).

clause A group of words containing a subject and a verb that is used as part of a sentence. An independent clause can stand alone as a sentence; a dependent or subordinate clause cannot stand alone: *Although he ran his fastest race.* When a sentence contains both a dependent and an independent clause (*Although he ran his fastest race, he lost to Juan*), the independent clause may also be called the main clause.

coherence The logical flow from point to point in an essay or paragraph.

collective noun A word that names a group of persons or things, for example, *class* or *committee;* it may take a singular or plural verb.

comparison and contrast Explaining by showing similarities (comparison) and differences (contrast) between two or more things.

complement A word or phrase that completes the verb. A subject or nominative complement is a word or phrase that follows a linking verb and belongs to the subject: Her paper is a *masterpiece.* An object complement completes the action of the verb and follows its object: The jury found the defendant *innocent.*

conclusion The end of an essay, summing up the main points and restating the thesis; it does not introduce new ideas.

conjunction A word used to connect parts of a sentence or to relate sentences. Coordinating conjunctions (*and, but, or, nor, for, yet, so*) link equal elements; subordinate conjunctions (such as *because, although, if*) link a dependent clause with an independent clause.

conjunctive adverb A word such as *thus, moreover,* or *however* that connects one independent clause to another.

coordinating conjunction See *conjunction.*

count noun A noun that refers to an individual entity or thing and can thus be counted: *a woman, the cars, an elephant.* See *noncount noun.*

cumulative adjectives A group of adjectives modifying a noun in such a way that each adjective modifies the rest of the expression: *a wonderful old Ford truck.*

D

deduction The type of reasoning that moves from a general proposition to a specific conclusion.

dependent clause A clause that functions as an adjective, adverb, or noun and that cannot stand alone as a sentence.

description Developing a topic by using sensory experience to show the reader what a person, place, or object is like.

draft The text of an essay in progress, from its first to its final version.

E

editing Making corrections and final additions or deletions to the final draft of a paper.

elliptical construction A phrase or clause in which clearly understood words are omitted: He is taller than you [are tall].

evidence Facts, examples, statistics, etc., needed to support an argument and to make it convincing.

exposition Writing that explains a topic.

F

figurative language The use of metaphor, simile, personification, and other imaginative devices to express a meaning beyond the literal.

freewriting A form of prewriting in which you jot down whatever thoughts you have about a subject as they occur to you.

future tense See *tense.*

G

gerund The *-ing* form of a verb used as a noun: *Making money* [gerund phrase] is his only concern.

I

idiom An expression that cannot be logically explained but is commonly understood.

independent clause A clause that can stand alone as a sentence; see *clause.*

indirect object See *object.*

induction The type of reasoning that proceeds from specific evidence to a general conclusion or hypothesis.

infinitive The form of a verb usually preceded by *to;* it sometimes functions as a noun: Sally decided not *to smoke* [infinitive as direct object]. Sometimes the infinitive can appear without *to:* He does nothing but *complain.*

interjection A word used as an exclamation: *No!*

intransitive verb See *verb.*

introduction The opening of an essay that expresses the writer's purpose, thesis, and tone and that captures the reader's attention.

irregular verb See *verb.*

L

linking verb Any form of the verb *be* as well as such words as *seem, feel, become,* and *look* that link the complement with the subject: Jack *is* a hunter.

M

modifier A word that describes or limits another word or word group.

mood The form of a verb that indicates whether the action or condition it expresses is a factual question or statement (indicative mood), a command or request (imperative mood), or a wish or condition contrary to fact (subjunctive mood).

N

narration A type of writing that tells a story.

nominative See *case*.

noncount noun A noun such as *furniture* or *rice* that cannot be counted and is never preceded by an indefinite article *(a, an)*. See *count noun*.

nonrestrictive A modifying phrase or clause that gives nonessential information about a noun; it is set off by commas. A restrictive modifier gives essential information about the noun it modifies and is not set off by commas.

noun A word that names something: *lady, squirrel, patience, writing* (common nouns); proper nouns, for specific names and places, are capitalized: *Michael, Nevada, Exxon.*

number A grammatical term used to establish the singular or plural status of nouns and verbs: *Colleges* is plural in number.

O

object A noun or pronoun that receives the action of a verb. The object may be direct (Susan hit *the ball*) or indirect (She gave *him* a kiss). Participles, gerunds, infinitives, and prepositions take objects to complete their meaning (turning the *corner*).

objective See *case*.

outline A diagram of an essay's organization in which the main points are listed as major items in a column, with subordinate points indented under the main points to which they belong.

P

paragraph A group of related sentences that develop one subject.

participle A verbal that may be in either one of two tenses. The present participle, which always ends in *-ing*, is used with forms of *be*

in verb phrases (is *sinking*) or as a modifier (*sinking* ship). The past participle, which ends in *-ed* for regular verbs, is used as part of a verb phrase (has *used*) or as a modifier (*used* car). See also *verbal.*

parts of speech The classification of words according to their function in a sentence: nouns, pronouns, adjectives, adverbs, verbs, prepositions, conjunctions, and interjections.

passive voice See *voice*.

past tense See *tense*.

person A grammatical term used to distinguish the person speaking (first person) from the person spoken to (second person) and from anyone or anything else (third person). Nouns, except those in direct address (*John,* please leave), are always considered third person.

persuasion A type of writing that aims to convince the reader to do or believe something.

phrase A group of words that can function as a noun, verb, or modifier and that does not contain a subject–verb combination.

phrasal verb Sometimes called a "two-word" verb, a phrasal verb consists of a verb plus one or two accompanying words that form an idiomatic construction (*break down, put up with*).

plagiarism Using the words or ideas of another without giving credit to their source.

possessive See *case*.

predicate The verb by itself (simple predicate) or the verb with all its modifiers, complements, and objects (complete predicate).

preposition A word that relates a noun or pronoun to another word in the sentence: *after, before, by, for, from, in, of, on, to, up,* and *with* are some commonly used prepositions.

present tense See *tense*.

prewriting Any device you use to get started before beginning the first draft of an essay.

principal parts The three basic forms of a verb: infinitive *(to eat)*, past tense *(ate)*, and past participle *(eaten)*.

pronoun A part of speech that stands for or refers to a noun.

proper noun See *noun.*

purpose Your reason for writing; your answer to the question "Why am I writing?"

R

regular verb See *verb.*

relative pronoun A pronoun that can introduce a subordinate clause: *who, whom, whose, that, which, what, whoever, whomever, whichever, whatever.*

report An essay in which a writer summarizes the content of another person's work.

restrictive See *nonrestrictive.*

review An evaluation in which a writer assesses the strengths and weaknesses of another's work by using supporting evidence.

revising The part of the writing process that enables you to alter and clarify what you have written by rethinking, rereading, and rewriting.

S

sentence A word group that expresses a complete thought, consisting of a subject and a predicate. A simple sentence contains one independent clause; a compound sentence has two or more independent clauses. A complex sentence contains one independent clause and at least one dependent clause. A compound-complex sentence contains two or more independent clauses and at least one dependent clause. Sentences also differ in purpose: declarative (statement), imperative (command), interrogative (question), and exclamatory (strong feeling).

subject The word or word group about which the predicate says (or asks) something in a sentence.

subjunctive See *mood.*

subordinate conjunction See *conjunction.*

T

tense The form of a verb that expresses time: present, past, future. Perfect tenses express completed action: present perfect (I *have run*), past perfect (I *had run*), future perfect (I *will have run*). The progressive tense expresses continuing action (I *am running*).

thesis A sentence that states your main point, usually placed in the introduction of an essay.

topic A specific aspect of a broad subject.

topic sentence A sentence that states the main idea of a paragraph, guiding and unifying it much as a thesis statement guides the development of the essay.

transition A word, phrase, or sentence that guides the reader from one point to another by linking sentences or paragraphs.

transitive verb See *verb.*

V

verb A word or word group expressing action, process, or being. Regular verbs form the past and past participle by adding *-d* or *-ed* to the infinitive: *walk, walked, have walked.* Irregular verbs (*drink, drank, have drunk*) do not follow this rule. A transitive verb requires an object to complete its meaning: He *wrote* [verb] a *letter* [object]; an intransitive verb does not require an object: he *sings* well. See also *linking verb, mood, tense,* and *voice.*

verbal A word formed from a verb and used as an adjective, adverb, or noun: *laughing.* Gerunds, participles, and infinitives are verbals.

voice A verb is in the active voice when the subject names the doer of the action: Joan *read* the book. A verb is in the passive voice when the subject names the receiver of the action: The book *was read* by Joan.

Glossary of
Usage

This glossary lists words that are commonly confused as well as usages that appear frequently, especially in speech, but are disapproved of by many dictionaries and books on style. Look over the entries, noting any usages with which you are unfamiliar, and refer to this glossary or to a good college dictionary whenever you are unsure of the way you are using a particular word. For a discussion of the varieties of writing referred to in this glossary, see **59.**

A

a, an Use *a* before a consonant sound, *an* before a vowel sound: *a* university, *a* horror; *an* uncle, *an* hour.

absolutely Often meaningless intensifier (*absolutely* the best cook) that is redundant with such words as *complete* and *perfect.*

accept, except See *except, accept.*

adapted, adopted *Adapted* means "changed"; *adopted* means "accepted":

> After the mayor *adopted* the housing rule, it was *adapted* to suit local needs.

administrate Use *administer.*

adverse, averse *Adverse* means "opposite" or "unfavorable": *adverse* criticism, *adverse* winds. *Averse* means "reluctant" or "disliking": He is *averse* to manual labor.

affect, effect *Affect* (to influence) is usually a verb; *effect* (result) is usually a noun. As a noun, *affect* is psychological jargon meaning "personal magnetism or impact." As a verb, *effect* means "bring about":

> His injury did not *affect* his performance.

> The protest had little *effect.*

> The new chair *effected* several changes.

> The schizophrenic exhibited very little *affect.*

afflict, inflict *Afflict* typically takes *with* and an animate object: He was *afflicted with* measles. *Inflict* takes an inanimate object: The judge *inflicted* the maximum penalty.

again, back Unnecessary after words meaning *again* or *back*, such as *refer, revert,* and *resume.*

> In reaching its decision, the court *referred* [not *referred back*] to a 1948 Supreme Court ruling.

ahold Use *hold*: Dan tried to get *hold* [not *ahold*] of himself.

ain't Most writers avoid this colloquial contraction.

all ready, already *All ready* means "fully prepared" or that everyone or everything is ready: The letters were *all ready* to be signed. *Already* is an adverb meaning "at or before this time": The book has *already* sold a million copies.

all right This spelling is preferable to *alright.*

all the farther Use *as far as:* This is *as far as* we can go.

allude A verb meaning "mention indirectly": He often *alludes* to Shakespeare. Do not confuse it with *refer,* "to mention directly." Also do not confuse the noun *allusion* with *illusion,* a false perception or impression.

a lot Two words; do not spell as one.

alternate(ly), alternative(ly) *Alternate* means "by turns, first one and then the other": *alternately* hot and cold weather. *Alternative* means "another choice," such as an *alternative* course of action.

altogether, all together *Altogether* is an adverb meaning "completely": *all together* is an adjective phrase meaning "in a group":

> The hikers were *all together* at the campsite.

> They were *altogether* unprepared for the storm.

alumnus, alumna, alumni A male graduate is an *alumnus,* and a female graduate is an *alumna; alumni* is the plural for both sexes (although *alumnae* is sometimes still used for female graduates). Do not use *alumni* to refer to an individual. To avoid confusion and the possible perception of unintended sexism, some people use the abbreviation *alum.*

among, between Use *among* with more than two, *between* with two.

amoral, immoral *Amoral* means without moral principles; *immoral* means contrary to such principles.

amount, number Use *number* for things that can be counted, *amount* for quantities of things that cannot be counted:

> A large *number* of books have been stolen.

> The old furnace wasted a large *amount* of fuel.

analyzation Use *analysis.*

and etc. See *etc.*

anyone, any one *Anyone* means "any person"; *any one* refers to a single person or thing from a group:

> *Anyone* can learn to spell better.

> Choose *any one* point of view and stick with it.

anyway, any way Use *anyway* to mean "in any case" or "nevertheless," *any way* to mean "any course" or "any direction." To mean "in any manner," use either one. *Anyways* is nonstandard.

> We played well but lost *anyway.*

> The traffic will be heavy *any way* you go at that hour.

> Do it *any way* [or *anyway*] you choose.

appraise, apprise *Appraise* means to set a value, as on real estate: The house was *appraised* at $140,000. *Apprise* means to notify, tell, or inform: The attorney was *apprised* of the facts of the case.

apprehend, comprehend *Apprehend* means to catch the meaning of something, whereas *comprehend* means to understand it fully.

as Often ambiguous when used to mean *since, when,* or *because:* She forgot her lines *because* [not *as*] she was nervous. *As* is often unnecessary: He was voted [as] the most likely to succeed. Do not use *as* to mean "whether" or "that": I can't say *that* [not *as*] I understand. See also *like, as.*

as regards Wordy—use *concerning.*

awhile, a while *Awhile* is an adverb; *a while* is a noun: wait *awhile;* wait for *a while.*

B

bad, badly Use *bad* as an adjective, *badly* as an adverb:

> I wanted a drink of water so *badly* that I was ready to do almost anything.

> It was *bad.* I feel *bad.* He looks *bad.*

basically Like *essentially* and *ultimately, basically* is overused and often adds little emphasis: [*Basically,*] the problem is serious.

being Often a weak connective in sentences: He writes well, *being* the son of a novelist. Instead of *being that* or *being as,* use *because:* He writes well *because* [not *being that*] he is the son of a novelist.

beside, besides *Beside* means "at the side of"; *besides* means "in addition to"; either may be used to mean "except":

The map lay *beside* the lamp.

Besides her regular job, she plays bass in a blues band.

No one *beside* [or *besides*] you had a key.

better Avoid as a synonym for *more: More* [not *Better*] than half of the workers were present.

between See *among, between.*

both Redundant with words such as *agree* or *together:* We [*both*] agreed to stop bickering.

but Avoid redundant combinations such as *but however* or *but nevertheless.* Use *that* rather than *but that* or *but what* in sentences such as "I do not doubt *that* [not *but that*] he will succeed."

C

can, may In strict usage, *can* expresses ability; *may* expresses permission:

May I go fishing?

Yes, if you *can* find your rod.

cannot Spell as one word unless you wish to place especially heavy emphasis on the *not.*

can't hardly, can't scarcely Avoid these double negatives; use *can hardly* or *can scarcely.*

case, line Both are often deadwood:

In [the case of] English, single adjectives usually precede nouns.

I would like to buy [something in the line of] a mystery.

center around *Center on* is more exact, but either phrase is usually roundabout and imprecise:

The story *concerns* [not *centers around*] a jewel thief.

climactic, climatic *Climactic* refers to climax (as in a story), *climatic* to climate (weather).

close to Not a substitute for *nearly* or *almost:* Nearly [not *close to*] fifty guests are coming.

complement, compliment *Complement* means "to complete": A good wine *complements* a dinner. *Compliment* means "to praise," as when you pay someone a *compliment.*

consist in, consist of *Consist in* means "to reside in" or "inhere": Virtue *consists in* doing good. *Consist of* means "to be composed of": The book *consists of* seven chapters.

continual, continuous *Continual* means "frequently repeated" and is not the same as *continuous,* "uninterrupted":

Robbery is a *continual* problem in our neighborhood.

Chicago suffered forty-three days of *continuous* subfreezing weather.

convince Use *convince* when someone changes his or her opinion; use *persuade* when someone is moved to take action:

The dean *persuaded* (not *convinced*) us to cancel the meeting.

could of An error for *could have.* See *of.*

council, counsel, consul A *council* is a governing body; *counsel* is advice or the act of giving advice; a *consul* is a government official in a foreign country:

The town *council* met last night.

Mr. Adamson *counseled* me to choose a career other than medicine.

The Iranian *consul* was expelled from the country.

couple *Couple* takes a plural verb when it refers to people, as does *pair:* The couple *are* [not *is*] in Bermuda.

credible, credulous, creditable All have to do with belief, but they are not interchangeable. *Credible* means "believable"; *credulous* means "naive"; *creditable* means "deserving praise."

D

data Originally plural for the rarely used singular *datum, data* is still used as a plural in much academic writing (to mean facts or pieces of information). But it often means a body of facts or information and takes a singular verb: The data *was* entered in the computer.

different *Different from* is standard usage (but *different than* is also used). *Differ from* indicates dissimilarity (Boys *differ from* girls); *differ with* indicates disagreement (She *differed with* his view of the film).

disinterested, uninterested *Disinterested* means "impartial"; *uninterested* means "not interested."

done Nonstandard as a substitute for *did:* They *did* [not *done*] the work already.

due to the fact that Use *because.*

E

each and every Use one word or the other.

economic, economical *Economic* usually concerns economics (*economic* policy), whereas *economical* always means "thrifty."

effect See *affect, effect.*

e.g. The abbreviation for the Latin *exempli gratia* ("for example"). Use *for example.*

elicit, illicit *Elicit* is a verb meaning "draw forth": The article *elicited* an angry response. *Illicit* is an adjective meaning "unlawful": The police cracked down on *illicit* gambling.

emigrate, immigrate *Emigrate* means to move out of a country; *immigrate* means to move in. An American who emigrates to England is, from the English standpoint, immigrating.

eminent, imminent *Eminent* means "prominent" or "famous"; *imminent* means "upcoming, about to happen":

> An *eminent* economist predicted *imminent* disaster.

enthuse A colloquial substitute for "be enthusiastic" or "show enthusiasm."

equally as *As* alone is sufficient. The film was [*equally*] *as* good as the book.

etc. An abbreviation of the Latin *et cetera* ("and other things"). It can be an evasive substitute for specifics: Work was delayed by rain, etc. Do not use *and etc.,* in which *and* is redundant.

everyone, every one See *anyone, any one.*

except, accept *Except,* meaning "other than," is not a substitute for *but.* Also, do not confuse *except* with *accept,* "to receive" or "to agree."

> The British might have scored a decisive victory, *but* [not *except*] they did not pursue the retreating American army.

> Everyone *except* Aunt Agatha *accepted* the invitation.

expect Informal when used to mean "suppose" or "think" as in "I *expect* it will rain." *Suppose, assume, think,* and *believe* are preferable.

explicit, implicit *Explicit,* meaning "expressed directly," is the opposite of *implicit* ("suggested," "expressed indirectly").

F

factor A factor helps to produce a given result, so *contributing factor* is redundant. *Factor* is often misused to mean "item" or "point": There are several *points* [not *factors*] in favor of the new proposal.

farther, further *Farther* usually refers to physical distance, *further* to additional time or degree.

> We managed to drive *farther* than we expected during the first three days.

The economists decided to wait for *further* developments before making a decision.

feature As a verb, *feature* should not be used to mean "contain" (The magazine *contained* [not *featured*] many recipes) but to mean "give prominence to" (The magazine *featured* an article by John Updike).

few, little; fewer, less *Few* and *fewer* refer to things that can be counted, *little* and *less* to things that cannot be counted: *few* apartments, *little* space; *fewer* calories, *less* food.

finalize Jargon for *complete*.

former, first; latter, last Use *former* and *latter* when you refer to one of two items; with three or more items, use *first* and *last*.

G

goes Not acceptable as an equivalent for *says*: Then he *says* [not *goes*], "I didn't mean it."

good, well *Good* is an adjective: The air smells *good*. *Well* is usually an adverb: The choir sings *well*. *Well* is also used as an adjective referring to health: I have stayed *well* since I started the new diet.

H

half Use *half a* (can) or *a half* (can), not *a half a* (can).

hardly See *can't hardly*.

hisself Nonstandard for *himself*.

hopefully Colloquial substitute for "I hope" or "it is hoped."

I

idea, ideal *Idea* (thought or notion) can be confused with *ideal* (a conception of something in its most perfect state): He did not have a clear *idea* of the ancient Greek *ideal* of heroic virtue.

i.e. The abbreviation for the Latin *id est* ("that is"). Use *that is*.

if and when Like *when and if*, a wordy and trite phrase. Use one word or the other.

illusion Sometimes confused with *allusion*; see *allude*.

imminent See *eminent, imminent*.

implicit See *explicit, implicit*.

imply, infer *Imply* means "to suggest"; *infer* means "to conclude." Writers imply; readers infer.

> The press secretary *implied* that the President would fire the attorney general.

> From the press secretary's remarks, I *inferred* that the President would fire the attorney general.

inflict, afflict See *afflict, inflict*.

in regards to The standard forms are *in regard to* or *as regards*. But *concerning* is usually preferable to either phrase.

inside of Use just *inside* or *within*.

irregardless Nonstandard for *regardless*.

its, it's *Its* is the possessive (belonging to *it*): The company issued *its* report. Compare *his, hers*. *It's* is the contraction for *it is* or *it has*. There is no such word as *its'*.

K

kind of/sort of Colloquial: The lecture was [*kind of*] interesting.

kind of a Drop the *a*: That kind of [*a*] story always amuses young readers.

L

latter See *former, first; latter, last*. Do not confuse *latter* with *later*.

lay, lie See *lie, lay*.

learn, teach Students learn; instructors teach:

> My grandfather *taught* me how to cast a fly.

> I *learned* to cast a fly before I was six years old.

leave, let *Leave* means "to depart or go away from"; *let* means "to permit." Do not use *leave* for *let*.

less See *few, little; fewer, less*.

let's us Since *let's* is the contraction for *let us*, do not add a second *us*.

liable See *likely, liable.*

lie, lay *Lie* means "to rest" or "to recline"; *lay* means "to put or place (something) down." The past of *lie* is *lay;* the past of *lay* is *laid:* She *laid* the book on the table and *lay* down to rest.

like, as In making comparisons, use *like* as a preposition; use *as, as if,* or *as though* as a conjunction introducing a dependent clause:

> *Like* Hamlet, he is indecisive.

> The lab researcher will examine the slides *as* she always has—slowly and carefully.

> After the race, all of the runners looked *as though* they might faint.

Some writers mistakenly go out of their way to avoid using *like:*

> This hotel looks *similar to* [preferably *like*] the one in Johnstown.

likely, liable *Likely* expresses probability; *liable* expresses obligation but is sometimes used loosely to mean *likely:* She is *likely* (not *liable*) to receive an award.

line See *case, line.*

loose, loosen, lose A *loose* screw (adjective); *loosen* a tie (verb); *lose* a bet (verb).

M

may, can See *can, may.*

media Because *media* is the plural of *medium,* most writers use a plural verb: The media *are* [not *is*] often accused of bias. Compare *criterion, criteria; phenomenon, phenomena.*

might of An error for *might have;* see *of.*

most Informal as a substitute for *almost,* as in "he comes here *most* every evening."

myself *Myself* can be used as a direct object referring to the subject of the sentence (I hurt *myself*) or as an intensive (I will do the job *myself*). Do not use it as a substitute for *I:* Two of us finished the puzzle: John and *I* [not *myself*].

N

nohow, nowheres Nonstandard forms. Use *in no way, not at all, nowhere.*

not too, not that Colloquial substitutes for *not very,* as in "I'm *not that* concerned with politics."

nowhere near Colloquial for *not nearly:* Sam's pizzas are *not nearly* [not *nowhere near*] as good as Tony's.

number, amount See *amount, number.*

O

of Do not use *of* for *have* in verb phrases: *could have, would have, might have, must have:* I should *have* [not *of*] attended the meeting.

off of Use just *off:* He would not get *off* [*of*] the subject.

oftentimes Use just *often.*

on account of Use this phrase as a preposition (*on account of* the rain), not as a conjunction (*on account of* it rained). *Because* or *because of* is preferable: *because of* the rain; *because* it rained.

opinionated An *opinionated* essay (as opposed to an essay of opinion) is one that unreasonably or obstinately maintains the writer's own opinions.

orientate *Orient* is simpler and preferable.

ought Do not use with auxiliaries such as *had* and *did:* Eve wondered if she *ought* [not *hadn't ought*] to leave.

outside of Use just *outside.*

P

party Except in law, *party* is a poor substitute for *person:* Would the *person* [not *party*] who requested a change in seating please come to the counter?

per Jargon for "according to": Use the insecticide *according to* (not *per*) the instructions.

percent, percentage Use *percent* with numbers (ten *percent*), *percentage* without numbers: A high *percentage* [not *percent*] of those responding rated inflation as the chief problem. Do not use *percentage* loosely for *part:* A large *part* [not *percentage*] of the work was done before we arrived.

persuade See *convince.*

plus *Plus* is technically a preposition meaning "with the addition of," not a conjunction:

> After the game, Bill was tired, *and* [not *plus*] his leg hurt.
>
> The principal *plus* the interest comes to $368.55.

practical, practicable Something *practical* works well in practice; something *practicable* can be put into practice but has not yet been shown to work:

> Conversion to solar energy is *practicable* in many parts of the country, but few systems have so far proved *practical.*

precede, proceed See *proceed, precede.*

predominant, predominate *Predominant* is the adjective (the *predominant* opinion); *predominate* is the verb: For twenty years, conservative opinion *predominated* in the court.

presently Use *now.*

previous to, prior to Use *before.*

principal, principle *Principal* can be an adjective or a noun: the *principal* cause; the *principal* of our school; the *principal* plus the interest charged by the bank. *Principle* is always a noun meaning "basic rule or truth": Although customs vary, the *principles* of good behavior are the same in both countries.

proceed, precede *Proceed* means "to go forward," "to continue"; *precede* means "to go before." *Proceed* is not a good choice if the meaning is simply "go."

Q

quite, rather See *rather, quite.*

quotation, quote *Quote* is the verb, *quotation* the noun: an apt *quotation* [not *quote*].

R

raise, rise *Raise* takes a direct object (*raise* something); *rise* does not:

> They *raise* the flag every day.
>
> Farmers *rise* early.

rather, quite Both can weaken the force of a strong modifier: a [*quite*] huge fireplace. *Rather* often adds no meaning and produces ambiguity: Does *rather clear* mean "very clear" or "a little clear"?

real, really *Real* is the adjective, *really* the adverb: a *real* distinction; *really* late. But *really* is often just an empty word: They [*really*] worked hard.

reason is . . . because Redundant. The reason is *that* [not *because*] he is shy.

refer back See *again, back.*

relevant If you call something *relevant* or *irrelevant,* be sure to say *to what* it is relevant or irrelevant.

respectfully, respectively *Respectfully* means "with respect"; *respectively* means "singly in the order given":

> They treated the ambassador *respectfully.*
>
> Her three children weighed *respectively* eight, nine, and ten pounds at birth.

rise, raise See *raise, rise.*

S

sensual, sensuous *Sensual* refers to bodily (usually sexual) pleasures; *sensuous* refers more generally to sensory appeal.

set, sit *Set* takes a direct object (*set* something down); *sit* does not (*sit* down).

shall, will The distinction between these words has largely broken down.

should of An error for *should have*. See *of.*

so Not a substitute for *very* (It was *so* cold); as an adverb, *so* requires some further explanation: It was *so* cold that the pipes froze.

some In writing, avoid the colloquial use of *some* for *somewhat:* I feel *somewhat* [not *some*] better today.

somewheres Nonstandard for *somewhere.*

stationary, stationery *Stationary* means "fixed in course or position"; *stationery* refers to writing materials.

supposed to, used to Be careful not to drop the *-d* from the end of *supposed* or *used* before *to.*

sure, surely *Sure* as an adverb is colloquial; in writing, use *surely:* We *surely* [not *sure*] enjoyed the concert.

T

teach, learn See *learn, teach.*

than, then *Than* is a conjunction used in comparisons; *then* is an adverb indicating time:

> The balloon rose faster *than* they expected.
>
> *Then* it drifted out over the lake.

their, there, they're Watch for misspellings: *Their* books are here (possessive adjective); *there* are my glasses (adverb); *they're* coming tonight (contraction of *they are*).

theirselves Nonstandard for *themselves.*

thusly Error for *thus.*

till, until Both are acceptable; *til* and *'til* are not.

to, too, two Spelling errors with these words are common but unnecessary. *To* is a preposition (*to* the fair) or the sign of an infinitive (*to* run). *Too* means either "also" or "excessively." *Two* is a number.

> John, *too*, found the path *to* the top *too* steep.
>
> It takes *two to* argue.

try and *Try to* is preferred by most stylists, though *try and* is common.

-type This suffix should usually be omitted in phrases: a temperamental *[-type]* person.

U

unique *Unique* means "single" or "without equal" and therefore does not need qualification: not *very unique* or *quite unique* but just *unique.*

used to See *supposed to, used to.*

utilize Often bureaucratic jargon for *use,* especially with reference to people.

W

ways Use *way* for distance: a long *way* [not *ways*] to go.

where Avoid using *where* as a substitute for *that;* I read in the paper *that . . .* [not *where . . .*].

whose, who's Be careful not to confuse the possessive *whose* (*Whose* notes are these?) with *who's,* the contraction for *who is.*

-wise Avoid this suffix, a common type of jargon: *gardenwise, profitwise.*

Y

your, you're *Your* is the possessive (*your* copy), and *you're* is the contraction for *you are.*

Index